Java for RPG Programmers

Phil Coulthard & George Farr

Java for RPG Programmers

Phil Coulthard & George Farr

ADVICE Press
480 California Avenue
Palo Alto, CA 94306

Java for RPG Programmers
by George Farr & Phil Coulthard

IBM Centre for Advanced Studies, Dr. Gabriel Silberman, Program Director
Sheila Richardson, IBM Retail Publishing Programs

Printed in the United States of America.

Published by   ADVICE Press, 480 California Avenue—Suite 104, Palo Alto, CA 94306.
Phone: (650) 321-2197 Fax: (650) 321-2199 info@advicepress.com
www.advicepress.com

Printing History

June 1998	First Book Edition
February 1999	Second Printing with minor changes
January 2000	Third Printing with minor changes

ISBN: 1-889671-23-1   [01/2000]

Dedications

For my relentlessly understanding wife Chris. To my wonderful and joy giving children Cassandra and Jennifer: Cassandra wants to learn to tap dance, while Jennifer just wants to get her teeth! So you know, I am the person living in the basement tapping on the keyboard all night. Also for my father, Frederick, and for my brother, Wayne.

— *Phil Coulthard*

To my loving wife, Diana, for encouraging the first book, putting up with the second one, and her unending support with the third.

To my beautiful children: Angelica who wants to quit her weekend paper route job! Michael who started calling me 'buddy' instead of dad, and AnnaLisa for putting up with both of them!!!

In addition, I like to dedicate this book to my Big brothers: Ibrahim and Elias. They continue to lead the way in education, career success and most importantly good family values

—*George N. Farr*

Thanks

There are many to thank on this project, from those who persevered through many arcane questions with ready answers and to those who happily reviewed chapters. We heartily thank the following fellow IBMers.

Barbara Morris	Jon Paris	Abe Batthish
Joe Sobura	Kimberly Mungal	Maha Masri
Sarah Ettritch	Susan Gantner	Rares Pateanu
Cheryl Pflughoeft	Paul Holm	Clifton Nock (double thanks to Clif for answering all those JDBC questions!)

In addition, we wish to thank the following customers and Java evangelists who also took an active interest in both the topic and the book.

Estrella Tan   Johnny Lee Lenhart

Finally, to the most important person involved in any major co-authored book project, the bartender! We heartily thank Jason Boucher at Jack Astor's.

FOREWORD
By Paul Conte

The AS/400, and the RPG programmers (you!) who have made it the most successful business system in the world, face the biggest change ever to occur in their intertwined histories.

As former AS/400 General Manager Bill Zeitler has said, IBM is "betting the ranch" on Java.

IBM has irrevocably linked the future success of the AS/400 to Java -- Java offers a way to add the graphical interface so urgently needed for AS/400 applications, it provides the core technology for IBM's attempts to sell the AS/400 as an e-business server, and it's the only viable answer IBM has to the Microsoft Visual Basic juggernaut. If you haven't already gotten the word, here it is: IBM is making the AS/400 a best-of-breed Java server, and is no longer basing the AS/400's future on RPG alone.

Considering IBM's bet on Java, the industry-wide rise of the Web, and Microsoft's push to capture the traditional business market, an RPG programmer has three choices:

1. Learn Java now

2. Abandon the AS/400 for Windows and learn Visual Basic

3. Become one of the last living RPG programmers doing maintenance on legacy applications

If the first choice is what you want to do, reading this book is one of the first steps you should take. Get yourself a copy of IBM's VisualAge for Java or Borland's JBuilder, prop this book up on your desk, and follow two of the best guides you'll find to lead you into the exciting world of Java programming. You'll never turn back.

Phil Coulthard and George Farr have spent years immersed in IBM's RPG development and working with AS/400 programmers. They're also key developers in IBM's Java platform and tools. They have the perfect combination of skills and experience to explain the practical use of Java for AS/400 development. Now they've delivered a unique book that presents Java and object-oriented programming in terms familiar to RPG programmers. No RPG programmer who wants to become proficient in Java should be without this essential resource.

—Paul Conte, Picante Software, Inc.

Table of Contents

Chapter 3 **Java's Language and Syntax** **85**

Chapter 9   **An Object Orientation** **269**

Chapter 10   **Exceptions** **313**

1

An Introduction to Java

What is Java?

Java: what is it, anyway? These days, you can't avoid hearing about, reading about, or wondering about Java. Well, we have good news for you. Java is, after all, just another programming language that you can understand and master.

The air is filled with hype surrounding Java. Much of the current buzz is well justified as things stand now, and our prediction is that soon Java will become even hotter. Chances are that Java is in your future and that knowing Java will enhance your career. Congratulations on taking the first concrete step on your journey to get familiar with Java by deciding to read this book. If you are doing so on your own time, sitting in your easy chair on your deck right now, all the better! Let the grass grow and the dog bark—you have some exciting new technologies to explore.

Will this be the first and last book you read on Java? Probably not. Once you get started and begin to write your own programs, you'll probably want to learn about more specific applications. *Java™ for RPG Programmers* will, however, give you a solid foundation in the structure, functions, and features of the language. On the strength of the introduction we provide, you will be able to delve deeper into the language with other books.

A note of caution is in order, however. We are, after all, describing what is probably an entirely new language to you, and we plan to offer comparisons to RPG as we go along. Hence, the book you hold in your hands is no small volume. (For that matter, neither are the RPG user guide and reference manuals!)

Java *is* much different than RPG. But so is programming your VCR, and you mastered that, didn't you? While Java and its rapidly growing list of related topics are too extensive to cover completely in these pages, you will certainly be able to hold your head up high at the water cooler after reading this book. You can then declare: "I, too, have drunk deeply from the cup of Java."

Hundreds of books about Java have flooded the market in the past few years. However, this one was written specifically for you, the RPG programmer. It will introduce you to the language from an AS/400 and RPG perspective, building the bridges of comparison for you, and using terms you are familiar with. We plan to leverage your existing knowledge and skill set, and we'll also provide you with a reasonable review of RPG IV as an added bonus.

Java is an object-oriented language. It is inconceivable that a new language today would not be object oriented; the benefits in productivity and quality are too great to ignore. These gains come from the capacity to reuse code and perform better problem domain modeling. Somebody on your team is going to have to become very good at doing object-oriented analysis and design in order to write efficient, high-quality Java code. Wish him or her well. Although this book does not examine object-oriented programming in any great depth, we will give you the basic concepts and techniques you'll need to grasp the subject, on the grounds that learning how to use the tools is the first step to becoming a carpenter.

If Java is, after all, just a programming language, then why all the fuss? There are a number of reasons:

- *The name.* Java *is* a cool name!
- *The Internet.* Java's original reason for existence is the Internet. The Internet is hot!
- *Portability.* Java comes closer than any preceding language at providing one hundred percent portable code.
- *Accessibility.* Java and its development tools are downloadable from the Web for free. Programmers like that.

Understanding each of these benefits serves as a good introduction to Java, so the following sections examine them in greater detail.

The Name

Java was originally designed by engineers from Sun Microsystems, Inc. The intent was to create a small-scale, interpreted language for programming small consumer devices. Reportedly known as *Oak* in its early days, it was originally an embedded language that quickly found a new use for Internet-related programming. It had all the attributes a programming language for the Internet could want: it was small, simple, easy to code, platform independent, and supported dynamic loading of code on demand. Thus, it was renamed and made publicly available as a programming language for the Internet in 1995. Java's big boost, however, came in early 1996, when Netscape Communications Corp. stepped up to support it as a programming language that could be processed by its Web browser. Suddenly, thousands of programmers and Web site owners wanted to learn and use Java.

What about the name? Well, can you imagine a developer in the ultra-cool UNIX and Internet world working with a hot, new language called Oak? Apparently, neither could the engineers. Legend has it that the name came from the coffee they drank in vast quantities while working so hard on the project.

The Internet

The original reason for Java's popularity, as we stated, was the Internet-specifically, the ability to program Web pages displayed by Web browsers such as Netscape's Navigator or Microsoft's Internet Explorer. Web browsers display text and graphics through HTML (*Hypertext Markup Language*), which is a tag-based language similar to UIM (*User Interface Manager*), the AS/400 source language for writing online help.

Java adds the ability to embed Java ***applets*** inside HTML pages. Applets are small applications that only run inside Web browsers, using the screen real estate of the browser window. They have the full power of a modern programming language behind them, so fully interactive, animated, live-data Web pages are made possible with relative ease.

Applets are the primary means by which Java is affiliated with the Internet. Another is Java's support for easy Internet communications programming. Indeed, it is possible to write a Web browser entirely in Java that performs the basic tasks of finding, retrieving, and displaying HTML files. In fact, Sun has done just that with its HotJava Web browser.

Portability

Java approaches more closely than any preceding language that elusive goal of *"write once, run anywhere."* It is possible to write completely portable applications in Java without too much sacrifice or pain. Why is this possible? Three reasons:

1. Java (like Basic, Smalltalk, and other languages) is interpreted rather than compiled. Thus, there are no chip-specific machine code instructions.

2. The interpreter for Java is well on its way to being ported to every single operating system, Web browser, and task-specific chip currently in production.

3. The Java language includes a rich set of functions that other languages leave to operating system APIs (Application Programming Interfaces). These built-in functions are part of the language specification, so they have to be ported with the interpreter. This means they are available to you on every platform.

Accessibility

How would *you* make a new programming language ubiquitous? Put a floppy CD-ROM in every box of cereal? Hire students to deliver it door-to-door? Sun chose the modern-day equivalent: they made Java available for free over the Internet. Imagine, then, that you are a pioneering programmer looking to "get into" Java. You can download the equivalent of a "compiler" for free or pick up a book at your local bookstore, and away you go. You might even take one of the numerous tutorials available for free on the Internet.

In order to get an idea of just how much information is available out there in cyberspace, visit the popular Yahoo! Web site (**www.yahoo.com**) and do a search for the word *Java*. Java is being discussed so widely because it offers the promise of learning something new on the ground floor, and even of making some money in your spare time by writing applets for Internet distribution, for the lowest possible cost of entry-nothing. Of course, you can pay for onsite education and robust development tools, but one of Java's most alluring features is that you do not have to make that investment.

WHAT ABOUT JELLO?

Will Java last, or is it just another hyped technology-of-the-day? That is a valid question and a valid concern. After all, we have seen many technologies come and go. Our time is limited and valuable, and making a large investment in something as foreign as Java can be construed as a large risk. What happens if, tomorrow or next year, something better comes along (perhaps called Jello, Juice, or Crumbs) and the industry jumps ship to it? Tell me, you are thinking, why is Java likely to survive?

We are of the opinion that Java is not a flash in the pan and that, indeed, it will last for a very long time to come. There is something different about Java. It is the right technology at exactly the right time, and the industry was hungry for Java without even knowing it. The confluence of events that has led to Java's meteoric rise does not happen very often in this industry. True, many different technologies have been thrown against the wall to see if they will stick. But, today, to have global success, a computer industry technology has to have the following going for it:

- *Large industry player buy-in*. Some niche products by niche players achieve great success, but the number of success stories is very small compared to the number of failures. The "big guys" must back up the niche product, or it won't gain critical mass.

4

- *Grass roots buy-in*. The technology must be enthusiastically endorsed by the development community. Developer demand exceeds supply in almost every computer industry technology. If IS managers are unable to draw upon a self-perpetuating pool of skilled individuals, they will face a difficult task keeping their projects staffed, and the technology will soon wither.

Java possesses these attributes in spades. Every single computer technology vendor has endorsed the language in a big way. Their support was driven primarily by the developer community's phenomenal buy-in, something on the order of 100,000 Java-related downloads were made from the Sun Web site in the language's first six months. At the time of this writing, it is estimated that there are 700,000 Java programmers, and at least eighty percent of Silicon Valley companies are either using or exploiting Java.

Consider the scenarios behind Java's success:

- The Internet was reaching both maturity and commodity status, programming for Web browsers remained difficult. Developers were looking for a mainstream way of programming interactive and compelling Web pages.

- Companies looking to the Internet were demanding more unique and compelling functionality for their Web sites. Looking for an edge, Netscape needed a Web scripting language for its industry-leading Navigator browser.

- Client/server was failing. Massive costs of deployment and maintenance were being reported. It proved increasingly difficult to keep up with operating systems and meet the expenses of managing applications.

- Companies like IBM and Sun were talking about network computing-putting more program functionality back on the server. But how to do that?

- There was no universal user interface language. Most enterprise applications need a new graphical user interface. Yet, which language should be used and which client platforms should be supported? Hundreds of options are available, each with its own pros and cons and degree of risk. One developer told us he had spent forty percent of his time for two years evaluating different options for his client/server project. RPG and COBOL has served us well for years, but will the next choice? Your job may depend on the answer!

- Developers are eager to learn new, strategic skills. But what to learn? CORBA? DCE? CGI? C? C++? TCP/IP? All of them, of course! Java does *not* replace these technologies, but it does offer a safe new skill if you want to choose just one.

- Java is accessible like nothing before it. You need only download the Java Development Kit (JDK); although rudimentary, the JDK enables you to start learning with no investment. Sun's brilliant decision to make Java and its associated software universally available ensured that the language would be widely embraced.

In our opinion, the world was ripe for Java. All the stars aligned. How often does this happen? Not very. Any Java wannabe that comes along now will be a very hard sell. The newcomer will first have to offer everything Java does: complete industry buy-in, complete portability, download-on-demand deployment, a reasonably easy programming model combined with full functionality, and complete scalability that ranges from toaster ovens to a toaster oven company's payroll. And, after mimicking all this, the new technology will have to add some other function, feature, or facet that the world decides it cannot live without. Something, by the way, that it would not be simple for Java itself to step up to.

Java is here for a long time. Your RPG and Java skills will keep you employed for many years. If nothing else, you will be able to service toaster ovens!

What about RPG?

NOTE: The comments that follow represent the authors' personal opinions, and not necessarily those of IBM.

At this point, you may be feeling some healthy concern about the longevity of your RPG investment in skills and code. Does this spell the end of RPG? Believe us, you could not kill RPG if you wanted to (and some do!).

RPG was, in its early days, what Java is today — the right thing at the right time. It offered a relatively easy way to meet the most pressing computer need of the period-generating reports. (Ironically, report writing is still a weak area in Java development today.) RPG quickly gained universal acceptance among industry and developers (within the IBM midrange world, of course. Is there another one?). The momentum fed on itself. . .and you see the result. RPG now runs businesses around much of the world. Like Java today, RPG has reached a critical mass and, as RPG programmers have always told IBM, RPG is a strategic part of your IS portfolio.

RPG is the flagship language of the AS/400. It is an easy-to-learn business application language. But Java shows strong signs that it is at least *capable* of replacing that mantra. C and C++ could not. They are for systems, rather than application programmers. COBOL, while very competent, offers no compelling advantages over RPG. Java, however, has much promise. IBM will not dissuade this. RPG is both a strength and a weakness of the AS/400-its downside is that it lends an "old world" image to the box. And as you know, attracting new blood to it is becoming increasingly difficult. To grow the AS/400 business, look for much hype around Java from IBM. Say, like books about Java for RPG programmers. Much of the hype will be true, too. So buy those books!

Java is a great fit for the AS/400, and IBM will promote it heavily. IBM, however, will continue to invest in and improve RPG. This is because you continue to demand us to do so, and our policy is not likely to change in the short term. RPG will continue to be used for many new applications, or at least parts of new applications where it fits best (for example, writing reports!). Besides, you will always have RPG code to maintain, and somebody will always be asking you to make improvements.

What role will Java play on the AS/400? Initially it will serve as a language for new applications, and for modernizing parts of existing strategic applications (especially the user interface). Some developers, especially those who write and sell applications, will rewrite entire applications in Java. Over time, as the language matures and the world evolves, more and more new investment on your part may well go into Java.

On the other hand, until Java offers the database performance and report writing capabilities that RPG does today, RPG will remain a strong part of the AS/400 landscape. People do not rewrite applications in a new language without a good business reason, and you may not see the need to rewrite existing RPG logic in Java, at least for the typical batch functions. That's fine; put Java to work where and when it fits best, and put RPG to work where and when it works best. When you need portability, object-oriented productivity, reuse benefits, graphical user interfaces, or off-the-shelf third-party code, consider Java. When you need the strengths of RPG or have existing working RPG code, use RPG. One thing is for sure, though: knowing both RPG *and* Java will be a very strong feather in your cap!

What about C and C++?

Will Java replace C and C++? No. These are system languages that enable efficient access to low-level operating system functions (see Figure 1-1). They heavily exploit the power of pointers-variables that hold memory addresses-to aid in their efficiency. Unfortunately, pointers are also very dangerous and require a lot of skill and tedious testing to ensure your code is bug free. Java chose not to implement pointers for security, simplicity, and error-reduction reasons. RPG historically does not have pointers either, although they have been recently introduced into the language. Why? To make it easier to access system APIs that need them! But if enough functionality were supplied with the language, the need to call the system APIs would be dramatically reduced and often eliminated. That is the route Java took. Of course, many system functions are obscure hooks into the system that do not lend themselves to a general purpose language like Java or RPG. Thus, applications that need low-level access will continue to be written in C and C++. Over time, the latter will be used more often than the former, as C++ is effectively a superset of C that adds built-in object-oriented capabilities.

Language options

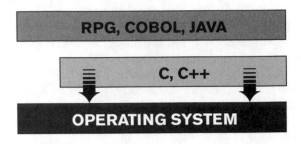

FIGURE 1-1

The "failure" of C and C++ has been the attempt to use them as effective business languages like RPG and COBOL, as opposed to systems languages for compiler and tool writers. They are simply too complex for this purpose. The learning curve necessary to write your first accounts receivable program in C or C++ is too steep, for instance. The result is likely have a pointer or memory management bug or two in it, to boot. This is not to say these languages *cannot* be used to write business applications-they certainly have been-but their complexity keeps them from becoming *mainstream* business languages. Mind you, many large applications may require a combination of languages: C++ for the server-side business logic and system exploitation, and Java for the client-side user interface. It's all a matter of the right *tools* for the job.

Now, it's time to return to the subject of learning Java before you get called into the office to fix a bug in your RPG code. (Well, perhaps a bug in somebody else's RPG code!)

APPLICATION MODELS

Java will find a home in many types of applications and parts of applications. Some of these include:

- Rewriting the user interface in Java, while leaving the business logic in RPG.

- Rewriting a piece of the business logic in Java.

- Adding a new functional piece to the application and writing it in Java.

- Obtaining a "Java bean" (explained later) off the shelf, and using it from an existing RPG application.

- Rewriting the "front end" of your application in Java and calling snippets of legacy RPG business logic-essentially, wrapping RPG with Java.

- Writing new Web browser Internet (the world) or intranet (your company) applications that call snippets of legacy RPG business logic.

- Writing Lotus Notes applications with Java applets mixed in.

- Writing entirely new Java applications from scratch.

What you'll see is that Java can play a role in at least two important places in your applications:

- *The client.* This can be a traditional command-line-initiated application, or a Web browser-based applet. It is also possible to have one code base that offers both command line invocation and Web browser invocation. The code runs on any client connected to your AS/400 server, including traditional Windows clients and the new network stations ("thin clients").

- *The server.* Like your present RPG applications, Java will serve as a competent business application language on the AS/400, easily enabling the writing of business logic, report generations, batch processing, and more. All of these capabilities will improve quickly over time. Note, however, that IBM will not provide a Java means of writing green screen display file user interface applications. It is assumed your user interface will be on the client and will utilize the power of graphic user interfaces (GUIs). Mind you, this will be simplified on the AS/400, because as of V4R2, Java GUI applications will run there. The user interface parts will be automatically distributed to your graphical workstation at runtime. This saves you the trouble of writing more complex client/server applications.

Most programmers will start with the client, rewriting the user interface piece first while retaining the existing logic on the server. Over time, that logic, too, may be rewritten in Java. Usually, this will be "from the outside in," whereby the outside skin is first redesigned in object-oriented fashion, and existing snippets of code are left in place and invoked as needed. We do recommend you continue your path to RPG IV and ILE. Why? Because this progression will offer you skills that you can transfer to Java (as you will see in the following chapters), and ILE's modularity will make it easier to replace "pieces" of your application with Java. (The first such "piece" may well be the user interface, for example.) Furthermore, unless you have a compelling business need (such as portability or retention/attraction of skills) to rewrite working RPG logic in Java, why do so? Better to upgrade it to RPG IV and ILE first, gaining the performance and functional enhancements they offer.

However, Java *is* a good choice for new applications and applications requiring portability. Once you have decided to use it, you'll need to make some choices, including:

- How to communicate between the client and the server.

- How to communicate between server Java and RPG.

- How much logic to put in the client versus the server.

- How and where to access the database.

- Whether to have a Web browser (applet) or application client interface.

These are *your* decisions to make-and here are some options you might choose:

- Use Rochester-supplied Java code called the AS/400 Toolbox for Java or Remote Method Invocation (RMI), a Java-supplied way to write distributed Java applications. Another option growing in popularity is the use of CORBA to distribute Java applications, especially in more advanced shops.
- Use Rochester-supplied classes called the AS/400 Toolbox for Java.
- Keep the client thin, but keep error checking and user responses in the client.
- If low throughput is sufficient, access data directly from the client. If high throughput is needed, access data from the server via stored procedures or even RPG programs.
- You can offer your users the choice of accessing the client code either from a client command line (application) or a Web browser (applet). This is easily done in Java.

These decisions of application architecture can wait for now. First, you must learn about the language itself. That's the focus of this book.

HOUSE OF JAVA

Java comes in its purest form as a Java Development Kit, or *JDK*. This "kit" contains a number of fundamentals, such as:

- A Java "compiler" that compiles Java source code into efficiently interpreted bytecode (as opposed to directly executable machine code). This is the **JAVAC** command.
- A Java interpreter that interprets or runs Java bytecode. This is the **JAVA** command.
- A set of Java class libraries or "packages", similar to reusable ILE service programs, for often-needed programming tasks.

These basic elements that define the language, together with their documentation, which is also part of the JDK (although it must be downloaded separately).

The JDK also includes a number of other useful command-line tools. However, it does *not* include an editor, an integrated development environment, or a visual design tool. And the JDK provides only the most rudimentary of debuggers. Nonetheless, with a decent personal computer editor (for example, the editor in CODE/400 for Windows) you have all you need for *basic* Java development. Figure 1-2 illustrates the pieces of the Java Development Kit:

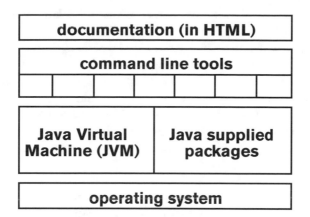

FIGURE: 1-2

Most programmers, however, will opt for any one of the numerous full-scale Java development tools that are already available, such as IBM's VisualAge for Java, Borland's JBuilder, or Symantec's Visual Cafe. These start with the basic JDK and add IDEs (integrated development environments), class hierarchy browsers, debuggers, visual design tools, wizards, and many more items to make the Java development task easier. Multiple-developer shops will also look for tools that offer built-in team support and versioning control. These are, again, covered by IBM's VisualAge for Java.
The JDK originates with Sun. Based on tremendous programmer feedback, the company adds enhancements and features to the language and, once or twice a year, releases a new "version" of the JDK (such as 1.1). In between versions come bug fix "releases" (such as 1.1.1) that appear numerous times each year. Other industry players betting heavily on Java (such as IBM, Oracle, and Netscape) work with Sun to define and even implement some specialized pieces.

In February, 1997, Sun released 1.1 of the JDK, and quickly followed up with several quality improvement releases (up to 1.1.5 as of this writing). Version 1.1 was a major delta improvement over its predecessor, 1.0. The next version, 1.2, no doubt will also be yet another major improvement, demonstrating that the JDK is maturing and improving very fast.

> **NOTE:** Because this book examines the basics of Java, all our samples were written using Sun's JDK on Windows 95. We happened to use the CODE/400 editor for entering the source, but you, of course, can use whatever tool you have handy. You can order a free trial copy of CODE/400 at **www.software.ibm.com/ad/varpg** if you are looking for a cheap and capable Windows 95 or WindowsNT editor.

Sun makes its JDK for both the Windows (32-bit) and Solaris operating systems publicly available at its Web site **www.javasoft.com** (follow the link for JDK). When you install it, be sure to follow the instructions in the readme file, especially the ones related to updating your PATH and CLASSPATH statements on Windows. Other operating system vendors license the JDK code from Sun and port it *as is* to their own operating systems. The IBM Hursley laboratory, for example, licenses and ports the JDK to the IBM operating systems AIX, OS/2, OS/400 and MVS. For OS/400, the IBM Rochester lab leverages that ported base and then integrates it deeply into the operating system for improved performance. Various Web browser manufacturers also license the JDK code in order to run Java applets embedded in Web pages.

As part of that license, the licensee agrees to stay current with the JDK, and must port a new release within about six months of a new release of the JDK. This ensures a reasonably current base across all the operating systems and Web browsers, as well as user program portability. This JDK now comes with most, if not all, of the major operating systems. It will come with OS/400 as of the Version 4, Release 2 (V4R2) release, although an initial port supporting V3R7 and V4R1 is available from the IBM Hursley Web site, for downloading, at **http://ncc.hursley.ibm.com/javainfo**.

You may get confused about who actually "owns" Java: Is it Sun Microsystems or JavaSoft? The answer is both. Sun is the parent company, and JavaSoft is a child company. Ultimately, Sun is the "owner."

Java Bytecode

Java achieves its portability because of its bytecode architecture. As illustrated in Figure 1-3, the Java source code you enter is compiled into bytecode using the JDK-supplied **JAVAC** command-line compiler. This compiler is really only the front half of a traditional compiler, in that an executable program is not produced as a result. Rather, it stops at what is referred to as the intermediate code in traditional compilers. This is an efficient (versus reading the source), compact version of the source, which is independent of any particular operating system.

The Java source code is contained in a file that ends with extension **.JAVA**, (dot java), while the Java bytecode is contained in a file that ends with extension **.CLASS** (dot class).

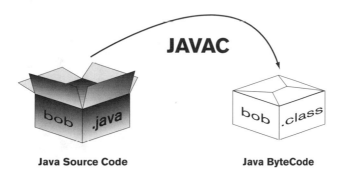

FIGURE 1-3

You can send a bytecode .class file to any operating system or Web browser that contains the Java interpreter, and run it there without change. The hard work is performed by the interpreter itself-it has to be ported. And it is the operating system and Web browser vendors that do this hard work for you.

> **NOTE:** The interpreter does have to call the operating system to run your Java instructions. For example, you may have a Java instruction to create a push button. This will be captured in the bytecode using its predefined operators and operands. When the interpreter runs these instructions, it calls the appropriate operating system API to create a push button. (However, in JDK 1.2, an all-Java version of the graphical user interface functions in Java is made available; this is explained in Chapter 12).

Recall that Java applications have their own windows and are invoked from the command line like RPG applications, whereas Java applets use the window of the Web browser and can only be run inside a Web browser. Applets then are small mini-applications that run inside the Web browser and, thus, the Web browser itself is the application for applets. In order to run a Java *application* you invoke the **JAVA** command and pass it the name of your bytecode .class file as a parameter (see Figure 1-4). For *applets* that run inside Web browsers, you need to use something called an **APPLET** tag in your Web page source, as we will describe soon.

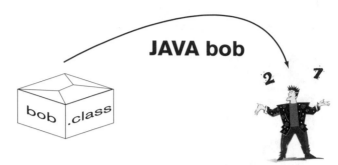

FIGURE 1-4

NOTE: Sun is now supplying a subset of the JDK called Java Runtime Environment, or JRE, for the operating systems it supports. The JRE consists of only the Java virtual machine (i.e., the interpreter) and the supporting runtime libraries or "packages." As such, it is intended as a distribution option for your applications in case you do not want to assume the existence of a virtual machine on your users' computers, or if you are worried that their version of the virtual machine may not match yours.

JAVA: THE LANGUAGE

Java is based to some extent on C++, Smalltalk, Ada, and other languages. It is most heavily influenced by C and C++, however, as anyone with a background in these languages will immediately recognize. It captures the best of these languages, while adding and subtracting functions to achieve robust functionality and easier programmability.

The working theme of the Java designers was, and is, **KISS** (*Keep It Simple, Stupid*). To that end, the language does *not* have:

- Pointer variables (it does have object references though, as you will see)
- Memory allocation and deallocation constructs
- Include files ("/**COPY** members," in RPG parlance)
- Make files (a language for facilitating C and C++ builds)
- Multiple inheritance (an OO construct that C++ uses)
- Method ("procedure") prototyping. In Java, you declare and define methods (that is, "subroutines" or "procedures") at the same time.
- Operator overloading, a complex function available in C++

The biggest plus, from the point of view of programmer productivity, is the absence of memory management functions. Instead of supplying built-in functions for getting and returning memory, Java offers automatic **garbage collection**. That is, when you declare variables, Java keeps track of where they are used at runtime, and frees up their memory when it determines your code no longer requires them. If you have written any C or C++ code or used the new memory allocation operation codes in RPG IV (`ALLOC`, `REALLOC,` and `DEALLOC`), then you know that you must take care to do the following:

- Allocate enough memory
- Reallocate the memory when more is needed
- Free up the memory when done with it
- Free up the memory once and only once

Memory management is very error-prone, and such errors are typically hard to reproduce as well as difficult to find. As the RPG IV reference manual states: "*misuse of heap storage can cause problems.*" Indeed. Garbage collection is a language feature Java picked up from Smalltalk, and one that, by itself, saves a significant amount of programmer time. Now just imagine if someone could manage your *real* memory! You would save even more time! Maybe in the next release.

In Java terms, KISS could also be interpreted to mean *Keep It Safe, Stupid*. That's because, in addition to a focus on ease of use, Java has a focus on security. An Internet language must be secure, as it is not considered polite for code that is downloaded to client workstations, to have the potential for obliterating the data maintained on those trusting, friendly little computers (no offense intended for ActiveX fans).

Java's extensive built-in security is designed to prevent problems that might arise from both malicious intent and poor programming. The most fundamental of these possibilities is the decision to not define pointers in the language. While this might be seen as a programmer plus (pointer programming, after all, is a battle-won skill) it also stands as a major sand trap for bad-boy hackers. Many malicious programs are written by accessing memory that the program is not supposed to utilize, which is done by clever manipulation of pointers. We could tell you more about this but then, of course, we would be creating a security problem ourselves. Suffice it to say, "see no pointer, do no evil."

NOTE: On the AS/400, pointers are not nearly as dangerous as on other systems, because each one encapsulates significant security information. That's why they are 16 bytes long on OS/400 versus four bytes on a typical 32-bit operating system.

THE INTERNET, HTML, AND JAVA APPLETS

As mentioned earlier, Java's initial role in life, which is still its main role, is that of a World Wide Web browser language. In this form, it is used to author applets that run inside Web browsers.

Applets resemble traditional applications, except that they are embedded inside HTML and share the Web browser user interface real estate with it. HTML stands for *HyperText Markup Language*, a tag-based language for formatting text, images, and other content that is intended to be displayed by Web browsers. The operation resembles the way UIM (User Interface Manager) is used to author online help pages or screens on the AS/400.

A tag has both a starting form and an ending form, and the "meat" or text for that particular tag goes between them. For UIM, the tags are special symbols that are prefixed by a colon (:). Typically, the ending tag is the same as the starting tag, but with an 'e' prefixed before it. For example, in UIM you start a list with :ul (*Unordered List*) and end it with :eul (*End Unordered List*). In HTML, the principle is similar, but the syntax is slightly different. Rather than denoting a tag with a colon, HTML denotes it by enclosing it in angle brackets. And rather than ending a tag with a prefixed *e*, it ends a tag with a prefixed slash (/). For example, a unordered list is started in HTML by <ul>, and ended with </ul>.

HTML includes many tags for partitioning and formatting text - for example, you can use tags for creating headings, paragraphs, lists and more, as well as for formatting text. Here is an example:

```
<html>
<head>
<title>My First Web Page</title>
</head>
<body>
<h1>This is a header</h1>
<hr>
<p>
This is a paragraph. Well, you see how simple it is! The following is an
ordered list...
</p>
<ol>
<li>Type in the starting tag inside angle brackets
<li>Type in the body between the tags
<li>Type in the ending tag with a slash in front
</ol>
</body>
</html>
```

NOTE: HTML tags are not case-sensitive. Some tags, like <hr> (*horizontal rule*) do not have an ending tag. Others, like <li> (*list item*), have an optional ending tag; the end is implied by the existence of the next tag.

Figure 1-5 shows how the preceding HTML appears in Netscape Navigator 4.03...

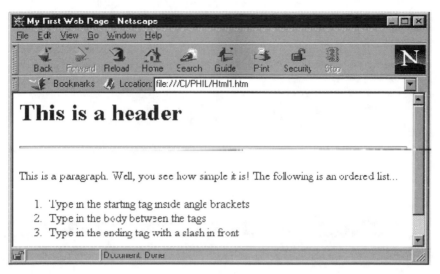

FIGURE 1-5

When you are creating UIM help pages on the AS/400, you must compile them with the **CRTPNLGRP** (*Create Panel Group*) command, and then use help specifications in your display file DDS in order for the AS/400 workstation manager to display your work. HTML is considerably easier. You simply create the HTML source with a text editor, save the file with the filename extension .htm or .html, and then open the source document directly with your Web browser. The Web browser interprets the HTML commands on the fly and displays the contents according to the instructions provided by the tags.

HTML provides plenty of tags to spice up your Web page, including those for formatting for fonts, graphics, and even audio. One all important tag is used to create a link between a piece of text or even an image, with an element elsewhere on the same page, or on another Web page. The text or image that represents the link is highlighted in several ways, depending on how the user has configured the browser. Most often, a textual link is displayed in the browser window in a different color than the rest of the text and is underlined as well. Images that function as links are usually surrounded by a black border. When you pass your cursor over the link, the cursor turns into a little hand. Clicking the mouse while over the link takes you to the referenced Web page. That is, the contents of the Web browser's window changes in order to display the referenced page. Clicking on the left arrow in the toolbar of the browser returns you to the originating page. The ability to jump quickly from one location to another is what puts the *hyper* in *hyper*text. You can author a complex *web* of pages that are easily traversed by the end user or reader.

Here is an example:

```
<html>
<head>
<title>
My Second Web Page
</title>
</head>
<body>
<p>
To see my first web page, click
<a href="file:///C|/PHIL/HTML1.HTM">here</a>
</p>
</body>
</html>
```

Figure 1-6 shows the result as displayed in Navigator.

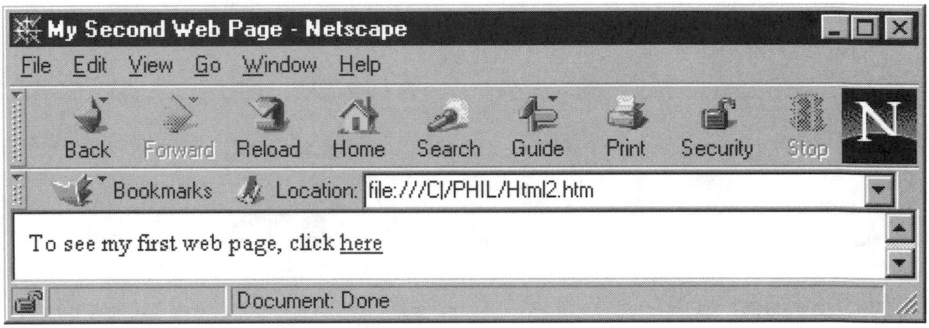

FIGURE 1-6

This makes authoring traditional *static* Web pages quite simple: you need only an editor, an HTML reference manual, and a Web browser. All of these are available for free on the Internet today. Of course, the example shown above presents a link to a local file on your hard disk. If you copy the preceding HTML, you have not made a link to a location on the Internet as yet. To do so, you need to connect your computer to the Net. Often, this is done by paying a monthly access fee to an Internet Service Provider (ISP).

Along with giving you access to the Net, it's common for providers to allocate space where you can install your HTML source files on their server. You then use their server's HTTP (*HyperText Transport Protocol*) software to make your HTML files accessible from the Internet. HTTP servers serve up Web pages to Web browsers (HTTP server software is often referred to as a *Web server*).

Your directory on the Web server and HTML files, graphics files, and other contents are assigned universal, unique URL (Uniform Resource Locator) addresses. These addresses enable your Web pages to be found by Internet surfers. They can display your page either by typing in its URL in their Web browser window, or by following a hypertext link as described above.

The important thing to remember about these links is that they can refer to any HTML file anywhere else in the world as long as that file's URL is known. A URL address consists of several parts:

- The protocol or prefix section of the URL denotes the part of the Internet on which the file resides. Web pages use the HTTP protocol, which corresponds to the prefix `http://`, whereas `file:///` is used to identify local files.

- The protocol is followed by the domain name for the HTTP server, such as www.ibm.com.

- The domain name is followed by the pathname section. This includes a series of file directories, separated by slashes, and ending in the actual filename of the Web page, graphic image, or other object to be displayed by the browser.

URLs can refer to many types of resources accessible through the Internet, in addition to HTTP files and local files. The tip to the Web browser as to what follows is the first part of the URL name, which designates the protocol being used to access the file.

Let's look at an example:

`http://www.software.ibm.com/ad/vajava.html`

This is the name of an Internet file `vajava.html`, in directory `ad`, at HTTP server "domain" `www.software.ibm.com`-the IBM software Web site.

How did IBM get its domain name `www.software.ibm.com`? It applied for it, from a regulating body that hands out unique names. Currently, that regulating body is called InterNIC or Internet Naming Information Center. InterNIC owns the job of assigning unique World Wide Web names to companies' resources, upon request. Often, InterNIC assigns blocks of unique names to Internet provider companies who, in turn, sell individual names to their customers who wish to set up their own Web sites. Large companies, however, will apply to InterNIC directly and get their own block of names. For more information, see `http://www.internic.net` on the World Wide Web.

NOTE: The infrastructure and underpinnings of the Internet are beyond the scope of this book. For general information about the infrastructure of the Internet and how it relates to the AS/400, consult the IBM redbook **Cool Title About the AS/400 and Internet** (SG24-4815-01). Another very good reference is the AS/400 manual **OS/400 TCP/IP Configuration and Reference V4R2** (SC41-5420-01).

HTML as an Internet User Interface Language

Choosing a Web browser interface for your applications is a good idea. With such an interface, your internal applications, such as accounts-receivable files, can be served on an *Intranet* that only employees of your company can access (and possibly only restricted employees within your company). Your external applications, such as product-ordering forms, can be made available to the *Internet* world at large.

Such filtering of access between external Internet files and internal Intranet files can be accomplished with a security device called an Internet firewall. A firewall is software or hardware that restricts access to a Web site to Web surfers with a particular computer IP "address" or within a particular block of IP addresses, or by means of passwords.

Regardless of whether you choose Intranet or Internet deployment for your files, the bulk of your application runs on the server. Typically, only the user interface part runs on the client. Furthermore, even these client- or Web browser-hosted pieces are downloaded *on demand* to the Web browser from your server, by your HTTP server ("Web server") software. This architecture offers a number of advantages over the traditional client/server option for adding graphical user interfaces to your applications. The architecture:

- Supports all clients, not just Windows, including the new thin client network stations.

- Removes the expensive requirement of installing and maintaining your programs on all user client workstations.

- Keeps the client *thin*, leaving most of your application code on the server, leveraging its scalability, security, backup infrastructure, and performance.

- Expands your application's reach: it becomes immediately accessible to the world at large (assuming you want this), or at least your company's internal world at large.

But there is a problem. We referred to these Web pages as *static*. That means they only display information to the user; they do not accept input from the user. This is pretty useless for *interactive* applications. How many AS/400 applications have you seen that are comprised entirely of UIM help panel groups, without display files to interact with the user, and that lack RPG code to process that information? There *is* a way, however, using conventional HTML, to define interactive Web pages. This involves special HTML tags for defining *forms*, which allow you to create input-capable fields such as text entry boxes and drop-down lists. Here is how forms are commonly used to receive data inputted by a user and process that data on the server side:

- You create a *form* in your HTML source document. That forms defines fields that ask the user for some form of input.

- As part of defining the form, you identify a server-side program. This program will be given as parameters the user's input from the HTML form.

- After entering data, the user presses a Submit button on the form, which sends the user input to the server program residing on the HTTP server.

- Your server-side program uses the user input to write a new file on your server, or adds the user input to an existing file. The program can even produce an entirely new Web page, passing that page to the HTTP server that, in turn, passes it to the Web browser that displays it to the user.

The server-side program used to process HTML form input is called CGI, or *Common Gateway Interface*. CGI was, prior to Java, the only way to allow users to interact with your Web browser pages. It is a mature and pervasive technique for producing interactive browser-based interfaces. If you have ever registered a software purchase online (that is, via the Internet), chances are you have used such a program to get your purchase information to the vendor.

Various languages are possible for writing the server side program, depending on the Web server (that is, the HTTP server) software package you are using and on the server itself. On the AS/400 for example, there are a few vendors that offer HTTP server software, including IBM's Internet Connection package. All offer CGI support, and all of them support RPG as a CGI server programming language. Again, see the AS/400 TCP/IP manual for more information.

You can also use a general scripting language called Perl. Perl is an interpreted language that works well for writing CGI programs, and is available on all major operating systems including the AS/400. It is quite an arcane language to learn, but it is available everywhere, and is always freely downloadable from the Web. Perl comes from the world of shareware-UNIX. To find out more, see the Web site `www.rgc.com/pub/languages/perl/CPAN.html` on the World Wide Web.

Do you have to learn CGI programming techniques to write interactive Web pages? No. Java has, to a large degree, replaced CGI. Furthermore, there is a new option for Web server software, called Java Servlets. This was originally defined and architected by Sun, but is rapidly being adopted by all major Web servers, including IBM's on AS/400 (look for it to be available after V4R2).

Servlets are just like CGI programs, but they are written in Java and run in the same address space as the Web server, versus starting up another job for each call to CGI program. This means they offer the programming advantages of Java, are more efficient than calling external CGI programs and, furthermore, easily support "state information" between client invocations.

Java as an Internet User Interface Language

You have learned how HTML can be used to write static Web pages that display information but that do not ask for information. You have also learned how HTML, together with CGI, can be used to write reasonably interactive Web pages. While we briefly mentioned Java's new role as a Web server CGI replacement via Java Servlets, that is a very small part of Java's role in this picture (and certainly not a heavily used role as yet).

So how else does Java fit into this picture? By far the biggest role of Java in relation to the Web is that of a *browser programming language*. That is, you can write Java code that actually runs *right in the browser!* This offers so many advantages over CGI that it explains the phenomenal acceptance of Java by the programming community from its inception. What are those advantages? Well, consider what it means to write server-side CGI programs that have to serve entire Web pages (HTML files) at a time to the Web browser:

- *Response time.* All correspondence with the user requires an entirely new page, served across the network or possibly the Internet. Even small error feedback mechanisms require the entire page to be resent, even with only slight delta differences.

- *User interaction.* Much like the 5250 displays of the past (surely they will be "the past" soon!) these applications cannot respond to graphical user interface "events" such as mouse moves and mouse clicks. They only respond when the "submit" button is pressed. This is even more restrictive than 5250 displays, which can at least respond to function and command keys as well as the Enter key.

- *Development effort.* Testing and debugging can be slow when there are problems with the results. This environment does not lend itself well to *rapid application development* (RAD).

- *Server load.* Much work, like verification of user input syntax, must be done at the server. In environments where there are potentially thousands of simultaneous users (for example, popular Internet pages) this can take cycles away from the server that are better used for business logic and serving of HTML Web pages.

Along comes Java. Java extends the HTML "language" by adding a new tag called **APPLET**. This tag refers to a Java program to be run by the browser when the tag is encountered while reading the HTML. These programs will most often contain user interfaces. The user interface usually does not have its own main window, however; rather, it uses the window of the Web browser (this is what distinguishes a Java application from a Java applet). Because these Java programs do not have their own windows and cannot be started from the command line, they are referred to as *applets* as opposed to traditional applications. Instead of a main window, the applet will insert user interface parts such as lists, push buttons, and entry fields into the Web browser's window at the point in the HTML where the **APPLET** tag was encountered.

The **APPLET** tag includes parameters for specifying how the HTML text will flow around the applet, and how much of the Web browser window the applet will occupy. There is also syntax for specifying hardcoded parameters to be passed into the Java program. Of course these applets are not traditional "program files" at all, but Java class files containing bytecodes that will be interpreted by the Web browser's built-in Java interpreter.

When the Web browser sees the **APPLET** tag inside an HTML page, it goes back to the HTTP server where the HTML page originated to find the referenced Java class. Once found and downloaded, the Java class is interpreted, or run, by the Web browser. If you have ever seen a "Java applet started" message when browsing a Web site, then you have encountered a Java applet.

We will go into more detail later about Java applets. For now, you need to know that they have the full power of the Java programming language at their disposal, except for some restrictions regarding access to the local client workstation's resources for security reasons. That is, an applet cannot read or write files on the local file system or call any local file system executables. It can do communications back to the server it came from, however. These restrictions are known as the "*sandbox*" that the Java applet must live within, which is a constraint not faced by a full-fledged Java application. If you write a standalone Java application that is invoked from the command line, you do not have these restrictions, because you are writing a traditional application and the end user must have taken explicit steps to put your application on his or her workstation.

NOTE: With the 1.1 release of the Java Development Kit from Sun, you can now choose to write applets that do not have the sandbox restrictions by using a special process called "*digital signatures.*" This allows you to sign your applet so users can be guaranteed it came from you untampered. If the users trust you, they can allow signed applets from you to access their workstation resources. This works well in Intranet environments, where you can predefine who is allowed to distribute signed applets for company-wide use, and you can identify which company staff are allowed to run them. (The flip side of signing is the ability to preauthorize only selected users to run the applet).

JAVA APPLICATIONS

Certainly, the prospect of being able to embed Java applets inside HTML Web pages is an enticing one. That is the fuel that has fed Java's wildfire acceptance. However, you can write full fledged applications with Java, as well. These might be server-side applications that run on the AS/400 and do business logic or data manipulation, or client-side applications that display full-fledged user interfaces, access the AS/400 for data, or call programs on the AS/400. These applications are invoked by running the **JAVA** interpreter on them. You pass to the interpreter command the name of the Java class file to be interpreted.

Java applications are still portable to all Java-enabled operating systems (which is pretty much all of them now). They have the advantage of having their own main window and user interface real estate. They also do not have the sandbox restrictions that were described for Java applets.

For servers such as the AS/400, you can only run Java applications (not Java applets). This is because the Web browsers run only on the clients. On the other hand, in order to create the client-side applets, your only prerequisite is the presence of Web browser on all of your users' workstations. This normally won't be a problem, although there are still some countries that do not have Internet access. In some countries, Internet access is prohibited, while others simply do not have the infrastructure in place yet.

Therefore, for the client part of your application you need to make a choice between applets and applications. You gain more function and options with applications, but you will have to look after distribution and servicing yourself, because you will not have a Web browser to automatically download the program for you. (There is work afoot, however, to define an Internet-based distribution system for Java applications.) A number of Java-written installation programs are available on the market now. Yet another option is to write Java code that can be used as either an application or an applet: you simply supply a little additional code for the application version for the main "frame" window, and then call your applet code. This is a great compromise.

SUMMARY

Here is a summary of the topics covered in this chapter:

- Beyond all the hype Java is, after all, a programming language.

- Java is an *interpreted* language (although traditional compilers for Java are starting to appear). Web browsers, by the way, are already using a technology called "**Just in Time**" (*JIT*) compilation that compiles a Java applet into machine code "on the fly" and then runs the machine code.

- Java is made available freely on the Internet as part of a Java Development Kit (JDK)

- Java source code is compiled via **JAVAC** into Java bytecode.

- Java can be used to write Web browser-based *applets*, or traditional *applications*.

- Java applets require the HTML **APPLET** tag, while applications use the **JAVA** command (or **JRE** if using the Java Runtime Environment).

- Java applets have, by default, a security restriction known as a ***sandbox***, which prevents them from accessing the local file system or any remote server other than the one from which they originated.

REFERENCES

- HTML online reference: `http://www.blooberry.com/html/`

- InterNIC home page: `http://www.internic.net`

- Perl home page:
  `http://www.rge.com/pub/languages/perl/CPAN.html`

- JavaSoft Web page for Windows JDK:
  `http://www.javasoft.com`

- IBM redbook about the AS/400 and the Internet:
  Title: **Cool Title About the AS/400 and Internet**
  Authors: Heikki Arhippainen, Richard Halleen, Lee Hargreaves, James Hudlow, Bernd Lindner, Brian R. Smith, S W Wu
  Document Number: SG24-4815-01

- IBM manual about the AS/400, TCP/IP and the Internet:
  Title: **OS/400 TCP/IP Configuration and Reference V4R2**
  Document Number: SC41-5420-01

2

The Java Onion

ILE RPG IV Review

It is our belief that it is easier for you to learn Java by comparing it with RPG IV ("ILE RPG") than by comparing it to RPG III. This is because new constructs exist, both in the RPG IV language and in the ILE (*Integrated Language Environment*) definition, that are more modern and a closer match to Java and its environment than RPG III. This belief is backed up by the experience of RPG programmers who have already made the journey to Java. They report back that the transition to Java is made far easier if you have a footing in ILE RPG. Many of the new concepts you need to learn in Java, such as modularity, free format expressions, and methods, are easier learned first through their counterparts in RPG IV — modules and procedures.

We also believe that you should be continuing your code migration to ILE RPG IV from RPG III, even if you are eventually destined for Java. Moving from RPG III to IV will give you short-term quality, maintainability, functionality, and performance benefits (the latter applies primarily if you are on RISC, where you need to be able to use Java on the AS/400 itself anyway). Such a progression will position your code base to make selective replacements with new Java code. This is not possible if you have a monolithic RPG III application model.

For these reasons, we have chosen to teach you Java by comparing it to RPG IV. However, we realize many of you have not yet made the transition to this greatly improved version of the language, so we will spend a little time at the beginning of this chapter reviewing the overall concepts of ILE and RPG IV. These are the "outer shell" concepts, not the internal language definition details. As we go deeper into the Java language, we will continually contrast it to appropriate details in RPG IV, and where there are new functions in the RPG language we will briefly review these before diving into their Java counterparts. You should find that this book will make you more comfortable not only with Java, but also RPG IV. You are going to end up with two very important skill sets, so start thinking about that salary increase now! If you are familiar with RPG IV and ILE, you can safely skip these RPG reviews, of course. And presumably you have already received half of your deserved salary increase!

In essence we will "peel the onion", looking first at RPG IV and then Java, from the outside in. (No crying, now!) This is an extensive chapter that covers a good deal of ground, but when you are done you will be well on your way to being familiar with the architecture and interfaces of Java applications (and of ILE RPG as well). Note that we use RPG IV, ILE RPG and ILE RPG IV terms interchangeably.

> **NOTE:** You may feel like you are "drinking from a fire hose" in this chapter as many new concepts are thrown at you. Do not despair: subsequent chapters will contain information and examples that will make these concepts clearer. You'll eventually "get it." Grab a "byte" to eat if you need to, then we will begin...

RPG IV Versus RPG III Applications

In a typical, traditional RPG III application, we might have a CL program that gets initial control and that calls the appropriate RPG program or programs as required. The RPG program, of course, is huge. It contains mainline code and includes dozens if not hundreds of subroutines. For large applications, there may be dozens or even hundreds of these RPG programs, but due to the overhead of calling them, each does a significant amount of work when called, usually driving an entire piece of the application. The CL program might put up a main menu and process the selected option by calling the appropriate RPG program. It also, of course, performs file overriding and library list manipulation.

Such a scenario is illustrated in Figure 2-1:

Traditional Application

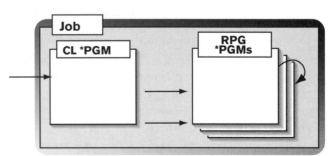

FIGURE 2-1

NOTE: The application is "scoped" to the job, so common resources, such as open data paths and file overrides, are available and applicable to all the programs in the job.

Now, we jump to what a typical ILE RPG application might look like, as shown in Figure 2-2:

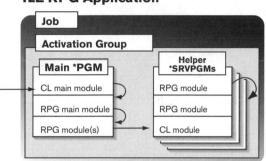

ILE RPG Application

FIGURE 2-2

We see some major differences here compared to the previous setup. First, ILE redefines the *compilation unit*: rather than compiling a source member directly into a program object (*PGM), in ILE you compile a source member into an intermediate module object (*MODULE) using the **CRTRPGMOD** command. These modules are not "shippable" and you cannot "call" them from the command line as you call a program. Rather, they are designed to be subsequently "bound together" into a program object using the **CRTPGM** command.

There is also a **CRTBNDRPG** (*Create Bound RPG*) command for creating single-module program objects in one step, but you should only use this as a short-term solution as you convert to RPG IV. The power of ILE is that modules compiled from different languages, such as ILE CL and ILE RPG (or ILE C, ILE C++ or ILE COBOL), can be "bound together" to form a single program object. This program object is no different than what you are used to—you call it from the command line or via a command (*CMD) object. The question is: which module gets control from the command line? The answer: by default, the first one specified on the **CRTPGM** command that created it. You'll learn more about this later.

Why, in RPG III, did we write such large programs? Performance, of course. It is simply too expensive to make calls between programs using the external CALL op-code. There is a downside to using these large programs. The disadvantages include:

- *Ease of Maintainance.* You are new to the job, and you have been given the assignment of fixing an identified bug in someone else's code. (Why is it "other" programmers always write terrible code? Why is the driver in front of you is always too slow and the one behind you always too fast?). Your supervisor says, Here is their twenty-thousand lines of source code, go for it!

- *Ease of Collaboration.* Suppose there are twelve of you working on a hot new project — but there is only one source member. Wait your turn to edit it.

ILE set out to improve on this development and application model. It strikes at the very heart of why we write large, monolithic programs-the performance of inter-program calls. By defining modules, as well as something else *very* important, ***procedures***, it allows us to write smaller pieces of code that contribute to the final program object. Each small piece of source code gets compiled into an intermediate (that is, not permanently required and not shipped) module object (*MODULE). These modules can call each other without the performance penalty commonly encountered with program calls. All these modules are eventually combined to form a single program object that you can ship. Here is how ILE solves the problems mentioned earlier:

- *Ease of Maintainance.* You are new, but you are good! You found the bug in that other programmer's code (ever wonder what others say about our code? "they are a programming God!", surely) because you only had to look at two thousand lines of code, not twenty thousand lines of code. And you did it before lunch. Take the rest of the day off.

- *Ease of Collaboration.* All twelve programmers get their own source member to work on. Their work is combined later by binding the twelve modules into one program object. (Of course, these twelve programmers need to talk once and a while to know what the other is doing!)

You are probably wondering: how do all of these modules "call" each other? Can one module call a subroutine in another one? No. Subroutines are simply disguised "goto" statements. You cannot "goto" another module. In V3R1, we are forced to write modules that each have "mainline" code, and we call those from other modules the same way we call programs today (but without the performance cost). As of V3R2, however, life is significantly better (well, we still have mortgages, sorry!). This release of RPG IV adds ***procedures.*** These resemble subroutines, but they allow code in one module to directly call a procedure in another (see Figure 2-3). They are "grown up" subroutines that allow multiple "entry points" into a module, as opposed to a single mainline entry point. They also offer numerous other advantages over subroutines, such as local variables (finally, RPG has local variables!).

In the end, once you have all your modules with their associated procedures, you bind all the modules together to form a single program. If you want to facilitate reuse of your procedures by more than one program object, you can either bind the same module into multiple program objects or, preferably, put them into a ***service program*** instead. Service programs (*SRVPGM) are new entities in ILE. Unlike programs, they cannot be called from the command line. Rather, they are intended to be called programmatically by code inside one or more program objects. Once again, it is the procedures inside the service programs that are called. (Note that like programs, service programs can consist of one or more modules.)

ILE RPG Modules

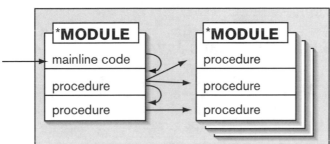

FIGURE 2-3

An important aspect of having these modules inside programs and service programs is that, if you change the source code for one module, you can recompile that module and selectively "replace" or "update" it inside the program or service program, using the **UPDPGM** and **UPDSRVPGM** commands. This avoids the need to recompile all of the source code that comprises the program or service program.

The intention of grouping these procedures into modules is that you can take a monolithic old program, divide it into smaller modules, and then bind them back together into a single program. Furthermore, you can take what was formerly a group of multiple programs and think about binding pieces of them together into a new, smaller collection of programs and service programs, thus reducing the amount of program to program calls you have to make. Commonly needed subroutines can be packaged as service programs instead of using the old copy-and-paste or /COPY tricks that lead to maintenance problems and bloated programs.

All of these new ILE constructs will be described in greater detail as we progress, and as we compare them directly to their counterparts in Java, when applicable.

Finally, in our initial ILE application picture, we show an ***activation group*** inside a job. These are also new constructs for ILE. You can have more than one activation group per job, and all of your application's resources can be scoped to one activation group as opposed to the entire job. Resourses in one activation group do not get shared with another activation group. This allows for more fine-grained control over important aspects such as file overrides and open data paths. Activation groups can be "named" so that they persist for the life of the job; they can also be defined so that they are created and destroyed with the life of the program. For performance reasons, it is very important to use ***named*** activation groups, which is *not* the default. You define this on the `ACTGRP` parameter of the **CRTPGM** or **CRTSRVPGM** commands. Activation groups are very important in order to understand and to master ILE, and all ILE books and manuals discuss them. However, they have no relevance to learning Java, so we defer detailed discussion of activation groups to these other ILE books.

THE OUTER SKIN: RPG VERSUS JAVA

RPG's Outer Skin

To recap the previous discussion, in ILE RPG IV, your applications will have one or more program objects that are each bound to one or more service programs (see Figure 2-4). Your programs and service programs are comprised of compiled modules.

FIGURE 2-4

Java's Outer Skin

In Java, your application is comprised simply of a number of ***class*** files (.class). Class files contain Java bytecode, which are compiled from Java source. Recall that bytecodes are not machine code that a traditional compiler produces, but simply a more effecient way to represent your source. It would be too slow to interpret source directly. Bytecodes are in binary format, so they are easier to parse. They remain, however, completely platform independent.

You will have a primary class file that gets invoked from the command line, and many additional class files that are used by this first class file, as shown in the following figure.

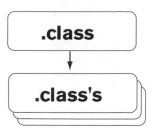

FIGURE 2-5

Compiling RPG

In RPG IV, both program objects and service programs are comprised of one or more **bound** modules. Each compilation unit-or module-is compiled from a corresponding source member, using **CRTRPGMOD** (*Create RPG Module*). The term *bound* implies that these modules are bound or "glued" together using the **CRTPGM** (*Create Program*) or **CRTSRVPGM** (*Create Service Program*) commands. This effectively takes multiple separate compilation units (that is, modules) and "binds" them into a single runtime unit (a program or a service program). Other service programs required by this program are "linked" into the program by specifying them on the **CRTPGM** command, as shown in Figure 2-6.

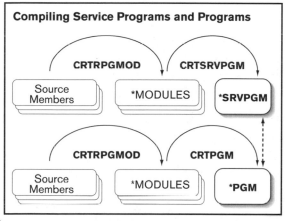

FIGURE 2-6

The inter-module procedure calls within the program and service programs, are done using a new **CALLP** op-code, thus providing better performance than a full external program call using **CALL**. This is because at bind time (**CRTPGM** or **CRTSRVPGM**) all calls between modules are resolved to actual addresses. The overhead to resolve addresses is done once at build time rather than every time when running the application. This is in contrast to traditional external program calls, where the program has to be found in the library list, then the authority has to be verified, and finally, if all is well, the external

33

program is initialized, loaded into memory, and called. Lots of overhead is required for every single call. This is what led to the creation of super-large, monolithic RPG programs; no expense was spared to *avoid* making external program calls. What better way to achieve this than putting all the logic in one program? You know this story well.

Compiling Java

As shown in Figure 2-7, you compile Java source code (.Java) into bytecode (.class) using the **JAVAC** "compiler." There is no "bind" step equivalent to ILE's **CRTPGM** that benefits runtime performance, but compile time checks are made on the referenced classes to ensure that they do indeed exist and have the referenced entry points.

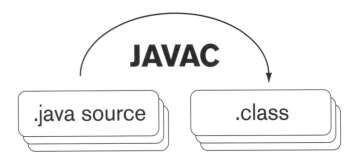

FIGURE 2-7

In traditional workstation or personal computer languages like C or C++, the concepts of ILE programs and service programs correspond to executables (.exe) and dynamic link libraries (.dll). The concept of modules corresponds to object (.obj) files.

In Java, again, you have only class files, no programs or service programs. Really, what you have with class files are Java's equivalent to AS/400 modules or workstation object files. That is to say, each class file is essentially a module-an "unbound" compilation unit. This is a consistent analogy to the Java compiler (**JAVAC**) as only the first half of a traditional compiler. It produces an intermediate representation of the source, called *bytecode*, as discussed earlier.

Whereas RPG and other traditional compilers will continue past that intermediate representation to produce machine code, Java stops at the intermediate phase, so that the result is still operating system independent (see Figure 2-8). Of course, ILE modules cannot be called from the command line, whereas Java class files apparently can. In fact, class files cannot be directly run, either. When you "run" one you actually invoke the Java interpreter on the command line and pass to it the name of the class file. It is the Java interpreter that can be run, not your class file explicitly. It is up to the interpreter, at runtime, to interpret the bytecode in the class and "run it" by calling the necessary system functions for that particular system. This is how Java achieves its portability.

ILE RPG Compilation

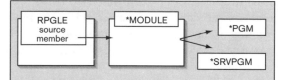

Java Compilation

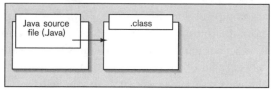

FIGURE 2-8

At runtime, when a Java class file being interpreted refers to or "calls" another class file, that class file is searched for and found. This ***dynamic loading*** of referenced code may seem like a throwback to pre-ILE, and indeed, it does have performance implications. However, dynamic loading has significant advantages, too, that Java seeks to exploit. In particular, it allows pieces of your application to be easily replaced with new editions, without requiring your entire application to be replaced. Remember, Java is first and foremost an Internet language, so these class files are often being located and retrieved from a remote server. The ability to place your application in one central server location and have all users automatically able to access it is one of Java's most significant advantages. The ability to selectively replace individual class files in that application as fixes are made is another big advantage. Further, because Java as an Internet language must always be concerned with security, the verification of each class as it is first referenced must be done to ensure its integrity at all times.

All of this discussion refers to Java that is traditionally interpreted on operating systems other than the AS/400. It applies, for example, to any client Java applications or applets that you write to interface to the AS/400. However, Java that runs on the AS/400 will be used as a server business language, like RPG, versus an Internet language. So AS/400 Java does have some optimizations that benefit such a role. For interpreted Java on the AS/400, inter-class information established at runtime is cached in order to benefit performance (but the cache is cleared if the referenced class file has been subsequently changed). The AS/400 also has a typical server language capability: it can be "statically compiled," which offers runtime performance benefits similar to that of ILE.

NOTE: In both cases we are referring to the operating system built-in Java support as of Version 4, Release 2 (V4R2) of the operating system.

Another important note about AS/400 Java is that you typically do not compile the **JAVAC** on the AS/400. You certainly can but, this step will usually be performed on your workstation—for example on Windows using the Sun JDK. The resulting .class file will then be copied or transferred to the AS/400 IFS (*Integrated File System*) where it will reside. Thus, you do not use SEU (*Source Entry Utility*) to create and edit your Java source, but rather workstation-based tools.

RPG IV Flow of Control

With RPG, in the main module of the CPP (*Control Point Program*) program object your program gets control from the command line in the first **C** specifications of the program's main module. This initial set of global **H, F, D, I, C** and **O** specifications is referred to as the ***main procedure***. This is a bit of a misnomer in that there is no formal procedure declaration or syntax. However, this is the convention you will read about in the **ILE RPG/400 Programmer's Guide**.

From that main **C** specifications point on, control is passed to other modules inside the main program or inside other modules by calling ***exported*** procedures in those. All modules other than the initial control point module may code an **H** specification **NOMAIN** keyword to indicate they only supply ***sub-procedures***, not mainline code. In RPG parlance, **NOMAIN** indicates there is no ***main procedure***. And ***sub-procedures*** refer to any procedure that is not a main procedure. We simply use the terms "main code" and "procedure" in this book.

> **NOTE:** Service programs are not callable directly from the command line. They must be linked to a program that calls the entry points, or procedures, inside the service program as required.

Figure 2-9 shows what a typical module looks like:

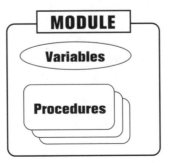

FIGURE 2-9

> **NOTE:** We use the terms *variable* and *field* interchangeably here and elsewhere in this book.

Procedures are a very important addition to the RPG language, and were introduced in V3R2. They are beefed up subroutines, in essence. However, when compared to subroutines, procedures offer the following significant advantages:

- *Parameter passing.* You can pass parameters to the procedure, thus reducing reliance on global variables.

- *Local variables.* You can declare variables with the new **D** (Definition) specifications right inside the procedure.

- *Return values.* You can return a value from a procedure by using calls to them inside expressions. Thus in effect you can create your own built-in functions.

- *Recursion.* Within a procedure you can call that same procedure again, recursively.

- *Exporting.* You can export procedures, allowing code in other modules to be able to call the procedure directly as a bound call. This allows your modules to have "multiple entry points" from the outside, which is important for service programs, for example.

- *Prototyping.* With a procedure you can first declare its ***signature,*** which is its name, parameters and return value. These "prototypes" are often defined in /COPY members so callers of the procedure in other source members can include the copy member to aid the compiler.

RPG procedures, and ILE, go hand-in-hand. What happened to subroutines, you might ask? Nothing! They still exist and you are still welcome to use them. But with the advantages of procedures, you will find using subroutines a step backward. In general, using subroutines are a *"sub"* standard practice, even though it is still *"routine."* Figure 2-10 shows is what a typical procedure looks like:

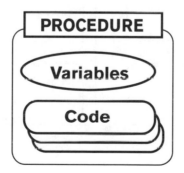

FIGURE 2-10

An RPG program will get control in the main code of its ***entry*** module, and will then call procedures that exist in:

- The same module

- Another module in the same program object
- Modules in bound service programs

Examples are shown in Figure 2-11 and 2-12:

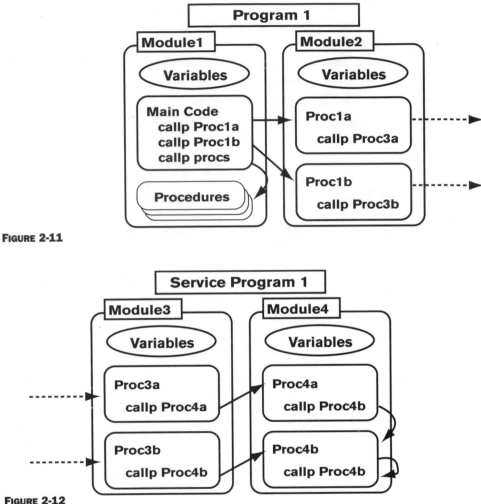

FIGURE 2-11

FIGURE 2-12

NOTE: There are two ways to call a procedure: using the **CALLP** op-code, or using **EVAL** or another op-code as part of an expression. You must use the latter alternative if the procedure returns a value that you are interested in. The **CALLP** op-code discards any returned value from the procedure.

Running an RPG Program

You call an RPG program from the CL command line by using the **CALL** command, and passing the parameters, as in

```
CALL PROGRAM1(100 200);
```

This passes control to your program. Specifically, it passes control to the ***entry*** module in your ILE RPG IV program that you specified on the *"Program entry procedure module (**ENTMOD***)"* parameter of the **CRTPGM** (Create Program) command. This defaults to the first module specified in the **MODULE** parameter list which does not have **NOMAIN** specified on the **H**-spec. Control goes to the main procedure, that is the first **C**-specs in that module (the ***Main Code*** area in Figure 2-11). This main procedure will not, as discussed, have a procedure declaration with begin and end, as sub-procedures do. It will contain up to the full complement of **H**, **F**, **D**, **I**, **C** and **O** specifications. The **C**-specs may then make calls to other procedures within the program object or any bound service programs.

RPG has modules that contain *global* variables and procedures. We think of file **F** specs as being global variables, too, as they implicitly define fields that are globally accessible by all procedures in the module. Procedures themselves contain the actual executable code, as well as *local* variables that are only accessible to that procedure.

NOTE: Procedures currently cannot contain F specifications. These must be declared at the module level prior to any procedures. Procedures contain only P (Procedure), D (Declaration) and C (Calculation) specifications.

Java's Flow of Control

How does this compare to Java? Java has class files (*dot*-class) that contain. . .what? Not procedures, and not global variables. Rather, Java class files contain ***classes.*** These are Java language constructs. They are similar to RPG data structures, in that there is language syntax for defining them, and you can declare variables inside them. But unlike data structures, you can also define procedures right inside the classes. In Java terms, these are known as ***methods***. It is inside these methods that you place all your executable code in Java. You can also define local variables inside methods that are local to that method only.

Defining Java Classes

Figure 2-13 shows what a class (called `Class1`) looks like, at a high level, inside a compiled .class (dot class) file:

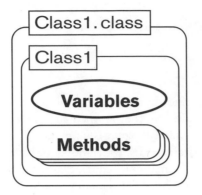

FIGURE 2-13

STYLE NOTE: The variables inside a class can be defined before or after the methods. Some advocate putting them after the methods (see Figure 2-14) because they are implementation details. Our feeling, however, is that it is more natural for programmers to see the variables first, so they have context when they see them later in use. It is simply a style choice, though, one that is entirely up to you.

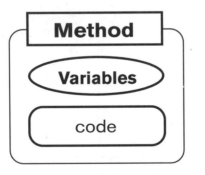

FIGURE 2-14

STYLE NOTE: Like classes, the variables inside a Java method can be declared anywhere. Well, almost anywhere-unlike the variables in a class, the variables in a method must be declared prior to their use. Convention for method variables is that they go at the top of the method, although many people prefer to embed the local variable declarations with their code, declaring variables just before they are first used.

A better analogy than an RPG data structure, to a Java class, is an RPG module. Java classes contain *global* variables that all methods can access. They also contain *local* variables inside each method which only method can access. The same applies to RPG modules as well. They can contain global variables at the top and local variables inside each procedure. The actual executable code of a Java program exists inside methods, and only inside methods. There is no Java equivalent to RPG's "mainline" code.

COMPARING ANATOMIES

RPG	Java	Comments
*PGM	Application	Program object = Application
*MODULE	.Class file	Module object = Class file
	Class	No RPG syntax for modules
Variables	Variables	Global variables or fields
Procedures	Methods	Functions
Variables	Variables	Local variables
Code	Code	Executable code

What does a Java class look like? The syntax looks like Figure 2-15:

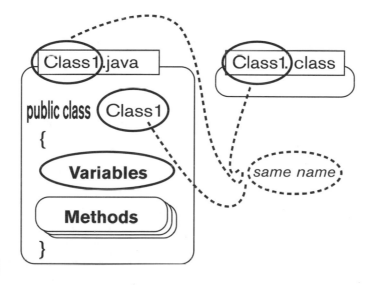

FIGURE 2-15

An interesting thing to note is that the name of the class must exactly match the name of the Java source file, and by extension, the name of the "compiled" Java class file as well. Furthermore, you are only permitted one class per Java source file. (You *can* have multiple classes, but in that case, each becomes a separate dot-class file after using **JAVAC** to compile. Good form requires that you define exactly one class per source file.) This would imply that the necessity of defining a class inside the source file, with the same name as the source file, is a bit redundant. However, there are good reasons for this:

- It reinforces the idea of a class as a language construct versus a file system object.

- It reinforces the idea that all Java code resides inside classes.

- It allows special keywords, like `public` in the previous example, in the syntax for the class.

- As of Java 1.1, classes can have inner, or nested, classes (we leave details of these to other books and the JDK documentation, however).

- It facilitates declaring instances of classes, or "objects," which we will describe shortly.

Suppose RPG had a module specification, such as **M**, and you had to define a begin-module and end-module specification as the first and last lines of every RPG IV source member. Also imagine that the begin-module-spec required you to define a module name that had to be the same name as the source member. This would be equivalent to Java's requirements for defining classes. At first, this might seem like redundant syntax, but it would offer the same benefits described for Java classes.

The "`public`" keyword, or *modifier*, in the previous example states that this class is freely accessible by all other classes that choose to use it. The default without using the term `public` means that it is only accessible by other classes in this *package*, a construct we will discover later in this chapter. To have a class accessible by the command line however, it must be declared `public`.

The syntax for defining a **Java class** is, therefore:

```
<modifier> class Name
{
    ...
}
```

Specifically, Java class syntax involves:

- The angle brackets around modifiers indicate that they are optional. You have seen `public`, but there are a few more (`abstract` and `final`) that you'll hear about in Chapter 9.

- The term `class` is not optional. It defines the *type* of Java construct you are defining.

- The *Name* is case-sensitive and totally up to you. By convention, the first character of the class name is in uppercase.

- The braces { and } define the beginning and end of the class *block*. You will see these used throughout Java for defining all blocks or "scopes." This syntax is lifted from C and C++.

- All Java source, including class definitions, are free format. Line breaks and redundant white space are ignored by the compiler. Thus, we could put every word on its own line if we wished!

The syntax for defining a **Java method** inside a class is:

```
<modifier> return-type name(<parameter-type parameter-name ...>)
{
    ...
    return return-variable;
}
```

SYNTAX NOTE:

- The list of modifiers is larger than that for a class. (These will be covered later.) As with classes, however, you need to code **public** to allow any other arbitrary user access to this method.

- The return type is the type of variable this method will return, much the same as RPG procedures require. (Note, however, that if it does not return a value you must specify the keyword **void**.)

- The name can be any name you want. By convention, method names are all lowercase except the first letter of any words other than the first, as in getName and getBillRate. Names in Java are *very* case-sensitive and they have no limit on length.

- The parameter list is a type-name pairing. If the method does not take parameters, just code "()" with nothing between the parentheses.

- As with the braces in classes, the braces { and } in methods are free form.

- The **return** statement is needed only if you return a parameter; otherwise, **return** with no parameter is acceptable. The type of the variable you return must match the return-type on the method declaration, as with RPG procedures.

SYNTAX NOTE: There are two predominant styles for Java braces:

The wrap-around brace style:

```
public void myMethod() {
    ...
}
```

Or the line-up brace style:

```
public void myMethod()
{
    ...
}
```

We prefer the latter, because this alternative makes it easier to line up the braces in an editor to ensure that you have not missed one.

Using Java Classes

Well, Dorothy, you are leaving Kansas now! Before you discover how Java's control flow compares to that of RPG, we have to take a brief detour and describe how classes are used in Java. We will describe classes in action: **objects**. We will then describe how program flow happens in Java by way of inter-operating of objects.

When you define a class, you are merely defining what the class will *look* like to the compiler. You have not defined something *directly* usable by other programmers. A class is merely a *template*; it does not reserve any memory or storage as yet. In order to use a class, programmers must declare an **instance** of it, just as you would declare an instance of a packed decimal or character data type by declaring a field of that type. In effect, a class defines a new data type to the compiler. For example, assume that you have defined a new class called MyClass. To subsequently use this class, you must define an instance of it, like this:

```
MyClass myclass1;
```

SYNTAX NOTE: all *statements* in Java end with a semicolon (;), including declarations.

This statement defines a *variable* to the compiler, of type **MyClass** and name myclass1. It will eventually be equated to an **instance** of the class MyClass-an **object**, in fact. The term **object** refers to a particular instance or usage of a class. It is with the usage of a class-an actual object- that the compiler finally allocates the memory needed to hold the variables defined in the class and in the methods of the class. Note that you can define more than one instance of a class, like this:

```
MyClass myclass1;
MyClass myclass2;
```

Each instance, or ***object***, is allocated unique storage by the compiler. This means that each object gets a unique copy of the variables declared in the class. It also means that in each case, the object can change its copy of the variables without affecting the other instances of the class.

Declaring a variable by specifying the class name as the type, as shown here, is the *first* step. But it is not the *only* step. You must further ***allocate*** a particular *object*. That is, you must ***allocate*** an *instance* of the class. In fact, in the examples shown so far, the compiler still has not allocated the memory for an instance of the class. It has merely noted that these variables will contain `references` to objects, or instances of this class type. Therefore, you have not really defined an instance as yet; you have simply defined an object variable that will contain an instance. You must explicitly allocate an instance of the class to which your variable can refer, by using the **new** operator. This can either be done at the time the variable is declared, or after. For example:

```
MyClass myclass1 = new MyClass();
MyClass myclass2;
myclass2 = new MyClass();
```

SYNTAX NOTE: The equals sign (=) is used in Java to equate a value to a variable. It is the assignment operator, just as it is in the **EVAL** op-code in RPG IV.

This assigns your variable to a new instance of your class. That instance, or object, is a piece of memory that is allocated by the **new** operator. Your variable (say, `myclass1`) is given the address of this allocated memory. Thus, object variables do not contain objects *per se*; they contain addresses of objects. Java calls these addresses ***references***. It is very important to think of object variables, such as `myclass1` and `myclass2` in the preceding example, as *references to objects*, versus actual objects. (Remember, too, that an object is an instance of a class or, simply put, some unique memory allocated somewhere.) This is a key Java concept. Unlike regular base data type variables, object variables require the second step of pointing them to an allocated class instance- an object. An ***object reference variable,*** then, like `myclass1`, contains the memory address or reference of an allocated object.

This concept of an object variable being a reference to an object carries the implication that you can change on the fly which instance of the class the variable points to:

```
MyClass myclass1 = new MyClass();
MyClass myclass2 = new MyClass();
```

At this point, **myclass1** and **myclass2** each point to separate objects in memory, as shown in Figure 2-16:

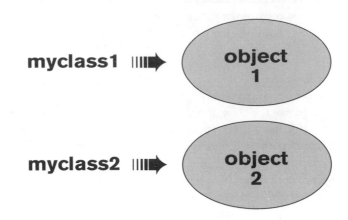

FIGURE 2-16

Now, consider this new line:

```
myclass2 = myclass1;
```

This line is interesting because it resets **myclass2** to refer to the same object in memory that **myclass1** does.

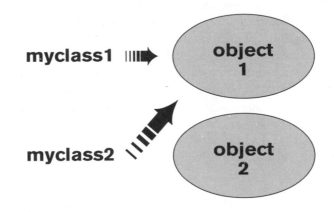

FIGURE 2-17

Changes made to variables using **myclass1** will affect what you see using **myclass2** now. So what happens to the second object in memory? If no other references exist to it, it will be vacuumed up by the *garbage collector*. This always runs in the background, looking for dead objects like this to reclaim. '

In summary: You *use* a class by declaring a variable and specifying the class name as the type, and then allocating an instance of the class with the ***new*** operator. This allocates unique memory for each of the global variables in the class. A particular instance is called an object. You can have multiple objects of the same class, but each has their own copy of the variables that are defined inside that class. A class is like a template that describes common information for all instances of that class:

- what the variable types and names are in each instance (and any initial values you specify).
- what methods, and their code, are available in each instance.

Recall our discussion of RPG service programs: there is one copy of them, but they can be used by many programs. Furthermore, each program that uses a particular service program gets its own copy of the global variables in the modules that comprise the service program. (Actually, two programs in the same activation group might share the same copy of the variables unless you specify a unique name for the activation group of the service program.) This concept closely resembles that of classes, except that your Java programs can have as many instances of a class as they like, while RPG programs can have only one "instance" of a service program, and hence its modules and their variables.

Another analogy to classes versus objects that you may find useful is that of compilable source. Source members (like RPG or DDS) can be compiled multiple times into multiple objects. The source itself is useless to an application. Only the compiled object can be used. Similarly, a Java class is not the important thing; rather, it is the instantiated objects of the class that are important to your application. Thus, you can roughly equate the `new` operator, which does the instantiation, as being analogous to a source compiler. If you want, you can instantiate (or compile) the same class (or source) as many times as you like, as long as each resulting object is given a unique name. Furthermore, each resulting object is totally independent of the others- they each hold their own data.

For all of us learning Java or other object-oriented languages, the concept of a class as being merely a ***template*** of something that must be "instantiated" in order to be used causes the greatest confusion initially. There are many other analogies, such as a class being a cookie cutter and the objects being the actual cookies. Don't worry; these concepts will become clear as you read the many examples throughout this book. You will be leaving a trail of cookie crumbs in no time!

Accessing Members in a Java Class

With an object variable, you can now access the variables and the methods inside that instance of the class. Collectively, variables and methods of a class are referred to as class *members*. Suppose you *already* have a class called Stack that manages integers on a last-in, first-out stack. It might have methods push and pop that put an integer on the top of the stack and remove the top item from the stack, respectively. Here is what the code that *uses* that class might look like (note that this code would exist in a method inside *another* class):

LISTING 2-1

```
Stack myList = new Stack();    // allocate instance of stack class
myList.push(100);              // stack contents: 100
myList.push(200);              // stack contents: 200, 100
int topValue;                  // declare an integer variable
topValue = myList.pop();       // topValue: 200, stack contents: 100
```

SYNTAX NOTE:

- Line comments in Java start with a double forward-slash (*//*).

- Java has "primitive" data types, such as "int" for integer, as well as object reference variables. These will be discussed in subsequent chapters.

Stack is a good example of the power of objects, as it is likely that your program will use more than one stack. Each one is another instance of the class Stack, that is, each one is a unique object.

Once you have an object (in this case, myList) you can call the methods inside that object by using the ***dot operator*** on the object. The dot comes after the name of the object, and the method name comes after the dot. Then, as with RPG IV procedure calls, you place the parameters inside round parentheses.

You can access variables inside the object in exactly the same manner, using the dot operator. Suppose the Stack class has an integer variable inside it called topIndex. This variable holds the array index of the top item in the stack. You could change that variable directly, as long as you qualify the variable reference with the object name. For example:..

```
myList.topIndex = 12; // change value of topIndex in object myList
```

Since multiple objects each have their own copy of the variables and methods in a class, it is very much necessary to tell the compiler which version of the variables or methods you want to use by identifying the object. If you come from a System/38 background, just think of this as object.variable versus object.library. You are *qualifying* the reference. Because variables defined at the class level have unique storage per class instance, they are usually referred to as *instance variables*. Their value depends on the instance, or object, of the class in which the reference is made to them. *Instance variable* is a better term than the one we have used to this point, *global variable,* and we will use this term from now on.

Since every variable and method in Java must exist inside a class, it follows that your code will be littered with these xxx.yyy and xxx.yyy() expressions. This is unavoidable. Imagine your RPG **C**-specs code having to qualify every reference to a data structure sub-field with the name of the data structure. That's life in an object-oriented world: You need to be "qualified" to do it!

Actually, not every member (variable or method) reference needs to be qualified with an object name. The exception occurs when you are referring to members in the current class in which you are writing code. If you are writing code in a method (remember, that is the only place you can write code) and you refer to a variable without qualifying that variable with an object name, the Java compiler will first look for that variable definition in the current method (local variable). If it is not defined there, the compiler will look for the variable definition in the current class in which the method is defined (instance variable). If it is not found there, you will get an error. Referring to an instance variable, (either to read or to write it), is equivalent to telling the compiler that you are referring to a variable in *this* class—in this class *instance*, actually. In fact, there is a special predefined object variable in Java called **this**. Sometimes you may need to use it. For example, if you define a local variable of the same name as an instance variable, and want to reference or use the instance variable, you will have to qualify it with **this**. For example:

LISTING 2-2

```
class Aclass
    {
    int george;  // instance variable
    int phil;    // another instance variable
    void aMethod()
    {
        int george;     // local variable
        george = 1;     // change the local variable
        this.george = 2; // change the instance variable
        phil = 3;       // No local "phil" so not ambiguous
    }
    }
```

In this example we have a class, called Aclass, that contains two class instance variables, george and phil, each of type integer. This class also contains a method called aMethod, which contains a local variable called george, and some Java logic to assign a value to all three variables- the two instance variables and the one local variable. Notice that since the

49

variable george is declared both locally and at the class level, the local variable "hides" the class instance variable. The only way to access the class instance variable, then, is to qualify it with the **this** special name to tell the compiler you are referring to the variable declared in "this" class instance.

Running a Java Program

We are back on track again. You now know how to define classes, declare and allocate instances of them (object variables), and invoke methods and change variables in them. In other words, you know how to use objects. We now review what Java flow of control looks like in a typical Java application, as shown in Figure 2-18.

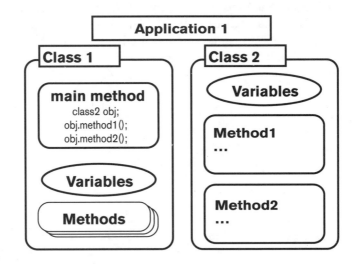

FIGURE 2-18

The main method (covered later) of the initial class gets control first. It then calls methods in its own class as necessary. It also instantiates instances of other classes (objects) and invokes methods on those classes as necessary. Continuing with the analogy of an RPG module to a Java class and an RPG procedure to a Java method, these other method calls are synonymous with procedure calls within other modules in RPG. All this is done in order to accomplish the desired task of the Java application, and when that has been done, the main method finally "returns" to the caller and the application ends.

Calling All RPG Procedures

In RPG, you have three ways to call a procedure:

- As part of an assignment statement where the returned result is saved in a variable.
- As part of an expression where the returned result is used in the expression but not saved.
- Using the **CALLP** procedure call op-code which runs the procedure and discards the returned value, if any.

Other notes:

- Procedure names can be up to 1024 characters long (more than 15 requires a continuation name specification) as of Version 3, Release 7. The names are case *tolerant* (although the *exported* names are allowed to be mixed case as of Version 4 Release 2).
- Procedure names must be unique within the module.
- Procedures can be defined to take optional parameters, which need not be specified on invocation, or can be passed the special value ***OMIT**.
- Procedure parameters passed inside parentheses are delimited on a call using a colon.
- If the procedure does not take any parameters, no parentheses are specified on the call.

Calling All Java Methods

In Java, you have the same three ways to call a method, although of course each uses a different syntax:

- As part of an assignment statement, where the returned result is saved in a variable.
- As part of an expression, where the returned result is used in the expression but not saved.
- By a simple direct call, which runs the method and discards the returned value, if any.

The following table compares the three invocation options in both languages:

RPG		Java
EVAL	myVar = myProc(p1 : p2)	myVar = myObject.myProc(p1,p2);
IF	myProc(p1 : p2) = 10	if (myObject.myProc(p1,p2) == 10)
CALLP	myProc(p1 : p2)	myObject.myProc(p1, p2);

Other notes:

- Java method names can be any length and are case-sensitive.

- Methods *cannot* be defined as taking optional parameters in Java.

- Method names need *not* be unique within a class, as long as the **signature** is unique. The **signature** is the combination of the method name plus the number and type of parameters.

- Method parameters are passed inside parentheses and are delimited on a call using a comma.

- If the method does not take any parameters, empty parentheses *must* be specified on the call. This is preferable to RPG's syntax in that it makes an obvious visual distinction between a variable reference and a method call. The following table gives examples of no-parameter calls:

RPG		Java
EVAL	myVar = noParms	myVar = myObject.noParms();
IF	noParms = 10	if (myObject.noParms() == 10)
CALLP	noParms	myObject.noParms();

Java Overload! Java Overload!

As we have indicated, Java allows you to have multiple methods with the same name, in the same class, as long as the number or type of parameters are different for each. This is a key concept in object-oriented languages like Java, and it is called method **overloading**. You are effectively *overloading* the name of the method with multiple definitions. This allows you to imply to users of your class that in each case the operation to be performed is the same—only the inputs are different. You might, for example, have a String class that has two methods for substring: one that takes a single "position" number and returns the substring from that position until the end, and another that takes a position number and a "length" number and returns the substring from the given position for the given length. This makes use of the substring method more intuitive than having two methods called, say, substring and substringWithLength. Note that under the covers, the single parameter version of substring will likely just invoke the multiple parameter version with the remaining length of the string supplied as the second parameter.

Method overloading is a particularly important feature of Java since the language does not allow you to define methods that take a variable number of parameters (or optional parameters). RPG procedures do allow for this, offsetting somewhat the need for overloading in RPG.

Prototyping RPG Procedures

To use a procedure in RPG, you must prototype it first. This involves the use of the new **D**-spec (Definition) with the **PR** definition-type. A prototype is essentially a pre-declaration of a procedure's name, return value (if any), and parameters (if any). This prototyping is done in your source prior to the definition of the procedure and, most commonly, it is in a copy member that all users of the procedure /**COPY** into their source at the top. Here is an example of a prototype for a procedure, SWAP, that returns nothing and takes in two "output" parameters (that is, the procedure changes them):

LISTING 2-3

```
DSWAP             PR
D parm1                       5I 0
D parm2                       5I 0
```

Here is another example of a prototype of a procedure, COMPARE, which does return a value (an integer), and which takes in two "input" parameters (that is, the procedure does *not* change them so we code the keyword **VALUE** to indicate that they are pass-by-value):

LISTING 2-4

```
DCOMPARE          PR          5I 0
D parm1                       5I 0 VALUE
D parm2                       5I 0 VALUE
```

Now, make note of the following:

- The name of the procedure is defined on the **PR** statement. You can specify keywords (in positions 44 through 80) that apply to callers of the procedure: **EXTPROC**(name), **EXTPGM**(name), and **OPDESC**. The first two allow you to define a name for external callers (code outside of this module) that is different than the internal name, while the last allows you to specify operational descriptors- useful information you can query about the passed in parameters (see **ILE RPG/400 Programmer's Guide** for a good description of this).

- The return type, if any, is also specified on the **PR** statement. You can also specify keywords that apply to the returned type (for example, **DATFMT**, **TIMFMT**, **DIM**, **LIKE**, **PROCPTR**). See the **ILE RPG/400 Reference** manual for more information (which, by the way, is available online in CODE/400 when editing ILE RPG source). The name on the **PR** spec is the name of the procedure, not the name of the returned value; there is no name associated with a return value.

- The input parameter definitions follow. The compiler takes any subsequent **D**-specs with blanks in positions 24 and 25 (where **PR** is) as parameter definitions.

- The parameter variable names are optional, and need not be the same as those specified in the actual procedure definition. You can use more meaningful names than you do in the actual procedure definition if you choose. The names can "float" anywhere between positions 7 and 21.

- The keyword **VALUE** indicates a pass-by-value parameter versus the default of pass-by-reference. This implies the procedure cannot change these variables.

- There are a number of other keywords possible on the parameter definitions. In addition to the keywords mentioned for the return value on the **PR** spec, you can also specify **CONST, NOOPT, OPTIONS(*NOPASS, *OMIT, *VARSIZE, *STRING), STATIC** or **VALUE**. Again, see the reference manual for descriptions of these.

Defining RPG Procedures

Having prototyped an RPG procedure with its parameters and return type as just described, the next step is to actually define the procedure. RPG procedure definitions start with a new specification type- the **P** (Procedure) spec. A begin-procedure specification and an end-procedure specification are located at the beginning and end of the procedure. These are indicated by a **B** and an **E** in position 24 of the P-spec, respectively. In columns 7 to 21, you place the name of the procedure, which must exactly match the name specified on the prototype.

```
PSWAP                   B
   *  . . .
PSWAP                   E
```

NOTE: The name of the procedure can "float" anywhere between columns 7 and 21. It need not be left-justified. Also, on the begin-procedure specification, you can specify keywords in positions 44-80. At this time, the only valid keyword for a procedure is **EXPORT**, meaning this procedure is to be accessible by code inside other modules.

If the procedure returns a value or takes parameters, you follow the begin-procedure P-spec with a *procedure-interface* specification, a **D**-spec with **PI** in positions 24 and 25. This procedure interface spec is similar to the **PLIST** with which you are already familiar for programs. It is basically a repeat of the prototype definition, the only difference being the use of **PI** versus **PR**. This is so the compiler can easily ensure the two are identical; after all, you must define a procedure's interface exactly the same way that you prototyped it for callers. Thus, the procedure interface repeats the name of the procedure on the initial **PI** spec, and defines the returned value type, if any, on the same spec. Any input parameters are subsequently defined in the following **D**-specs, with positions 24 and 25 blank. These will be a complete repeat of their prototype definitions: copy and paste!

Having defined the return value and parameters (if any) with the procedure-interface specs, you would define any needed local variables with **D**-specs and an **S** (for "Standalone") or **DS** (for "Data Structures") in positions 24-25. Then, the logic follows in the **C**-specs and finally in the `return` statement. You cannot define any other specs, such as an **F**-spec, locally in a procedure; these are defined only at the top of the module.

The following is an example procedure that will compare two integer numbers (integer is one of the new data types in RPG IV):

LISTING 2-5

```
      * COMPARE procedure
 PCOMPARE           B
      * Procedure interface
 DCOMPARE           PI              5I 0
 D parm1                            5I 0
 D parm2                            5I 0
      * Local variables
 D retval           S               5I 0
      * Logic
 C                  if        parm1 > parm2
 C                  eval      retval = 1
 C                  else
 C                  if        parm1 < parm2
 C                  eval      retval = -1
 C                  else
 C                  eval      retval = 0
 C                  endif
 C                  endif
      * Return statement
 C                  RETURN    retval
      * Procedure end
 PCOMPARE           E
```

Prototyping Java Methods — Not!

Java- unlike RPG, C, and C++- does not require or allow you to prototype your methods prior to defining them. In fact, Java does not even have the concept of copy-members, which is where these prototypes typically are placed. When you define a Java class and the methods inside it, you declare and define the methods in one step, as shown in the following example

LISTING 2-6

```java
public class Testing
{
   public void swap(int parm1, int parm2)
   {
     // code to swap the parameters
   }
   public int compare(int parm1, int parm2)
   {
     // code to compare parameters and return -1,0 or 1
   }
}
```

If you do not have prototypes that can be included, how does the compiler verify the parameter and return types on calls to methods? It does this as part of its dynamic loading of classes: when a class is referenced or used in another class, both the compiler, and later the runtime, will verify all method calls to an object of that class are correct. It does this by actually going out and getting the .class file object from the system as it needs it.

Defining Java Methods

As we have seen, in a Java method you define the return value, the method name, and the parameters all in one statement. Following this initial statement, the method body is enclosed in braces, and it contains local variable declarations and logic, and finally ends with a **return** statement (if the method returns a value). The following example shows the Java method equivalent to the RPG COMPARE procedure example just shown:

LISTING 2-7

```java
int compare(int parm1, int parm2)
{
    int retval;
    if (parm1 > parm2)
      retval = 1;
    else if (parm1 < parm2)
      retval = -1;
    else
      retval = 0;
    return retval;
}
```

As you see, the return value int (integer) is specified first, followed by the name of the method and, in parentheses, the type and name of any parameters, separated by commas. Any modifiers (such as **public**) come before the return value. If the method does not return a value, you have to specify the language keyword **void**. The list of modifiers, which are described throughout this book, are:

Modifier	Description
public	Method accessible by all
private	Method only accessible by this class
protected	Method only accessible by this class and those that extend it (see Chapter 9)
static	Method can be used without instance of class
abstract	Empty method;- will be coded by a class that extends this one (see Chapter 9)
final	Method cannot be overridden by classes that extend this one (see Chapter 9)
native	Method implemented in other language
synchronized	Only one thread of execution is allowed to run this method at a time (see Chapter 11)

NOTE: Parameters passed to Java methods are passed by value (primitive types), compared to the default in RPG, which is pass-by-reference. This has serious implications: pass-by-value means that the contents of the parameters are copied at call-time, while pass-by-reference means that the parameter addresses are passed at call-time rather than a copy of the values. This means Java methods cannot alter the contents of passed parameters. There was an example previously of a Java method called "**swap**," which implies the method will swap the values of two given integers. This is easy enough to do in an RPG procedure, but in Java, the pass-by-value rule makes it difficult-any changes to the passed in variables will be ineffective. For base or *primitive* variable types (such as **int** for integer) the only reasonable circumvention is to pass the values as arrays of one item each. Java does pass arrays as references, as it turns out; more on this in the coming chapters.

RPG Code Reuse Through Service Programs

Recall the discussion of an ILE RPG application at the beginning of the chapter? Such an application generally contains an RPG program object bound to one or more service programs. The RPG program flow is between procedures in the modules that comprise both the program object and the bound service programs. When you bind an RPG program using **CRTPGM**, you specify the service programs the program object will use. However, the service programs are not physically copied into the program object, they are simply "linked" to it. The same service program can be "linked" to more than one program object, as shown in Figure 2-19.

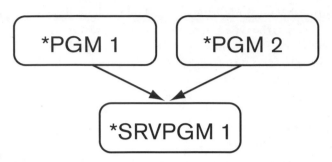

FIGURE 2-19

For commonly needed functions, using a service program can reduce the overall storage requirements, as using a service program does not affect the physical size of a program the way /COPY statements or bound modules do. Each program using the common service program receives its own copy of the variables in it at runtime (as long as the programs are in separate jobs or the service program uses a named activation group or specifies *CALLER for the activation group and the program using it uses a uniquely named activation group). Service programs are the best examples of code reuse: there is only one copy of both the source and the object on the system, no matter how many programs use it. This is also a big plus for maintenance, if the service program has to be updated. In many cases, it can be replaced without requiring the reconstruction of all programs that use it.

Distributing Your RPG Service Programs

Once you have an ILE RPG service program that contains a number of useful procedures, the time will come when you want to either sell it or at least package it up for reuse by others. This is easily done. For anyone who wants to use your service program in their own program, you would need to supply two things:

- The service program object itself (*SRVPGM)
- A copy member with the prototypes for the exported procedures

A user of your service program would then:

- Include the copy member in their source (/COPY) so the compiler would be able to find the prototypes in order to perform parameter number and type checking;
- Specify the service program name on the BNDSRVPGM parameter of the **CRTGPM** command when creating a program that uses your service program.

For your own maintenance purposes, you may want to investigate the use of the *binder language*. This is a source member language for naming all the exported procedures in your service program. You can then specify this on **CRTSRVPGM**'s `SRCFILE` and `SRCMBR` parameters. Here is a short example of some binding language source, for exporting a procedure called `RJUSTIFY`:

LISTING 2-8

```
STRPGMEXP SIGNATURE('RJUSTIFY')
   EXPORT SYMBOL('RJUSTIFY')
ENDPGMEXP
```

Actually, making procedures available to users of the service program involves two steps (*both* are required):

- Specifying `EXPORT` on the **P**-spec (procedure begin). This makes the procedure accessible to code in other modules;
- Specifying the procedure in the binding source, or specifying `EXPORT(*ALL)`, when creating the service program. This makes the procedure accessible to users outside of the service program. This is equivalent to Java's "`public`" modifier for methods.

Another ILE construct worth investigating is the use of *binding directories* (*BNDDIR). When creating programs and service programs, you can either specify all of the modules and service programs explicitly with the **MODULE** and **BNDSRVPGM** parameters, or externally, by specifying a binding directory on the **BNDDIR** parameter. Binding directories list modules and service programs. You create a binding directory with the **CRTBNDDIR** (*Create Binding Directory*) command, and populate it with module and service program names using the **ADDBNDDIRE** (*Add Binding Directory Entry*) command. This is a good way to ensure that your programs and service programs are always recreated properly, without having to rely on all programmers knowing exactly what module and service programs are needed when recompiling and recreating the objects.

Java Code Reuse through Packages

Java, like all object-oriented languages, is big on code reuse. OO majors in it. Java classes are all about code reuse. Imagine that you have a class called `Stack` for managing a stack of numbers. It is a common class, and it will be used by many other Java classes. They all get the benefit of it. As with service programs, there is only one copy of this class on your system, no matter how many others use it, and every instance gets its own copy of the variables so has a "private version" of them, at runtime.

It almost sounds as though classes could be equated to service programs and not to modules as we have previously done. Well, consider that service programs can have multiple modules. Then imagine that you have a service program not for Stacks, but for data structures in general, and that it is comprised internally of multiple modules. Say that there is one module for Stacks and one module for Queues, and one module for LinkedLists. This would be a general purpose service program that any program needing these structures could use. In Java this would be implemented not as one class, but as a collection of related-use classes. In the same way, in RPG it would be implemented not as one module, but as a collection of modules. In RPG or any ILE language, then, you would use a service program to package these related modules up into a single entity. Java has a similar mechanism for grouping related classes which is called, appropriately enough, a *package*. For example, as shown in Figure 2-20, we might define a package called dataStruct containing classes for common data structure algorithms such as stacks, linked lists, and queues.

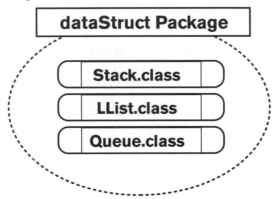

FIGURE 2-20

In Java, *packages* are a defined part of the language, as opposed to a file system object such as *SRVPGM and DLL objects. In the source file where a class is defined, you can optionally define the package of which this class is part. In fact, you will almost always define all the classes you write to be part of a package in Java. This is, among other things, a convenient way to group your classes; soon enough, you will have dozens, hundreds, or even thousands of classes that will benefit from grouping.

Defining a Java Package

Inside the source file for a class, you define the package to which this class will belong by using the **package** Java statement, as shown in Figure 2-21:

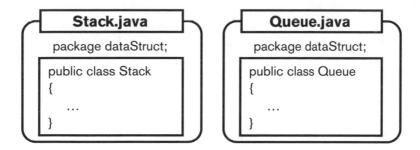

FIGURE 2-21

Note the "`package dataStruct;`" statement at the top of both source files. This is what creates a package. The **`package`** statement is essentially a compiler directive, informing the **JAVAC** compiler that this class is to be considered part of the `dataStruct` package (in this example). All classes that specify the same name on the **`package`** statement are considered to be part of that package after compiling. This statement must, if specified, be the first statement in your Java source file. If this statement does not produce some kind of file system package object, then why bother with using packages? Three reasons:

- *Grouping.* As we have discussed, it is always helpful to partition numerous items into a smaller number of groups. This helps to present a mental picture of the functionality at a glance.

- *Name qualification.* When you use a class inside a package, you typically have to fully qualify the class name with the package name, as in `dataStruct.Stack`. This allows two classes to have the same name as long as their package names are unique.

- *Privacy.* Classes in the same package can have accessibility rights that outside classes do not have.

Since classes, like AS/400 ILE modules, are designed to be small and concise, it is important to have a grouping mechanism. Imagine if you did not have ILE programs and service programs, but only module objects. You would quickly become overwhelmed with the number of modules on your system. Besides that, finding and using the appropriate module for a given job would be difficult.

STYLE NOTE: The Java convention for package names is to at least start them with lowercase letters.

Using Java Packages

The opposite of *defining* a Java package is *using* a Java package. If you have source code that needs to use the classes defined in a package, you have two choices:

- Qualify all reference to the classes with the package name, as in

```
dataStruct.Stack myList = new dataStruct.Stack();
```

NOTE: Package.class name qualification is consistent with object.member name qualification syntax.

- Import the package using the Java **import** statement at top of the source file, after any package statements, as in

```
import dataStruct.*; // import all classes in dataStruct package
```

The **import** statement can also be used to import a single class from a package, as in

```
import dataStruct.Stack; // just import the Stack class
```

There is no performance implication to importing all classes or importing one class, so in most cases you will simply import them all.

When you **import** a package, you have full, unqualified access to all classes in the package. This frees you from the tedium of prefixing the package name to all class names used in the package. You still can fully qualify each class name with its package name, if you wish. If you do fully qualify each class name, then you do not need to use the **import** statement since the Java compiler knows the package by the qualified names. Why would you want to do this? If you are importing two packages, and want to use a class that has the same name in both, then you would have to import one of the packages and refer to the classes in the other using full package name qualification.

If you do not specify a package statement in your class source file, then your class is considered to be part of the ***default package***—that is, the "unnamed" package. There is exactly one of these, and all classes without **package** statements are placed there. This unnamed package is always imported implicitly for you by Java.

Java Package Naming Conventions

It is important to choose package names that are as unique as possible in order to minimize the chance for collision with other package names. This becomes particularly important as Java packages become available on the market for global reuse and resale. To this end, the Java language allows package names to be multiple-part names, with each name separated by a dot. This allows for some clever naming conventions for all your packages. For example:

```
bobs.packages.dataStruct
bobs.packages.taxTables
bobs.packages.mathRoutines
```

In fact, Java has a standard convention for naming packages that will ensure universal uniqueness. The general rule is to take you company's URL address, such as **ibm.com**, which already is unique to the world, and reverse it, as in

```
com.ibm.dataStruct
com.ibm.taxTables
com.ibm.mathRoutines
```

Initially, the convention involved uppercasing the first section of this name, as with **COM**. However, in the summer of 1997, JavaSoft announced a change in convention to lowercase.

Packages and the File System

Packages do not have unique file system objects as service programs and classes do. However, there are rules for the location where classes inside a package must exist in the file system. Each dot-separated part of a qualified package name must correspond to a directory in the file system. This is the convention that the Java compiler and runtime (virtual machine) will follow when looking for package-qualified classes. So, for example, if you have package `com.bob.myPackage`, and your classes are "rooted" in the directory `myJava`, then your file directory structure must look like Figure 2-22:

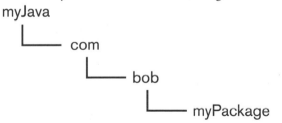

FIGURE 2-22

All of the classes inside the `com.bob.myPackage` package, then, must exist in the directory `myJava\com\bob\myPackage`. (Notice that each dot-separated part of the package name becomes a separate subdirectory of the same name.) Also keep in mind that these names are *very* case sensitive. The Java runtime will look for subdirectories with exactly the same case as the package name, just as it does when looking for a class.

CLASSPATH versus Library List

The equivalent to the AS/400 library list in Java is the CLASSPATH environment variable (this is called a system value on the AS/400). The CLASSPATH environment variable is where you list all the directories that the Java compiler and virtual machine will search when looking for a class. When working with packages, you specify the root directory (such as myJava in the previous example). Java will then automatically search the children directories according to the package naming. On Windows 95, then, your CLASSPATH statement in your autoexec.bat file might look like this:

```
SET CLASSPATH = .;c:\myJava
```

NOTE: You can specify multiple directories, which are comma separated.

When your packages are ready for distribution, you may distribute in this directory structure. Or you may "zip" your packages up into a single ZIP file (compressed) or JAR (*Java Archive File*) from which the JVM (Java Virtual Machine) can read directly. This process involves a lot of TLAs (Three Letter Acronyms)!

ZIP Files

You will use ZIP files when packaging applications as opposed to applets. ZIP is an industry-standard compression technology initially created by PKWare Inc. You can use any ZIP capable tool, such as PKWare's ***PKZIP*** or the commonly-used Windows-only WINZIP utility, to "zip up" or compress your subdirectory tree.

NOTE: You can obtain copies of these utilities at **www.shareware.com** or **www.winzip.com.** Please remember to pay the developers the token shareware fees that they request.

You give the ZIP file any name you wish, and users can set up their CLASSPATH environment variable to point directly to the ZIP file. For example, on Windows 95, you might edit your autoexec.bat file to contain

```
SET CLASSPATH = .;c:\myJava;c:\myJava\myPackage.zip
```

The JVM *class loader* will load classes directly from the ZIP file if they are found there.

JAR Files

You will typically use JAR files when packaging applets rather than applications. JAR files make use of ZIP compression technology, but they also use the all-Java tool JAR that comes with the JDK. This tool compresses not only Java files but other files such as audio and image clips, that are often required by applets. Using a JAR file can significantly reduce the overall download time of an applet and its associated files, as all the files are loaded at once in a compressed (smaller) format.

The JVM *class loader* for applets (inside a Web browser) can load classes and resources directly from a JAR file. You do not use CLASSPATH for applets; rather, you use an **APPLET** tag inside your HTML Web page source, with a **CODE** parameter pointing to the applet class, and a **CODEPATH** parameter identifying the host directory location of the files. When using JAR files, you also need to code an additional **ARCHIVE** parameter pointing to the JAR file.

LISTING 2-9

```
<APPLET code=CoolApplet.class
        codebase="http://www.mycompany.com/coolstuff"
        archive="cool.jar + cooler.jar"
        height=500
        width=300>
</APPLET>
```

NOTE: You can, in fact, use JAR files for applications as well as applets. Indeed, many may find JAR files more convenient because the "**JAR**" command for producing them comes with the JDK. If you do choose to use JAR files, your CLASSPATH statement in Windows 95 might look like this:

```
SET CLASSPATH = .;c:\myJava;c:\myJava\myPackage.jar
```

Like ZIP files, you specify the actual JAR file name in the CLASSPATH, and the Java runtime will read classes and packages directly from it.

Distributing Your Packages

For applets, distribution is easy. You place your files in a directory on your Web server (for the AS/400, this will be an IFS file system directory) and include an HTML page that points to the applets and resources with an **APPLET** tag. To update, just replace the files on the server.

For applications, you need to use another option for distributing your Java files. That is because you won't have the benefit of the Web server and Web browser to automatically download your code to the users on demand. Using a traditional installation package will work, but these are almost always specific to a few operating systems, meaning you will require separate installation code for each operating system you choose to support. In other words, you can write once/run anywhere, but you can install it on only a few systems. Some interesting new technology is in the works for this, however, including a technique called "push technology" that allows Web servers to "push" Java applications to the clients on demand, much the same way that a Web browser "pulls" them down on demand. Another option is to make use of written-in-Java installation utility, such as InstallShield Java Edition from InstallShield Software Corporation.

RPG Static Variables

In RPG, when you define local variables in your procedures, you can use the **D**-spec to specify a keyword on those declarations called **STATIC**. This keyword changes the variable's content lifetime from the life of a particular procedure call, to essentially for as long as this module is active. The variable is initialized when the program or service program is first activated (either to its type default or to the value specified with the **INZ** keyword), and never again. Each call to the procedure picks up the value for this variable from the last call to the procedure. This is in contrast to non-static variables (officially known as "*automatic*" variables) that are initialized each time the procedure is called.

> **NOTE:** It is implicit that global variables defined at the top of the module, before any procedures, are always static.

For recursive calls, where a procedure calls itself, static variables still keep their current value for each recursive invocation of the procedure. Non-static variables are reinitialized with each recursive invocation of the procedure because each invocation gets its own copy.

Static variables in RPG are only valid inside procedures. They can be only data structures or stand-alone fields.

Static variables are useful when you wish to create lasting-value variables (as with global variables) but wish them to be scoped only to one procedure. Static variables are similar to a constant, except that you have the option of changing them. To test-drive a static variable, declare a packed decimal variable in a procedure, increment the variable by a value of one inside the procedure, and return the current value of it. Create another procedure identical to the first but, this time, declare the variable static. Here is an example of how to use a static variable in RPG:

LISTING 2-10

```
     *-------------------------------------------------------
     * PROCEDURE: TESTLOCAL
     * PURPOSE  : Test use of non-static variables. Note inz(0)
     * RETURNS  : Current value of the non-static variable
     *-------------------------------------------------------
P TESTLOCAL       B
D TESTLOCAL       PI              5P 0
     * Local Variables
D counter         S               5P 0 INZ(0)
     * Logic
C                 EVAL      counter = counter + 1
C                 RETURN    counter
P TESTLOCAL       E
       *-----------------------------------------------------
     * PROCEDURE: TESTSTATIC
     * PURPOSE  : Test use of static variables. Note INZ(10)
     * RETURNS  : Current value of the static variable
     *-----------------------------------------------------
P TESTSTATIC      B
D TESTSTATIC      PI              5P 0
     * Local Variables
D counter         S               5P 0 STATIC INZ(10)
     * Logic
C                 EVAL      counter = counter + 1
C                 RETURN    counter
P TESTSTATIC      E
```

Call the procedure a couple of times. Then, compare the results to when you do not use the **STATIC** keyword, as shown in the following example:

LISTING 2-11

```
     * Prototypes of needed procedures
D TESTLOCAL       PR              5P 0
D TESTSTATIC      PR              5P 0
     * Global variables
DVALUE            S               5P 0
     * Main logic
     * Test non-static version
C                 EVAL      VALUE = TESTLOCAL
C      VALUE      DSPLY
C                 EVAL      VALUE = TESTLOCAL
C      VALUE      DSPLY
     * Test static version
C                 EVAL      VALUE = TESTSTATIC
C      VALUE      DSPLY
C                 EVAL      VALUE = TESTSTATIC
C      VALUE      DSPLY
     * End of program
C                 MOVE      *ON          *INLR
```

67

To compile this, you might want to use a CL program like the following:

LISTING 2-12

```
        PGM         /* Beginning of CL program */
        CRTRPGMOD   MODULE(COULTHAR/TESTILE) +
                    SRCFILE(COULTHAR/QRPGLESRC)
        CRTPGM      PGM(COULTHAR/TESTILE) MODULE(COULTHAR/TESTILE)
        ENDPGM
```

When you call the program from the command line, you will see that the first two calls return 1, indicating that the variable is always reinitialized to zero. The second two calls return 11 and 12 respectively, indicating that the variable is retaining its previous value between calls. (In order to distinguish the variables in this example, the static variable is initialized to 10.)

Java Static Variables

In Java, you can also have static variables. Just as with RPG, you specify the **STATIC** *modifier* keyword for them, as in:

```
static int counter = 10;
```

However, you cannot specify this *modifier* on local variables in a method the way you can for local procedure variables in RPG. Rather, it can only be specified for variables defined at the class level. Defining a variable in a class as static means that the variable will always have only one value regardless of the number of instances (objects) declared with that class. In other words, all objects of the class will share the same value for that variable. Furthermore, the modifier **STATIC** allows you to directly access the variable without requiring an object. You can simply qualify the reference with the name of the class, as in the following example.

LISTING 2-13

```
class TestStatic
{
    static int counter = 10;
}
....
TestStatic.counter = TestStatic.counter + 1;
```

For this reason, static variables are referred to as *class variables* rather than *instance variables*. They are scoped to the class itself, not a particular instance of the class (object). They are also referred to by the class name itself, not a particular instance of the class.

How might you use such a variable? Imagine that you have a class called Customer, and that Customer contains variables about the customer's information, such as company name, address, contact name, and so on. If this class represents a record in a database, you will probably need a unique key field, such as "customer number." Each time a new customer object is created, you will want to automatically assign the next available number to that customer. To do this, you would define a static variable in the Customer class called nextNumber, and you would initialize it at program start time to a number stored in the database somewhere. Then, whenever a customer is created, you would assign it that value for the customer number, and increment the customer number (and possibly update the database value as well). Again, the idea is that static class variables pertain to the class, not to any particular instance of that class.

Java Static Methods

Java allows not only variables to be defined as static, but also methods themselves, as in:

LISTING 2-14

```
class TestStatic
{
    static int counter = 10;
    // static method...
    static int getNextCounter()
    {
        counter = counter + 1;
        return counter;
    }
}
```

What does it mean to have a static method? It means, like variables, that the method can be used (called) directly without needing an instance of the object.

```
int value;

value = TestStatic.getNextCounter();
```

These are called *class methods*. They are very useful because, as you recall, Java does not allow you to write standalone functions. All code must exist inside methods which, in turn, must exist inside classes. If you do have a helper function that does not really need to be associated with a unique instance of a class, you can define it as static in a Helper class, for instance, and use it directly as though it were a standalone function. The only difference is that you must qualify each reference to the helper function with the name of the class. But at least you are not required to instantiate an instance of that class.

Static methods can only operate on local variables in that method, as well as on static variables in the class. They cannot reference instance variables in the class (non-static variables). This makes sense because the method can be used without an instance of the class having been defined. Class variables and class methods give you the benefit of traditional global variables in RPG, as well as the benefit of name scoping that a class offers; because the variables are always qualified by class name, you can safely reuse that variable name in other classes.

Finally, we have seen from experience that RPG programmers who are in the early stages of first learning Java have trouble initially understanding the differences between static methods and non-static methods. They are just not clear about when to use one versus the other. Here is some help with the concept: if your method *will* use any class instance variables, it should *not* be static. If however, your method can do its job *without* using any of the variables in the class (as opposed to local variables in the method), it may as well be static. Our previous example of a "compare" method should have been defined as static because all of the information it needs is passed into it as parameters, so it has no dependency on any instance variables in the class.

The tough part really comes when thinking of a non-static example. In order to "think OO" you need to think about writing classes and methods that act on instance variables in the class rather than always taking their information in as parameters. For example, the compare method might be part of a class called YearsOfService, and that class could have an instance variable called "years" defined as type int (for integer). It might then also have a compare method that took in only one parameter and then compared the parameter to this instance variable:

LISTING 2-15

```
public class YearsOfService
{
    int years; // instance variable
    public YearsOfService(int years)
    {
        this.years = years;
    }
    public int compare(int compareTo)
    {
        int retval = 0;
        if (compareTo > years)
          retval = 1;
        else if (compareTo < years)
          retval = -1;
        return retval;
    }
} // end class YearsOfService
```

In this sample code, note the use of the special method called "YearsOfService," which is the same name as the class. This is an example of a ***constructor***, a method that you can always optionally specify for initializing your instance variables to a user-specified value. You simply specify your parameter on the **new** operator, and it is passed in to this constructor method if it exists. (Constructors are discussed later in this chapter.)

If you find yourself writing only static methods that do not use instance variables, you are probably still thinking too "procedurally." Instead, you need to think about how you can better utilize instance variables in your class in order to store state information.

RPG Scoping

In RPG, all variables declared at the top of the source member are scoped to the entire compilation unit (program for **CRTBNDPRG** or **CRTRPGPGM**, or module for **CRTRPGMOD**). That means the variable can be accessed directly by any mainline or procedure code in the source.

Similarly, all procedures are scoped to the compilation unit. You can invoke a procedure defined in a module either from the mainline logic, or from within any other procedure in that module.

You can extend that scoping by defining variables or procedures as exported, using the **EXPORT** keyword on the definition. With this use of the **EXPORT** keyword, all modules in the program or service program have access to the variable or procedure. Local variables defined inside procedures are, of course, only accessible to the code within that procedure.

This scoping affects not only accessibility, but also naming conflicts. You must take care not to define two variables or procedures in the same scope and with the same name. If you define two global variables with the same name you will, of course, get a compiler error. Even if you define a variable and a procedure with the same name, you will still get a compiler error. However, if you define one global variable and one local procedure variable with the same name, you will not run into a compiler error. What this does is effectively "hide" the global variable to the code inside the procedure. When local code references this variable name the local code will always be referencing the local variable — there is no way to force the code to reference the global variable of the same name instead. Occasionally, this referring to the local version of the variable is what you want to do, but more often, it is a bug that leads to interesting results. For this reason, you should observe good style by using a naming convention for global variables. For instance, you might consistently use uppercase for global and mixed case for local, or prefixing all global variable names with some common string such as "g_".

Java Scoping

In Java, class variable and method names are scoped to that class, and local method variables are scoped to that method, just as in RPG. Java also will not allow two variables at the same level to have the same name. However, it does allow a variable and a method to have the same name. This is because methods are always referenced with parentheses even if they take no parameters. Therefore, the compiler can always distinguish their usage. (This would be a good change for the ILE RPG language definition, too!)

Java, like RPG, allows you to hide a variable defined in a higher scope with a variable of the same name in a lower scope. However, as discussed previously, you can force the use of a class scoped variable by using "`this`." name qualification.

Java has an additional variable scope that RPG does not—that of blocks. Inside any Java code you can start a new block simply by using the brackets { and }. Any variables defined inside this block are scoped only to this block (the next chapter covers blocks in more detail). Here is an example:

LISTING 2-16

```
void method1()
{
    int variable = 1;
    {
        int variable = 2;
    }
}
```

The use of blocks gives the Java programmer additional flexibility. Also recall that local variables can be declared anywhere within the code. The scope of the variable starts at the line where it is declared, extends down into any subsequent nested blocks, and ends at the end of the current block.

Java Accessor Rights

In Java, you give your classes names. This is in contrast to RPG, where modules are not given names as far as your source code references to them are concerned (they are given file system names, but you never refer to these names inside your source code). All variable and method names within a class definition are scoped either to that class or to the embedded block within a method. But what is the scope of the class name itself?

Java differentiates between the *scope* of a name (where it can be referenced without name qualification), and *access control* to a name (that is, a variable, method, or class name). Any name inside a class has scoping access (that is, non-qualified name access) to all names in the current scope or above and extending up to the class level. The class itself is, by default, scoped to the package it is in- any code inside the package can refer to that class name without qualification (className versus package.className). Access control, on the other hand, refers to the visibility or accessibility of *qualified* names. These are names qualified by dot syntax-for example, package.class, class.variable or class.method().

The key difference between Java and RPG in this context is that of name qualification. RPG does not have this. You can only refer to names without qualification, so the compiler looks up the scope hierarchy until it finds the first definition of that name. If it finds the name definition, you can use it. Java, on the other hand, allows you to explicitly define the particular class, variable, or method to which you are referring. Theoretically, then, this ability to explicitly qualify names with their unambiguous scope allows all Java code access to all classes, variables, and methods: you need only qualify the reference sufficiently in order for Java to unambiguously find that name. This is considered bad form in object-oriented languages such as Java. One of the tenets of OO is that of *encapsulation*—you want to give users of your package "black box" access to only selected methods, variables, and classes. This allows you to "hide" the implementation details, and subsequently change them in further revisions without worry of breaking existing user's code. Restricting creative users from accessing your "internal" variables, methods, and classes is, therefore, important for this goal. Thus, while users could access any variable or method in theory, in practise we restrict access to some of these.

Java has defined syntax that explicitly restricts who can access each part of your package. Actually, so does RPG; through the use of its **EXPORT** keyword, you can explicitly decide what variables and methods the public is allowed to see. With service programs, RPG actually allows you to divide the world into two camps: the modules within the service program (which is equivalent to the classes within your package), and the users of the service program (that is, the users of your package). By using binding source, you subset the list of exported procedures that are open to access by the end-user world of your service program. Similarly for Java, you can divide the world up into the classes that make up your package, and the users of your package. By default, all classes, class and instance variables, and methods are accessible by all the classes in the package-and no other code outside of this. This is called "package" access control. This is equivalent, then, to the **EXPORT** keyword in RPG. You can further qualify the level of accessibility by using access control modifiers in the definitions of your variables and methods:

- *public.* The world, including the end user classes, are allowed access to this variable or method.

- *private.* Only the code inside this class is allowed access to this variable or method.

- *protected.* Only this class or classes that *extend* (see Chapter 9) this class are allowed access to this variable or method.

Notice that classes, like variables and methods have, by default, package access. You cannot specify all of these modifiers for classes, but you can specify `public` for a class, indicating that it is usable by the world at large. If I use somebody else's package, I am only permitted to use those classes in the package that are defined as `public`. Inside each of those classes, I am allowed access only to the variables and methods defined `public`. As shown in the following table, this is equivalent to the variables and procedures listed in the binding source for a service program. All `EXPORT`ed names are available to all other modules in the service program (package access), while only the subset listed in the binding source are available for users of the service program (public access).

Java	RPG
package (default)	`EXPORT` keyword, but not listed in binding source
public	listed in binding source
private	*no* `EXPORT` keyword
protected	not applicable

It is safe to say, then, that in Java the public does not have access to your private parts! This is certainly considered good form.

It is considered very good form in Java and other OO languages to define all your instance variables as private or protected, and to supply `getXXX()` and `setXXX()` methods for retrieving and setting the variables. These methods are affectionately known as "getters" and "setters," and more officially as ***mutators*** and ***accessors***. The reason for using these is, again, one of encapsulation. Variables are almost always implementation details that are best left "hidden." This gives you the flexibility to later change the variable type, length, name, and so on, while keeping the get and set method interface constant, and therefore not disrupting any users. Also, it is a matter of data integrity. Only your class code should have direct access to the variables; you do not want to run the risk of someone changing them to unexpected values. Think back to the stack example. It has a `topIndex` variable that represents the index of the top entry in the stack array. No code but the `stack` class code should ever change this! This is similar to your database-end users not being able to edit the data using SEU. Instead, they must call your RPG program to access the data. Only by restricting access to your data and your variables can you ensure that the state of the data is always valid. Furthermore, only through this means can you isolate users from implementation changes.

Class Constructors in Java

Java class constructs are, as you have seen, similar to RPG modules. Typically, you define one per source file, and they contain variables and methods (procedures). The important differences you have seen so far are these:

- Classes are named *language* constructs.
- Classes can have multiple instances (objects), each with its own variable contents.

There is another important difference. Classes can have a special method called a **constructor**. A constructor is a method in the class, which the compiler and runtime recognize, and that has the same name as the class. Unlike regular methods, constructors do not specify any return type on their definition line because they cannot return values. What does a constructor do? It is called by the Java runtime when the object is first created. This is your opportunity to initialize variables and do any setup that your class requires and that your methods assume.

Because you can initialize your class-scoped instance variables when you declare them, you might wonder: What is the value add of a constructor? There are at least three reasons why you might use a constructor:

- Complex variable assignments that cannot be easily made in declaration assignment statements.
- Initial state operations or logic, such as opening a file.
- User control (programmer user that is) over the initial instance variable values. This is done by letting users pass in parameters which you use to initialize your variables.

You can also have more than one constructor. Because they must all have the same name as the class, the difference is in the number of parameters. A *default* constructor takes no parameters, but you can define other constructors with as many parameters as you need. Recall that Java allows you to *overload* methods-that is, -supply more than one method with the same name as long as the number or type of parameters are different. This applies nicely to constructors. You may have versions of your constructors that take differing parameters, giving users the freedom to use defaults or specify explicit initial values. Imagine, for example, that you have defined a class called AS400, which connects to an AS/400 from a Java client. It might have a number of constructors: one that takes an AS/400 name and prompts for the user ID and password; one that takes an AS/400 name and a user ID and prompts for the password; and one that takes an AS/400 name, user ID, and password, and does not prompt at all (unless the password is expired).

The users specify the parameters to a constructor as part of the **new** operator statement, as in:

```
AS400 myHost = new AS400(); // take defaults
AS400 myHost = new AS400("SYSTEM1", "BOB", "ABABA"); // supply defaults
```

NOTE: One constructor can call other constructors, allowing you to abstract out common code. You do this by calling the "this()" method-with the appropriate parameters, if applicable. For example:

LISTING 2-17

```
class AS400
{
    private String userId; // String is a built-in class
    private String password;
    boolean connected = false; // boolean is a built-in type
    AS400() // default constructor
    {
        userId = "phil";
        password = "greatguy";
    }
    AS400(String id) // constructor with one parameter
    {
        this(); // call default constructor
        userId = id;
    }
} // end AS400 class
```

You might have code in another class that "instantiates" instances of this class with lines of code like:

```
AS400 host1 = new AS400(); // call default constructor
AS400 host2 = new AS400("PHIL"); // call one-parameter constructor
```

The key here is that *you do not explicitly code a call to a constructor.* Rather, you simply code the "**new**" operator as usual, possibly passing in parameters, and the Java runtime implicitly calls the appropriate constructor for you. That is, the runtime looks for a constructor method in your class that matches the number and type of parameters specified with the **new** operator (after the name of your class and between the parentheses that follow) and calls that method for you, passing in the **new** parameters to the method. Constructors are really just a short form equivalent to supplying a method called init, say, that you would instruct users to call in order to initialize your object's state or variables.

Constructors, like methods, allow you to specify access modifiers. However, they have additional responsibility in a constructor-they affect who is allowed to instantiate your class. If you specify **public**, this class can be created by anyone. If you specify **protected**, this class can be created only if it is extended by another class (as explained in a later chapter). The default is public if the class is tagged as **public**, and package otherwise (only code in this package can instantiate this class with this constructor).

There is a subtlety to constructors: if you do not define any, Java will supply a default one with no parameters that does nothing. If you supply even one constructor, however, it will not do this. Therefore, if you supply one constructor that takes one parameter, and a user tries to instantiate your class without any parameters, he or she will get an error message stating that no default constructor exists. In this case, if you want to allow a no-parameter "**new**" operation you must explicitly supply a no-parameter constructor as well, even if it is empty.

Calling an RPG Program: the Mainline

As mentioned earlier, you can invoke an RPG program from the command line using the AS/400 CL **CALL** command. This gives control to the program object listed on the **CALL** command, and passes to it any parameters you have specified. The module inside the ILE RPG program that gets control is the one defined on the *"Program entry procedure module (***ENTMOD***)"* parameter of the **CRTPGM** command which, by default, is the first module found that does not have **NOMAIN** keyword specified on the **H**-spec. The mainline code found in the **C**-specs at the top of this module gets initial program control.

Calling a Java Program: the "main" Method

In the case of a Java application (and in contrast to an applet) you also invoke the Java applications from the command line, but you do so by calling the Java interpreter — **JAVA** — and passing to it the name of the Java class you wish to invoke. Typically, the initial class file you call will not be part of a named package, so you call it directly as in JAVA MyClass (note that the class file name is case-sensitive). However, if you wish to call a class that is part of a package, you must qualify the call with the package name, as in JAVA myPackage.MyClass. In this case, Java will search the CLASSPATH environment variable for a directory that has a subdirectory named myPackage, and look inside that subdirectory for MyClass.class. It will also search inside any ZIP or JAR files named on the CLASSPATH, as discussed earlier.

Can you simply call any class like this directly? No! By the same token, you cannot call into any module directly inside an RPG program, either. When the Java interpreter invokes a class from the command line using the JAVA interpreter as described above, it looks inside that class for a method called main. Actually, the interpreter searches not just any method called main, but one that specifically looks like this:

```
public static void main(String args[])
{
 ...
}
```

Java looks for exactly one such method with exactly this signature. If it does not find such a method, you will get an error message. Of course, if there were two such methods, you would have gotten an error message at compile time (**JAVAC**). The break down of the signature is shown in the following table (all parts are mandatory):

Part	Description
`public`	This method is publicly accessible.
`static`	This method does not require an instance of the class to be created first.
`void`	This method does not return any values.
`main`	This is the name of the method, and is case sensitive.
`String args[]`	This is an array of strings, one for each parameter specified on the command line.

We will cover the parameters shortly. Typically, this initial class, which contains the `main` method, instantiates classes from packages and invokes them. Because the method returns no value, no return statement is required. When the last line of the `main` method is done executing, the program ends. The following table presents some analogies here to ILE RPG:

RPG	Java	Comments
program object	main class file	File system objects where control begins
service programs	packages	RPG program uses service programs, Java application uses packages of classes
entry module in program object	main class	Main class can have any name. Typically not in a named package
mainline code	`main` method	Gets control from command line
other modules in program object	other classes `main` needs that are not in named packages	
other modules in service programs	classes in named packages that `main` uses	

Illustrated pictorially, you have something like Figure 2-23:

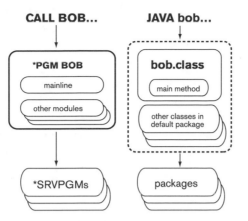

FIGURE 2-23

Command-Line Parameters in RPG

In RPG, you specify the parameters to your main program object on the **CALL** command. The RPG entry module will define the parameters that it expects, either by using the traditional ***ENTRY PLIST** C-spec statement, or by using the new RPG IV way of using **D**-spec prototyping. For example, if you have a program in which the entry module accepts a six-character string, you could define the parameters traditionally as:

```
C          *ENTRY          PLIST
C                          PARM                       KEYCHAR          6
```

You could also define the parameters with new ILE prototyping syntax as in:

```
DMAIN            PR                        EXTPGM('PRTCUST')
D KEYCHAR                     6A

DMAIN            PI
D KEYCHAR                     6A
```

Both options are equivalent. Notice that, in the latter, the **PR** specification defines the prototype, while the **PI** specification defines the actuals. It is the variable name (KEYCHAR) in the latter that is important.

D-specs (Definition) are new for RPG IV and are used to define fields, or prototypes like this. Why use this technique over our trusty ***ENTRY** technique for defining command line parameters? The advantage is that you could place the **PR** specifications inside a **/COPY** member and use it when calling this program from another program, using the **CALLP** op-code. This would give you the advantage of letting the compiler verify that you have gotten the parameters correct in the call.

NOTE: In RPG you can define command-line parameters to be of any valid type and each are explicitly defined in your ＊**ENTRY** or **PR D**-spec.

Command-Line Parameters in Java

In Java applications, you pass parameters on the command line with the **JAVA** command. You specify the parameters, after the name of the Java class to invoke, with blank delimiters. Each word or token specified becomes one parameter. Each parameter is accessible to your Java main method as an entry in the args array of strings. Unlike RPG, every parameter is passed to Java as a string, and you must explicitly convert it to the required data type yourself. (This will be covered in more detail later.) In order to pass a string with embedded blanks as a single parameter, you must enclose the string in quotes on the command line. For example:

```
JAVA bob hi there "George and Phil"
```

This fills "String args[]" array entry 0 (arrays are zero-based in Java) with "hi", array entry 1 with "there" and array entry 2 with "George and Phil."

Writing to the Command Line in RPG

Very often, it is either necessary or worthwhile to write information out to the command line. It is a time-honored debugging trick, for example, to spit out "I am here" messages so as to track your flow of control in a program (this is not so widespread anymore, thanks to the proliferation of source-level debuggers, but we all still do it occasionally). Also, almost all language introduction books start out with a simple little "hello world" program that writes this string out to the screen. The first page of the book is rarely the place to introduce display files or GUI constructs!

In RPG, a common way to write simple output like this is by using the **DSPLY** op-code. This has not changed for RPG IV, so we will not cover well-worn ground here. However, by using **DSPLY,** you could write a simple introductory and obligatory "hello world" RPG IV program, with the additional twist that it prints whatever is passed on the command line, as:

LISTING 2-18

```
 * Prototype of this program main entry
DMAIN              PR                      EXTPGM('HWORLD')
D STRING                        1000A     OPTIONS(*VARSIZE)
 * Definition of this program main entry
DMAIN              PI
D STRING                        1000A     OPTIONS(*VARSIZE)
 * Global variables
DOutString         S            52A
 * Main logic
C                  EVAL        OutString = 'Input: ' +
C                                %TRIMR(%SUBST(STRING:1:45))
C      OutString   DSPLY
 * End of program
C                  MOVE        *ON          *INLR
```

Notice that the **DSPLY** op-code has the nasty restriction of only being able to display a maximum of fifty-two characters. Calling this program with CALL HWORLD 'hi there' results in the following:

LISTING 2-19

```
                    Display Program Messages
Job 008338/COULTHAR/QPADEV0014 started on 97/07/25 at 10:34:37 in subsystem
DSPLY  Input: hi there
```

Writing to the Command Line in Java

In Java, the equivalent to **DSPLY** is called "writing to standard output." It involves using a Java supplied class called **System**, and a static object variable inside of that class called **out**, and finally a method of out called **println** —which is short for "print line." Here is an example:

```
System.out.println("Hello world");
```

By now, you are familiar with static variables, and you see here that object variables can also be static. In this case, "out" is a static object variable in the System class. Because the object is static, you can use it directly without having to first instantiate an instance of class System using **new**. Rather, you simply qualify access to it with the class name. The method **println** prints a line of text to the screen-to the command line, actually, where **Java** was invoked. In fact, it is written to a special "file" called *standard output*. This is not a file on disk. Typically, the contents of the standard output file get displayed on the invoking command line (the "console"). But, in graphical applications or in applets where there is no command line, to see this output you have to be running inside a shell that captures and displays it. For example, the VisualAge for Java product has a "console" that displays any information written to standard output while the application or applet is running inside the product.

You will quickly become very familiar with `System.out.println` as you begin to learn Java. Most of your simple starter applications will use it to display dynamic information to yourself. The method `println` takes any number of strings or variables, separated by plus signs (+), and displays them. This means that `println` automatically converts variable contents from their native type to string format, which is very useful. For objects, `println` does this by trying to call a method in the object called `toString()`. You must supply this method for this to work with objects or instances of your classes.

Here, then, is the Java equivalent of the RPG program that displays the passed-in string:

LISTING 2-20

```
// main class
public class HelloWorld
{
  // main method
  public static void main(String[] args)
  {
    // print first parameter passed
    System.out.println("Input: " + args[0]);
  }
}
```

After compiling the code (we are running on Windows 95) with `Javac HelloWorld.java`, running it looks like this:

LISTING 2-21

```
C:\JAVA>java HelloWorld "hello world!"
Input: hello world!
```

Some things to note about this example are:

- `args[0]` is the Java syntax for the first entry in array args (arrays are zero-based).
- It will fail if you do not pass in at least one parameter, because `args[0]` will not be defined.
- Any parameters after the first will be ignored.
- A multiple-word input string must be passed with quotation marks surrounding it.

A more robust version of the preceding program will check to make sure that there is at least one parameter, concatenate all of the parameters in a temporary string first, and print, like this:

LISTING 2-22

```
// main class
public class HelloWorld
{
  // main method
  public static void main(String[] args)
  {
    String outString;
    // build up output string
    if (args.length > 0)
      {
        int idx;
        outString = "Input: ";
        for (idx=0; idx<args.length; idx=idx+1)
        {
          outString = outString + args[idx] + " ";
        }
      }
    else
      outString = "No input given";
    System.out.println(outString);
  }
}
```

Don't be scared! This example presents a number of functions we have yet to discuss, such as the **if** and **for** statements. This is just a morsel to whet your appetite for the meat to come in subsequent chapters. Come back and revisit this little sample later on, and you will be amazed at how easy it is to read and understand. For now, though, just to convince you that it works, here are some sample runs:

LISTING 2-23

```
C:\PHIL\JAVA>java HelloWorld
No input given
C:\PHIL\JAVA>java HelloWorld a simple test
Input: a simple test
C:\PHIL\JAVA>java HelloWorld "helloWorld!"
Input: helloWorld!
Congratulations! You have written your first running Java code!
```

SUMMARY

You covered a lot of ground in this chapter, both from an ILE RPG point of view and from a Java point of view. You have learned that:

- A Java application is comprised of Java source files (.java) that are compiled via **JAVAC** into Java classes containing bytecodes.

- A Java source file contains one class (typically) with variables and methods that use those variables.

- Flow of control starts with a Java main class containing a Java `main` method, and continues via object method calls through to other Java classes.

- A class is used by instantiating an instance of it (an **object**) with the **new** operator, unless the class contains static variables or methods, in which case they can be accessed directly by qualifying them with the class name.

- Java classes are similar to ILE RPG (RPG IV) modules, Java methods are similar to ILE RPG procedures, Java packages are similar to ILE RPG service programs, and the main initial class is similar to an ILE RPG program object.

- Two Java methods in the same class can have the same name, as long as their **signatures** are different. This is called method **overloading**. A method signature is defined as the number of parameters and the type of the parameters, collectively.

- Java classes can have special methods called **constructors**, which are implicitly called by the Java runtime when an object is created with the **new** operator. These constructor methods have the same name as the class and do not specify a return type. There can be multiple constructors as long as their signatures are different. Java will call the appropriate constructor that has the same number and type of parameters as you specify with the **new** operator.

- Java and RPG IV both have syntax for exporting methods or procedures for external users, or hiding them for internal use only. In Java, this is done with method modifiers **public** and **private**.

- Command-line parameters can be printed to a Java class and its easy to print out to the command line (console) in Java.

Raid the refrigerator again, take a nap, and we will rejoin you in the next chapter!

3

Java's Language and Syntax

OVERVIEW

In the previous chapters, we provided you with an overview of:

- How Java applications compare to RPG applications
- What Java is and the reasons for using it
- Java flow of control compared to the RPG IV language

In this chapter, we will begin to examine Java in more detail, with a focus on the language's core syntax. Subsequent chapters will build on this by moving into other core areas of the language. Finally, starting with Chapter 9, we will begin looking at some of the more interesting Java capabilities, such as OO, threads, exceptions, database access, user interfaces, and so on. While the previous chapter was a high-level introduction to the "layout" of the Java language (and of RPG IV), the next few chapters go deeper into language reference details. Then we will move into higher-level capabilities. Imagine that you are on an inverted Java bungee cord: we went high, we are going deep, and then we will go high again.

This chapter covers the following topics:
- Basics
- Comments
- Variable Naming and Keywords
- Statements
- Expressions and Operators
- Arithmetic Manipulations

I WANT TO BE FREE! THE JAVA BASICS

Unlike RPG, which is column-oriented, Java is a free-form language. All redundant white space is ignored by the compiler, including line breaks. For example, the following are equivalent:

```
void myMethod(int parameter1) { return; }

void myMethod(int parameter1)
{
    return;
}
```

Freedom in Java, as in other realms, is best enjoyed by observing a few rules. To aid in programmer readability, you'll probably want to set some standards in your shop that are related to indentation and style rules. The rules themselves are not as important as using them consistently, but a good start on a set of Java coding standards can be found at **www.ambysoft.com**.

Another important aspect of Java code is that all statements end in a semicolon. This is a result of the free-form style of the language: the compiler needs a definitive way to determine the end of one statement and the start of another. Thus, in our example the **return** statement ends in a semicolon. Again, white space is not important, so the following are equivalent:

```
return;
return      ;
```

The next pervasive syntactical note to keep in mind about Java is that curly braces are used to delimit the beginning and end of blocks. In the previous example, you will notice that the body of the method myMethod starts with an opening brace { and ends with a closing brace }. As you will see, these braces are used to delimit classes, methods, and bodies of statement blocks. Every opening brace must eventually be followed by a closing brace.

So, "brace yourself" to see many semicolons and a lot of free space.

COMMENTS

We know that, as a responsible programmer, you always document your code with meaningful comments. (Don't you?) Here we will show you how to continue that tradition (or perhaps start it).

The process of specifying comments in RPG IV has not really changed from RPG III. To specify a comment, you put an asterisk (*) in column 7 of any RPG specification. The spec type itself in column 6 is optional for comment lines, as the following shows:

LISTING 3-1

```
C*  This is one style of comments in RPG IV
    *************************************************
    *   This is another one                         *
    *************************************************
```

In RPG IV, you can also place line comments after column 80 (the RPG IV source member length minimum is 100, compared to 80 for RPG III).

In Java, you have three types of comments at your disposal:

Comment Type	Description
/* comment */	Multi-line comments surrounded by '/*' and '*/'
// comment	Single-line comments using the double-slashes
/** comment */	JavaDoc comments surrounded by '/**' and '*/'

Like C and C++, Java uses /* to indicate the start of multi-line comments and */ to end them:

```
/* this is a multi
line comment */
```

Everything between the comment delimiters is commented out, no matter how many lines they cross. This form of markup is often used for comment blocks such as:

```
/*-----------------------------*
 * Please read these comments  *
 * as they are very important! *
 *-----------------------------*/
```

You cannot nest these block comments inside each other, as in /* outer /* inner */ outer */. Also, because it is easy to forget the ending delimiter, even the best of us have been known to accidentally comment out large chunks of code in Java. A good editor (such as those in VisualAge for Java, VisualAge for RPG, or in CODE/400 on Windows) will eliminate this problem. These editors show comments in a different color than the rest of the code, so you will see at a glance when lines have been inadvertently commented out.

Double-slashes // are used for a line comment. All text after // is ignored to the end of line, as in:

```
// show comment example
int myVariable = 10; // define and initialize variable
```

The final kind of Java comment is a refinement of the multi-line comment. These are called *JavaDoc* comments, and they use a double asterisk to start the multi-line comment, as in:

```
/** Hey you,    *
   * read this! */
```

This comment is otherwise identical to the multi-line type with two exceptions: it can also be used by the **javadoc** command to generate API documentation from the code, and it recognizes special "tags" within the code to aid the generated output. The following section describes this comment style in more detail.

JavaDoc Comments

We all know the importance of documenting our code, both internally and externally. Typically, it's done as a benefit to the poor followers who have to maintain the brilliant (yet indecipherable) code we leave behind. In Java, the need is even more pressing. This is because Java is all about reuse of code, and such reuse is accomplished by supplying our compiled classes and packages to others for their benefit. Since the code we supply is compiled, these users have no access to the internal comments. Therefore, they must rely on some form of external documentation to tell them how to use the classes and, most importantly, what the methods are and exactly what parameters they expect. What the methods do and what they return is also of vital importance to other programmers hoping to use it. Notice that RPG IV service programs have a similar need. However, for these we have at least the copy member that contains the exported procedure prototypes as a form of documentation. Java has no concept of copy members or included files.

With this in mind, Java supplies an easy way to embed important API informational type comments right in your code where it belongs, and yet extract those comments out to produce external HTML documentation. This is a very good thing! It means that these comments can double as both internal and external, and that a consistent format for the information can be achieved.

The JDK or Java Development Kit includes a utility command called *javadoc*. This utility generates API documentation from source code that contains JavaDoc comments, as we briefly described already. For example, in order to generate documentation for a class called Extract, you would type the following:

```
c:\> javadoc Extract.java
```

The argument passed to **javadoc** is a series of Java package names or source files. **Javadoc** parses the JavaDoc style comments contained in the source files and produces a set of HTML pages describing the classes, interfaces, constructors, methods, and class-level variables. Specifically, it produces the following files:

File type	Description
Package list	An index list of all packages is put in a file called `packages.html`
Index	An index of all classes and members found is put in a file called `AllNames.html`
class hierarchy	A list of all classes found and their hierarchy is put in a file called `tree.html`
List of methods	One file per class that lists the class and its methods

When **javadoc** parses a documentation comment, leading (*) characters on each line are discarded. For lines other than the first, blanks and tabs preceding the initial (*) characters are also discarded. The following example illustrates JavaDoc comments in a Java source file:

LISTING 3-2

```
/** This is the <U>scan package</U>
 *  this is the second line.
 *  @author  George & Phil
 *  @version July 22,1999
 */
```

Comments can include embedded HTML tags. In our example, the HTML <U>scan package</U> produces underlined text for "scan package." The first sentence of each comment should provide a concise, yet complete, description of the declared entity. This sentence ends at the first period. It is important to be concise and describe the complete entity because **javadoc** copies this to the member summary at the top of the HTML file. (Notice that the term *member* refers collectively to methods and class-level variables.)

Besides parsing HTML tags, **javadoc** recognizes a special set of tags, called keywords, that starts with the at sign (@). These tags provide additional information such as "*See Also*" references, an author name, or a version number for this text. In the preceding example, we used two tags: **@author** to describe the author name, and **@version** to identify the date for this version of the files.

The following table summarizes the tags that **javadoc** recognizes:

Tag Name	Description
@author	Formats and creates the given "Author" entry. The text has no special internal structure. A comment may contain multiple **@author** tags. This tag can only be used in a class or interface documentation comment.
@see	Adds a hyperlinked "See Also" entry to the class. The class name can be qualified by the package name.
@version	Formats and adds the given "Version" information. The text has no special internal structure. A comment may contain at most one **@version** tag. This tag can only be used in a class or interface documentation comment.
@since	Adds a "Since" entry. This tag means that this change or feature has existed since the release number of the software specified by the since-text.

Tag Name	Description
@deprecated	This identifies this as an obsolete method. You should list the replacement. If the member is obsolete and there is no replacement, the argument to **@deprecated** should be "No replacement".
@return	Adds a "Returns" section, which contains the description of the return value.
@param	Formats the given parameter name and its description in the parameters section of a method description. The description may be continued on the next line.

Each tag must start at the beginning of a line. Try to keep tags that have the same name together within a comment. For example, put all **@author** tags together so that **javadoc** can tell where the list ends. The following is an example of a documented class:

LISTING 3-3

```
/**
 * A cool class.
 *
 * @author Phil Coulthard and George Farr
 * @version 1.0
 * @see YourClass
 */
public class MyClass
{
    /**
     * Constructor
     */
    public MyClass()
    { } // empty for now

    /**
     * Shows a message
     * @param   message The message string to show
     * @return void
     * @see     MyClass#MyMethod2(String message)
     */
    public void myMethod(String message)
    {
        System.out.println(message);
    }
    /**
     * Shows a message in quotes
     * @param   message The message string to show
     * @return String object containing quotes
     * @see     MyClass#MyMethod(String message)
     */
    public String myMethod2(String message)
    {
        String newMessage = "'" + message + "'";
        System.out.println(newMessage);
        return newMessage;
    }
} // end class MyClass
```

We then create a new subdirectory to hold the results of **javadoc**, and run **javadoc** against our class source file by using the directory option (-d) to put the output in our new subdirectory:

```
C:\JAVA> md html
C:\JAVA> javadoc -d html MyClass.java
```

Then, we need to copy the image files that the generated HTML uses to an images subdirectory of our new html subdirectory:

```
C:\JAVA> cd html
C:\JAVA\html> md images
C:\JAVA\html> copy c:\jdk1.1.5\docs\api\images\*.* images
```

Now, finally, we can open one of the generated HTML files by typing start MyClass.html. In our example, this causes Netscape 4.03 to open the file. Part of the result is shown in Figure 3-1:

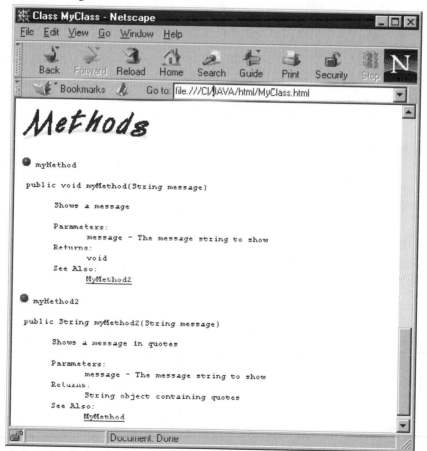

FIGURE 3-1

For more information about **javadoc**, consult the JDK documentation.

VARIABLE NAMING

An important feature shared by RPG IV and Java is the ability to reference data that is stored in memory by using descriptive symbolic names (called fields or variables) rather than numeric memory cell addresses. Each field that you use in your program must have a unique name. RPG IV limits field names to 4096 characters (as of V3R7) and ignores case for field names. On the other hand, Java allows variable names to have unlimited length. Java names are *very* case sensitive. Case sensitivity is a key point that the RPG programmer must consider. Its importance cannot be overemphasized. All referenced and declared names must match letter-for-letter. Furthermore, the source file name must match verbatim the defined class name inside the source file, including the case. Otherwise, the compiler will generate errors that you may not be able to diagnose easily. It bears repeating that, as a Java programmer, you must be especially sensitive!

Naming Syntax for Fields and Variables

For RPG IV names, the first character must be alphabetic. It can include the special characters $, #, and @; the remaining characters can be alphabetic or numeric, including the underscore _ character. For Java names, the first character can be any valid letter, the underscore, or dollar sign. Remaining characters can contain both letters and digits. Furthermore, Java names can actually include Unicode characters as well, if you so desire. Go ahead, give that variable a nice Arabic name! An interesting note about the $, # and @ sign in RPG names is that these are variant characters, meaning they are actually different characters for a number of codepages, such as German and Swedish. Thus, when working in these codepages you do not use these characters as shown here and in the reference manuals, but rather their equivalents in the source codepage or CCSID.

Keywords

Keywords are identifiers or names that are reserved by the language, and that carry special meaning within it. For example, in RPG IV the `CONST` and `INZ` keywords on the D specification tell the compiler that the field you are defining is a constant and that its initial value is supplied by the parameter. The RPG IV reference manual describes all of the keywords you can use on the H, F, and D specifications. Further, all of the op-codes are keywords. RPG IV also has other special words called *figurative constants*. You have used these since the inception of the RPG language. They include `*ZERO`, which initializes a field to zeros, or `*BLANKS,` which initializes a character field to blanks. The other figurative constants or special words are listed in the RPG manuals.

Keywords are used by Java and all other languages. Language designers decide on their names, usage, and meanings for each specific language. Because keywords and figurative constants have special meaning, you cannot use them as names of fields or variables in your programs.

The following table lists the reserved keywords in Java:

abstract	default	goto	null
synchronized	boolean	do	if
package	this	break	double
implements	private	throw	byte
else	import	protected	throws
case	extends	instanceof	public
transient	catch	false	int
return	true	char	final
interface	short	try	class
finally	long	static	void
const	float	native	super
volatile	continue	for	new
switch	while		

The two special words `const` and `goto` are not used in Java. They may be assigned meanings in future versions of the Java language but, in truth, their reserved status is to aid C and C++ programmers from accidentally using them.

STATEMENTS

Programmers use *statements* to control the sequence and frequency of execution of different segments of a program. Because of RPG's fixed-form nature, the compiler can easily analyze and parse the syntax of the values present in their fixed-column locations. Unlike RPG, Java is a free-form language. There are many more variations of what makes up an executable statement, what indicates a block of consecutive statements, and what ends an executable line of code. The following sections cover four different types of statements in Java:

- Expression
- Block
- Empty
- Labeled

Expression Statement

With the simple arithmetic *operators* plus, minus, multiply, and divide (+, -, *, /) you can build simple arithmetic expressions in both Java and RPG. For example, X + 1 or Y + 2 / 3 are simple expressions, whereas X and Y are variables. RPG and Java would be very limited if they used only these four basic operators. As you will see later in this chapter when we cover expressions, both RPG and Java have a rich set of operators for creating *expressions.* The following examples demonstrate different expressions that you may use in your programs:

```
1.8 / 3
X+2-3+I
amountDue > 0
```

You can also assign expressions in a program to a variable. To do this, you use a field on the left-hand side with the assignment operator (equals sign) as follows:

```
myvalue =  1.8 / 3
result  =  X+2-3+I
```

Notice in these examples that the white space between the operators is generally not important, although consistent use of it does aid readability. This last example shows how you might code some sample expressions in your program. However, they are not syntactically correct for Java statements. Can you guess why not? To make these valid *expression assignment statements* you must (as we mentioned in the introduction to this chapter) end each statement with a semicolon. In Java, the semicolon is a statement terminator. It is not a separator, as it is in languages such as Pascal. Obviously RPG, our column-oriented language, has no construct like the statement terminator. However, even for RPG, these expressions are valid only when used with the new **EVAL** op-code, with its free-form factor two syntax.

In summary, an *expression statement* consists of an expression that is executed for its side effects. For instance, the previous example showed assignment expressions that had the side effect of altering the value of a variable (the left-hand operand). A method or procedure call can have the side effects of the call.

Block Statement

A Java *block statement* groups together a sequence of one or more statements. The group is delimited by enclosing it with a starting brace '{' and a closing brace '}'. A semicolon (;) is used to end each statement in the sequence, as usual. There is no (;) after either brace. Braces can be used to group declarations and statements together into a single entity, or block. They are syntactically equivalent to single braces that surround the statements of a class or method. You can also group multiple statements together after an `if` or `while` structure. For example, we can block the *expression statements* that we used in our previous example as follows:

```
{
  myvalue =   1.8 / 3;
  result  =   X+2-3+I;
}
```

This block is syntactically correct. The compiler will not issue any errors for it. However, it would be more typical for you to block a group of statements in order to make them look equivalent to a single statement. You can then apply an `if` or a loop condition before the block. The compiler will execute the block only if the condition is met. Another reason to use blocks is to define a set of variables locally in the block. If you try to reference one of these variables outside the block, the compiler will indicate that it is not declared. For example, the `if` statement syntax in Java is as follows:

```
if (expression)
   statement;
```

In order to condition the previous block of code example, we would code an `if` with its expression above the block. This indicates to the compiler that we want the block to execute only when the expression evaluates to `true`. To use an `if` condition with a block of code, you would code as follows:

```
if (expression)
   {
     float myvalue; // declare a float type variable called myvalue
     int    result;  // declare an integer type variable called result
     myvalue   = 1.8 / 3;
     result    = X+2-3+I;
   }
```

It is important to note that the block is treated as a single statement. That is, either all or none of the statements inside it are executed in our example. If we only had one statement to execute after the `if`, we would not need the braces. For example, the following `if` statement is syntactically correct:

```
if (x == 2)
   x = x+1;
```

You normally use a block statement when you want to execute more than one statement after an `if` or `while` condition. Notice also that braces are optional when we have one statement to execute. In other words, we could have coded our example as follows:

```
if (x == 2)
   {
      x = x + 1;
   }
```

NOTE: In the preceding examples, the double equals sign `(==)` is used to distinguish comparisons such as this one from assignment statements that use their single equals sign `(=)`. Note also that assignment statements are not allowed inside a conditional expression like this. Only expressions that evaluate to `true` or `false` are allowed.

Empty Statement

The simplest kind of Java statement is an empty one. You now know that Java statements must be ended with a semicolon. What, then, happens if we have statements like the following:

```
if (x == 2)
   ;
for (i = 0;i < 10;i = i+1)
{
   ;
}
```

Are they syntactically correct? (Do not worry about the syntax of the `for` statement for now.) The answer is: yes. A semicolon on its own with nothing preceding it is just another Java statement. In this case it is called the ***empty statement***. Empty statements are very rarely used, but they appear occasionally as the `true` part of an `if` statement even when all we are interested in is the `else` part. For example:

```
if (x > 2)
   ;
else
   // interesting statements
```

This, however, is more elegantly coded by negating the conditional expression. Also notice that an equivalent to the empty statement is an ***empty block***, as in {}. For example:

```
if (x > 2)
   {}
```

Labeled Statement

Java labels are similar to an RPG **TAG** operation code, with the tag name specified in factor one. In Java, you can have one or more labels separated by a colon (:). The following example shows a label definition:

```
ReturnPoint:      while (x>10) {...}
```

In RPG, a **TAG** can be specified on any line. In Java too any line can be labeled. However, the compiler will only recognize labels at the beginning of loops or blocks, such a while-loop, when used as a target with the **break** statement. Also, label names are independent of all other kinds of names used in the program. For example, you can have a variable defined as an integer and, in the same block of code, also have a label with the same name. The compiler can distinguish between both entities. The most common use of labels is with the **break** statement. The following example illustrates this usage:

LISTING 3-4

```
int index = 1;
int index2 = 1;

outerLoop: while(true)
{
    index = index + 1;
    index2 = 1;
    innerLoop: while(true)
     {
        index2 = index2 + 1;
        if (index2 == 3)
          break outerLoop;
     }
}
```

First, we define two loops, one outer and one nested inner. We label the outer loop as outerLoop and we are then able to exit directly from that outer loop use a labeled **break** statement, as shown. If we did not specify the outerLoop parameter with **break**, then we would only have exited the innermost loop. Note that you are not "jumping" to a labeled statement, but rather "exiting" from a labeled loop. This should be used sparingly, as some will argue it is not a good structured programming style. It is better, they say, to test a variable's value in the **while** loop expression and set the variable in the loop body to force exit. (We will cover **if**, **for**, **while**, and **break** statements in detail in the next chapter.)

The following example summarizes all of the Java statement types we have discussed:

LISTING 3-5

```
public class Statement
{
    public static void main(String args[])
    {
        int x = 8;
        for (int i=0;i<10;i++)
        { }
        label1:
        while(x<0)
        {
          break label1;
          ;
        }
        if (x == 10);
          ;
        {};
        {
          System.out.println("I am in a block!");
        }
        label0:;
        label2:label3:label4:;
    }
}
```

To get extra credit for this lesson, take a little pop quiz by considering each statement. Decide which one is syntactically correct and which one the Java compiler will flag as an error. We will step through the example and discuss each line. The first structure is a **for** loop with all header information correctly specified. It includes an empty block. This is syntactically correct in Java.

Next, we have a label statement with a loop that breaks out of the label. Again, this is correct. Notice that on the line after the **break** label1; statement there is an empty statement specified. We indicate this with nothing other than a semicolon. Next, we have a correctly specified **if** statement with an empty body: if (x==10); . Then, there is an empty block followed immediately by an empty statement. Both are valid in Java, and so is the block that includes the print statement. Finally, we define several labels; we separate each one with a colon. This is also correct!

As it turns out, the Java program in our example compiles cleanly. It is not terribly useful, but it is valid. It demonstrates many of Java's syntax rules and statement types.

EXPRESSIONS AND OPERATORS

Expressions in RPG and Java are used to fetch, compute, and store values. We refer to those that compute and store values as *computational expressions,* and those that simply fetch a value without altering it as *fetch expressions*.

The following examples illustrate the distinction between the two types of expressions. Assume that the `while` loop expression must evaluate to `*ON` ('1') or `*OFF` ('0') in RPG, and to `true` or `false` in Java:

RPG				Java
C		DOW	(*IN99)	`while (in99)`
C		ENDDO		`{`
				`}`

The RPG expression (`*IN99`) will return 0 or 1 and end the loop if it is 0. The Java expression (`in99`) will return `true` or `false` and end the loop if it is `false`. (The variable must be declared boolean in this case. See the data type chapter for more information on data types, including boolean.) Both of these are *fetch expressions*. They do not alter any variable.

The following example illustrates a *computational expression*:

RPG				Java
C		EVAL	x = x + 1	`x = x + 1;`

This expression computes the value `x + 1` and stores the result of the computation back into x.

In the following sections, we will discuss *computational expressions* and their associated operators in both RPG IV and Java, as well as *fetch expressions*.

Computational Expressions

Operators are commonly classified by the number of values (operands or parameters) on which they operate. This distinction is useful because many operators have different (although related) meanings, depending on whether they are combined with two operands or only one.

For example, if you remember algebra from your school days, you know that you can use -1 as the equivalent of 0-1, right? In the first case, the minus sign acts on the single numeric value, performing negation; in the second, it is operating on two numeric values. An operator that acts on a *single* operand is known as a **unary** operator. An operator that acts on two operands is known as a **binary** operator. In this example, the minus sign can be used as either a binary operator or a unary operator.

Arithmetic Operators

Arithmetic operators are the simplest and, probably, the most used in all languages. The following table lists all of the arithmetic operators used in both RPG and Java:

Java	RPG Op-Code	RPG Expression
+ (addition)	ADD or Z-ADD	+
- (subtraction)	SUB or Z-SUB	-
* (multiplication)	MULT	*
/ (division)	DIV	/
% (modulus or remainder)	MVR	
		** (exponent)

The binary arithmetic operators are (+), (-), (*), and (/), and the modulus operator (%). In RPG, you use the **MVR** (*Move Remainder*) operation code to accomplish what the (%) operator provides in Java. An important point to remember is that RPG IV, through free-form factor two, supports free-form expressions that very closely match what Java supports. In addition, to make things easier in RPG IV, many new operators have been introduced in the language that we will use in our comparison to Java. In all of the examples we use in this chapter, you can still use the fixed-form operation codes provided. However, because you are already familiar with these and not the free-form operators, our examples will include free-form expressions with the newly introduced operators.

Consider the following examples, which show different expressions using the various binary arithmetic operators in both languages, but using RPG's new **EVAL** op-code:

RPG			Java
C	EVAL	X = X+1	X = X + 1;
C	EVAL	X = X / 2	X = X / 2;
C	EVAL	A = A + 2 * 3	A = A + 2 * 3;
C	EVAL	A = (A - 3) / 2	A = (A - 3) / 2

In the first example, the additive operator (+) adds the value contained in X to the numeric literal 1 and places the sum back in variable X. The (+), (-), (*), and (/) arithmetic binary operators are similar in the way they operate.

The next example uses the division operator to divide x by 2. The next two examples show expressions that use the additive and multiplicative operators. In the first case, given that the precedence of (*) and (/) are higher than (-) and (+), the number 2 is multiplied by 3, the result is added to the variable A, and then the result is stored back in A.

In the last example, the parentheses — (and) — force the addition to occur before the multiplication. As you will see later in this chapter when we cover operator precedence, the parentheses have higher precedence than any of these arithmetic operators.

The binary operator (%), remainder or modulus, produces a pure value that is the remainder from an implied division of its operands. As we mentioned earlier, this is equivalent to using the **DIV** operation code in RPG followed by the **MVR** operation code. Consider the following example:

RPG					Java
C	X	DIV	60	minutes	minutes = X / 60;
C		MVR		seconds	seconds = X % 60;

In this example we calculate the number of minutes and seconds, given a value in seconds. If x contains the value 185 seconds, the division operation produces a value of 3 minutes and the remainder produces a value of 5 seconds.

The only operator we have not yet discussed is the exponentiation (**) operator. This operator is used in RPG IV, but not in Java. Instead, Java provides a method supplied in its Math class that supports this function. This function is covered later in this chapter.

Assignment Operators

Once a variable has been declared, you can assign a value or a field to it using the assignment operator (=). In fact, we have used this simple form of assignment operator in the previous section. To assign the value zero to the field x, you code as follows:

RPG				Java
C		EVAL	X = 0	X = 0;

In the case of RPG, the **MOVE** operation code could be called an assignment operator because it accomplishes the same function. However, you should try using the new **EVAL** operation code instead. This way of coding is more structured and flexible.

To reduce the number of assignment statements, the Java language allows the stringing of variables together. If you want to assign three variables to the same value, you can string them all together in a single statement as follows:

```
A  =  B  =  C  =  25;
```

In this example, all variables will contain the value 25. RPG does not support this structure in its free-form format. As can be expected, Java takes this concept one step further and introduces other related assignment statements. With an expression such as x = x +1; the language designers noticed that the variable on the left-hand side is repeated on the right hand side of the assignment operator. They shortened this construct to x += 1; and produced a new set of variations for assignment statements. These variations are shown in the following table. The combination of (+) and (=) operators creates a new operator, the (+=) operator.

Operator	Example	Meaning
=	A = A+B	assignment
+=	A += B	A = A + B
-=	A -= B	A = A - B
/=	A /= B	A = A / B
*=	A *= B	A = A * B
%=	A %= B	A = A % B
^=	A ^= B	A = A ^ B
&=	A &= B	A = A & B
|=	A |= B	A = A | B
<<=	A <<= B	A = A << B
>>=	A >>= B	A = A >> B
>>>=	A >>>= B	A = A >>> B

Given that there are many other binary operators in Java, the language designers introduced the new (x=) operator where (x) stands for other supported binary operators. These include not only the arithmetic operators we have seen, but *all* binary operators: (+), (-), (/), (*), (%), (^), (&), (|), (<<), (>>), and (>>>).

The general rule is as follows: if expression1 and expression2 are expressions, then expression1 x= expression2 is equivalent to expression1 = expression1 x expression2 where x stands for one of the operators mentioned. Obviously, both forms are allowed in Java (and in C and C++ as well). This format is a shorthand version that accomplishes the same thing with less typing. It hails originally from C, where the design philosophy was: less is more.

Incrementing, Decrementing, and Unary Operators

Java provides two unusual operators, also borrowed from C, for incrementing and decrementing variables. The increment operator (++) adds one to its operand, while the decrement operator (--) subtracts one from its operand. These are most commonly used to increment or decrement the index of an array or other incrementing value inside a loop. The following example illustrates a **while** loop that uses the (++) operator for incrementing its index:

RPG			Java
C	EVAL	IDX = 1	`idx = 0;`
C	DOW	(IDX <= 10)	`while (idx < 10)`
C*	:	Some code	`{`
C	EVAL	IDX = IDX +1	`    // some code`
C	ENDDO		`    idx ++;`
			`}`

The preceding example also shows an RPG **DOW** (Do While) loop that is similar to Java. The primary difference between them is in the way we increment the index. In RPG, a common way to do this is to use the **EVAL** operation code and add one to the index. You can also use the **ADD** operation code to increment the field by one. In Java, using the traditional assignment statement with the (+) operator is valid, too, as in
`idx = idx + 1;`

These operators are unusual in that both (++) and (--) can be used as either *prefix* or *suffix* operators. In the preceding example, we used the (++) as a suffix operator; that is, the (++) is placed after the operand. To use it as a prefix operator, we would code the expression as follows:

`++idx;`

What is the difference between these two forms? When the (++) and (--) are prefix operators, the operand will be incremented or decremented by one *before* its value is used in the expression. When used as suffix operators, the operand will be incremented or decremented by one *after* its value has been used in the expression. Consider the following examples:

LISTING 3-6

```
a = 5;
b = 5;
x = ++a + 50; // x is 56 after execution
y = 50 + b++; // y is 55 after execution
```

In the first case, the (++) operator prefixes the variable a. The operand a is incremented by one (changed to 6) *before* it is used in the expression. This value, in turn, is added to 50, and the sum 56 is placed in the variable x. In the second case, 50 is added to the content of operand b, which is 5, and the sum of 55 is placed in the variable y.

There is something else that is unique about these operators. Unlike all other arithmetic operators, they have side effects on their operands even when used in fetch expressions, such as the right-hand side of an assignment statement! Beware of this!

In the preceding example, for instance, both a and b are effected by the statements. At the end, both have been incremented. The difference between prefix and suffix use is relative to the target of the assignment statement but, as far as the variables a and b are concerned, both had the same effect of increasing their value by one. In our example, as part of the expression evaluation, the value of b is incremented to 6; however, the increment occurs after the expression has been evaluated because the (++) operator is used as a suffix. These operators are similar to that in C and C++, with the exception that C and C++ do not allow the operand to be of type float. Notice also that these operators can only be applied to variable operands; they cannot be applied to expressions. For example, expressions like (a+b)++ or (a+b)-- are invalid. Both of these operators are considered unary operators because they are used with one argument or operand.

The following table lists the RPG and Java arithmetic operators:

Operator	RPG Operator	Java Operator
Increment	N/A	++
Decrement	N/A	--
Unary plus	+	+
Unary minus	-	-

These operators take exactly one argument — that is, they are ***unary operators***. The following examples illustrate how to use the unary minus and plus operators in both RPG and Java:

RPG			Java
C	EVAL	X = -X	X = -X;
C	EVAL	X = +X	X = +X;

It's interesting to note that the unary plus operator really does nothing, while the unary negation operator actually negates the given operand. Thus if y is set to -1, then -y evaluates to 1, while +y evaluates to -1.

Relational and Logical Operators

RPG and Java have several operators for testing equality and magnitude. All ***relational expressions*** using these operators return a "boolean" value of **true** or **false**. For example, to test if variable X is greater than 10, you can have an expression such as X > 10 in both languages. This expression is most useful when doing a block of code based on an equality test or a test for magnitude. For example, the same test expression X > 10 can be used on the **if** or any loop statement expression. The following example illustrates relational expressions used on an **if** statement.

RPG		Java
C	IF (prefix = 'A')	if (prefix == 'A')
C*	some code	{
C*	more code	// code
C	ENDIF	}

In the example, we test to see if the `prefix` variable is equal to the character (A). If it is, then the expression evaluates to **true** and the body of the **if** structure is executed. Otherwise, control is transferred past the end of the **if** block. Notice that the equality operator is (=) in RPG and (==) in Java (the (=) operator is only used as the assignment operator in Java).

Expressions that result in boolean values of **true** or **false** can be combined by using *logical operators* to form a more complex test. For example, if we want to test for variable x being greater than 10 but less than 20, we can have an RPG expression such as: (X>10) AND (X<20). This syntax combines both sub-expressions using the **AND** operator. The equivalent of the **AND** operator in Java is the (&&) operator. As you will see, Java almost always uses doubled-up characters such as == and && in its logical or boolean binary expression operators. Notice that Java, when an expression needs to be enclosed in parentheses, as with the **if** operator, these combined expressions need to be enclosed in outer parentheses, as in if ((x>10) && (x<20)) ....

As expected, both RPG and Java provide *logical operators* to combine relational tests. These operators in RPG are: **AND**, **OR**, and **NOT**. Java has an additional operator that is not supported in RPG, namely the ***exclusive OR*** operator (^). In this case, both sides must not be the same; that is, one or the other but not both evaluate to **true**. As mentioned earlier, Java uses the (&&) operator for the **AND** combination. The Java equivalent of the **OR** operator is the (||) operator. In the case of the (&&) operator, the expression is **true** only if both expressions are **true**; if either expression is **false**, the entire expression is **false**. You can use the single (&) operator, as well. The difference between these two operators is in the internal expression evaluation. For the (&) operator, both sides of the expression are evaluated regardless of the outcome. For the (&&) operator, if the left side of the expression is **false**, the entire expression is obviously **false** and the right side is never evaluated. We recommend always using the doubled up version, as sometimes the right-hand side is not valid if the left hand is **true** — for example ((x != 0) & ((y / x) > 0)). In this case, if x is equal to 0 (left sub expression is **false**) then we would be dividing y by 0 in the right hand sub expression.

The following tables summarize the available relational and logical operators in both RPG and Java:

Relational

RPG XX	RPG Expression	Java	Description
EQ	=	==	equal
NE	<>	!=	not equal
GT	>	>	greater than
LT	<	<	less than
GE	>=	>=	greater than or equal
LE	<=	<=	less than or equal

Logical

RPG XX opCodes	RPG opCodes	Java	Description
ORxx	OR	`||` or `|`	logical or
ANDxx	AND	`&&` or `&`	logical and
NOT		`!`	logical not, or negation
		`^`	exclusive or

The (`|`) and (`||`) operators are similar to the (`&`) and (`&&`) operators. You can use either one of them. The **OR** expressions result in **true** if either or both operands evaluate to **true**. If both operands are **false**, the expression evaluates to **false**. As with (`&`) and (`&&`), the operator (`|`) evaluates both sides of the expression regardless of the outcome. With the (`||`) operator, if the expression on the left side is **true**, the expression is obviously **true**, and the right side is never evaluated. In general, the (`&&`) and (`||`) operators are the most commonly used. As you will see in the following section on bitwise operators, the operators (`&`) , (`|`) and (`^`) are used with bit manipulations, as well. The "not" operator (`!`) is a unary operator that negates the *boolean* expression following it, as in if (`!(x > 10)`). So if the expression operand evaluates to **false**, after negation it evaluates to **true**. Compare this to the "not equals" operator (`!=`), which is a binary operator comparing two operands, returning **true** if both have different values.

Bitwise Operators

The RPG language does not support ***bitwise operators***. Java on the other hand, has seven bitwise operators that allow you to perform operations on individual bits in integer values. All of these operators are inherited from the C and C++ languages, and, yes, you too can be a "bit" "wiser":

Bitwise operator	Meaning
&	Bitwise AND
|	Bitwise OR
^	Bitwise Exclusive OR
~	Bitwise negation
< <	Left Shift
> >	Right Shift
> > >	Zero fill right shift

It is very important to keep in mind that bitwise operators work only on integer types. Using any other type causes a compiler error. The bitwise (`&`) operator is often used to mask off some set of bits. It produces a value that is the ***bitwise and*** of its operands. The bitwise (`&`) works on bits, whereas the logical (`&&`) works on boolean values. Traversing each operand bit by bit, if the corresponding bit in *both* of the operands are 1s, the corresponding bit in the result variable is set to 1. Otherwise, the corresponding bit in the result variable is set to 0. This is similar to the *logical and* where the resulting value is `true` if both operands evaluate to `true`, otherwise `false`. Here is an example:

LISTING 3-7

```
public class Bit
{
    public static void main(String args[])
    {
        int firstNum  = 14;
        int secondNum = 12;
        int result;
        result = firstNum & secondNum;
        System.out.println("The result is : " +  result);
    }
}
```

In this example, we perform a bitwise (&) on two integer operands that contain the values 14 and 12. Knowing this, the internal representation of these two operand fields and of the resulting field is shown here in bit format:

```
firstNum  == 14 == '00000000 00000000 00000000 00001110'
secondNum == 12 == '00000000 00000000 00000000 00001100'
------------------------------------------------------------
result    == 12 == '00000000 00000000 00000000 00001100' (after &)
```

In this case, only the third and fourth bits have a 1 in both operands. That means that all of the values of the `result` field will be 0 except these positions. This value evaluates to $2^2 + 2^3$ which equals 12. Therefore, the `println` method will print the value 12.

If you have followed the example so far, then the other bitwise operators will be just as easy to understand. The **bitwise OR** operator (|), like the (&) operator, works on any integer type and traverses the operands bit by bit. A 1 is returned in the result value at each bit position when *either* of the two operand values have 1 in the same bit position. Otherwise it is 0. By comparison, the **exclusive OR** operator (^) returns a 1 at each bit position when the two values have *opposite* values in the same bit position. Here is an example of these:

LISTING 3-8

```
public class OrxOr
{
    public static void main(String args[])
    {
        int firstNum  = 14;
        int secondNum = 12;
        int firstResult, secondResult;
        secondResult = (byte) (firstNum | secondNum);
        System.out.println("The first result is: " +  secondResult);
        firstResult = (byte) (firstNum ^ secondNum);
        System.out.println("The first result is: " +  firstResult);
    }
}
```

In this example, we use the operand values of 12 and 14 again. Here are the bit values of the operands and two results after doing a *bitwise or* and *bitwise exclusive or*:

```
firstNum      == 14 == '00000000 00000000 00000000 00001110'
secondNum     == 12 == '00000000 00000000 00000000 00001100'
-------------------------------------------------------------
firstResult   == 14 == '00000000 00000000 00000000 00001110' (after |)
secondResult  ==  2 == '00000000 00000000 00000000 00000010' (after ^)
```

All this talk about twiddling of bits might have you wondering how to print out the binary version of an integer variable. This is jumping ahead a bit, but there are classes in Java that mimic each of the built-in data types and that supply some cool methods. The one we want is the Integer class, and the method is the static method toBinaryString, which takes an integer as input and outputs a string containing its binary or bitwise value. You might want to create your own static method called printBits in your own helper class that, in turn, uses this Integer method:

```
public static void printBits(String name, int x)
{
    System.out.println(name + " == " + x + " == " +
                       Integer.toBinaryString(x));
}
```

Calling this with the firstNum and secondNum variables we have been using so far gives us the following output (note that leading zero value bits are not printed):

```
firstNum == 14 == 1110
secondNum == 12 == 1100
```

Before we move on to the next topic, which is shift operators, let's review another simple bitwise operator: the inverse operator (~). It is similar to the logical negation operator (!), but at the bit level. That is, it negates whatever the value is in each bit of the operand. So 1s become 0s and 0s become 1s. So imagine in the previous examples we did this:

```
firstNum = ~firstNum;
secondNum = ~secondNum;
```

We would get the following before and after results:

```
firstNum  == `00000000 00000000 00000000 00001110' (before)
secondNum == `00000000 00000000 00000000 00001100' (before)
-----------------------------------------------------------
firstNum  == `11111111 11111111 11111111 11110001' (after ~)
secondNum == `11111111 11111111 11111111 11110011' (after ~)
```

Shift Operators

The **shift operators** will complete our discussion of bitwise operators. As you work with the bits that makeup an integer number, there are some operations that may require you to shift the bit values to the right or to the left. In Java, this operation is performed with the left bitwise shift operator (<<) and the right bitwise shift operator (>>). The following example illustrates how these operators work:

LISTING 3-9

```
public class Shift
{
    public static void main(String args[])
    {
        int firstNum = 2;
        int firstResult, secondResult;
        firstResult = (firstNum << 2);
        System.out.println("The first result is : " + firstResult);
        secondResult = (firstResult >> 1);
        System.out.println("The second result is : " + secondResult);
    }
}
```

We start by initializing the variable firstNum to the value 2. This is represented internally by the following sequence of bits shown for firstNum:

```
firstNum    == 2 == `00000000 00000000 00000000 00000010'
-----------------------------------------------------------
firstResult  == 8 == `00000000 00000000 00000000 00001000'
secondResult == 4 == `00000000 00000000 00000000 00000100'
```

The first operation we perform on the variable is shifting left twice. Then, we use the result from the first operation to shift right once. As a result, the internal representation for each of the variables firstResult and secondResult is as shown. Notice that shifting left is equivalent to multiplying by the corresponding power of 2, and shifting right is equivalent to dividing by the corresponding power of 2 with possible truncation in both cases. These operations are generally more efficient than using multiplication or division, however.

Unlike the inconsistencies found in some implementations of the C and C++ languages, Java always preserves the sign bit (the leftmost bit) after performing the right bitwise shift. To handle this situation, Java introduces a new bitwise operator, the shift right operator (>>>). The difference between the (>>>) and the other shift right operator (>>) is that the (>>>) operator does not preserve the leftmost sign bit. In other words, the operator always sets the leftmost bit to 0.

Conditional Operators

The **conditional operator** (? :) is also called a **ternary operator**. This operator is similar to the one in C and C++. RPG IV does not have it. This operator, a short version of the if statement, is used to choose alternate values for a variable, based on an expression that evaluates to **true** or **false**. The following example shows how to use this operator and compares its use to the if statement (the if statement is explained in more detail in the following chapter):

```
result = (idx == 20) ? 30 : 35;
// same as...
if (idx == 20)
  result = 30;
else
  result = 35;
```

The conditional *boolean* expression, written with the ternary operator (?:), provides an alternate way to write similar constructs. The boolean expression before the (?) is evaluated first. If it is **true**, then the expression between the (?) and (:) is evaluated and its value is assigned to left hand variable (result in our example). Otherwise, the expression between the (:) and (;) is evaluated, and its value is assigned to the left hand variable.

Conditional expressions are only suitable when you want to return one of two values, depending on the value of a boolean expression. Conditional expressions are compact; they save you keystrokes. Once you become accustomed to their notation, as with the increment and decrement operators (++, and --), you will find them clearer to read than their longer equivalents.

Operator Precedence

So far, we have introduced all of the Java and RPG operators that you can use in expressions. In this section, we will discuss **operator precedence**: the order of evaluation of multiple operators in expressions. That is, these are the rules that govern which operator is evaluated first, second, third, and so on. Operator precedence is important in any programming language; it determines the final result of an expression, which depends on the order in which operands are evaluated.

The following table summarizes operator precedence in RPG IV:

( )

Built-in functions, user-defined procedures

unary +, unary -, NOT

**

*, /

binary +, and Binary -

=, <>, >, >=, <, <=

AND

OR

In an earlier program example, we saw the expression 'A + 2 * 3'. If the value of A is 4, then what would the result be after evaluation? Will it be 18 or 10? If we add first, then the final value will be '4 + 2', or 6, multiplied by 3, which gives the result 18. However, if we multiply first, then the value will be '2 * 3', or 6, with 4 added to this value which gives the result 10. This is why operator precedence has to be established.

As you can see in the table, the multiplication operator has higher precedence and, therefore, the value of the expression we gave is 10. Multiplication (*) will be done first, followed by addition (+). In fact, this is the logic that the compiler uses to establish the evaluation of any given expression in a language. High-precedence operators are evaluated before low-precedence operators. What happens if you have operators with the same precedence? For example, what would the expression (X / 4 * 3) evaluate to? If X is equal to 12, then will the result be 1 or 9? The result depends on how the compiler parses and evaluates the line for operators of the same precedence. Is parsing done from left-to-right, or right-to-left? For the multiplication and division operators, RPG and Java parse and evaluate from left-to-right. This means that the preceding expression in both languages evaluates to 9.

Operators	Associativity
`++, --, ~, !, -, (type cast)`	R
`*, /, %`	L
`+, -`	L
`+ (concat)`	L
`>>>`	L
`>>, <<`	L
`<, <=, >, >=`	L
`instanceof`	L
`= =, !=`	L
`&`	L
`^`	L
`&& |`	L
`| |`	L
`?:`	R
`=, *=, /=, %=, +=, -=, <<=, >>=, >>>=, &=, ^=, |=`	R

This table shows the precedence of Java operators. Again, operators in the top of the table have higher precedence than those appearing below them. For operators that have equal precedence, the *Associativity* column indicates which ones will be evaluated first. For example, in the case of the (*) and (/) operators, evaluation is done left-to-right, as indicated by the **L** in the column. On the other hand, the operators (++), (--), (~), (!), (-), and (type cast) are evaluated from right-to-left.

> **NOTE:** We will discuss 'type casting' in the Data Types chapter, 'string concatenation' in the Strings chapter and 'instance of' in the Object Orientation chapter.

Fetch Expressions

As mentioned earlier in this chapter, ***fetch expressions*** are the most elementary type of expression. Their primary use is to construct or fetch values without performing any computation on them. For example, accessing a field in a class and assigning it to another field, or executing a call to a method that returns a value, are examples of *fetch expressions*. In the following three sections we will discuss the different kinds of fetch expressions.

Null Expressions

The ***fetch expression* null** produces a special object reference value that does not refer to any object, but is assignment-compatible with all *object reference* types. These are simply any variable declared to be of a class type, as described in the previous chapter. It is the default value for these type of variables before they have been assigned to an object by use of the **new** operator. Keep in mind that, if you subsequently assigned an object reference variable to **null**, the object it was pointing to will be left "dangling" if no other variables point to it. Hence, it will be swept up by the garbage collector. The special value **null** is most easily thought of as a language-supplied constant, but in reality it is actually an expression, a fetch expression. This is splitting hairs, though, and not of much consequence. (Notice, however, that **null** is not considered a zero as it is in C and C++.)

If you have need to determine if an object reference variable has yet to be assigned to an object, you can compare it to **null**, as in:

```
if (myObject != null) // not instantiated yet?
  myObject = new MyClass(); // instantiate it now
```

Method Call and Array Index Expressions

A method call expression is a primary expression that invokes a method. This is similar to a procedure call expression in RPG IV. A method call expression fetches a value returned by the method or the procedure. Similarly, an array index expression produces an array element when it is evaluated. The following illustrates both of these expressions:

```
myVariable = myObject.myMethod(); // call method myMethod in myObject
y = myEmployeeArray[i]; // retrieve i'th entry of array myEmployeeArray
```

OTHER MATHEMATICAL FUNCTIONS

Earlier in this chapter, we introduced the basic math operators that are used in expressions. These include (+), (-), (*), (/), and (%). However, RPG and Java support many other mathematical functions, such as the built-in functions in RPG and supplied methods in Java. The Java supplied class Math contains methods for performing basic numeric operations, such as exponentiation, logarithms, square roots, and the trigonometric functions.

To help ensure portability of Java programs, the definitions of many of the numeric functions in the Math class supplied by Java are implemented using certain accepted published algorithms. These algorithms are available from the well-known network library netlib as the package "Freely Distributable Math Library" (**fdlibm**). These algorithms, which are written in the C programming language, were rewritten in Java and supplied as the Java math class. The Java math library is defined with respect to the version of **fdlibm** dated January 4, 1995.

Here we look at an example of the RPG %ABS (*absolute*) built-in function:

LISTING 3-10

```
D FirstNum        S              4S 0 INZ(40)
D SecondNum       S              4S 0 INZ(65)
D Result          S              4S 0
C                 EVAL     Result = FirstNum—SecondNum
C        Result   DSPLY
C                 EVAL     Result = %ABS(FirstNum—SecondNum)
C        Result   DSPLY
```

We declare two fields, FirstNum and SecondNum as zoned (4,0) and initialize them to the values 40 and 65 respectively. On the C-spec, we perform two different calculations using the EVAL operation code. In both calculations, the field with the larger value, SecondNum, is subtracted from the field containing the smaller value, FirstNum. In both cases, the subtraction results in a value of -25. The %ABS built-in function then returns the absolute value of -25, which is 25. Thus %ABS returns the positive value of a given negative number. It has no affect on positive numbers.

The same result can be accomplished in Java by using the Math class, which is found in the Java.lang package. The following illustrates the same example written in Java:

LISTING 3-11

```
public class ABS
{
    public static void main(String args[])
    {
        int firstNum  = 40;
        int secondNum = 65;
        int result1, result2;

        result1 = firstNum—secondNum;
        result2 = Math.abs(firstNum—secondNum);

        System.out.println("The first result is: " + result1);
        System.out.println("The absolute value is: " + result2);
    }
}
```

As in the RPG example, we declare two fields of type integer and initialize them to 40 and 65. In the first case, we just do the subtraction. In the second case, we subtract and then use the abs method to return the absolute value. Again, this gives us -25 and 25, respectively. This is just one example of the many different methods available in the Math package.

Another straightforward math function in RPG and Java involves retrieving the square root of a given number. The special RPG operation code **SQRT** does what you need. In the following example, we declare a field with the value of 9 and use **SQRT** in order to find its square root:

LISTING 3-12

```
D*Name+++++++++ETDsFrom+++To/L+++IDc.Keywords++++++++++
D Test            S             4S 0 INZ(9)
D Result          S             4S 0
C*
C                 SQRT    Test          Result
C     Result      DSPLY
C                 MOVE    *ON           *INLR
```

The expected result of 3 is returned. It is just as simple to do this in Java. The Math class contains the method sqrt for just this purpose. This method is available only for fields with a double data type (data types are covered in Chapter 5). The following example illustrates the Java way of getting the square root of the value 9:

LISTING 3-13

```
public class SqRoot
{
    public static void main (String args[])
    {
        double firstNum = 9;
        double result;
        result = Math.sqrt(firstNum);
        System.out.println("The result is: " + result);
    }
}
```

As you see can see from the example, we use the static method **sqrt** with the value 9 as a parameter. This results in the value 3 being returned.

We have shown you only a couple of examples of the available methods in the Java `Math` class. There are many more that you can use, including the following:

Method	Description
abs(double)	Returns the absolute value of a double value.
abs(float)	Returns the absolute value of a float value.
abs(int)	Returns the absolute value of an int value.
abs(long)	Returns the absolute value of a long value.
acos(double)	Returns the arc cosine of an angle, in the range of 0.0 through pi.
asin(double)	Returns the arc sine of an angle, in the range of -**pi**/2 through **pi**/2.
atan(double)	Returns the arc tangent of an angle, in the range of -**pi**/2 through **pi**/2.
atan2(double,double)	rectangular coordinates (b, a) to polar (r, theta).
ceil(double)	Returns the smallest (closest to negative infinity) double value that is not less than the argument and is equal to a mathematical integer.
cos(double)	Returns the trigonometric cosine of an angle.
exp(double)	Returns the exponential number (eg, 2.718) raised to the power of a double value.
floor(double)	Returns the largest (closest to positive infinity) double value that is not greater than the argument and returns the greater of two double values.
max(float, float)	Returns the greater of two float values.
max(int, int)	Returns the greater of two int values.
max(long, long)	Returns the greater of two long values.
min(double, double)	Returns the smaller of two double values.
min(float, float)	Returns the smaller of two float values.
min(int, int)	Returns the smaller of two int values.
min(long, long)	Returns the smaller of two long values.
pow(double, double)	Returns of value of the first argument raised to the power of the second argument.
random()	Returns a random number between 0.0 and 1.0.
rint(double)	Returns the closest integer to the argument.
round(double)	Returns the closest long to the argument.
round(float)	Returns the closest int to the argument.
sin(double)	Returns the trigonometric sine of an angle.
sqrt(double)	Returns the square root of a double value.
tan(double)	Returns the trigonometric tangent of an angle.

NOTE: These methods are all static and, therefore, resemble traditional standalone functions in other non-OO languages. The exception is that in order to call them, you must qualify the method name with the class name as in `Math.xxxx()`.

In many cases, a method listed in the table may have an equivalent RPG procedure, code, built-in function, or operation code that performs the same function. Let us look at an example that does not, however. In Java, there is a method that returns the maximum value of two numbers. How can this be accomplished with RPG? We can simply write a routine or *procedure* that, when it is given two values, returns the largest one:

LISTING 3-14

```
D*Name+++++++++ETDsFrom+++To/L+++IDc.Keywords++++++++++
D First             S              4S 0 INZ(9)
D Second            S              4S 0 INZ(22)
D Third             S              4S 0 INZ(2)
D Result            S              4S 0
D MAX               PR             4S 0
D  First                           4S 0
D  Second                          4S 0
C*
C                   EVAL      Result = MAX(First:Second)
C      Result       DSPLY
C                   EVAL      Result = MAX(First:Third)
C      Result       DSPLY
C                   MOVE      *ON             *INLR
 * Start of procedure MAX...
P MAX               B
D                   PI             4S 0
D  First                          4S 0
D  Second                         4S 0
C                   IF        First>Second
C                   RETURN    First
C                   ELSE
C                   RETURN    Second
C                   EndIF
P MAX               E
```

In our example, the body of the procedure called MAX contains an **if** structure that performs the comparison. If the first number is larger, then this value is returned using the **RETURN** operation code. Otherwise, the **else** part is executed and the second number is returned. This procedure is similar to the Java supplied max method. In Java, we simply call the static method Math.max and pass it the two values. Compare the RPG code with the following example that shows the equivalent Java code for returning the maximum of two numbers:

LISTING 3-15

```
public class Max
{
     public static void main (String args[])
     {
          double firstNum = 9;
          double secondNum = 22;
          double result;
          result = Math.max(firstNum, secondNum);
          System.out.println("The result is: " + result);
     }
}
```

Notice that the max procedure is already written for you. The body of the RPG code is very similar to that of Java.

Finally, when we discussed arithmetic operators earlier in this chapter, we mentioned that RPG has an exponentiation operator, whereas Java does not. The following example illustrates an expression that uses exponentiation in RPG:

LISTING 3-16

```
D*Name++++++++++ETDsFrom+++To/L+++IDc.Keywords++++++++++
D FirstNum        S               4S 0 INZ(2)
D exp             S               4S 0 INZ(4)
D Result          S               4S 0
C*
C                 EVAL      Result = FirstNum ** exp
C     Result      DSPLY
C                 MOVE      *ON           *INLR
```

In this example, we declare the field FirstNum and initialize it to the value 2. In addition, we declare the field exp to hold the exponent value. In the body of the code, we have an expression that takes the field FirstNum and raises it to the power of the field exp. The result is placed in the field Result. After executing this program, the **DSPLY** operation outputs the value of 16, which is the result of 2^4.

Although Java has no standalone exponentiation operator, it does have a static method called **exp**, again in the Math class. As an exercise you may try experimenting with it.

SUMMARY

- There are three kinds of comments in Java: multiple-line, single-line, and JavaDoc.
- **Javadoc** is a tool supplied in the JDK that helps you document your classes and methods and converts the comments in a Java source file into an HTML document that may read by any Web browser.
- Java fields must start with a letter, underscore, or a dollar sign, whereas RPG must start with an alphanumeric character, #, $, or @ characters.
- RPG field name lengths can be up to 4096, whereas Java variable name length is unlimited.
- There are four kinds of Java statements:
  - Expression statement
  - Blocked statement
  - Empty statement
  - Labeled statement
- Two kinds of expressions in Java, *computational* and *fetch* expressions. Computational expressions use operators and cause side effects, whereas fetch expressions are used to fetch a value, but do not do any computation on them.
- Java has seven bitwise operators that mask or compare bit values in integral variables.
- Use the shift right operator (>>>) when you do not want to preserve the leftmost sign bit. If the leftmost sign bit is required to be preserved, then use the (>>) operator.
- Java has a whole class (java.lang.Math) that comes with the JDK and has methods to cover a variety of math functions, including things like sin, cos, tan, abs, sqrt and many other useful methods.

4

Structured Operations and Statements

CONTROL STRUCTURES

Structured operation codes (op-codes) and statements form the smallest executable unit in RPG and Java programs. They control the order in which statements will be acted upon by the computer. *Control structures* can be divided into four basic categories: *sequence*, *decision*, *loop*, and *transfer*. As with life, programs benefit from control! Especially, conditional control!

Sequence structures (op-codes or statements) allow control, in both languages, to flow from one statement to the next in the order in which they were written in the program. That is, flow is sequential. Examples of sequence of structures in RPG are the ADD, MOVE, SUB, and EVAL operation codes. Examples in Java are the expression statements such as assignment. These statements (or op-codes) execute consecutively. They do not cause the flow of control to shift. When control comes to the end of a program, it usually terminates. These concepts were covered in the previous chapter.

Decision structures allow control to flow in a different path, depending on the result of a conditional statement. You can conditionally select alternate paths for your program. Decision control structures include:

- if conditional statement
- select (RPG) or switch (Java) conditional statement

Loop structures allow control to flow iteratively for a specified number of times, or until a condition is met. These include:

- `do` (RPG) and `for` (Java) loop statements
- `do-while` (RPG) and `for` (Java) loop statements
- `do-until` (RPG) and `do-while` (Java) loop structures

Transfer structures allow control to flow to another part of the program. Transfer control structures include:

- `goto` (RPG) statement
- `leave` / `iter` (RPG) and `break` / `continue` (Java) statements
- `return` statement
- `try-catch` and `throw` (Java) statements

The following table shows structured op-codes that are available in RPG and their equivalent Java statements. Some less-common statements are not shown because they are not available in both languages.

RPG	Java	Description

`IFxx/IF`
`ENDIF/END`
	`if` (expression)
	{
	  // statements;
	}
		Enables you to execute a code fragment based on a boolean test.

`SELECT`
 	
`WHENxx/WHEN`
  `OTHER`
`ENDSL/END`
	`switch` (test)
	{
	  case value:
	  break;
	  default:
	}
		Enables you to switch a case (in Java) or **SELECT WHEN** (in RPG) based on the value of an expression.

`DO`
`ENDDO/END`
	`for` (init; expression;
	increment)
	{
	  // statements;
	}
		Loop specific number of times based on an initial value, expression, and increment. Loop while the expression is **true**.

`DOWxx/DOW`
`ENDDO/END`
	`while` (expression)
	{
	  // statements;
	}
		Loop while the expression is **true**.

`DOUxx/DOU`
`ENDDO/END`
	`do`
	{
	  // statements
	}
	`while` (expression);
		Loop until the expression is **false**. Body is executed at least once.

RPG	Java	Description
GOTO and TAG		Java disallows it. RPG has it and allows it. Our advice... do not use it!
LEAVE ITER	break; continue;	Break/**LEAVE** transfers control out of the inner most structure. Continue/**ITER** ends the current iteration of the loop, and starts the next.
RETURN	return statement	Return to caller.
*PSSR, INFSR, and error indicators	try/catch statement	Catch all program and file exceptions. See chapter 10.
send escape msg	throw statement	Causes an exception to be thrown. See chapter 10.

ALTERNATE PATHS: DECISION STRUCTURES

Let's turn our focus to the RPG op-codes and Java statements that can alter the flow of control, such as if and **select / switch**.

If, Then What? Else, of Course

The use of conditions and conditional statements to form a decision structure, such as the **if** op-code or statement, is important (although not always required) in the construction of an RPG or Java program. A condition is an assertion or test that concerns the value of a data item or more complex expressions. The conditional statement is the primary mechanism through which alternate paths of control can be developed within a program. The flow of control through a conditional statement depends on the determination of the truth or falsity of the assertion at program execution.

The **if** conditional op-code or statement enables you to execute different parts or blocks of code based on a simple test. The **if** statement in Java is nearly identical to the **if** statement in C. RPG, on the other hand, has two forms of this statement: a fixed form that was inherited from RPG III, and a free-format factor two form that enables you to write more *expressive* expressions. The **if** structures in RPG and Java are written differently, but they are the same in function. The following illustrates the two forms of the RPG **IF** statement:

RPG Fixed Form				RPG Free Form		
C	NUM	IFLT	2	C	IF	NUM<2 AND
C	*IN99	ANDEQ		*IN99		
*ON				C*	:	
C*		:		C*	:	
C		ENDIF		C	ENDIF	

The *second* column illustrates the free-format **IF** statement in RPG. In this format, you first specify the **IF** op-code and then specify the expression that you want to be evaluated in the free-format factor two entry. The expression forms two conditions: the NUM field must be less than 2 and indicator 99 must be ***ON**. If both conditions are **true**, then the body of the **IF** op-code is executed. If any one of these conditions being evaluated is **false**, then the body of the **IF** op-code will not be executed, and control will be passed to the next operation found after the **ENDIF** op-code. (For a review of expressions and their rules of construction, refer to the previous chapter.) The *first* column of this example illustrates the fixed-format **IF** statement in RPG. In this format, the **IFxx** structure is used, where **xx** can be: **EQ**, **GT**, **LT**, **GE**, **LE,** and **NE**. The disadvantage of using the fixed format is that there is a need for additional op-codes (**ANDxx** or **ORxx**) to build each condition. The Java **if** statement, as you may have guessed, is closer to the free-format version of the RPG **IF** op-code.

The following illustrates the simplest form of the **if** statement in Java:

```
if (num<2 && IN99=='1')
  {
    // statements;
  }
```

Notice that the expression part is often coded with parentheses around the sub expressions or conditions, as in:

```
if ((num<2) && (IN99=='1'))
```

Because the && operator has precedence over the other operators, however, this is simply a style preference that aids readability. Also notice that the braces are optional if only a single statement exists after the **if** :

```
if ((num<2) && (IN99=='1'))
   System.out.println("Wow, I get it now!");
```

A problem will result if you add a second line later, but forget to add the braces, as in:

```
if ((num<2) && (IN99=='1'))
   System.out.println("Wow, I get it now!");
   System.out.println("Well, maybe not!");
```

This will compile, but you will get an unexpected outcome. The second statement will be executed *regardless* of the outcome of the **if** test because it is *not* part of the **if** body. If the body has more than one statement, you must enclose the block with braces. To prevent this type of error, always use braces, even for single statement blocks.

You can see that both languages allow you to specify an arbitrarily complex expression. If the expression evaluates to **true**, the following block of statements within the structure are executed. However, what if you want to have another condition to test? That is, what if you want the program to do something else if the conditional expression is **false**? Both languages give you the ability to specify an optional **else** part that supplies the statements to execute if the test condition of the **if** expression is **false**. The following example illustrates the use of the **ELSE** op-code in RPG IV that works in complement to the **IF** op-code:

RPG Fixed Form				RPG Free Form			
C	NUM	IFLT	2	C		IF	NUM<2 AND *IN99
C	*IN99	ANDEQ		C*		:	
*ON				C		ELSE	
C*		:		C*		:	
C		ELSE		C		ENDIF	
C*		:					
C		ENDIF					

Next we show a similar example using the Java **else** clause:

LISTING 4-1

```
if ((num < 2) && (IN99 == '1'))
   { // start if block
     // statements
   } // end if block
else
   { // start else block
     // statements
   } // end else block
```

In both examples, the block of statements after the **else** statement executes if the **if** expression evaluates to **false**. The biggest difference in both examples is the use of the block statement in Java to indicate the start and end of an **if** or **else** body. As mentioned in the previous chapter, you can think of the closing brace '}' in Java as an equivalent to the **ENDIF** op-code in RPG. It indicates the end of the code block in an **if** or **else** body. The starting brace '{' does not have a matching op code in RPG IV other than being the first executable statement after the **IF** or **ELSE** op-codes. So, as we have seen in both RPG and Java, the **if** structure allows for an *either-or* kind of condition by providing an **else** clause. If the **if** expression evaluates to a **true** condition, the body of the **if** op-code or statement block is executed; otherwise, the **else** op-code or statement body block is executed.

An interesting situation arises when you have more than two conditions. Let's take a look at an example in which you are testing for an age. You would like to have conditions perform one set of instructions if the person is at least 65 years old, a second set if the person is less than 65 but not younger than 12, a third set if the person is less than 12 but not younger than 2, and a default set if the person is 2 or less. That adds up to a total of three different conditions (there could easily be more), and a *default* condition that is processed if all three previous conditions are **false**. Both languages support this kind of testing by allowing you to nest the **IF** statements. The following illustrates the nesting feature in RPG:

LISTING 4-2

```
...+... 1 ...+... 2 ...+... 3 ...+... 4 ...+... 5
    C* Assign Ticket Prices for the Zoo based on age
    C                     IF        Age>=65
    C                     EVAL      Ticket=10
    C                     ELSE
    C                     IF        Age>12
    C                     EVAL      Ticket=20
    C                     ELSE
    C                     IF        Age>2
    C                     EVAL      Ticket=5
    C                     ELSE
    C                     EVAL      Ticket=0
    C                     ENDIF
    C                     ENDIF
    C                     ENDIF
```

This situation resembles the **if** statement in its simplest form. All you have to do is add another **if** op-code or statement after the **else** op-code or statement with the new condition you want to test. For more complex conditions, additional **else if** structures can be added. What follows is the previous example written in Java:

```
// Assign ticket prices for the zoo based on age
if (Age >= 65)
  Ticket = 10;
else if (Age > 12)
  Ticket = 20
else if (Age > 2)
  Ticket = 5;
else
  Ticket = 0;
```

Notice, as is commonly seen in Java, that the **else** and **if** statements are lumped together on the same line to aid readability. The rule to always remember, however, is: *an* **else** *always matches the most previous* **if**. Sound reasonable? You can easily get in trouble by using **if** statements as the body of the **if** statement itself. For example:

```
if (Age < 65)
  if (Age > 12)
    Ticket = 20;
else
  Ticket = 10;
```

It may look as if the **else** matches the outer **if**, but it does not. Instead it matches the inner **if**. Once again, you need to remember the rule. Or, you can avoid the situation altogether by writing these kind of **if-if** statements as single **if** statements with compound expressions, as in:

```
if ((Age < 65) && (Age > 12))
   Ticket = 20;
else
   Ticket = 10;
```

Too Many IFs? Time to Switch!

One of the most common programming methods in any language is to test a field against some value. In the case of the **if** decision structure, if the test evaluates to **true**, then a block of statements is executed and control passes to the end of the structure. For a **false** condition, the block of statements is ignored and, if an **else-if** block is specified, the next test is performed. Again, for this test, the block is either ignored or executed depending on the condition result. If there are more **else-if** blocks, then more testing is done until an expression evaluates to **true**. Once there is a **true** condition, the block is executed and control passes to the end of the structure. If none of the tests succeed, then all the blocks are ignored unless a default **else** block is specified. Control first passes to the default **else** block of statements and then to the end of the structure.

You can use the **if** op-code or statement to solve this kind of problem. However, both Java and RPG provide you with a more elegant way of doing multiple tests such as the one described. Take, for example, the following code:

LISTING 4-3

```
if (day == MON)
{
    // do something
}
else if (day == TUE)
{
    // do something
}
else if (day == WED)
{
    // do something
}
else if (day == THUR)
{
    // do something
}
else if (day == FRI)
{
    // do something
}
else
{
    // default code
}
```

Here we use the **if** statement to determine what day of the week it is. The code in this Java example is very long and you can imagine what the equivalent code written in RPG IV would look like with five **if** and four nested **else** statements. Luckily, both languages provide a structure specifically for problems of this type that involve deeply nested **if-else** statements. In fact these nested statements can often be syntactically correct and yet not express the intended logic of the programmer. Incorrect **else-if** matching bugs are hard to find and modifications to the statements are risky to make.

As an alternative to **if-else** statements, Java and RPG offer the **switch** statement and the **SELECT** op-code, respectively. These give the same results as the **if** statement, but they have a simplified structure that is more readable and maintainable. We will now redo our example using the **switch** statement in Java and the **SELECT** op-code in RPG:

RPG		Java
C	SELECT	`switch (day)`
C	WHEN day = MON	`{`
C*	*do something*	`    case MON:`
C	WHEN day = TUE	`        // do something`
C*	*do something*	`        break;`
C	WHEN day = WED	`    case TUE:`
C*	*do something*	`        // do something`
C	WHEN day = THUR	`        break;`
C*	*do something*	`    case WED:`
C	WHEN day = FRI	`        // do something`
C*	*do something*	`        break;`
C	OTHER	`    . . . .`
C*	*default code*	`    default:`
C	ENDSL	`        // default code`
		`} // end switch statement`

The first important point to note is the improved readability of the **SELECT/switch** structure compared to the nested **if** statements. Also, if you look at the previous example, you can almost map the structures one to one between the languages. The **switch** statement maps to the `SELECT` op-code, and the **case** statement maps to the `WHEN` op-code. In Java you have to use the **break** statement to indicate the end of the case statement body. However, in RPG there is no need to do this because the compiler finds the end of the `WHEN` operation body when it encounters the next `WHEN` or `OTHER` operation codes. The default statement in Java maps to the `OTHER` operation code in RPG. Finally, the very end brace '}', which ends the case statement in Java, maps to the `ENDSL` operation code in RPG. It's straightforward mapping! The following table summarizes the mappings we discussed:

RPG SELECT	Java Switch
`SELECT`	`switch`
`WHEN` or `WHENxx`	`case`
`OTHER`	`default`
`ENDSL`	`end brace '}'`

The RPG **SELECT** op-code and Java's **switch** statement seem to be very similar. However, they differ in the expression that is tested. Here are descriptions of this important distinction:

- In the Java **switch** statement, the expression is only specified once, as part of the "**switch (expression)**" syntax. The result of the expression is then compared to each of the **case** statement values until a match is found. If found, that **case** body is executed. If no match is found, the **default** body is executed if it exists. Otherwise, the **switch** statement completes without doing anything. The expression must resolve to a value of type byte, character, short, or integer. Java does not allow you to use other types such as long, float, strings, or objects within a switch. Further, the **case** statements can only test for equality with the expression value.

- The RPG **SELECT** op-code is superior in function in this regard. The **WHEN** op-code allows you to specify any valid expression you like, and each **WHEN** can specify a different one. RPG simply selects the first **WHEN** that evaluates to **true**. Further, the expression is open to any data type available.

There is, in fact, an additional important difference! Did you notice that the RPG **SELECT** statement in our example was more compact than the Java **switch** statement? This is primarily because of the Java requirement to end each **case** statement block with a **break** statement. RPG, on the other hand, implicitly defines the end of a **WHEN** op-code when it see another one or an **OTHER** or **ENDSL** statement. This use of **break** makes Java more verbose than RPG. But there are more sinister implications than size of code. What do you think will happen if you forget to insert the **break** statement in Java to terminate the **case** clause? Rather than implicitly ending the block of code at the next **case** statement, Java will continue to execute all statements until it finally finds a **break** statement or the end of the **switch** statement. This can lead to some nasty bugs that are quite time consuming to track down. Why this behavior (inherited from C, by the way)? It is actually by design. It allows you to group cases together that have common code. For example, let's say that you want to execute one block of code for MON, TUE, and WED; and another one for THUR and FRI. Here is how we exploit that **break**-less behavior to do it:

LISTING 4-4

```
switch (day)
{
    case MON:
    case TUE:
    case WED:
        // first block of code
        break;
    case THUR:
    case FRI:
        // second block of code
        break;
    default:
} // end switch statement
```

The Conditional Operator '?:'

In the previous chapter, we introduced the '**?:**' conditional or *ternary* operator. Under certain circumstances, you can use a shorthand version of the **if** statement to indicate alternate paths through the code. This operator is similar to the one found in C and C++ . RPG IV, on the other hand, does not support it. There are advantages to using this operator, even though we already have the **if** statement. They are compact format and less typing. However, if you are more comfortable using the **if** statement, then just use it. The same results will be produced. The following example illustrates an **if** statement that does a simple test of age < 2. If the test is **true**, then a boolean variable (described in next chapter) is set to **true**; otherwise, the variable is set to **false**:

```
if (age < 2)
    freeTicket = true;
else
    freeTicket = false;
// ternary equivalent
freeTicket = (age < 2) ? true : false;
```

Because we described this in the previous chapter, we will simply point out that in some cases it is a valid alternative to more tedious **if** statements.

Loop Structures — They Get Around

The three most common loop structures that are available in all modern languages are also available in both RPG and Java: the **for** loop (**DO** in RPG), the **while** loop (**DOW** in RPG), and the **do...while** (or until) loops (**DOU** in RPG). Their syntax is a bit different and there is a little difference in semantics too!

131

The following table summaries the different loops that are available in both languages. In the next section we will describe all three loops. Notice that the `do until` and `do while` loops in RPG still have both the fixed format form that they inherited from RPG III, and they have the free format factor two form that was introduced in RPG IV. Because the free format form is more structured than the fixed format form, and because we want to encourage you to use the free format form in your future RPG IV programming, we use it in the examples only when we compare RPG loops to Java.

RPG					JAVA
C	start	DO	limit	index	`for (initialization; condition;`
C*		:			`increments)`
C		ENDDO			`{`
					`    // body`
					`}`
C		DOW	expression		`while (expression)`
C*		:			`{`
C		ENDDO			`    // body`
					`}`
C		DOU	expression		`do`
C*		:			`{`
C		ENDDO			`    // body`
					`} while (expression);`

Going "for" a Loop-Just "DO" It

The `DO` loop in RPG and `for` loop in Java are used when a known definitive number of iterations are required to execute a block of statements or operation codes. This kind of loop structure is called a ***determinant loop***. In this kind of loop, there is a starting and ending value and an index that controls iteration steps for the loop. As you see in the next RPG example, the starting value is specified in factor one (defaults to 1 if not specified) and factor two contains the ending or limit value (defaults to 1 if not specified):

LISTING 4-5

```
C*      FACTOR 1    OPCODE    FACTOR 2    RESULT
C*      --------    ------    --------    ------
C       Start       DO        End         Idx
C*                  :
C*                  loop body
C*                  :
C                   ENDDO
```

The result column contains the index field. (If not specified, RPG generates an internal field to contain your index.) To delimit the end of your `DO` loop block, use the `ENDDO` operation code after the last op-code in the body of the loop. The example shows that if the `Start` field contains the value 1, and the `End` field contains the value 10, the loop will iterate 10 times. It starts with a value of 1 in the index field `Idx`, incrementing it for each iteration until `Idx` becomes 10 in value. The increment value by default is 1 because we did not specify it. However, we could use factor two of the **ENDDO** operation code to tell RPG a negative or positive increment, or a step value to add or subtract after each loop iteration.

The Java **for** statement contains all the functionality that RPG provides. The general format for the Java **for** statement is:

```
for (expression)
{
  // statements
}
```

The **for** statement expression consists of three main parts, which are separated by semicolons:

```
for (initialization; condition; increment)
```

These pieces are typically used as follows:

- *Initialization*: a specification of the initial value of the index variable (can also declare it here).

- *Condition*: a boolean expression. Loop continues while expression is **true**. Loop executes zero times if expression is **false** on initial run. Typically this is a comparison of the index value to a predetermined maximum value, such as the dimension limit on an array.

- *Increment*: an assignment or increment statement of your choosing, but typically increments the index value.

In Java, unlike RPG, all management of the loop indexing is your responsibility. The only thing Java gives you in terms of built-in support in the **for** loop is the promise to keep looping as long as the boolean conditioning expression is **true**. Absolutely everything else is up to you. So, if you want to have an index variable and increment it per loop iteration, it is your job to take care of that. Let us now look at an example of a typical simple **for** loop in Java that loops through all elements of an array and prints out the contents. In Java, arrays start at index zero, and they support a special built-in variable called **length**, which represents the number of items in the array:

```
char myCharArray[] = new char[20]; // declare an array of 20 characters
int  idx;
for (idx = 0; idx < myCharArray.length; idx++)
{
  myCharArray[idx] = ' '; // set idx'th character to blank
}
```

In this example, we first declare an array of 20 characters (arrays are covered in Chapter 6), then declare an integer index variable called idx. We then loop through the array, assigning a blank character to each position in the array. In this example, we do the following:

- Initialize our indexing variable to zero: idx = 0;
- Keep looping as long as the indexing variable is less than the size of the array: idx < myCharArray.length;
- Increment our indexing variable by one after each iteration: idx++.

The following example runs backwards through the array:

```
char myCharArray[] = new char[20]; // declare an array of 20 characters
int  idx;
for (idx = myCharArray.length-1; idx >= 0; idx--)
{
    myCharArray[idx] = ' '; // set idx'th character to blank
}
```

In this example, we initialize the indexing variable to the size of the array minus one (to account for the zero-based indexing in Java arrays), and decrement the variable by one until we hit zero. Notice that, in both examples, we have declared the index variable outside of the **for** loop. It turns out that we can actually do this as part of the initialization section of the **for** loop, as in:

```
char myCharArray[] = new char[20]; // declare an array of 20 characters
for (int idx = myCharArray.length-1; idx >= 0; idx--)
{
    myCharArray[idx] = ' '; // set idx'th character to blank
}
```

Notice how we declare and initialize the idx variable in one shot. This is handy, but because of Java's scoping rules, it does mean that the variable is not accessible outside the scope of the **for** loop. It *is* accessible, however, in all three parts of the **for** expression and in the body of the loop itself.

Another point to make about the **for** loop is that, like all Java multi-statement structures, the braces are optional if the block or body has but one statement. For example:

```
for (int idx = 0; idx < salaries.length; idx++)
    System.out.println("Salary is: " + salaries[idx]);
```

Again, however, we caution you about not using braces due to the risk of adding additional statements later and forgetting the braces (in which case the first statement remains the only one executed per loop iteration). We do show you examples with and without the braces, however.

As it turns out, all three parts of the **for** statement are optional in Java. For example, we can legally define a `for` loop with none of the three parts (although the two delimiting semicolons are still required), as in:

```
for ( ; ; )
   System.out.println("looping...");
```

What does this mean? Because Java agrees to loop as long as the condition expression is not **false**, this loop will simply run forever. Of course, we humbly recommend not writing infinite loop programs! What is very interesting about the `for` loop construct, though, is that it is a completely general construct-that is, the initialization part can contain any statement, the conditional part can contain any boolean expression, and the increment part can contain any statement. It is merely convention-although a convention we recommend you follow-that these are used for index initialization, loop termination checking, and index incrementing or decrementing. The initialization part and the incrementing part actually allow multiple statements to be specified. However, they must be separated by commas, not the usual semicolons. This gives tremendous flexibility. For our first example, let's go back to the `for` loop, which initialized a character array to all blanks. Because the body of the loop is very small, we actually have the option of performing it in the third part of the `for` expression, as follows:

```
for (int idx = 0; idx < myCharArray.length; myCharArray[idx]=' ', idx++)
{
}
```

You will notice that we put the assignment statement together with the `idx++` statement-comma separated-in the increment part. This is perfectly legal, and you will see it done often. The two statements are separated by a comma. Because we do all the necessary work in the increment part, we have no need for a body. So we use an empty block. We could also use an empty statement-a simple semicolon. In fact, to be really concise, we could also increment the `idx` variable right in the assignment statement, as follows:

```
for (int idx = 0; idx < myCharArray.length; myCharArray[idx++]=' ')
   ;
```

You often see this kind of compact **for** statement in Java code. There is a trick to its interpretation. The expression idx++, uses the current value of idx as the index into the array and then increments it after. (This was discussed in Chapter 3.) Compact **for** statements are also commonly used to find the first non-blank character in a character array, as follows:

```
char myCharArray[] = {' ', ' ', 'a', 'b', 'c'};
int idx;
for (idx = 0; myCharArray[idx] == ' '; idx++)
   ;
System.out.println("first blank char position = " + idx);
```

In this example, we declare the index variable idx outside the **for** loop so we can access it later. Our **for** loop then initializes the index to zero, loops as long as the array character indexed by it is blank, and increments the index each time. In this case, the output result is 2. Note that myCharArray is declared as an array of characters and initialized to contain the five characters blank, blank, a, b, and c. This implicitly sets its length to five. The number 2 that we get as a result is zero-based; in fact, so is the third position. Of course, if the input is an array of all blank characters, this example runs into trouble. The terminating condition stays **true** until the index variable is beyond the limit of the array. This results in a runtime "exception," which is not at all unlike an "unmonitored exception" error in RPG:

```
java.lang.ArrayIndexOutOfBoundsException: 5
```

To fix this, we need the condition expression to also check for end of array:

```
for (idx = 0;
     idx < myCharArray.length && myCharArray[idx] == ' ';
     idx++)
   ;
```

Now we have a robust and compact example to check for the first non-blank character. What we did here was to put each of the three parts of the **for** statement on its own line. Because Java is a free-format language, this is perfectly legal and is often done for readability. Your subsequent code will want to check if idx is greater than the array's length, which will determine if the array was all blanks or not:

```
if (idx >= myCharArray.length)
   System.out.println("All blank array!");
else
   System.out.println("first blank char position = " + idx);
```

How would you find the last non-blank character, which is another common programming requirement? The procedure follows:

```
for (idx = myCharArrar.length-1;
     idx >= 0 && myCharArray[idx] == ' ';
     idx--)
   ;
```

In Java, as you will see in Chapter 6, you can have multiple-dimension arrays. Imagine, then, that you have a two-dimensional array called `raster`, and that you want to initialize it to one for each position. The `for` loop can handle this easily. It is an array's best friend! Two dimensional arrays are declared using two sets of empty brackets and the `new` operator, which specifies the length for each dimension. Note that `arrayVariable.length` gives the length of the first dimension and `arrayVariable[x].length` gives the length of the x'th row. Here then is a fully compilable example:

LISTING 4-6

```
public class TestFor
{
    public static void main(String args[])
    {
        int raster[][] = new int[3][2]; // matrix 3 by 2
        for (int x=0; x < raster.length; x++)
        {
            for (int y=0; y < raster[x].length; y++)
            {
                raster[x][y] - 1;
                System.out.println("raster " + x + "," + y + " = " +
                                   raster[x][y]);
            }
        }
    } // end main method
} // end TestFor class
```

This results in the following output:

```
raster 0,0 = 1
raster 0,1 = 1
raster 1,0 = 1
raster 1,1 = 1
raster 2,0 = 1
raster 2,1 = 1
```

This example illustrates the ability to nest **for** loops. That is, the body of one **for** loop can be yet another **for** loop. This means the inner loop is executed for its duration multiple times, once per iteration of the outer loop. This example is a little bit longer than necessary. Here is the smallest possible version of this nested **for** loop for initializing a two-dimensional array (without the `println` statement):

```
for (int x=0; x < raster.length; x++)
   for (int y=0; y < raster[x].length; raster[x][y++] = 1)
          ;
```

Looping for a While

Now that you have mastered the **for** loop, you will find the **while** loop to be a breeze. It is a subset of the **for** loop's functionality and brings nothing new to the table-except ease of use. The **while** statement is a lot simpler than the **for** statement described earlier. This is because the **while** loop only takes an expression for evaluation and does not have as many parameters as the **for** loop allows. Its use is for those cases where the termination of the loop is not predetermined, and you simply want to loop *while* a given condition is **true**. You will decide in the body of the code when to set that condition to **false**. (If this procedure is not performed correctly you will have an infinite loop.) This is called an ***indeterminant*** loop, because you can't predict when it will end. It is especially useful when reading or asking for input, because the end will be determined by the end of file or by a user-initiated action.

In the free-format **DOW** operation code in RPG, you specify an expression in the free-format factor two to be evaluated each time the loop iterates. If the expression evaluates to **true,** the next iteration is executed. However, if the condition or the expression specified in factor two is **false**, the **while** loop is terminated and control is transferred to the operation after the **ENDDO** op-code. The following illustrates the syntax of **DOW** in RPG IV:

LISTING 4-7

```
C*      Factor 1     opcode    Factor 2      Result
C                    DOW       expression
C*                   :
C*                   loop body
C*                   :
C                    ENDDO
```

The **while** loop for both Java and RPG executes zero or more times. This point becomes important in contrast to the next section where we describe the **DOU** (*do until*) loop, which executes one or more times.

The equivalent in Java to RPG's **DOW** op-code is the **while** statement, which has the following syntax:

```
while (expression)
{
    // statement(s)
}
```

The expression is any boolean expression evaluating to **true** or **false**. The loop iterates as long as the expression is **true**. In Java, the expression is very often a variable of type boolean (described in Chapter 5), which itself evaluates to **true** or **false**. This makes it a perfect match for the condition expression. The variable is usually declared and initialized to **true** first, then set to **false** inside the loop when some ending condition is met, such as reading the end of file:

```
boolean notDone = true;
while (notDone)
{
    // read input
    if (input.eof()) // end of file for input?
        notDone = false;
}
```

In fact, you will usually see the boolean variable initialized to **false** and its negation checked in the condition expression, which accomplishes the same thing:

```
boolean done = false;
while (!done)
{
    // read input
    if (input.eof()) // end of file for input?
        done = true;
}
```

The **while** loop is actually equivalent to the **for** loop, in that one can be completely mapped to the other. All you do is move the initialization part of the **for** loop outside, preserve the condition expression, and move the incrementing part to the bottom of the **while** loop body. Here is a typical **for** loop:

```
for (int x = 0; x < myArray.length; x++)
{
    myArray[x] = 1;
}
```

Here is the exact equivalent, but as a `while` loop:

```
int x = 0;
while (x < myArray.length)
{
    myArray[x] = 1;
    x++;
}
```

So when do you use the `for` loop and when do you use the `while` loop? It is your decision, really, because they are functionally equivalent. In general, though, the `for` loop is used when you can predict the number of iterations of the loop, and `while` is used when you cannot.

Looping "Until" Done

The last loop structure we will cover here is the **do until** loop. This is the `DOU` (do until) op-code in RPG, and the `do while` statement in Java. Here is the syntax in RPG:

LISTING 4-8

```
C*      Factor 1     opcode    Factor 2     Result
C                    DOU       expression
C*                   :
C*                   loop body
C*                   :
C                    ENDDO
```

The `DOU` operation code is exactly the same in syntax as the `DOW` operation code, except for the name of the operation code. On the `DOU` operation, just like the `DOW` operation, you specify an expression in the free-form factor two. If both the `DOW` and `DOU` are similar, why have two of them? The answer is that the `DOU` operation expression is evaluated *after* the body of the `DOU` structure has been executed, in contrast to *before* for `DOW`.

The Java equivalent to `DOU` is `do while`. Here is the syntax for it (note the ending semicolon):

```
do
{
  // statement(s)
} while (expression);
```

As with RPG's `DOW` versus `DOU`, Java's `do while` statement is functionally identical to the `while` statement. The difference that the condition expression is not evaluated until the *end* of the loop, which guarantees at least one iteration of the loop. Our experience is that programmers tend to use one or the other of these exclusively. That underlines their equivalent functionality. Consider the job of reading input from a file (hey, you have done that, right?). You have to read until the *end of file*. Which loop structure is best? That's up to you. Both have pros and cons. If you use `while`, you must do the initial read outside the loop to initialize the *end of file* flag. Then, you must do the subsequent reads inside the loop, as follows:

```
boolean eof; // a variable that will be true or false
eof = myFile.getRecord(); // get the first record from the file
while (!eof)
{
    // ... process record
    eof = myFile.getRecord();
}
```

The disadvantage here is clear. You have to duplicate the record read statement. That can create bugs later on if that statement is changed in one place but not the other. Alternatively, you could code this using `do while` (or `DOU` in RPG), and avoid the redundancy, as follows:

```
boolean eof; // a variable that will be true or false
do
{
    eof = myFile.getRecord();
    if (!eof)
        {
        // ... process record
        }
} while (!eof);
```

The disadvantage of this approach is that the `if` statement adds complexity to ensure that the last read does not result in *end of file*. Again, the choice is completely a personal decision. (Our preference is `while` versus `do while`, but what do we know!)

TRANSFER STRUCTURES

Our attention will now turn to those statements that directly alter flow of control by explicitly transferring control to another statement.

If You Continue, I Will Need a Break

We have shown you the looping constructs in RPG and Java, and how their termination is determined by a conditional expression at the top or bottom of the loop. The language runtime evaluates the expression at each iteration of the loop, and continues iterating as long as the expression evaluates to `true`. Controlling when the loop ends is usually a simple matter of setting the appropriate variables to force the expression evaluation to `false`. This is the preferred and structured approach. However, for reasons of completeness, both languages offer alternative shortcuts to this. They take the form of the `LEAVE` op-code in RPG and the `break` statement in Java. Both of these, when used in the body of a `switch`, `while`, `do,` or `for` structure, force the immediate end of the loop. Control is then passed by default to the statement after the loop structure. The Java `break` statement also allows an optional tag parameter to force exit of a loop labeled with that tag. In addition, both languages offer a shortcut to force iteration of the loop from within the body, thus skipping all subsequent codes in the body. This is done by using the `ITER` op-code in RPG and the `continue` statement in Java. The `continue` statement, like the `break` statement, allows an optional tag value to explicitly identify the loop to be iterated. The `continue` statement is valid inside `while`, `do,` and `for` structures in Java.

Both `break` and `continue` apply to the inner most loop structure. That is, they exit or iterate the inner most loop. In a nested loop, to exit or iterate a more outer loop, you use the optional tag value to skip to a labeled outer loop. We caution you that both of these constructs for forcing termination and iteration offer nothing new in function over a little bit of proper `if-else` coding, and can be avoided. They make for some nasty maintenance problems, and are really nothing but special case *goto* statements. Some people avoid them altogether. Other people insist that they can offer a more readable and elegant looking solution than nasty use of conditioning. Our preference is to not use them by default. In our years of experience with C and C++ programming, where they also exist, we have found them to be very rarely worth using. But then again, they are another tool to put in your programming toolbox.

In this contrived example of RPG's `LEAVE` op-code, we search an array for an entry that contains the name MIKE. If found, we perform our duty and then break out of the loop:

LISTING 4-9

```
C                   MOVE      1DX             I
C                   DOW       IDX<=10
C                   IF        RECORDS(IDX)='MIKE'
C                   EVAL      SALARY(IDX)  =  SALARY(IDX)+999
C                   EXCEPT    HEAD1
C                   LEAVE
C                   ENDIF
C                   ADD       1               IDX
C                   ENDDO
C                   MOVE      *ON             *INLR
```

As the example illustrates, the `LEAVE` operation does not take any values in factor one, factor two, or the result field. You simply specify the operation code alone. If the record being evaluated has the name MIKE in the `DOW` loop, we increase his salary (his lucky day) and output to the printer. We then terminate the loop by doing a `LEAVE`. The `LEAVE` operation transfers control from within the `DOW` loop to the statement following the **ENDDO**. The RPG **ITER** op-code is very similar. We could use it in the same way we specified the **LEAVE** operation. In the case of **ITER**, control from within the loop structure will be transferred to the **ENDDO** operation code to force another iteration of the loop, unless its **ENDDO** conditioning indicator is off.

Here is the same example written in Java using its **break** statement. (To compare strings in Java, you must use the equals method that is discussed in a subsequent chapter.) We also add in some additional contrived code to illustrate the use of **continue**:

LISTING 4-10

```
int idx = 0;
while ( idx < 10 )
{
  if (!records[idx].equals("MIKE"))
    {
      idx++;
      continue;
    }
  else
    {
      salary[idx] = salary[idx] + 999;
      System.out.println(records[idx]);
      break;
    }
}
```

In this case the **continue** statement is used to force control back to the **while** statement. At this point, the conditioning expression will be evaluated and, if **true,** another iteration of the loop will be forced. The **break** statement is used to force an exit from the **while** statement, and control jumps to the statement following the end brace of the **while** body.

The **break** and **continue** statements allow an optional label to identify the loop to exit or iterate:

LISTING 4-11

```
OuterLoop: while ( idx < 10 )
{
  for (int idx2 = 0; idx2 < 100; idx2++)
    {
      if (myArray[idx][idx2] != 1)
        break OuterLoop;
      else
        continue OuterLoop;
    }
}
```

This is typically used to force your way out of deeply nested structures, and is in contrast to the procedure of setting a variable and checking that variable in the remainder of the code in all structures.

Go to Where?

The purpose of control structures is to tightly control the flow of logic so that complex problems become simple to follow. With transfer structures, you can pass the flow to another part of a program. In structured programming, this transfer is usually at the exit point of a control structure or to a well-defined point in a program. The transfer logic is therefore limited and easy to follow. However, the `GOTO` op-code or statement is an example of a transfer structure that does not follow the structured programming design. In fact, it is the root cause of what is termed "spaghetti code," which refers to code that flows all over the place and does not seem to have any predictable path. With the advent of structured programming practices and language support, the use of `GOTO` has fallen out of favor. In fact, Java designers decided to not even include it in the language, although the word is reserved. It is interesting that they took such a strong stand on `GOTO` while still advocating use of `break` and `continue`, which are quite similar.

RPG IV, however, still has a `GOTO` op-code for historical reasons, and its syntax remains the same:

LISTING 4-12

```
C     99              GOTO      EXIT
C*                              :
C     EXIT            TAG
C*                              :
C                     MOVE      *ON        *INLR
```

In this example, if the conditioning indicator 99 is on, you want control to transfer to the `EXIT TAG` to turn the last indicator (`LR`) on and do some clean up before termination. Notice that a cleaner and more structured replacement for the `GOTO` and `TAG` operation codes is the `IF` or `IFxx` and `ENDIF` operations.

Return to Caller

In RPG IV, the **RETURN** operation code does more than its predecessor in RPG III. The **RETURN** operation code is used to return a value to the caller from a procedure. (These procedures are new in RPG IV V3R2 of the system.) The following example illustrates the use of the **return** statement/op-code in both Java and RPG respectively. As you may notice, both are almost identical:

RPG

```
C         CALLP     VAL = tripleval(FLD)
C* mainline code
C* ...
C* tripleval procedure:
P tripleval      B
D                PI        5I0
D   parm1                  5I0
C                RETURN    parm1*3
P tripleval      E
```

Java

```
val = tripleval(fld);
...
int tripleval(int parm1)
{
    return parm1*3;
}
```

In both cases, we have a method (Java) or a procedure (RPG) that returns three times the value that is passed to it. Notice the Java code is simpler than its counterpart RPG code. In the case of RPG IV, you have to define the **PI** or *Procedure Interface* for the procedure (this is simply the **PLIST** for the procedure) as well as the start of the procedure and the end of it with the P-specs.

This example illustrates the use of **return** with an expression. However, both Java and RPG allow the return with no value at all. In the case of Java, the **return** statement must be in a method declared with **void** return type or in a constructor. In the case of RPG, on the Procedure Interface (**PI**) line, no type would be specified, to indicate that the procedure does not return anything. In Java, a method that returns nothing does not have to explicitly code a **return** statement. It is implicit when the end of the method is reached. Also notice that you can specify more than one return statement in a method, perhaps for different conditions. For example, a method that returns the maximum of two given numbers might look like this:

```
int max(int value1, int value2)
{
    if (value1 > value2)
      return value1;
    else
      return value2;
}
```

This is a common practice and, in this case, is perfectly acceptable. However, you must be careful in cases where you have common code to be executed before returning. You then must duplicate that code for every imbedded **return** condition, an error prone practice. So, as with the use of **break** and **continue**, using multiple **return** statements in a single method is something to be done sparingly. An alternative implementation to the max method with a single **return** statement would be:

```
int max(int value1, int value2)
{
  int returnValue;
  if (value1 > value2)
    returnValue = value1;
  else
    returnValue = value2;
  return returnValue;
}
```

This is more code, but arguably it is safer in the long run.

Notice that, in the case of RPG, the **RETURN** operation behaves just like its counterpart Java statement only if it is used in a subprocedure. If, however, the **RETURN** operation code is used in the main line code, the behavior is different than Java's. The following occurs if **RETURN** is used in the main line procedure:

- The halt indicators are checked. The program ends abnormally if a halt indicator is on.
- If the halt indicators are not on, then the *Last Record* indicator (**LR**) is checked.
- If it is on, then normal termination occurs.
- Finally, if none of the above indicators is on, the return goes back to the calling routine and all data are preserved for the next time the program is called (better performance).

NOTE: This description is not a change from RPG III. Programmers used the **RETURN** operation code in the mainline to avoid total shutdown of the program and, thereby, increased their performance by avoiding the startup performance penalty.

In Java, you can specify a **return** statement in your "main" method as well, which signifies the end of the program. It does not have the same implications, however. The program ends whether a **return** statement was entered in the main, or whether the end of code was reached in main. You will see in the chapter on threads, however, that there is a preferred way to exit your programs versus **return**. We recommend using `System.exit(nn);` where *nn* is a number. (It is readable by calling programs.)

SUMMARY

In this chapter, we introduced you to the control flow statements in Java and compared them one for one with RPG's. We covered the following:

- RPG and Java have the most common structured statements available in most modern programming languages, including:
  - ✓ `if` and `else` structure
  - ✓ `SELECT` and `switch` op-code and statement respectively
  - ✓ Loops (including `DO/for`, `DOW/while`, `DOU/do-while`)
  - ✓ `LEAVE/break` and `ITER/continue`
  - ✓ `return` statement for returning from RPG procedures or Java methods

- Use `if` statement if the number of expressions to be tested are few. For deeply nested `if-else` conditions, consider using the `switch` statement in Java and the `SELECT` op-code in RPG IV.

- RPG's `WHEN` op-code is more powerful than Java's `switch` statement since it allows you to specify any kind of expression with any data type. In Java's `switch` statement the expression can only be a primitive data type of byte, char, short, and int.

- `GOTO` op-code is available in RPG but not in Java.

- Use the `DO/for` loop when you have a predicable number of iterations you want the loop to go through.

- Use the `DOW/while` loop when you want to iterate zero or more times through the loop.

- Use the `DOU/do-while` loop when you want the body of the loop to execute at least once.

- Use `break` and `continue` sparingly in Java, for forcing exit or iteration of a loop.

- Java supports other transfer statements, including `try/catch` and `throw,` for dealing with exceptions. These are discussed in Chapter 10, which is the *Exceptions* chapter.

5

Data Types and Variables

INTRODUCTION

A base part of most languages today is the offering of a variety of standard data types, such as binary, integer, float, characters, and so on. As with RPG fields, in Java the type of every variable used must be declared at compile time. A data type defines the set of values that an expression can produce, or that a variable can store or contain. As you will see when we cover arithmetic and string manipulations, the data type of a variable is what establishes the operations that may occur on the variable. For example, if you declare a field or a variable as a character, you cannot perform arithmetic operations on it. If you declare a field as numeric (no matter what type of numeric it is), you cannot do string manipulations on it, such as substringing, concatenating, or scanning. If you do attempt to manipulate a data item in a way that is inconsistent with its type, the compiler will inform you of the problem by issuing an error message at compile time. Both languages have different forms of declarations, which we will discuss shortly.

Both RPG and Java are *strongly typed* languages. This means every variable and every expression has a type that must be known at compile time. This allows the compiler to determine what operations can be used with certain variables, and what values can be stored in them.

Review of RPG Types

Figure 5-1 depicts the data types available in RPG as of Version 4 Release 2:

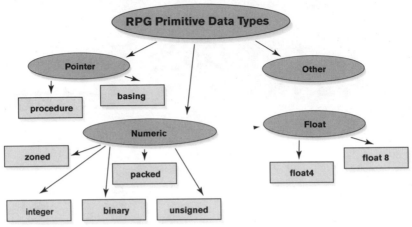

Categories of types are shown in the circles. Actual language data types are shown in square boxes. All types in a particular category support similar operations. The "Other..." category shown in Figure 5-2 includes the following:

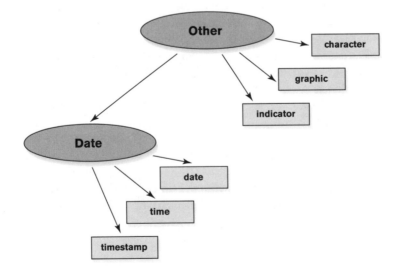

The following table includes the different data types or categories that RPG allows:

Data Type	Description
Numeric	Can be binary, zoned, packed, integer, unsigned or float
Character	One or more characters
Graphic	One or more double byte (DBCS) characters
Date	Date data type
Time	Time data type
TimeStamp	Consists of Date and Time combined
Indicator	Can contain a '0' or '1'
Basing Pointer	Contains a memory address
Procedure Pointer	Contain an address to a procedure

The **numeric** category in RPG can be one of many data types. You can choose from **integer, binary, unsigned, float,** and the famous **packed** and **zoned** types. The **character** data type in RPG is a straightforward, fixed length, character field. **Graphic** is its counterpart for double byte languages, such as Chinese or Japanese. Three new data types that were introduced in RPG IV are **date**, **time**, and **timestamp**, which are self-explanatory. The **indicator** data type is new for V4R2 of RPG, and can contain a zero or a one. In addition, **pointer** data types were introduced in V3R2 and V3R6, and are used to hold either a memory address (basing) or procedure address. They are useful when calling certain system APIs that were previously only accessible from ILE C.

Introduction to Java Types

Variables in Java, like fields in RPG, must be defined with a type. Java has two distinct flavors of types:

- **Primitive types**. These are similar to RPG's data types in that they are predefined in the language and have built-in language support in the form of operators and conversion rules.

- **Reference types**. These are variables whose type is defined to be that of a class in Java, either Java supplied or user defined. Reference variables, as we have seen in Chapter 2, are equated to an instance of the class type they are defined as. Because they contain the memory address of a class instance or object, they are said to *refer* to an object; hence, the term reference variable. These reference variables distinguish Java as an object-oriented language, compared to the primitive-only data types in RPG.

We limit our discussion in this chapter to **primitive** types in Java, which compare to RPG's data types. We introduced you to reference types in Chapter 2, and we will discuss them in more detail in Chapter 9. It is interesting to note, however, that all of Java's primitive types are also available as classes in the `java.lang` package. These classes are wrappers of the primitive types with methods for converting to and from them. They are of value in those cases where the code expects only objects. Also of interest is that arrays and strings are both implemented as objects in Java, so variables of these are, in fact, reference variables.

The chart in Figure 5-3 displays the eight primitive data types in Java broken down by category as they were for RPG:

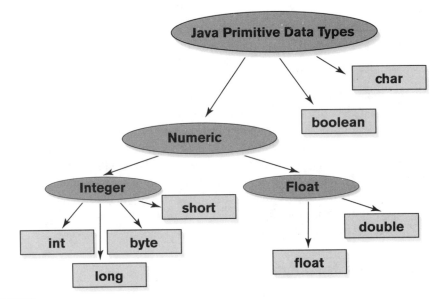

FIGURE 5-3

Primitive data types in Java are subdivided into the following categories:

- *Numeric* types consisting of those that do not have decimals and those that do. The former are in the integer sub category and include one-byte (*byte*), two-byte (*short*), four-byte (*int*), and eight-byte (*long*) length types. The latter are in the float sub category and include four-byte (*float*) and eight-byte float (*double*) types. Note that in both RPG and Java, numeric data types are signed, which allow both positive and negative numbers. However, there is an exception to this in RPG: the unsigned data type that allows only positive numbers. Thus, although otherwise identical to RPG's integer data type, it does allow larger positive numbers.

- *Character* data type, unlike RPG, is always a single character long, unless you define an array of characters in RPG. Also unlike RPG, a character in Java is actually two bytes long as it is based on the 16-bit Unicode encoding standard that encompasses all international characters. In contrast, a character in RPG is one byte long and is based on the EBCDIC encoding standard. In RPG then, the complex use of codepages is required to support international characters properly, but not in Java.

- *Boolean* data type, which supports two values: `true` and `false`. These are reserved words in Java and only assignable to boolean variables. Boolean is analogous to RPG indicators, where '1' is `true` and '0' is `false`.

A brief comparison of the data types in the two languages follows:

RPG	Java	Comments
numeric (no decimals)	short or int	depends on length. Note RPG has no match to Java's *byte or long* data types.
numeric (with decimals)	float or double, or `java.math.BigDecimal` class	Depends on length. BigDecimal is a java supplied class, not a primitive
float (length 4)	float	Both are IEEE standard
float (length 8)	double	Both are IEEE standard
basing pointer	object reference	Both are memory addresses, but Java does not permit address math
procedure pointer	not available	
character (length one)	char	Single character only
character (length n)	`java.lang.String` class	Covered in later chapter
graphic	`java.lang.String` class	Covered in later chapter
indicator	boolean	'1' = `true`, '0' = `false`
date	`java.util.Date` class	See Chapter 8
time	`java.util.Time` class	See Chapter 8
timestamp	`java.util.Date` class	See Chapter 8

As you can see, there are some RPG types that the Java designers chose to implement, not as a primitive data type, but rather as a class. These will be discussed in subsequent chapters. Also note that some data type comparisons between the languages depend on the defined length of the particular variable in RPG. We will go into more detail on each of the primitive data types after we cover some syntactical details.

DATA DECLARATION

Data types are put to use in two places in a language: in explicit fields, or in variables that you define; and in implicit fields or variables the compiler generates to process expressions. Now that you have had a glimpse of what the types are in Java, it is important to show you how to define variables of this type. The syntax is completely different from RPG's, but arguably easier. Let's review both.

Defining Fields in RPG

How do you declare a field in RPG IV? There are three ways:

- On the C, I, or O specifications, by supplying length information.
- Using the `DEFINE` operation code.

- On the D (Definition) specification, which is new in RPG IV.

Why so many? The first two are inherited from RPG III, and the third is new for RPG IV. Before RPG IV, you had no choice other than to define fields on the I-spec, E-spec, and the C-spec. The new *Definition* specification introduced by RPG IV adds structure to your RPG code. It allows you to define all your fields, data structures, arrays, and tables in one area in your source code. So why did RPG not drop the other two methods? The simple answer is upward compatibility. Existing applications written in RPG III must run "as is" after converting them to RPG IV. An example follows:

LISTING 5-1

```
*8901234567890123456789012345678901234567890123456789012345678901234567890
FQSYSPRT    O    F    80           PRINTER OFLIND(*INOV)
D FIRST           S              5A   INZ('PHIL ')
D AGE             S              2B 0 INZ(25)
D*-------------------------------------------------------------------
C       *LIKE          DEFINE   FIRST           LAST            +5
C                      MOVE     'COULTHARD '    LAST
C                      MOVE     'ONCE WAS '     AGETEXT              9
C                      EXCEPT   RESULT
C                      MOVE     *ON             *INLR
C*-------------------------------------------------------------------
OQSYSPRT    E              RESULT
O                          FIRST           5
O                          LAST            15
O                          AGETEXT         24
O                          AGE             26
```

The following example illustrates defining fields that use the three different methods:

- Fields FIRST and AGE are defined using the D-spec. The name goes in columns 7 to 21. Material is more readable because it is not necessary to left justify it. Names in RPG IV can be upper or lower case, although the compiler converts them to upper case. The s in column 24 indicates this is a standalone field (compared to, for example, a data structure or constant). The length is defined in columns 33 to 39, the data type in column 40, and the decimals in columns 41 to 42. The keyword **INZ** is used to initialize the values of the variables.
- Field LAST is defined on a C-spec using the **DEFINE** op-code to pick up the attributes of the previously defined FIRST field. The length is incremented by five over FIRST's.
- Field AGETEXT is defined on a C-spec at the time of first use by specifying a length.

The resulting output of this example is:

```
PHIL COULTHARD ONCE WAS 25
```

(Yes, and the AS/400 was once a new computer!) Newcomers to RPG IV are encouraged to do field definitions on the D-spec because the code is easier to read and easier to maintain (It is no longer necessary to hunt for field definitions because now they are all at the top of the program.) The RPG IV equivalent to the **DEFINE** op-code is the **LIKE** keyword on the D-spec; the field LAST in the example could have been declared as:

```
D LAST              S              +5      LIKE(FIRST) INZ(*ALL' ')
```

This example also shows how to use the **INZ** keyword to initialize all positions of a variable to a specified value by using ***ALL** followed immediately by the value. Finally, Figure 5-4 shows what this new D-spec looks like when prompted in CODE/400:

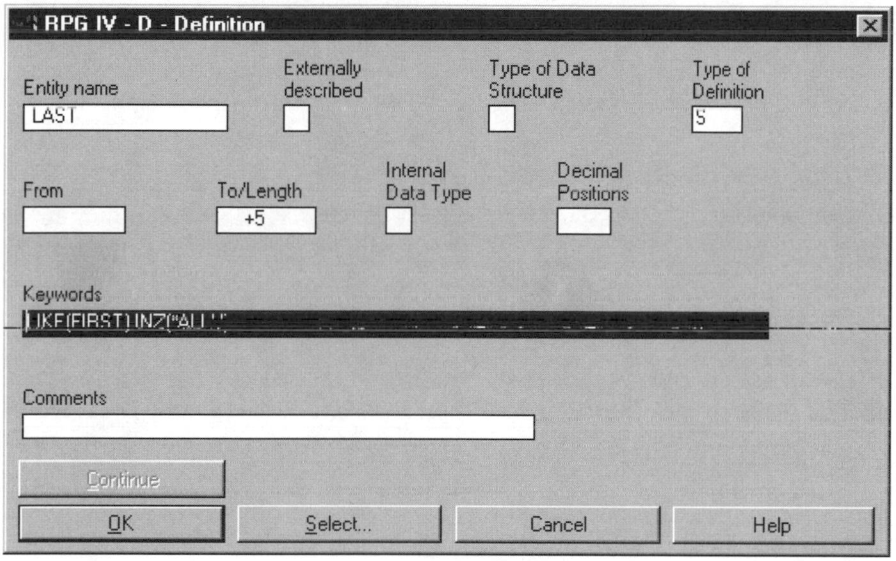

FIGURE 5-4

The data type must be a single character entry that represents one of the RPG built-in data types:

Data Type	Description
A	Character. Specify the *VARYING* keyword for a variable length field (**new for V4R2**)
B	Numeric (Binary format)
D	Date
F	Numeric (Float format)
G	Graphic (Fixed or Variable-length format) . Specify the *VARYING* keyword for a variable length field (**new for V4R2**)

Data Type	Description
I	Numeric (Integer format)
N	Character (Indicator format) (**new for V4R2**)
P	Numeric (Packed decimal format)
S	Numeric (Zoned format)
T	Time
U	Numeric (Unsigned format)
Z	Timestamp
*	Basing pointer or procedure pointer

NOTE: If the data type column is blank on the D-spec, the type defaults to character if the decimals column is blank as well, or packed otherwise (unless it is a subfield, in this case it defaults to Zoned).

Defining Variables in Java

In Java, variables can be defined in two places: at the class level, such that they are available to all methods (similar to RPG's *global* variables); or inside a method, such that they are available only to the code inside that method (similar to RPG IV's *local* variables inside procedures). This is an important distinction to keep in mind.

Unlike RPG, Java has only a single syntax for defining variables. There are, however, a number of optional parts. In its simplest form, a variable declaration in Java looks like this:

```
type name;
```

The data type comes first and is followed by a name of your choosing. The statement ends with a semicolon, as do all Java statements. Here is an example:

```
int myVariable;
```

This defines a variable (we call it a "field" in RPG; again, we are using "field" and "variable" interchangeably in the book) named myVariable, of type int (integer). It is really that simple. The valid types are the eight Java reserved words for built in primitive data types. They are shown on the following chart:

Data Type Keyword	Description
char	character (single)
boolean	boolean (**true** or **false**)
byte	numeric (one byte long)
short	numeric (two bytes long)
int	numeric (four bytes long)
long	numeric (eight bytes long)

Data Type Keyword	Description
`float`	floating point (single precision: 4 bytes)
`double`	floating point (double precision: 8 bytes)

These are the valid types for variables that are a primitive type. Note that for object reference variables, the type will be the name of a Java class or interface (these are described in Chapter 9).

To initialize a variable at the time you declare it, you simply equate it to a value, as in:

```
int myVariable = 10;
```

The value to which it is initialized can either be a literal variable that is also already defined, or it can be an expression (for example, `myVar + 2`). In either case, the resulting type must be the same or compatible with the defined type of the variable. It's really quite easy. Unlike RPG, you don't have to worry about the following:

- *Columns*. Java is free form.
- *Name length*. No appreciable limit to names in Java.
- *Case*. Names are very case-sensitive in Java, unlike RPG IV where they are case tolerant. Thus, in Java the names `abc` and `ABC` are different, while they would be the same in RPG.
- *Length*. You do not specify a length for your variables in Java because that is predefined by the type.
- *Location*. With RPG IV, your D-spec variables must be declared at the top of the program or the top of a procedure. In Java, class-level variables can be declared before or after the methods (we prefer before), while method level variables can be declared anywhere in the code as long as they are declared before use.

Java variable names are not shortened by convention, but are as long as is wished to be descriptive. Lower case is used except for the first letter of words other than the first word. An example would be `interestRate` or `variablePayRate`.

Java variables specified at the class level, versus inside a method, can also be specified with optional ***modifier*** keywords before the data type. An example follows:

```
private int myVariable = 10;
```

In this case, we have specified the modifier `private`, indicating this variable is not accessible (either to read or to write) by code outside of this class. The list of modifiers is:

Modifiers	Description
`public`, `private`, or `protected`	Accessibility of the variable. `Public` means all can access, `private` means only this class, and `protected` means this class or those that extend it (see Chapter 9). The default is **package**, meaning this class or others in this package can access it. There is no language modifier keyword for this default however.
`static`	This variable is initialized only once and has only one value, regardless of the number of instances of this class. Can be accessed via `classname.variable`, versus `object.variable`. Only class level variables support this. Static variables are known as "**class variables**" as there is one value per class, not one per object.
`static final`	This variable is a **constant**, and cannot be changed. By some conventions, constants always have uppercase names to distinguish them from non-constants.

`Static` and `static final` variables can also be defined as `public`, `private`, or `protected`. For classes that are not extendible (see Chapter 9), you should always define your non-static and non-constant variables as `private`, which will force users of your class to go through your methods. However, also note that local variables inside a method are always private to that method; and no modifiers are needed or allowed.

We should also point out there are two other modifiers: `transient` and `volatile`. However, these are *very* rarely used, and you need not worry about them. Briefly, though, the former deals with the persistence of a variable when you serialize it to disk (an advanced topic not covered in this book), while the latter deals with the behavior of a variable in a multithreaded application, but is not often used.

VARIABLE SCOPE, LIFETIME, AND EXTERNAL ACCESS

The discussion of data types leads to the discussion of variables, which in turn leads to the discussion of *variable scope* (that is, which code *inside* this RPG compile unit or this Java class has access to the variable), *variable lifetime* (when is the variable allocated memory and initialized, and when is that memory freed) and *external accessibility* (the question of whether code *outside* of this RPG compile unit or Java class can access the variable). The following sections discuss these three aspects of Java variables one at a time.

Variable Scope

In RPG III, the question of variable scope is an easy one. All variables are global to the program in which they are declared (and one source member equals one program after compiling). The only rule is that a variable cannot be accessed prior to being defined, but after being defined, all code whether global or in a subroutine, can access that variable.

In RPG IV, V3R2 or V3R6 or above introduces procedures. These now allow local variables to be defined in the procedure itself (recall the discussion in Chapter 2). These variables are not accessible by any code outside of the procedure. However, global variables declared in the mainline area of the compile unit are accessible by the procedures in that module, as they were for subroutines. The compile unit has also changed in RPG IV. Rather than being a source member compiling into a program object directly, they are compiled into intermediate module objects, which are then bound into a program object or service program object. Thus, code in one module cannot, by default, access global variables in another module-even if they end up in the same program object.

In Java, we mentioned that variables can be declared at the class level or at the method level. Basically, method-level or local variables are only accessible by the code contained in that method, while class-level variables are accessible by code in any of the methods in that class. In fact, within a method you can also have parameter variables. These resemble locally declared variables except that they are passed in by the caller rather than being defined within the code or body of the method. Otherwise, they are just like local variables. Thus, we can roughly equate global variables in RPG IV modules to class-level variables in Java, and local variables in RPG IV procedures to local variables in Java methods. Furthermore, since RPG IV procedures also support the passing in of parameters, we can equate RPG IV procedure parameter variables to Java method variables. (By *equate,* in this context, we are talking about the scope or direct accessibility of the variables.)

However, moving further beyond parameters, Java has something called ***blocks***, which are one or more statements contained inside curly braces ({)and (}). You have seen these already in relation to class definitions and method definitions, which are special cases of blocks. However, you can also have blocks defined directly inside methods, and these blocks can have their own variables that are local to that block. For example:

```
int myVariable;
myVariable = 10;
{
    int mySecondVariable;
    mySecondVariable - 20;
}
System.out.println("mySecondVariable =   " + mySecondVariable);
```

In the preceding example, the variable mySecondVariable inside the braces or block has its own scope. This means it is not accessible to the code outside of that block. In this case, then, you will get an error since the println method call is trying to access an inaccessible variable. Notice that Java does not allow variable "hiding" in blocks-that is, you cannot redefine myVariable from the outer block as this could lead to subtle programming errors. Blocks like this are simply to aid program readability. There are other examples of blocks, such as the **for** statement, and you can declare variables in them that are local to that statement block, as in:

159

```
for (int index = 0; index < 10; index++)
{
    System.out.println("index = " + index);
}
```

Any attempt to reference the `index` variable after the last curly brace of the `for` statement will result in an error. A variable declared inside a block is only accessible inside the block in which it is defined. RPG has no equivalent to Java's local blocks. The general scoping rule in Java, then, is that code can only access any variable in the current scope (block) or *higher*, up to the class level.

Variable Lifetime

When do variables come to life, and how long do they live? For RPG III, as you know, they come to life when the program is first called and they live until the program is ended (by either setting the **LR** indicator to ON or by ending the job). Global variables in RPG IV have the same lifetime, although you can now subdivide a job into named ILE *activation groups*, and variables will not live past the life of these. The new local variables inside RPG IV procedures only come to life when the procedure is called, and they die immediately when it ends. These are sometimes called *automatic variables* since their death is automatic with the ending of the procedure. However, if you specify **STATIC** for a local variable in RPG, that variable's value persists for the life of the program or service program it is in.

For Java, for methods and nested blocks inside methods, these *automatic* or *local* variables "come to life" when the method is called or the block is entered. If an initialization has been specified, it is applied at that time. When the block ends or the method ends, the variable goes away, just as with RPG IV procedures. (By the term "come to life" we really mean, "when the variables get allocated actual storage in memory.")

For Java class-level variables, life is more interesting! Non-static class-level variables (that is, *instance variables*) come to life when an instance of the class (object) is instantiated with the **new** operator. Each class instance gets its own memory allocation for the instance variables, so they are totally independent of each other. If your instance variable declaration includes an initializer (for example, " = 10"), that initial value is applied at the same time as the object is created, and hence its instance variables come to life. For static class-level variables (that is, *class* variables), there is but one allocated memory location for the variable, regardless of the number of instances of the class—be it zero or be it one hundred.

Since the life and values of a static variable are not dependent on-or even related to-instances of the class, it stands that static variables come to life or are allocated memory as soon as the Java runtime "knows about" the class. This typically occurs when the class is first referenced in any way or is explicitly loaded into memory by one of the various means of doing so. The important thing to remember is that static variables will be alive as soon as you first possibly need them. Recall that in Java, unlike RPG, local variables in a method cannot be static.

Variable External Access

When we talk about scoping of a variable, we are talking about what code has *direct* access to it. In this case, we are talking about code in the same *compilation unit* as the variable. In RPG III, a compilation unit is a program object; in RPG IV it is a module object; and in Java it is a class. However, there is the ability in both RPG IV and in Java for code outside of a variable's compilation unit to access that variable.

In RPG IV, this is accomplished by specifying the **EXPORT** keyword on the variable definition specification. This allows other modules in the final program or service program to access this variable, providing they define it as well but with the **IMPORT** keyword. This tells the compiler that this variable is allocated in another module but that you intend to access it in this module. In a service program, you can even go farther and make your exported variables (and procedures!) available to other *programs*, if you specify as much in the binding source for the service program (as described in Chapter 2).

In Java, the equivalent to RPG's **EXPORT** keyword is the use of the **public** modifier on your class-level variables. This tells the compiler that you want any code in any other classes to have access to this variable. Think of this as being equivalent to exporting your variable, via **EXPORT** and binding source, from an RPG IV service program for all the world to use. However, good form dictates that you will rarely if ever do this for non-static variables, as you should prefer to force users to go through your getXXX and setXXX methods to access your instance variables. To prevent such world access to your variables, you can instead not specify any modifier, giving your variable package access. This allows only other classes in this package access to your class. Since we equate a package to a service program, this is equivalent to **EXPORT**ing your variable in RPG but not specifying it in the binding source. To completely restrict other classes, you use the **private** modifier, indicating only your class code has access. (This should be your default!) Note there is also a **protected** mode, limiting access to classes that *extend* or *subclass* this class-a topic we will discuss in Chapter 9.

Assuming that you have made a variable available to outside classes, that outside code cannot simply use the variable name as is. Whereas RPG forces the external code to **IMPORT** the variable, Java forces the external code to *qualify* the variable name. For static variables, the variable name must be qualified with the class name separated by a dot. For non-static variables, the variable name must be qualified with the class instance or object name, again separated by a dot. This *dot operator* tells the compiler that the variable is not part of this class, and further, tells the compiler (and actually the runtime) exactly in which class or class instance the variable can be found.

Variables: An Example

At this point it would be helpful, no doubt, to see an example of Java variables in action. Consider the following:

LISTING 5-2

```
public class Widget
{
    public  static final int TYPE1 = 1; // constant
    public  static final int TYPE2 = 2; // constant
    public  static       int nextID= 0; // class
    private              int id;        // instance
    private              int type  = 0; // instance
    public Widget() // Constructor. Note name == class name
    {
        id = nextID; // references instance and class vars
        nextID = nextID + 1;
    }
    public boolean setType(int newType)
    {
        boolean inputOK = true; // local
        if (newType >= TYPE1 && newType <= TYPE2)
          type = newType; // references instance variable
        else
          inputOK = false;
        return inputOK;
    }
    public String toString()
    {
        String retString; // local
        retString = "Type = " + type + ", ID = " + id;
        return retString;
    }
} // end Widget class
```

This example class has two constant variables (TYPE1 and TYPE2), one static variable (nextID) and two instance variables (id and type). It also has a constructor method (Widget) and two other methods (setType and toString). All access one or more of the class-level variables. The last two methods also declare their own local variables (inputOK and retString), while setType accepts a method parameter (newType). The following example shows the class in use:

LISTING 5-3

```
public class TestWidget
{
    public static void main(String args[])
    {
        Widget.nextID = 1000; // set class variable
        Widget myWidget = new Widget(); // object 1
        myWidget.setType(Widget.TYPE1); // call method
        Widget myWidget2 = new Widget(); // object 2
        myWidget2.setType(Widget.TYPE2); // call method
        System.out.println(myWidget); // calls toString method
        System.out.println(myWidget2); // calls toString method
    }
} // end TestWidget class
```

Compiling and running this test class gives us the following output:

```
C:\JAVA>JAVA TestWidget
 Type = 1, ID = 1000
 Type = 2, ID - 1001
```

First, notice the `toString` method. This is a special method for Java in that, if you supply one in your class, Java will implicitly call it when you specify an instance of your class on the `System.out.println` method, which we do in our `TestWidget` class. This method simply creates a `String` object (these are covered in Chapter 7) that displays some interesting variable values. Including a `toString` method in your class is a good idea to make debugging easier, if nothing else.

This `Widget` class example highlights a few of the items we have been discussing. It represents an item of which we will need a large number. Each unique `Widget` will be identified by a type (we use constants `TYPE1` or `TYPE2` to make this less error-prone) and by a unique identifier. The assignment of a unique identifier is solved by using a static variable (`nextID`), since there is only ever one value for a static variable. We simply use and increment this variable in our constructor so each `Widget` instance gets a unique value. The problem is we need to "seed" this static variable at the beginning of the program, outside of our class. That is why we made it public, and you see in the `TestWidget` class that we seed it to 1000. The type is set per `Widget` by calling the method `setType` and passing in one of the defined constants for a value. Notice that the instance variable type is set to this value (if it is valid). Because id and type are instance variables, each `Widget` instance gets to maintain its own independent values for these, which is what we want. Also notice that we made these instance variables private, as we do not want to risk external code (outside of this class) *directly* changing any of `Widget`'s values.

Take note in `TestWidget` how we qualify the references to the static variables in the `Widget` class by qualifying them with "`Widget.`" Without this, Java would look for these variables in the `TestWidget` class. Also note how we instantiate two instances of `Widget` by using the **new** operator, and then invoke the `setType` method on each one in order to independently change the instance variables of each object.

We remind you that as an RPG III programmer, you are not familiar with either local variables or parameters (as shown in the `setType` method). However, as an RPG IV programmer (V3R2 or higher) you do have both, through the use of procedures, as described in Chapter 2. However, while RPG's global variables are directly equivalent to class-level static variables, the concept of instance variables that have different values per class instance is totally foreign to RPG. In essence, RPG gives you exactly one instance of each module in your programs.

Another thing to watch for in Java versus RPG is variable initialization. In RPG, the compiler does supply reasonable defaults for fields on which we sometimes rely. Java has a similar supplied default value for class-level variables, but *not* for local variables. Rather, a local variable must be initialized or assigned a value before it is first referenced, or the compiler will issue an error message. A good rule is to *always* initialize a variable explicitly, even if it is to zero.

LITERALS BY DATA TYPE

We have shown you an example of an int (integer) variable initialization in Java, so you are familiar with the syntax:

```
int myVariable = 10;
```

However, let us round out this example with examples of initialization for each data type. It is important to know this, because any literal value you specify at initialization time (or assign later, for that matter) must be consistent with the variable's data type. Each data type, both in RPG and Java, has an explicit syntax for literal values.

We humans learn by example, so we will teach the syntax of literals by example. First, the non-numeric data types:

RPG Type	Example	Java Type	Example
character 1	`'a'` or `X'7D'`	char	`'a'` or `'\''`
character n	`'abc'`	String	`"ABC"` or `"c:\\mydir"`
graphic	`G'oK1K2i'`		
indicator	`'0'` or `'1'` or `*OFF` or `*ON`	boolean	**True** or **false**
date	`D'97-12-11'`		See Chapter 8
time	`T'11:33;01'`		See Chapter 8

RPG Type	Example	Java Type	Example
timestamp	`Z'1997-12-11.33.01'`		See Chapter 8
basing pointer	`*NULL or %ADDR(myVar)`	object reference	`null` or `new MyClass()`
procedure pointer	`*NULL or %PADDR(myProc)`		

The character data type takes a literal enclosed in single quotes. In Java, this can be but one character, while in RPG it can be multiple characters. RPG allows hexadecimal numbers if they begin with the letter x. Java also allows special character values, if they are preceded by a slash, which is called an *escape sequence*. Examples are:

Escape Sequence	Description
\n	newline character
\t	tab
\b	backspace
\r	carriage return
\f	form feed
\\	backslash
\'	single quote
\"	Double quote
\ddd	Octal number, not to exceed 377
\uxxxx	Unicode number; - must be 4 digits

For numerics, here are some examples:

RPG Type	Example	Java Type	Example
		byte	`10 or -10`
integer 5	`10 or -10`	short	`10 or -10`
integer 10	`10 or -10`	int	`10 or -10`
		long	`10 or 10L or -10 or -10L`
unsigned	`10 or 20`		
binary	`10 or 10.1`		
packed	`10 or 10.1`		
zoned	`10 or 10.1`		
float 4	`10 or .12 or 1234.9E12`	float	`10 or 12.1 or 1.234E12`
float 8	`10 or .12 or 1234.9E12`	double	`10 or 12.1 or 1.234E12`

165

The non-float values in Java are simple integers that must not be larger than the capacity of the data type. However, long data type literals do allow an optional *L* character after them (this character can be upper- or lower case). This tells the compiler that these are indeed long values, which can be important in expressions, where casting between data types can happen implicitly. By default, these literals are assumed to be base 10 decimal numbers, but you can also specify octal (base 8) or hexadecimal (base 16). For octal, use a leading zero, as in 035. For hexadecimal, use a leading 0x or 0X as in 0x1d.

Float-type literals in Java are decimal numbers followed by an optional decimal point followed by an exponent. The literal can followed by an *F* for single precision float or *D* for double precision float—the default is double. The exponent part consists of an *E* or *e*, followed by a positive or negative decimal number.

Numeric Data Type Ranges

When programming with numeric data types it is important to know the limits to each data type, so that you can choose the appropriate data type to avoid overflow or truncation.

In RPG, when you define a numeric data type variable and specify a length or decimal type, you do so by specifying how many decimal "digits" the variable will hold. You do not specify how many bytes of memory to allocate—that is done implicitly by the compiler based on the number of digits that you indicate (the exception to this rule is the float data type, where you do specify the number of bytes—4 or 8). This digit length is a rather unique means of describing length and underscores RPG's role as a business language as opposed to a scientific or general language. Java, on the other hand, does not burden you with the business of specifying lengths at all. Rather, it supplies a number of different numeric types for you, each of which represents a different predefined length or capacity. This implies that you have to know what the limit is for each data type in order to choose the correct one for your particular case. You could simply always choose the largest—long for integers and double for floating-point—but for large numbers of variables this will be a waste of computer memory, as these large variables take up more space than their smaller cousins.

In order to determine the limits for each data type you do, in turn, have to know the underlying size of each in bytes. Thus, in the end, you are forced to think in terms of numerical limits, rather than the number of digits as you usually do in RPG. Let's review, then, the RPG data type ranges:

Type	Bytes	Range
binary 4,0	2	-9,999 **to** 9,999 (four 9s)
binary 9,0	4	-999 ,999, 999 **to** 999,999,999 (nine 9s)
zoned 30,0	30	-30 9s **to** +30 9s
packed 30,0	16	-30 9s **to** +30 9s

Type	Bytes	Range
integer 5	2	2^{15} = -32,768 **to** 32,767
integer 10	4	2^{31} = -2,147,483,648 **to** 2,147,483,647
unsigned 5	2	2^{16} = 0 **to** 65535
unsigned 10	4	2^{32} = 0 **to** 4,294,967,295
float 4	4	1.175 494 4 E-38 **to** 3.402 823 5 E+38
float 8	8	2.225 073 858 507 201 E-308 **to** 1.797 693 134 862 315 E+308

Note how integer types allow a maximum value of 2 to the power of *n-1*, where *n* is the number of bits in the allocated memory length. For unsigned, since one bit is not required to store the sign, it is 2 to the power of *n*. Thus, if you are still using binary data type but specifying zero decimal positions, it is to your advantage to switch to the integer data type. Furthermore, it is more efficient in internal expression evaluations than is binary.

Let us now compare these ranges to those of Java's built-in numeric types:

Type	Bytes	Range
byte	1	2^7 = -128 **to** 127
short	2	2^{15} = -32,768 **to** 32,767
int	4	2^{31} = -2,147,483,648 **to** 2,147,483,647
long	8	2^{63} = 9,223,372,036,854,775,808 **to** 9,223,372,036,854,775,807
float	4	1.402 398 64 E-45 **to** 3.402 823 47 E+38
double	8	4.940 656 458 214 465 44 E-324 **to** 1.797 693 134 862 315 70 E+308

NOTE: The ranges given for float and double in both languages are positive numbers. The negative number range is the same.

Float Versus Packed

What are floating-point fields, and why would you use them? You can see that for Java, float and double are the only primitive data types that support decimal points. Since your RPG code is riddled with packed decimal fields, your first inclination may be to use float or double in your Java code in place of packed. Or use int or long for zero decimal packed numbers. However, as the range tables showed, even a long data type in Java does not hold integers as big as packed decimal can.

Also, floating-point fields (whether single- or double-precision) are somewhat less efficient than packed fields. Why is this? Because floating point fields are designed to hold arbitrary values without benefit of previous knowledge about the number of decimals. That is, you do not tell the compiler at definition time how many decimals the data will contain; you simply specify whether it is to be four bytes or eight bytes long. Any valid floating-point number can be assigned to that variable during runtime. This makes for great flexibility, but it also means that the internal storage of these numbers has to be flexible. That means, as always with flexibility, a performance cost in order to interpret the data at runtime; the internal format of the data essentially must be converted every time it is referenced. Compare this to packed decimal, where you tell the RPG compiler at field definition time exactly how many decimals any data contained in the field will have. This allows the compiler to store the data in a fixed format every time, and allows mathematical operations to exploit this knowledge for very fast evaluations (mind you, most hardware today offers built-in support for floating-point manipulation).

Therefore, in cases where you are dealing with a predetermined number of decimals, (such as with amounts of money) floating-point is not a good choice. Floating-point fields are a good choice when dealing with data for which you cannot predict the exact decimal precision, such as with scientific data, real-world measurements like the size of a human hair, and so on. It is also of value even when the number of decimals can be hard-coded, but the size of the number cannot. For example, if the number may become extremely huge or extremely small (yes, well below one), float or double can handle it. It is hard to imagine what type of data would need to allow for numbers bigger than $1.7 * 10^{308}$!

However, this discussion is about RPG, where we have a choice between packed and float. In Java we have no such choice, as there is no equivalent data type to packed. However, for your business applications that deal with pay rates, unit costs, unit prices, and so on, it is hard to imagine the need for the power of floats with their attendant costs. It is too bad Java did not see fit to support a built-in packed decimal data type, but clearly the designers were not coming from an RPG background!

So on the surface, it appears you are stuck with float or double. However, these have other perhaps more serious concerns than performance—that is, their propensity to produce high-precision results after a mathematical operation. You do not want to be billing your customers in ten-thousands of a cent, for instance! Let's look at a Java example. Imagine you have widgets to sell for $1234.56, and you decide to have a sale where you are offering 23 percent off. What might the calculations for the new price look like? Try this:

LISTING 5-4

```
public class TestFloat
{
    public static void main(String args[])
    {
        double unitCost = 1234.56;
        double discount = 0.23;
        System.out.println("unitCost = " + unitCost);
```

LISTING 5-4

```
        unitCost = unitCost - unitCost * discount;
        System.out.println("saleCost = " + unitCost);
    }
}
```

The result is the following:

```
C:\JAVA>java TestFloat
unitCost = 1234.56
saleCost = 950.6111999999999
```

Can you imagine sending this bill to your customers? To circumvent this problem, you might try writing your own complicated code to force the decimal precision and make some decision on rounding, but this is ugly code. Really, then, float and double are not good choices for monetary values.

However, all is not lost! The Java designers did supply, at least, a Java class to "emulate" the mathematical behavior of a packed decimal data type. While not a built-in type, it is at least something that can offer accurate results with methods for easily setting the decimal precision. The class is called `BigDecimal`, and you find it in the `java.math` package. This class offers you complete control over rounding behavior on divide and decimal-point adjustments, and offers a very complete set of mathematical and conversion functions in the form of methods. We do recommend that you use this class, and in fact the AS/400 Toolbox for Java product maps packed decimal database fields to this class in its two database packages. If your packed decimal operations on the AS/400 use half-adjust, then even that rounding option is available to you.

To understand this class and its documentation in the JDK, you have to be familiar with its terminology and architecture. An instance of a `BigDecimal` class is really the following:

- An integer value like 123456, with no limit on the number of digits ("precision") in that integer value.
- A decimal position (*scale*) within that integer value. This is specified in terms of number of digits to the right of the decimal point.

When you create a new `BigDecimal` object, you have three choices for the initial value: a string like "1234.56", a `BigInteger` object (another class in `java.math`) or a double value. If you get your value from the user, it will probably be as a string. Using a string sets both the integer value (123456) and the scale (2 in our example since there are two decimal positions). Alternatively, you can use the static method `valueOf(long val, int scale)` to return to you a new `BigDecimal` object with the integer value and scale you specify:

```
BigDecimal unitCost = BigDecimal.valueOf(123456, 2);
```

Once you have a BigDecimal object, you can perform all the usual mathematical operations on it via methods like add, subtract, divide, multiply, abs, and negate. You can also use comparative methods like compareTo, min, and max to compare it to another BigDecimal value. (Note that compareTo ignores trailing zeros in the decimal portion, so 1234.00 is considered equal to 1234.0000. If you do not want this, use the equals method.) There are also methods for converting a BigDecimal object to other data types such as integer (intValue), long (longValue), double (doubleValue), BigInteger (toBigInteger) and, of course, string (toString).

How does BigDecimal deal with the growing precision problem as seen in the example involving the 23 percent discount? It will, by default, give you more decimal points after a multiplication than you started with (specifically, it will give you back the sum of the decimal points of the two operators). However, it supplies a very useful method called setScale to set the number of decimal points after an operation like multiply. This method will simply move the decimal point but leave the non-decimal part of the number unchanged. For example, if you start with 1234.5678 and call setScale(5) you will get 1234.56780. But what if you call setScale(2)? This will give you back either 1234.56 or 1234.57, depending on the *rounding* behavior you ask for! This behavior can be specified as the second parameter to setScale, and must be one of the eight constants defined in BigDecimal. It's likely that you will only ever use two of these, however-either BigDecimal.ROUND_DOWN (which gives you 1234.56-i.e., a simple truncate) or BigDecimal.ROUND_HALF_UP (which gives you 1234.57-i.e., rounds up if truncated digits are greater than 5). Let's revisit our example, then, this time using BigDecimal instead of double:

LISTING 5-5

```
import java.math.*;
public class TestBD
{
    public static void main(String args[])
    {
        BigDecimal unitCost = new BigDecimal("1234.56");
        BigDecimal discount = new BigDecimal(".23");
        System.out.println("unitCost = " + unitCost);
        // unitCost = unitCost - unitCost * disCount
        unitCost = unitCost.subtract( unitCost.multiply(discount) );
        System.out.println("unitCost after discount = " + unitCost);
        unitCost = unitCost.setScale(2, BigDecimal.ROUND_HALF_UP);
        System.out.println("unitCost after setScale = " + unitCost);
    }
}
```

This gives the following result:

```
C:\JAVA>java TestBD
unitCost = 1234.56
unitCost after discount = 950.6112
unitCost after setScale = 950.61
```

There are only two methods in `BigDecimal` that may cause truncation of data from the decimal part of the number: `setScale` and `divide`. All other operations increase the number of decimal digits if required. Note that the non-decimal part of the number is never truncated, but rather simply grows as much as necessary to hold the result. For `setScale` and `divide`, you should choose `BigDecimal.ROUND_HALF_UP` if you normally use the half-adjust operation modifier in RPG; otherwise you should choose `BigDecimal.ROUND_DOWN`. However, there are a total of six *additional* rounding options for you as well: `ROUND_CEILING`, `ROUND_FLOOR`, `ROUND_HALF_DOWN`, `ROUND_HALF_EVEN`, `ROUND_UNNECESSARY`, `ROUND_UP`.

Note in the previous example how we nested a `BigDecimal` method call as a parameter to another `BigDecimal` method:

```
unitCost = unitCost.subtract( unitCost.multiply(discount) );
```

This is possible because the `multiply` method returns a new `BigDecimal` object, which is then passed in as a parameter to the `subtract` method. This method also returns a new `BigDecimal` object, which we then equate back to our original `unitCost` object reference variable. In fact, all the `math` methods return new objects rather than changing the object on which they are invoked. That is why you must code `object = object.method(xxx)` when using the `BigDecimal` class. It is *read-only* or, in Java-speak *immutable*. No method has any impact on the object on which it is directly invoked, but rather, the method returns a new object altogether. If the returned object is equated to the source object variable, then the very original object in memory is lost and will eventually be swept up by the garbage collector. (You will learn about another immutable class in a couple of chapters: the `String` class.)

BOOLEAN DATA TYPE

Since the boolean data type in Java is somewhat foreign to you as an RPG programmer, we believe that it is worth a brief description. In both RPG and Java, you have expressions that evaluate to **true** or **false** and so affect the flow of control in your program. For example:

```
if (amountDue > 0)
   // do something
```

The notion of **true** or **false** is intrinsic to computing, and is the end result of any conditional expression, no matter how complex. In RPG and DDS, this notion is imbedded in indicators, with their 0 or 1 states (or ***OFF** or ***ON**). The Java boolean data type is roughly equivalent to RPG indicators, but rather than using 0 or 1 to indicate state, special keywords **true** and **false** are used. Therefore, you can initialize and set boolean variables to these:

```
boolean myFlag = true;
myFlag = false;
```

This is very similar to RPG indicators. However, where boolean variables go beyond indicators is in their affinity to expressions in Java. Because they hold only values that expressions evaluate to anyway, they can be used directly *as expressions*! For example, all of the following are valid:

```
if (myFlag == true)
  // ....
if (myFlag)
  // ...
if (myFlag == false)
  // ...
if (!myFlag)
  // ....
```

This is quite handy. Boolean variables can be used anywhere an expression or sub-expression is allowed, including **while** and **for** loop conditionals. Most interestingly, boolean variables can be assigned an expression! That is, they can be assigned the resulting **true** or **false** value of an expression, as in:

```
myFlag = (amountDue > 0); // will be true or false
```

This can all make for elegant and compact code. Here is another little example to show how to convert between integer and boolean values:

LISTING 5-6

```
// boolean test;
int y = 0;
if (test)
  y = 1;             // Boolean to integer
y = (test) ? 1 : 0; // Boolean to integer (option 2)
test = (y!=0);       // Integer to boolean
```

172

CASTING AND NUMERIC CONVERSIONS

Casting is the process of converting a variable's value from one data type to another. RPG's way of converting numeric fields from one type to another is very straightforward, as the next example illustrates:

LISTING 5-7

```
     FQSYSPRT    O    F    80          PRINTER OFLIND(*INOV)
     D DS1              DS
     D   INT5                      5I 0 INZ(25)
     D   BIN9                      9B 0 INZ(22)
     D   ZONE9                     9S 0 INZ(30)
     D   PACK9                     9P 0 INZ(40)
     D*-----------------------------------------------------
     C                 MOVE      BIN9           INT5
     C                 EXCEPT    RESULT
     C                 MOVE      PACK9          INT5
     C                 EXCEPT    RESULT
     C                 MOVE      ZONE9          INT5
     C                 EXCEPT    RESULT
     C                 MOVE      *ON            *INLR
     C*-----------------------------------------------------
     OQSYSPRT    E             RESULT
     O                         INT5                15
```

As you see in this example, we declare a number of fields with different types and initialize them. In the body of the code on the C-specs you see multiple moves from one numeric field to another followed by an exception output. The compiler determines the types of these fields and does the appropriate conversion as needed. In this example, then, each instance of binary, packed, and zoned is converted to integer. What happens if the value being moved will not fit in the result? It is truncated.

Java is somewhat similar to RPG in this respect. That is, in most cases you can simple move data between data types with no unique syntax being required other than an assignment statement:

```
short myShort = 10;
int   myInt = 30;
long  myLong;
myLong = myShort;
myLong = myInt;
```

This is perfectly legal and common practice. However, you will notice that we are only doing safe conversions here, from a smaller type to a larger type. Thus, the result will always safely fit in the target variable. What if the target type is smaller than the source type? For example:

```
long myLong = 40000;
short myShort = myLong;
```

This will fail. In fact, it will not even compile. Contrast this to RPG, where it is legal at compile time, and at runtime the result is simply truncated if necessary. But sometimes we want to do this because we know that the resulting value will fit in the target. There is a way to force Java to allow the conversion and simply truncate the result if necessary (but, of course, you should avoid these situations!). This involves some simple syntax called *casting*, which looks like this:

```
long myLong = 20000;
short myShort = (short)myLong;
```

The syntax involves specifying the resulting type in parentheses before the variable or operation:

$$(target\ type)\ source\text{-}value$$

This is simply a directive to the compiler that you know what you are doing and you will take responsibility for the risk of truncation. Casting like this is required, as we said, for any conversion from one data type to another of lower precision. It is allowed in all other cases as well, but not required.

The following table summarizes where casting is necessary in all the numeric type to type conversions:

	byte	char	short	int	long	float	double
byte		Cast					
char	Cast		Cast				
short	Cast	Cast					
int	Cast	Cast	Cast				
long	Cast	Cast	Cast	Cast			
float	Cast	Cast	Cast	Cast	Cast		
double	Cast	Cast	Cast	Cast	Cast	Cast	

Read this table by scanning across the rows. You see that converting from a data type specified in the left-hand column to any data type in the columns across the top does not require a cast for those target data types that have higher precision. There are but two apparent anomalies: a cast is required from char to byte and from short to char. The first anomaly occurs because char is actually a two-byte signed integer and byte is but one byte, so precision can be lost. The second occurs because char is signed and byte is not, so even though they are both two bytes, there is potential for corruption with negative or large positive values. So these are not anomalies after all. To be safe, just always cast-you have nothing to lose, if you know truncation will not occur.

NOTE: If you are using a `BigDecimal` object, you cannot use this primitive type casting technique. Rather, use the supplied methods in the `BigDecimal` class named xxxValue(), where xxx is each of the numeric primitive types. For example:

```
double myDouble = myBigDecimalObject.doubleValue();
```

Now that we have demonstrated how RPG does conversion with the **MOVE** operation code, what about other operations such as numeric operation codes or the **EVAL** op-code that allows expressions in factor two? Take a look at the following example:

LISTING 5-8

```
...+... 1 ...+... 2 ...+... 3 ...+... 4 ...+... 5 ...+... 6 ...+...
     FQSYSPRT    O    F   80          PRINTER OFLIND(*INOV)
     D DS1              DS
     D INT5                       5I 0 INZ(25)
     D FLT4                       4F   INZ(10)
     D FLT8                       8F   INZ(10)
     D BIN9                       9B 0 INZ(28)
     D ZONE9                      9S 0 INZ(80)
     D PACK9                      9P 0 INZ(40)
     D*-------------------------------------------------------------
     C               EVAL      INT5 = ((BIN9+ZONE9/PACK9)*2)+FLT4
     C               EXCEPT    RESULT
     C               MOVE      *ON             *INLR
     C*-------------------------------------------------------------
     OQSYSPRT    E             RESULT
     O                         INT5                  15
```

As with the **MOVE** operation code, you do not have to tell the RPG compiler of your intentions for field conversions. The compiler will do the conversion and expression evaluation internally before placing the result into the target field. In this case, our target is INT5, an integer of length 5. Actually, RPG introduced in V3R7 a new set of built-in functions to allow you to have more control over converting fields. For example, the **%INT** and **%INTH** built-in functions convert a field to an integer value, and **%FLOAT** converts a numeric field to float.

What happens in Java? Say we want to add int, short, and byte field values together and divide the result by a float number, and perhaps even assign the result of the expression to a double field:

LISTING 5-9

```
public class TestEXPR
{
    public static void main(String args[])
    {
        byte   byt  = 30;
```

175

LISTING 5-9

```
        short   sht  = 20;
        int     int1 = 20;
        float   flt  = 10;
        double dbl = (double)(((byt+sht-int1)*2)/flt);
        System.out.println(dbl);
    }
}
```

In this example, we declare different numeric fields. The highlighted line defines the final expression. It consists of adding the byte and short fields and then subtracting the result from an integer field. We then multiply by two, and finally divide the result by a float field. The most important thing in this example is that we are casting the final result to a double. The result of executing this is the value 6, which is the result of the operation. Under the covers, a series of rules is used to convert the intermediate results to a common format, usually that of the highest precision of all the operands:

- If at least one of the operands is of type double, the intermediate result is double (if the other operand is not also double, it is implicitly cast to double) and eight-byte math is used.

- If at least one of the operands is of type float, the intermediate result is float (if the other operand is not also float, it is implicitly cast to float) and four-byte math is used.

- If at least one operands is of type long, the intermediate result is long (if the other operand is not also long, it is implicitly cast to long) and eight-byte math is used.

- If none of the above, the intermediate result is integer (all operands are implicitly cast to integer) and four-byte math is used.

Casting is often done, both implicitly and explicitly, in Java. Another place this happens is on the **return** statement of a method. If you define a method's return type to be integer, your actual returned value can be a byte, character, short, or integer value without explicit casting. However, if you return a long value, you must explicitly cast it:

```
public int testThis()
{
    long retValue = 20000;
    return (int)testThis;
}
```

JAVA DATA TYPE CLASS WRAPPERS

Java supplies class "wrappers" for its primitive data types. These are classes, in the `java.lang` package, that allow you to work with each of the data types as objects instead of primitives. All of the operators are emulated via methods in the class. Furthermore, the classes supply some interesting and worthwhile additional methods and constants. The classes are:

- `Boolean`
- `Byte`
- `Character`
- `Double`
- `Float`
- `Integer`
- `Long`
- `Short`

These classes come in handy when an object is needed yet you have a primitive. For example, you may have an array of mixed values-some integers and some objects. This is not legal, of course, so you would instead use these class wrappers to produce objects from your integer values (we will cover arrays in Chapter 6).

All of these classes contain constructors that accept a primitive type value as input for conversion to an object. Most importantly, they all supply methods to convert to and from a string, such as the methods `parseInt` and `valueOf` in the `Integer` class. You will use these often, as Java only accepts user input in the forms of strings, so conversion is essential. Here are the methods supplied by each class to convert from a string, convert to a string, and convert to a primitive type:

Class	From a String	To a String	To a Primitive
Boolean	valueOf(String)	toString()	booleanValue()
Byte	valueOf(String) decode(String)	toString()	byteValue(), doubleValue(), floatValue(), intValue(), shortValue(), longValue()
Character		toString()	charValue(), getNumericValue()
Double	valueOf(String)	toString()	doubleValue(), byteValue(), floatValue(), intValue(), longValue(), shortValue()
Float	valueOf(String)	toString()	floatValue(), byteValue(), doubleValue(), intValue(), longValue(), shortValue

Class	From a String	To a String	To a Primitive
Integer	valueOf(String) parseInt(String)	toString() toBinaryString(long) toHexString(long) toOctalString(long)	intValue(), byteValue(), doubleValue(), floatValue(), longValue(), shortValue()
Long	valueOf(String) parseLong(String)	toString() toBinaryString(long) toHexString(long) toOctalString(long)	longValue(), byteValue(), doubleValue(), floatValue(), intValue(), shortValue()
Short	valueOf(String) parseShort(String)	toString()	shortValue(), byteValue(), doubleValue(), floatValue(), intValue(), longValue()

Note that the valueOf(String) methods all throw the exception "NumberFormatException" if the input string is not valid. This is Java's equivalent to sending an escape message on the AS/400, and you must "monitor" for these using *try/catch-blocks*. We do not cover this until Chapter 10. We mention it now so we can show you the following example of a program that accepts a float value as a string from the command line, then converts it to a primitive float using the Float class:

LISTING 5-10

```java
public class TestConvertFloat
{
    public static void main(String args[])
    {
        Float floatObject;
        if (args.length != 1)
          return;
        try
        {
            floatObject = Float.valueOf(args[0]);
        }
        catch(NumberFormatException exc)
        {
            System.out.println("Invalid input!");
            return;
        }
        float floatValue = floatObject.floatValue();
        System.out.println("input = " + floatValue);
    }
}
```

Note that args[0] represents the first parameter string passed in the command line. The result of compiling this and running it with various inputs is:

LISTING 5-11

```
C:\JAVA>javac TestConvertFloat.java
C:\JAVA>java    TestConvertFloat 1.2
input = 1.2
C:\JAVA>java    TestConvertFloat 1.02
input = 1.02
C:\JAVA>java    TestConvertFloat 0000.12
input = 0.12
C:\JAVA>java    TestConvertFloat 1.2e4
input = 12000.0
C:\JAVA>java    TestConvertFloat -1.2e4
input = -12000.0
C:\JAVA>java    TestConvertFloat abcdef
Invalid input!
```

Another useful thing about these classes is that there are constants for the minimum and maximum values these data types allow-for example, Integer.MAX_VALUE and Integer.MIN_VALUE. Numerous other useful methods exist, such as a number of isXXX() methods in the Character class, for instance isSpaceChar(). Many of these methods are static and take their target as a parameter, so they do not require an instance of the class. The class then just becomes a convenient place to group these related traditional-style functions. It is worth your time to peruse the JDK documentation pertaining to these classes.

SUMMARY

- Java has two categories for data types: primitive types and reference types.

- Java has eight primitive data types: boolean, char, byte, short, int, long, float, and double.

- Java does not have an equivalent data type to RPG's binary, packed, or zoned. However, the class `java.math.BigDecimal` works well as a packed decimal replacement.

- Character data type in Java represents one character, whereas RPG's character data type can be looked at as an array of one-byte characters. The equivalent in Java is the `String` class.

- Character and string data in Java is Unicode based, versus RPG's EBCDIC base. (Information on the Unicode standard can be found on the Web at **www.unicode.org**).

- Float, integer, unsigned, and indicator data types are all relatively new in RPG IV.

- Java has but one way to declare variables, versus the numerous options in RPG.

- In both RPG IV and Java you can declare a variable as either global or local.

- Java global variables are at the class level, can be static or non-static, and can be specified as public or private dictating accessibility by other classes.

- Static variables have a single value per class, whereas non-static variables a unique value per class instance or object.

- Procedures are equivalent to Java methods. Procedures in RPG IV were introduced into the language in V3R2 and V3R6.

- Casting in Java is implicit when converting to a higher precision data type, but requires explicit cast syntax when converting to a lower precision data type.

- There are class wrappers for each of the primitive data types that offer string conversion and other useful methods.

6

Arrays and Vectors

REFERENCE VARIABLES AND OBJECTS

As we have discussed, Java programs contain two types of variables:

- ***Primitive types.*** As discussed in the previous chapter, these are defined to be one of the primitive data types boolean, byte, char, short, int, long, float or double. These are similar to RPG fields.

- ***Reference types.*** As discussed in Chapter 2, these are defined to be of a class type. The class can either be a Java-supplied class or a user-defined class.

Reference type variables can be declared as one of the following types:

- ***Class type.*** This can include any of the classes Java supplies in its java.xxxx packages, or one of your own classes. This can also be the Java-supplied String class described in Chapter 7. Here are some examples:

```
MyClass myVariable;
String myString;
```

- ***Interface type.*** Interfaces are special kinds of classes that define only method names and parameters (***signatures***) without supplying the code for them. They are much like the prototypes for RPG IV procedures, and are discussed in Chapter 9. For example:

```
MyInterface myVariable;
```

- *Array type.* Arrays are declared by using the square brackets ([) and (]), one pair per dimension, along with the primitive or reference type that describes each element of the array. Arrays will be discussed in detail later in this chapter. Here are some examples:

```
int myOneDimensionalArray[];
int myTwoDimensionalArray[][];
MyClass myArrayOfObjects[];
```

Once you have declared a reference type variable, it can be assigned values as follows:

- **null.** This is the initial default value assigned to reference variables until such time as they are assigned to an instance of a class or array. You can also explicitly assign **null** to an object reference if you wish to "free" the object to which it currently points, and you can compare it to **null**. For example:

```
if (myObject == null)
  myObject = new MyClass();
...
myObject = null; // done with the object, free it up
```

- **Object.** These are instances of classes that are created by using the **new** operator, as in:

```
myObject = new MyClass();
```

As discussed in Chapter 2, this allocates memory for the object, and assigns the address of that memory location to the reference variable. Parameters can be specified with the **new** operator, like this:

```
myObject = new MyClass(100, true, "My Name");
```

In this case, Java will search the class MyClass for a constructor with the number and type of parameters (*signature*) that matches those specified. If found, this constructor is called. Otherwise an error occurs.

- **Arrays.** Array variables can hold arrays of the primitive or class type defined. It might seem surprising at first glance, but arrays are in fact objects in Java. Therefore, they are created using the **new** operator, as are all objects. For example:

```
int myArray[] = new int[100];
MyClass myArrayOfObjects[] = new MyClass[100];
```

The number 100 in these examples indicates that an array of 100 elements will be created. Note that after creating the array object, such as myArrayOfObjects, you must further instantiate objects for each element, as in:

```
for (int idx=0; idx < 100; idx++)
  myArrayOfObjects[idx] = new MyClass();
```

In other words, not only is the array itself an object, but in this case so are all of its elements. Thus, all must be instantiated.

NOTE: As the example shows, array elements are referenced using `[index]` notation, prefixed with the name of the array variable.

Object Reference Operators

Once you have declared and instantiated an object reference, you can perform operations on the object, including:

- Accessing class-level variables inside the object, using dot notation. For example:

  ```
  myObject.limit = 100;
  ```

- Invoking methods on the object, using dot notation, as in:

  ```
  myObject.setLimit(100);
  ```

- Casting between object types (see Chapter 9).

- Using the **instanceOf** operator to tell you if the object is an instance of a specified class name (again, covered in Chapter 9).

- Compare memory addresses of two object references, using (`==`), (`!=`), or the conditional operator (?:), as in:

```
if (myObject == myOtherObject)
    ...
else if (myObject != myYetAnotherObject)
    ...
myNewObject = (myObject == myOtherObject) ? myObject : myOtherObject;
```

In summary, variables in Java are either primitive (or base) data types like integer, or object references. These object references are in fact "pointers" to instances of classes. Arrays, which are covered next, are cases of object references that are used heavily in Java programs, and so have special support in the language.

NOTE: There are no explicit pointers or pointer arithmetic in Java. This is unlike RPG, where pointers and pointer arithmetic is supported. Java just contains reference type variables, which are like pointers in that they hold memory addresses. However, you cannot increment, decrement, or otherwise mathematically manipulate these memory addresses. They can only be assigned and compared. This gives you most of the benefits of pointers but with added security, ease of use, and strong type checking.

ARRAYS

As a seasoned programmer, you know you need a raise. Sorry-we mean *arrays*. Both RPG and Java support arrays, but with some noticeable differences between the languages. In both languages, arrays are of a fixed size that is determined at compile time. That size cannot be altered by the code at runtime. However, both languages have alternatives to arrays in order to solve this limitation. The following table highlights the differences and similarities between the two languages in terms of their support for arrays:

RPG	Java
✘ One dimension only	✓ Multiple dimensions
✓ Fixed in size at compile time	✓ Fixed in size at compile time
✓ Can initialize at declaration time (*Compile Time Array*)	✓ Can initialize at declaration time
✓ Can initialize by assigning values in the code (*Runtime Array*)	✓ Can initialize by assigning values in the code
✓ Can initialize by reading from a file (*Pre-Runtime Array*)	✘ No built-in support for initializing from a file
✓ Can use older style "tables"	✘ Only arrays, no tables
✓ Can simulate two-dimensional arrays using multiply occurring data structures (*MODS*)	✓ No need to simulate; arrays of two and more dimensions are supported. Further, a *MODS* can be implemented easily as an array of objects, where the object type is a class with the same variables as the data structure
✘ Have to use dynamic memory APIs to create dynamic sized arrays	✓ Can use supplied Vector class to achieve the same thing, and much easier to use

There are two major areas in which you can compare the array support in these languages: in number of dimensions and initialization. The first difference is that RPG only supports one-dimensional arrays, whereas Java has multiple-dimensional arrays. The second difference is that RPG allows arrays to be initialized at "pre-runtime" from a file, as well as by hard-coded "compile time" values and dynamic runtime assignments. Java only supports the latter two, although initializing array values from a file could be easily coded in Java, as you will see in an example later in this chapter.

In terms of function, RPG compile and runtime arrays are comparable to those in Java. The size of the arrays in both languages must be defined at compile time. This means that you hard-code the size of your array in your source, and cannot change the size dynamically at runtime. This is fine for those cases when the programmer knows at compile time the size of the array that will be used. But in other situations, it would be nice to have the option to grow dynamically and not worry about limits.

In fact, Java has another kind of a single-dimensional array, a *Vector*, that can dynamically grow and shrink at runtime. Do you think that there is a similar functionality to vectors in RPG? If you answered yes, you are right! In V3R1, IBM introduced the new pointer data type in RPG IV, and with it three new operation codes: **ALLOC, DEALLOC,** and **REALLOC** to help at runtime in allocation, de-allocation, and re-allocation of memory, respectively. (We will see a complete example of this when we cover vectors later in this chapter.) Finally, RPG has tables. Tables have been in the language since its inception, but with the introduction of arrays and *multi-occurring data structures (MODS),* their usage has diminished. Speaking of *MODS,* these are equivalent in Java to an array of objects of a user-defined class that has the same variables as the data structure in RPG.

Having completed this fast introduction to arrays, let's take a closer look at the array types in both RPG and Java, and where appropriate, compare them to each other.

Declaring Arrays

In Java, the syntax for declaring an array variable is essentially the same as declaring any variable, but with the added notation of square brackets to identify it as an array versus a simple scalar variable. Look at the following examples:

```
int oneDimArrayOfInts[];
int anotherOneDimArrayOfInts [ ];
long twoDimArrayOfLongs[][];
char[] twoDimArrayOfChars[];
```

These show how you define an array with an element or component type that all elements will have: a name, and a number of dimensions. In the first line we define oneDimArrayOfInts as a one-dimensional array variable that will hold primitive data of integer type. This does not create the array; it only gives the array elements a type, and the array variable a name. In addition, it tells the compiler that the array will be one-dimensional.

This is the tricky part when compared to RPG: We have not "created" an array at all-we have only "created" a reference variable that will eventually "point" or refer to an array object. We next declare anotherOneDimArrayOfInts simply to show that white space is not important in the syntax. In the next line, we define twoDimArrayOfLongs as a two-dimensional array variable that will contain elements of type long. We know it is two-dimensional because there are two pairs of square brackets, [] and [], and each pair indicates a dimension. That is the rule in Java. Thus, number of bracket pairs in Java is equivalent to the **DIM** keyword in RPG.

Finally, the twoDimArrayOfChars array variable is defined as a two-dimensional array of character type. If you notice in the example, you can specify the square brackets after the name of the array or after the type of the array. In fact, you can mix between both the name and the type. Either way, just remember the following rule: the number of paired brackets determines the number of array dimensions.

Creating or Instantiating Arrays

In Java, we must emphasize the difference between declaration and creation. We cannot overstate that in Java, arrays are objects. Not only must you *declare* them, you must also *create* them using the familiar **new** operator. Any attempt to reference *declared* array variables that are not yet *created* will result in a compile time error. It turns out that you can define, create, and initialize an array in Java all in one step, in two steps, or in three steps.

Now that we have seen how to *declare* array variables that tell the compiler what type the elements will be, the name of the array variable, and the number of dimensions in the array, let's look at how to *create* the array. The following lines expand our previous examples:

```
int oneDimArrayOfInts[]          = new int[1000];
int anotherOneDimArrayOfInts [  ] = new int[1000];
long twoDimArrayOfLongs[][]       = new long[10][10];
char[] twoDimArrayOfChars[]       = new char [20] [20];
```

The main difference here is the use of the **new** operator to create the arrays at declaration time. Notice that when we use the **new** operator keyword, we also tell the compiler the size of the array in the brackets. In this case, oneDimArrayOfInts and anotherOneDimArrayOfInts will both contain 1000 elements, twoDimArrayOfLongs will be 10 x 10 in size, giving it 100 elements, and finally, twoDimArrayOfChars is another two-dimensional array, but of size 20 x 20, giving it 400 elements. Notice that you do have a choice here. You can use the **new** operator at declaration time, as we did here, or you can defer creating the array until the body of the code. It's your choice.

At this point, you now have actual array objects whose elements can be assigned, referenced and compared. We will discuss how to do this shortly.

Compile Time Initialization of Arrays

Compile time arrays are supported by both RPG and Java. These are arrays in which the elements are initialized at the same time the array is declared. The syntax of initializing array elements as part of the declaration clearly differs between these two languages. In RPG, with compile time arrays, you define the array with its dimension on the D-spec and initialize it using the **CTDATA** keyword following the RPG source code, as shown in this example:

LISTING 6-1

```
D*
D   employee              3A        DIM(4) PERRCD(2)
D                                    CTDATA
**CTDATA employee
ABCDEF
GHIJKL
```

The main keywords used with compile time arrays are:

D-Spec Keyword	Explanation
DIM	Specifies number of elements the array is to contain
CTDATA	Compile time data records
PERRCD	Number of elements per record

All RPG arrays use the **DIM** keyword. This keyword tells the compiler the number of elements in the array. As we mentioned earlier, RPG supports only one dimension, and therefore, only one parameter is supplied (but it is designed to allow multiple parameters in the future in the event RPG IV steps up to supporting multiple dimension arrays). The example shows an array of four elements. The **CTDATA** keyword indicates to the compiler that the array is a compile time array, and therefore, the compiler should be looking for the **CTDATA** employee record at the bottom of the RPG source code. Finally, the **PERRCD** keyword tells the compiler that each record consists of two elements. Doing the math (four three-character elements in the array but only two lines of **CTDATA** data records), we see how each data record supplies the data for two elements in the array. Since each element is three characters long and each data record is six long, we get:

```
employee(1) = 'ABC'
employee(2) = 'DEF'
employee(3) = 'GHI'
employee(4) = 'JKL'
```

Now we compare this to what Java offers in terms of compile time arrays. Here is the same example in Java:

```
String employee[] = {"ABC", "DEF", "GHI", "JKL"};
```

Notice that in Java, character variables are only of length one, while the supplied `String` class is used for strings of multiple characters. Thus, in our example we use an array of `String` objects. The more complex alternative is a two-dimensional array of characters. The syntax shown here is the special syntax Java supports for defining, creating, and initializing arrays in one step. In this case, the initial values are supplied between curly braces ({) and (}), with each element's initial value separated by commas. The literal values supplied must be consistent with the declared element type of the array. Also, don't forget the ending semicolon, as always.

When you specify initial values within an array declaration in this way, Java performs the **new** operation and defines the array size for you. The array size is implicitly determined by the number of comma-separated elements in the initialization part. These types of compile time arrays are often used to hold constant data, and so are defined as **final**:

```
final String employee[] = {"ABC", "DEF", "GHI", "JKL"};
```

Runtime Initialization of Arrays

If you have used arrays in any language, then you already know what *runtime arrays* are. These are perhaps the most common type of array. With runtime arrays, you initialize the values of the elements in a separate step from declaring the array.

Thus, as the name says, runtime arrays are loaded (or initialized) at runtime during program execution. Your program code initializes them by assigning values to the elements, typically in a loop that stops at the size of the array. Here is an example of how this is done in RPG:

LISTING 6-2

```
D   newarr          S              5I 0 DIM(10)
D   value           S              5I 0 INZ(10)
D   idx             S              5I 0 INZ(1)
C                   DOW            idx < 11
C                   EVAL           newarr(idx) = value
C                   EVAL           value = value + 10
C                   EVAL           idx = idx + 1
C                   ENDDO
```

We first declare the array `newarr` to contain integer values of length 5 with zero decimal points. We define the array to be of size 10. Note that because we do *not* use the keywords **PERRCD, CTDATA, FROMFILE,** or **TOFILE** we know this is a runtime array in RPG. The field called `value` is initialized to 10 on the D-spec as well as the field `idx`, which we use as our index to control the **while** loop. Notice that the loop will iterate ten times starting at index value one. The field `value` is assigned to the array element and then it is incremented by 10 each time it goes through the loop. As we can see, in RPG array indexing starts at one, and array elements are referenced using `arrayName(index)` notation.

Now, let's look at the Java equivalent of this example:

LISTING 6-3

```
int newarr[] = new int[10];
int value = 10;
for (int idx=0; idx<10; idx++)
{
    newarr[idx] = value;
    value += 10;
}
```

This code accomplishes the same result as the RPG code. Notice the difference in the indexing of the array. In RPG we use parentheses, while Java uses square brackets. Using array elements in your source code is no different than using any other regular field, except that with arrays, you have to index them. An important difference that you may have noticed between the RPG and Java examples is the fact that we initialize the index field to one in RPG and to zero in Java. In Java, the index of the first element of an array is zero, and the last location is the size of the array, minus one. Officially, RPG arrays are "one-based" and Java arrays are "zero-based." Therefore, to loop through all the members of the array, the RPG program uses the loop index value 1 to 10, whereas Java uses 0 to 9.

Again, in both RPG and Java, the length of the array is fixed and established at compile time. If for any reason the index value being used is less than one or greater than the size of the array, RPG then generates a runtime error, "index out of bound." Similarly, if it is less than *zero* or greater than *or equal* to the size of the array, Java generates an *IndexOutOfBoundsException* error and terminates the program.

Since arrays in Java are objects, Java supplies arrays with a ***length*** member variable in order to retrieve the length of the array (that is, the number of elements). Knowing this, the previous example could have and should have been coded as follows to use the built-in variable:

LISTING 6-4

```
for (int idx=0; idx < newarr.length; idx++)
{
    newarr[idx] = value;
    value += 10;
}
```

Notice that we specify the name of the array first and follow it with a dot, and then specify the member variable `length` to retrieve the length of the array.

Initializing Multiple-Dimension Arrays

Now that we have seen the different types of arrays and the different ways to declare and initialize them, we will look at a few examples of array manipulations. As you know, each value of an array is called an array element. To access an array element you specify the name of the array with the index of that element placed between parentheses () for RPG, and square brackets [] for Java. In the case of Java, since the language does support multidimensional arrays, you specify as many sets of square brackets as there are dimensions in the array. For example, if array `employee` is two-dimensional, then to access the first element in it you specify `employee[0][0]`.

It is most important to think of multiple-dimension arrays as arrays of arrays. Thus, for two dimensions, each element of the first dimension is like another array. When using compile time initialization, each element's initial value for the first dimension will be a valid initialization value for another array. You will then have nested sets of curly bracket values. Furthermore, when using the `length` variable, you use it per dimension. Here, then, is an example of initializing a two-dimension array in Java using compile time initialization syntax, and then looping through the array to print out the values:

LISTING 6-5

```
class TestMultiArray
{
    public static void main(String args[])
    {
        int ctArray[][] = {{ 1 , 2 , 3 },
                           { 4 , 5 , 6 },
                           { 7 , 8 , 9 }};
        for (int xIdx=0; xIdx < ctArray.length; xIdx++)
        {
            for (int yIdx=0; yIdx < ctArray[xIdx].length; yIdx++)
            {
                System.out.print(ctArray[xIdx][yIdx] + " ");
            } // end inner for loop
            System.out.println();
        } // end outer for loop
    } // end main method
} // end TestMultiArray class
```

This illustrates an example of an array 3 x 3 in size, using a compile time array and assigning it the values 1 to 9. Note that each row of the array's initial values is surrounded by curly brackets {}. In the body of the code, we have two different loops to go through the three rows and three columns in the matrix. The example simply loops nine times, printing all of the elements of the array. The statement following the inner loop is a print of a new line in order to force the output to a separate line. The following output is produced by running the example:

```
C:\JAVA>java TestMultiArray
1 2 3
4 5 6
7 8 9
```

Here is the same example as a runtime array, which gives us the same output result:

LISTING 6-6

```
class TestMultiArrayRT
{
    public static void main(String args[])
    {
        int rtArray[][] = new int[3][3];
        int value = 1;
        for (int xIdx=0; xIdx < rtArray.length; xIdx++)
        {
            for (int yIdx=0; yIdx < rtArray[xIdx].length; yIdx++)
            {
                rtArray[xIdx][yIdx] = value++; // assign and increment
                System.out.print(rtArray[xIdx][yIdx] + " ");
            } // end inner for loop
            System.out.println();
        } // end outer for loop
    } // end main method
} // end TestMultiArrayRT class
```

Getting the hang of it? In this case, we create the same loop but use it to initialize as well as print out the value of each element. Note the use of value++ which, as you recall, assigns the current contents of variable value to the left-hand side, then increments those contents by one.

Think you could handle expanding this example to three dimensions? Or the previous example using compile time arrays? Any guess as to what the initialization statement might look like? Let's have a look:

LISTING 6-7

```
class TestThreeArray
{
    public static void main(String args[])
    {
        int ctArray[] [] []
            = { { { 1 , 2 , 3 }, { 4 , 5 , 6 }, { 7 , 8 , 9 } },
                { { 10, 11, 12}, { 13, 14, 15}, { 16, 17, 18} },
                { { 19, 20, 21}, { 22, 23, 24}, { 25, 26, 27} } };
        for (int xIdx=0; xIdx < ctArray.length; xIdx++)
        {
            for (int yIdx=0; yIdx < ctArray[xIdx].length; yIdx++)
            {
                for (int zIdx=0; zIdx < ctArray[yIdx].length; zIdx++)
                {
                    System.out.print(ctArray[xIdx][yIdx][zIdx] + " ");
                } // end inner for loop
                System.out.print("   ");
            } // end middle for loop
            System.out.println();
        } // end outer for loop
    } // end main method
} // end TestThreeArray class
```

The output of this is the following (it's difficult to show three dimensions in two-dimensional space!):

```
 1  2  3    4  5  6     7  8  9
10 11 12    13 14 15    16 17 18
19 20 21    22 23 24    25 26 27
```

Arrays Are Objects

As we described earlier, Java uses references (or if you like, pointers) to point to objects. Array references are no different than any other Java object. For example, you can point to one array object with an array reference, and later point to another array object using the same reference. The following example illustrates this:

LISTING 6-8

```
class TestArrayObjects
{
    public static void main(String args[])
    {
        int arrayOne[][] = { { 1 , 2 }, { 3 , 4 } };
        int arrayTwo[][] = { { 5 , 6 }, { 7 , 8 } };
        int tempArray[][];
        tempArray = arrayOne;
        for (int xIdx = 0; xIdx < tempArray.length; xIdx++)
        {
            for (int yIdx = 0; yIdx < tempArray[xIdx].length; yIdx++)
                System.out.print(tempArray[xIdx][yIdx] + " ");
            System.out.println();
        }
        tempArray = arrayTwo;
        for (int xIdx = 0; xIdx < tempArray.length; xIdx++)
        {
            for (int yIdx = 0; yIdx < tempArray[xIdx].length; yIdx++)
                System.out.print(tempArray[xIdx][yIdx] + " ");
            System.out.println();
        }
    } // end main method
} // end TestArrayObjects class
```

In this example, we declare and initialize two arrays, arrayOne and arrayTwo. We then declare but do not create a third array, tempArray, of the same dimensions as the first two. In the body of the code, we first assign tempArray to arrayOne and loop through printing the contents, then re-assign tempArray to arrayTwo and loop through again printing the contents. This results in the following output:

```
1 2
3 4
5 6
7 8
```

You may be inclined to think that each assignment of tempArray to another array results in a copy of the contents from one array to another. This is not the case, specifically because arrays are in fact objects in Java, and array variables are, therefore, reference variables. Thus, assigning a reference variable is the same as changing the object it points to in memory. So our tempArray assignments simply change the array to which the tempArray variable points, with no copying of array contents. This means changes made to the array elements of tempArray will also affect the original array to which it points. That's because after an array assignment, a statement like tempArray = arrayTwo results in one array in memory but with two variables referencing the array.

If you did want to copy the contents of an array, you would first have to instantiate a new instance of an array for the target using the **new** operator, then loop through both arrays, copying the contents. While this is easy enough to code, there is in fact an easier way if you do actually want to create a duplicate copy of an array. Java supplies a useful static method in its System class called arraycopy to handle this for you. It takes as input a source array, an index position from which to start copying, a target array, an index position in the target array where the copying starts to go, and a length indicating how many elements to copy. This works well for single-dimensional arrays, but for multiple-dimension arrays, you must be careful to call it per dimension, in the right order. For those, we recommend you simply use your own code loop instead for peace of mind. Here is an example usage for a single-dimensional array:

```
int arraySrc[] = {1,2,3,4};
int arrayTgt[] = new int[4];
System.arraycopy(arraySrc, 0, arrayTgt, 0, 4);
```

Pre-Runtime Arrays in RPG

As we mentioned earlier, RPG supports *pre-runtime arrays,* whereas Java does not. Nevertheless, since we are comparing arrays between RPG and Java, we will touch on this to make our comparison complete. If you know at compile time what data you want stored in your array, then the answer is clear as to which RPG array type to use- compile time arrays are the best choice (for both languages, actually). If your data is not known at compile time, then the answer will be to use either pre-runtime or runtime arrays. What's the difference? If the initialization data being read resides in a file on disk, then use pre-runtime arrays, since the main feature of this kind of an array is to read the data from a file at the start of runtime (i.e., at load time) and write it back to the file at termination time. However, if the source of the data is coming from the keyboard or any other input medium, then your best bet is a runtime array.

Here is an example of a pre-runtime array in RPG:

LISTING 6-9

```
FSTATE       UF    F    70          DISK
     D STATEARR          S                2A   DIM(20)
     D                                         PERRCD(1)
     D                                         FROMFILE(STATE)
     D                                         TOFILE(STATE)
```

This example illustrates how you can load the two-character prefix of a state into a pre-runtime array. The main keywords that are used with pre-runtime array are the following:

D-Spec Keyword	Explanation
DIM	Specify the number of dimensions.
FROMFILE(filename)	Read from this file at program load time.
PERRCD	Number of elements per record in the file.
TOFILE(filename)	Write to this file at termination of the program.

The list shows that, as with compile time arrays, you use the DIM keyword to define the dimension and number of elements in the array and the PERRCD keyword to tell the compiler the number of elements per record in the file. The two other keywords, FROMFILE and TOFILE, specify the file name *from* which you want to load the data to the array you are defining, and the file *to* which you want to write the data at termination. As you see in the example, other than specifying these extra keywords, the actual definition of the array is the same as a compile time array. As shown in the example, we first define the file STATE which is holding the data with which the array will be initialized. Following that, on the **D**-spec, we define the array STATEARR as a twenty-element array of two characters each, using the DIM keyword.

We mentioned earlier that pre-runtime arrays do not exist in Java; however, could we simulate them? The answer is absolutely yes! While Java does not have built-in support for RPG style pre-runtime arrays, it is possible to code your own. The way we will code it in Java is to define a class that will simulate the main keywords that RPG supports for pre-runtime arrays, namely: FROMFILE and DIM. We assume PERRCD of one for simplicity. Here is one possible implementation:

LISTING 6-10

```java
import java.io.*;
public class PreRun
{
    private String filename;
    private int    Dimension;
    private BufferedReader instream;

    public void FromFile(String filename)
    {
        this.filename = filename;
        try
        {
          instream = new BufferedReader(
                      new InputStreamReader(
                        new FileInputStream(filename) ) );
        }
        catch (IOException exc)
        {
          System.out.println("Error Reading " + exc);
        }
    } // end FromFile
    public void Dim(int dim)
    {
        Dimension = dim;
    } // end Dim method
    public void LoadPreRun(String tempArray[])
    {
        String line = new String(); // save compiler warning
        int  idx = 0;
        while ( idx < Dimension)
        {
            try
            {
              line = instream.readLine();
              line.trim();
              tempArray[idx] = line;
              idx++;
            }
            catch (IOException exc)
            {
              System.out.println("Error Reading " + exc);
            }
        } // end while loop
    } // end LoadPreRun method
} // end PreRun class
```

In this class, we implement two of the four keywords since the **TOFILE** keyword can be implemented just like the **FROMFILE,** except that the readLine method call turns into a writeLine method. The class PreRun defines three different methods. First, the FromFile method receives the file name as a parameter and simply opens the stream file from which we will be reading in the data and storing it in the pre-runtime array. Chapter 14 will describe in more detail the steps you need to follow for stream file access. Note we are not using a database file here, but rather a flat file or stream file. We leave database files to you as an exercise after reading the Database Access chapter. The FromFile method is a simulation of the **FROMFILE** keyword used by RPG. In fact, in RPG all of this is done for you implicitly. In other words, by simply telling the compiler the file from which you want to load the pre-runtime array data, the compiler generates the appropriate code for you without requiring you to do any extra coding. In the case of Java, we supply the file name to the method and we open the file in the class.

The next step is to simulate the **DIM** keyword in RPG. This is very simple. We define in our class a method Dim that will set the dimension of the array by assigning the value passed to the method to an instance variable (or global variable, as it is known in RPG). The reason we do that is to allow the other methods to be able to access this field. Remember that in RPG, the dimension must be known at compile time. This is why we simulate the dimension by having a fixed number passed to the method. Finally, the most interesting method that makes the body of the pre-runtime array simulation is the LoadPreRun method.

This method simply loads the array with the required values from the specified file name. Note that the file name has been defined as an instance variable, so we can access it globally from all other methods. The code in the method starts with a main **while** loop that loops as long as we have elements to be loaded from the file. Each element is read from the file, trimmed of any leading and trailing blanks, and then the value is placed in the array.

How would you use this class? The following application illustrates this:

LISTING 6-11

```
public class MainRead
{
    public static void main(String args[])
    {
        int arraysize = 5;
        String prerun[] = new String[arraysize];
        String filename = "TXT.TXT";
        PreRun myfile = new PreRun();
        myfile.FromFile(filename);
        myfile.Dim(arraysize);
        myfile.LoadPreRun(prerun);
        for (int idx = 0; idx < arraysize; idx++)
        {
            System.out.println("Array (" + idx + "): " + prerun[idx]);
        }
    } // end main method
} // end MainRead class
```

197

In this application, we define an array prerun to be our pre-runtime array as well as to define the file name. In this example we call the file "TXT.TXT." We have pre-edited this file for the purpose of this example and entered five elements into it (MA, MO, AR, CA, WY-one per line). In the code, we first instantiate the class using the **new** operator. We then start simulating the RPG keyword by simply referencing the object, followed by the method that is equivalent to the RPG keyword. For example, in RPG you specify the keyword **DIM(5)** which says: "Declare the array as single-dimensional with five elements." In Java, we simply reference the object myfile and then call the Dim method, as shown in the preceding example. Finally, we call the LoadPreRun method passing in our array, and this method initializes the array with the contents of the stream file on disk.

Unbalanced Arrays

So far, the multiple-dimension arrays that we have used have been rectangular. This means they have the same number of elements in each dimension. Java's multidimensional arrays are actually arrays of arrays. This means that each dimension does not have to be the same length. In fact, each element in a given dimension, if it is another array, can have differing numbers of elements. This is an ***unbalanced array***. However, the main restriction in unbalanced arrays is for the dimensions to be specified left to right. What does that mean? If you are declaring, say, an array of ten elements, and each element of the array is actually another array of unknown length, you can do that as follows:

```
int myArray[][] = new int[10][];
```

In this case, you specify the first left dimension as ten; however, you leave the second unknown dimension to be declared or created after in the body of the code. The example is perfectly legal in Java. However, you cannot do the opposite and specify the second dimension before the first, like this:

```
int myArray[][] = new int[][10];   // NOT VALID!
```

This is the left-to-right rule in Java. It is legal to specify the left dimension and leave the right, but not legal the other way. The fact that multidimensional arrays in Java are arrays of arrays explains this restriction. You create the left array first, and as you proceed in the code, you can create the rest left to right. Let us look at the following example that uses unbalanced arrays:

```
boolean ubArray[][] = new boolean[3][];
for (int idx = 0; idx< ubArray.length;idx++)
{
    ubArray[idx] = new boolean[idx+1];
}
```

In this example, we create an array of size three for the first dimension and unknown for the second dimension. As you see in the example, we loop three times, building up the second dimension of the array. In the body of the **for** loop we use the **new** operator to create the second dimension. This is, in fact, a new array for each element. The result of this is an array containing the following values:

```
false
false false
false false false
```

As you can see, we start with the first row having only one element, the second row having two elements, and finally the third row with three elements. This is a result of using idx+1 as the size parameter when creating the new array for each row.

VECTORS

In the previous section you learned about single- and multidimensional arrays. One important restriction in arrays that applies to both RPG and Java is that their length must be determined ahead of time and can never change. Note that in Java you can dynamically declare an array. Yes, this is more powerful than what is allowed in RPG, as it allows you to defer creation until you know the length. However, once you create an array, you cannot change the length. In other words, existing arrays have fixed length and cannot grow or shrink. As you tackle more complex applications, you sometimes do not know at any time, whether at compile time or runtime, how many elements you will want to store. To help with this, Java supplies a utility class, called Vector, in its java.util package. Java has vectors as an alternative when you need to use single-dimensional arrays that can grow or shrink dynamically. As you will see later in this section, RPG supports that as well, but more coding is required in order to dynamically allocate and manipulate storage.

> **NOTE:** Vectors are adjustable arrays that can increase or decrease its size in response to the number of elements they need to store.

Variables of the Vector class are (you guessed it) objects in Java, just as arrays are. In fact, the Vector class contains many supplied methods to help you with adding, removing, and searching elements. The following example illustrates a simple vector with three elements:

LISTING 6-12

```
import java.util.*; // import all classes in java.util package
class TestVector
{
    public static void main(String args[])
    {
        Vector myFirstVector = new Vector();
        myFirstVector.addElement(new String("Ford"));
        myFirstVector.addElement(new String("GM"));
        myFirstVector.addElement(new String("Chrysler"));
        for (int idx = 0 ; idx < myFirstVector.size() ; idx++)
        {
            System.out.println(myFirstVector.elementAt(idx));
        }
    }
}
```

In this example, we first define and create the Vector variable myFirstVector. We then add elements to it. Notice the use of the String class as we add the elements. (Not to worry; we have not covered strings yet. This is the topic of the next chapter.) For now, all you need to know is that the **new** keyword with the String class creates a String object, and the addElement method adds that string to the vector. For example, in the first case we send the string "Ford" as the parameter to the String class constructor to build for us a *new* string object with that value. The reference of that object is used as the input parameter to the addElement() method of the Vector class. This same thing happens three times, adding three strings to the vector, after which we use the **for** loop to print the content of the vector. Our loop ends at myFirstVector.size() which in our case is three.

NOTE: Vectors can only contain objects, not primitive type values. To use primitive values, you must create an instance of their wrapper classes, such as java.lang.Integer.

In this example, we use two methods that the Vector class supports, namely the addElement method and the size() method. There are many more methods that the Vector class supports; The most commonly used methods are listed in the following table:

Method	Description
addElement(Object)	Adds specified object to the end of this vector, increasing its size by one.
capacity()	Returns the current capacity of this vector. Capacity is the potential size of a vector, versus its actual size or element count.
clone()	Returns a copy of this vector. All elements are copied.

Method	Description
contains(Object)	Tests if the specified object is an element in this vector.
copyInto(Object[])	Copies the elements of this vector into the specified array.
elementAt(int)	Returns the element at the specified index (zero-based).
elements()	Returns an enumeration of the elements of this vector. See Chapter 9 for information on enumerators.
ensureCapacity(int)	Increases the capacity of this vector to the given number.
firstElement()	Returns reference to the first element of this vector.
indexOf(Object)	Searches for the first occurrence of the given parameter, testing for equality using the equals method on each element.
indexOf(Object, int)	Searches for the first occurrence of the first parameter, beginning the search at the zero-based index specified in the second parameter. Again, tests for equality using equals.
insertElementAt(Object, int)	Inserts the specified object at the specified index.
isEmpty()	Tests if this vector has no elements.
lastElement()	Returns the last element of the vector.
lastIndexOf(Object)	Returns the index of the last occurrence of the specified object in this vector. Useful for repeated elements.
lastIndexOf(Object, int)	Searches backwards for the specified object, starting from the specified index, and returns an index to it.
removeAllElements()	Removes all elements from this vector, and sets its size to zero.
removeElement(Object)	Removes first occurrence of the argument from this vector.
removeElementAt(int)	Deletes the element at the specified index.
setElementAt(Object, int)	Sets the element at the specified index to the specified object.
setSize(int)	Sets the size of this vector.
size()	Returns the number of elements in this vector.
toString()	Returns a string representation of this vector.
trimToSize()	Trims the capacity of this vector to be the vector's current size.

For a complete and up-to-date list of these methods, look up the online documentation in the JDK (Java Development Kit).

We have seen a straightforward and simple example of a vector. Let's look at a slightly more complex example that uses a few vector methods. Suppose we write a program that accepts commands from the console and acts appropriately depending on the commands entered. Think of this little program as a program that can be used with a car rental company. When customers return a car, you want the program to accept the command A for adding a returned car name and serial number. When customers come to rent a car, what you want to do is pop a car from the top of the vector and remove its entry. The final command that you want this program to accept is a D. This displays the content of the vector to see how many cars you have on your lot (that is, not rented). Let us build this program in small parts. Here is the first part:

LISTING 6-13

```
String command, carName;

InputStream incmd = System.in;
DataInputStream inlinedata = new DataInputStream(incmd);
BufferedReader inFileStraem = new BufferedReader( new
InputStreamReader(inlinedata));
try
{
  command = inFileStream.readLine();
}
catch (IOException exc)
{
  System.out.println("File error: " + exc);
}
if (command.equals("A"))
  // Add a car
else if (command.equals("R"))
  // Remove a car.
else if (command.equals("D"))
  // Display the content of the vector
```

First, we need to start by creating two strings: one to hold the command entered and one to hold the car information. Next, we need to read the command and the car name (if applicable, depending on the command entered) from the console. As you have learned, you can access the standard output stream through the System class. This was shown in all of the preceding examples that used with the print and println methods.

Similarly, you can access the standard input stream through the System class. The standard input stream lets you accept user input through the console window. In our example, you need to define the input stream as using the DataInputStream class to read in the data as shown in the previous example. The reason we use BufferedReader is to take advantage of the readLine method, which reads a whole line at once from the console. As shown in the example, since the readLine method can throw *exceptions*, we therefore need to use a *try/catch-block* to monitor for that. These are explained later in the exception handling chapter (Chapter 10), but really, catch is equivalent to the MONMSG command in CL programs. This is all we need to do to get the input from the console.

Next we use if/else statements to test for the type of the command that was entered, using one of the String class methods, namely the equals method. On the three if statements we test for four possible commands: A, R, D, and E for adding, removing, displaying, and ending, respectively. In the first case, to add an element to the vector we need to read the car information from the screen and store it in the carName String object that we created and then add it to the vector. This is very simple; the following example illustrates what needs to be done:

LISTING 6-14

```
try
{
  carName = inFileStream.readLine();
}
catch (IOException exc)
{
  System.out.println("File error: " + exc);
}
vec.addElement(carName);
```

We first have to read in the car information and assign it to the string variable carName. This is done using the readLine method, just as we did when we read in the command string. Then we use the Vector class addElement method to add an element to the vector. Next, we need to remove a car's information if the command entered is an R. The only line of code required here is to call the removeElement method. Here is the code required:

```
vec.removeElementAt(0);
```

The third possible command that can be entered is to display the content of the vector to see the number of cars that are on the lot and may be available to be rented. This can be done with a simple for loop to go through the whole array and print it. Here is the code required:

```
for (int idx = 0; idx < vec.size(); idx++)
  System.out.println("Car:" + vec.elementAt(idx));
```

As before, the `Vector` class can locate an element at a specified position using the `elementAt` method as shown. We supply as a parameter to the method the index of the element we want printed, which is the current loop index we use to loop through all of the elements in the vector. In addition, we took advantage of the `size()` method in the looping expression. This method returns the size of the vector we are dealing with.

The last command that you can enter is E which simply forces the condition on the **while** loop to **false** and the program terminates. This is all we need to do to accomplish the goals of the car rental program. Here is the entire example:

LISTING 6-15

```
import java.util.*;
import java.io.*;
class VecMain
{
    static Vector vec = new Vector();
    public static void main (String args[])
    {
        String command, carName;
        command = carName = " ";
        InputStream incmd = System.in;
        DataInputStream inlinedata = new DataInputStream(incmd);
        BufferedReader InFileStream = new BufferedReader(
            new InputStreamReader(inlinedata));
        while (!(command.equals("E")))
        {
            try
            {
                System.out.println();
                System.out.println("Enter command:");
                command = inFileStream.readLine();
            }
            catch (IOException exc)
            {
                System.out.println("File error: " + exc);
            }
            if (command.equals("A"))
            {
                try
                {
                    System.out.println("Enter car name:");
                    carName = inFileStream.readLine();
                }
                catch (IOException exc)
                {
                    System.out.println("File error: " + exc);
                }
                vec.addElement(carName);
            }
            else if (command.equals("R"))
                vec.removeElementAt(0);
            else if (command.equals("D"))
                for (int idx = 0; idx < vec.size(); idx++)
                    System.out.println("Car:" + vec.elementAt(idx));
        } // end while loop
    } // end main method
} // end VecMain class
```

This example can be modified to add more information for the car returned or removed, such as the customer's name, address, and credit card number. Additionally, rather than a car name, which is not unique, it should take a license plate number, which can then be used to index a good deal of information about that car. In fact, instead of entering the number from the console, you may want to come back to this example and expand it to do input/output from a database, after you have read the database chapter (Chapter 13). Also, some error checking is always welcome.

As we mentioned before, there are many other methods that can be used with vectors as listed in a table earlier. The way you use all of the methods listed is similar to the way we used them in this example.

Simulating Vectors In RPG

So far, we have been talking only about Java. What about RPG? Does RPG have anything similar to what Java offers in terms of dynamically allocating and de-allocating storage? The answer, perhaps to your surprise, is yes. In RPG IV, we can perform the same functions that we have accomplished in the car rental program example. Since this is a recent enhancement to RPG, let's code the same car rental program we have written in Java, but now write it using RPG IV. (If you are not interested in learning about dynamic memory allocation in RPG, then please feel free to skip this section.)

In RPG IV, the main features we will be using are the newly introduced memory management operation codes (`ALLOC`, `DEALLOC`, and `REALLOC`) as well as the new pointer data type. We will use these to build and maintain a linked list of data structures. Before we start building up the source code, let us first examine (see Figure 6-1) how we will be arranging the link list that will hold the car information as well as point to the next car:

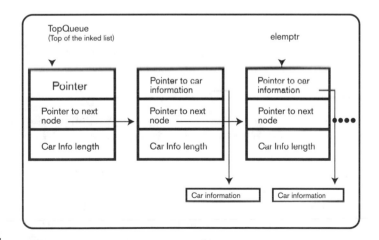

FIGURE 6-1

As Figure 6-1 shows, we will declare a data structure that will contain three fields. The first one is a pointer that will be used to point to the car information. The second one will be another pointer to be used to point to the next node in the linked list. The last one will contain the length of the car information we entered to allow us to allocate the exact amount of memory as the size of the car information field. Another important variable is elemptr, which will be used to point to the last element. This way, when we add or remove, we know the address of the last element in memory. In addition, the first element will be declared physically in memory and will be pointed to by the field TopQueue to tell us where the link list starts. This way we know the start of the list in order to do all operations required on it. In addition, as we build an element when a car is returned, we will create space and store the car information in that element, then we will use the first element of this data structure to point to it. With this design, let's create our global data definitions for this program. The following example illustrates all of the required definitions for our program:

LISTING 6-16

```
HNOMAIN
D AddCar          PR
D   name_parm                    42A
D RemoveCar       PR
D DisplayCar      PR
D*------------------------------------------------
D elem            DS                    BASED(elemptr)
D   CarName@                    *
D   next@                       *
D   name_len                   5U 0
D*------------------------------------------------
D   nameVal       S             42A    BASED(CarName@)
D   elemSize      C                    %size(elem)
D*------------------------------------------------
D   TopQueue      DS
D                               *      INZ(*NULL)
D                               *      INZ(*NULL)
D                              5U 0    INZ(0)
D*------------------------------------------------
D elemptr         S             *      INZ(%ADDR(TopQueue))
D*------------------------------------------------
D COMMAND         S             1A
D carName         S             42A
```

First, we declare the prototypes for the three procedures that will be used to add, remove, and display the elements for our car rental program: AddCar, RemoveCar, and DisplayCar. Since the work involved to perform the addition or removal of a car as well as the displaying of all cars requires more coding in RPG, we decided to have a standalone service program that will contain all three procedures to do the work for us. The main data structure in this program is TopQueue, which represents the top of our linked list. This is the one that is being pointed to by the field elemptr at the start of the program. We also have another data structure, elem, which is declared based on the pointer elemptr and is used as a skeleton for the data structure. It contains the same fields as the TopQueue data structure.

Notice that elemptr is initialized to the TopQueue address using the built in **%ADDR** as the parameter of the **INZ** keyword. The namVal field is also a based field that is defined to be used with the car information field. Remember that the car information is also being allocated storage to store the information the user enters on the screen. In addition, we have the field elemSize to be used when we add a new element in our list. Since we need to know the size of the storage to be allocated when a new car is added, elemSize will be used with the **ALLOC** op-code to allocate the appropriate number of bytes required. The last two fields declared are COMMAND and carName, which will be used to hold the command entered and the car information respectively. These two fields will be used for the same purpose they served in the Java example we showed earlier.

Let's begin by writing the main program which will read the command from the screen and call the appropriate procedure. The main subprocedure is illustrated in the following example:

LISTING 6-17

```
C      'CMD:A,R,E,D'  DSPLY                       COMMAND
C                     DOW         COMMAND<>'E'
C                     SELECT
C                     WHEN        COMMAND='A'
C                     CLEAR                       carName
C      'CarName?'     DSPLY                       carName
C                     CALLP       AddCar(carName)
C                     WHEN        COMMAND='R'
C                     CALLP       RemoveCar
C                     WHEN        COMMAND='D'
C                     CALLP       DisplayCar
C                     ENDSL
C                     CLEAR                       COMMAND
C      'CMD:A,R,E,D'  DSPLY                       COMMAND
C                     ENDDO
C                     MOVE        *ON             *INLR
```

As you see in the example, we start by prompting the user for a command. Like the Java example we gave earlier, the only allowed entries are A, R, E, and D for adding, removing, ending, and displaying, respectively. Next, we do a main loop that will run until the user enters E to end the program. The body of the code uses the **SELECT** operation code with **WHEN,** first to test the command that has been entered, and then to call the appropriate procedure. We will have to write three different procedures in order to complete this program:

- The first procedure, AddCar, will take the car information as a parameter and add it to the linked list.

- The second procedure, RemoveCar, will simply remove a car from top of the list.

- The last procedure, DisplayCar, will simply display the linked list in its entirety.

207

If the user enters the E command, the program sets on **LR** and terminates. Let's examine the service program that has all three procedures just described:

LISTING 6-18

```
P*------START OF PROCEDURE----------------------
PAddCar          B               EXPORT
D                PI
D   carName                      42A
C                ALLOC    elemSize         next@
C                EVAL     elemptr=next@
C                EVAL     next@=*NULL
C                EVAL     name_len=%len(%trimr(carName))
C                ALLOC    name_len         carname@
C                EVAL     %subst(nameVal:1:name_len)=carName
P                E
P*------START OF PROCEDURE----------------------
P DisplayCar     B               EXPORT
D   TmpElem@     S               *
D   carName      S               40A
C                EVAL     Tmpelem@=elemptr
C                EVAL     elemptr=%ADDR(TopQueue)
C                DOW      next@ <> *NULL
C                EVAL     elemptr = next@
C                EVAL     carName = %SUBST(nameVal:1:name_len)
C                DSPLY    carName
C                ENDDO
C                EVAL     elemptr=TmpElem@
P                E
P*------START OF PROCEDURE----------------------
P RemoveCar      B               EXPORT
D       Top@     S               *
D       Temp@    S               *
C                EVAL     Temp@ = elemptr
C                EVAL     elemptr= %ADDR(TopQueue)
C                EVAL     elemptr=next@
C                DEALLOC                   carname@
C                EVAL     Top@=next@
C                DEALLOC                   elemptr
C                EVAL     elemptr=%ADDR(TopQueue)
C                EVAL     next@=Top@
C                EVAL     elemptr = Temp@
P                E
```

Let's examine each procedure individually:

1. First the AddCar procedure. The procedure declares a procedure interface (PI in column 24-25) that enables it to receive the carName parameter. The carName parameter that is passed contains the car information that was entered by the user. The **ALLOC** operation on the first line allocates memory equal in size to field elemSize specified in factor two and places the pointer of this newly allocated memory in field next@. As we go through this code, go back to our picture of the

initial design. Since next@ is always pointing to the next element, after we allocate new storage for this element on hand, we store that address in elemptr (remember this is the field that points to the last element in the link list) and then reset next@ back to *NULL. This is now the last element and it points to nothing.

2. Next, we get the length of the car information which we are just about ready to store so that we can allocate the exact required memory and not waste any of it. This is done with the **ALLOC** operation code on the following line.

3. Finally, we store the car information and return to the main subprocedure.

4. The other two procedures, DisplayCar and RemoveCar, do not require any parameters to be passed to them. The DisplayCar procedure starts by saving the elemptr field in a temporary field so we do not lose track of the last element in the linked list. Then the DisplayCar procedure assigns the top of the list to it the elemptr field.

5. The next step is to go element-by-element through the linked list and display its content. This is done by retrieving the car information values and using the **DSPLY** op-code to display it out to the screen. Once it is displayed, the next@ pointer, which points to the next element, is used to jump to the next element and print it and so on, until we get to next@ being null, in which case we go to the end of the list with the job accomplished.

6. The last procedure, RemoveCar, starts by saving the pointer elemptr in a temporary field so that we do not lose track of the last element in the linked list. We then reset it to the address of the top of the list. Remember that the top of the list does not contain the first element, but rather it points to the first element with the field next@.

7. The next line of code assigns the value next@ to elemptr to point to the element to be removed. We start by removing the car information and clearing up the storage; then we save the next@ pointer so that, once we remove the element, we are able to reconnect it to the top of the list.

8. Then we deallocate the storage being pointed to by clemptr.

9. Finally we reset elemptr to the top of the list and re-establish the connection with the saved pointer in Top@.

10. The last thing we do is recover the elemptr saved value to make it point back to the last element in the list.

That's it! Yes, RPG does have the same capability for dynamically allocating storage like Java's Vector class. However, as you have seen, many more steps in RPG in order to simulate what Java provides. Then again, an enterprising person could write and sell a generic Vector service program, written in RPG IV (via procedures and memory allocation op-codes) and supporting all methods found in Java's Vector class.

PARAMETER PASSING

How do you pass arrays as a parameter? Or can you do that in RPG and Java? The answer is yes you can, for both languages. The only difference between the two languages is whether they allow passing arrays by value, reference, or both. *Pass by value* would mean that the calling program passes the array and its values to a called procedure. If the called procedure alters the values of the array, the original values in the calling program will not be affected. This is not the case for *pass by reference,* where the address of the array is passed to the called procedure and, therefore, any alteration to the array values will be reflected in the original program.

Let's take a look at RPG IV, where both call by value and reference are allowed. The following example illustrates pass by value:

LISTING 6-19

```
 D Week            S             9A   DIM(7) CTDATA PERRCD(1)
 D PASSBYV         PR
 D                               9A   DIM(7) VALUE
   *
 D i               S             1P 0 INZ(1)
   *
 C                 DOW      i<=7
 C     Week(i)     DSPLY
 C                 ADD      1              i
 C                 ENDDO
 C                 CALLP    PASSBYV(Week)
 C                 MOVE     1              i
 C                 DOW      i<=7
 C     Week(i)     DSPLY
 C                 ADD      1              i
 C                 ENDDO
 C                 ADD      1              i
 C                 ENDDO
 C                 MOVE     *ON            *INLR
 P PASSBYV         B
 D                 PI
 D weekp                         9A   DIM(7) VALUE
 C                 DOW      i<=7
 C                 Move     *Blanks        weekp(i)
 C                 ENDDO
 P                 E
** CTDATA week
 Monday
 Tuesday
 Wednesday
 Thursday
 Friday
 Saturday
 Sunday
```

In this example we declare an array, Week, to be a compile time array. As you can see, in the prototype definition, the keyword **VALUE** is specified to indicate passing by value. In this example, we initialize the array to the days of week and we first start by displaying the values in the array before we call the procedure to indicate the initialization value. Once we do that, we call the procedure PASSBYV, which is defined in the same example. In the procedure, we try to clear out the array values by moving blanks to it. Once the call is returned to the caller, we do the same loop to display the content on the array. You will notice that the original values of the array are unchanged, as expected since the array was passed by **VALUE.**

This would not be the case if we simply removed the keyword **VALUE** from the previous example. This one slight change would suddenly make the clearing of the array in the procedure affect the array in the mainline code, such that the second displaying of the elements would result in all blanks. Usage of **VALUE** or not in RPG affects all parameter types the same way, whether they are arrays or not.

In Java this is not the case. As we mentioned in Chapter 2, Java does not support pointers. Therefore, Java methods normally cannot change a parameter's value. In other words, Java normally passes parameters to methods using ***pass by value,*** similar to indicating the **VALUE** keyword for RPG parameter passing. As it turns out, Java does pass non-primitive types such as objects, arrays, and vectors, by reference. This lets the method change the content of the parameter. If you like, you can even think of the object *reference* itself as being passed by value as well. That is, object reference variables are, after all, memory addresses. Therefore, when you pass an object- including an array which after all is an object- you are passing a memory address. That address itself is passed by value, and so if you reset the object to which the variable points, perhaps by equating it to another object or a new object created with the **new** operator, that address change will *not* be reflected in the calling code. However, any changes made to the object the variable points to, by invoking methods on the object or changing elements in an array, *are* reflected to the caller.

Here is an example to illustrate all of this:

LISTING 6-20

```java
public class TestArrayParameters
{
    public static void main(String args[])
    {
        int arrayBefore[] = { 1,2,3,4,5 };
        printElements("before", arrayBefore);
        changeArrayElements(arrayBefore);
        printElements("after element changes ", arrayBefore);
        changeArrayReference(arrayBefore);
        printElements("after reference change", arrayBefore);
    }
    public static void changeArrayElements(int givenArray[])
    {
        for (int idx = 0; idx < givenArray.length; idx++)
            givenArray[idx] *= 10;
        return;
    }
    public static void changeArrayReference(int givenArray[])
    {
        givenArray = new int[5];
        return;
    }
    public static void printElements(String prompt, int array[])
    {
        System.out.print(prompt + ": ");
        for (int idx = 0; idx < array.length; idx++)
            System.out.print(array[idx] + " ");
        System.out.println();
    }
} // end TestArrayParameters class
```

The example has a main method that first declares an array called arrayBefore and initializes to a set of five numbers. Next, we print the values as we did with the RPG example to show that initialization worked as expected, but we do this by calling a little helper method called printElements, which is shown at the bottom of the class. Next, we call another supplied method called changeArrayElements which, as you can see, changes each element by multiplying it by ten. To see if that affected our mainline array, we then call printElements again. Next we call another supplied method called changeArrayReference. This method changes not the elements this time, but the actual array variable itself, pointing it to an entirely new array. If this affects the calling code, then we would expect our last call to printElements to show all zeros since it is a new array. Here is the result of running this test case:

```
C:\JAVA>javac TestArrayParameters.java
C:\JAVA>java TestArrayParameters
before: 1 2 3 4 5
```

```
after element changes : 10 20 30 40 50
after reference change: 10 20 30 40 50
```

We see that our call to changeArrayElements did in fact change the contents of our array in the mainline code. However, the call to changeArrayReference had no affect on our mainline array variable arrayBefore- it still points to the same array in memory as it did before the call. Thus, we see array contents can be changed, but array addresses cannot be changed. Again, the address of the array itself is passed by value.

Using Arrays Instead of Primitives for Simulated Pass By Reference

Remember that primitive values like integers are always passed by value in Java. That means you cannot write a method to swap the values of two integer variables, for example. The swap will have no affect on the caller's values of those variables. *Pass by value* effectively means a copy of the parameter values is passed to the method. However, we see one possible circumvention for this: Instead of passing primitive values, we could pass array objects- arrays with only one element, since we have just seen that array elements can be effectively changed by methods. Here, then, is a swap method that works in Java:

LISTING 6-21

```
public class TestSwap
{
    public static void main(String args[])
    {
        int value1 = 10;
        int value2 = 20;
        int value1Array[] = new int[1];
        int value2Array[] = new int[1];
        value1Array[0] = value1;
        value2Array[0] = value2;
        System.out.println("value1 = " + value1 + ", value2 = " + value2);
        swap(value1Array, value2Array);
        value1 = value1Array[0];
        value2 = value2Array[0];
        System.out.println("value1 = " + value1 + ", value2 = " + value2);

    }
    public static void swap(int value1[], int value2[])
    {
        int temp = value1[0];
        value1[0] = value2[0];
        value2[0] = temp;
        return;
    }
} // end TestSwap class
```

The important method here is swap, which takes two single-element arrays and swaps the first element of each. The trick to using this method with primitive values is to first move those values into the first element of a couple of arrays created for this purpose and then, after calling swap with those arrays, moving the values back into the primitive variables from the arrays. This is shown in the main method of our example. While this is not a pretty thing to have to do, it *does* work, as you see in the following output:

```
C:\JAVA>java TestSwap
value1 = 10, value2 = 20
value1 = 20, value2 = 10
```

SUMMARY

- Arrays, vectors, and strings are objects in Java.

- RPG has three kinds of arrays: compile time, pre-runtime, and runtime.

- Java has two kinds of arrays: compile time and runtime.

- RPG does not support multiple-dimension arrays, only those with one dimension.

- Java does support multiple-dimensional arrays as well as unbalanced arrays.

- The main rule for unbalanced arrays is to define them left to right.

- Vectors in Java can shrink and grow on demand.

- RPG IV supports new dynamic allocation of memory as well as pointer data type.

- Parameters are passed by value in Java, whereas in RPG they are passed by reference by default.

- To circumvent the pass by value problem for primitive type variables, you can use single element arrays.

7

String Manipulation

INTRODUCTION

In Chapter 5 we talked about primitive data types, and one of them was the char (character) type. We mentioned that you can create a string using an array of type char. However, Java has a better way of dealing with strings—the String class in the java.lang package, which is always imported and hence always available to you. Throughout the book you already have seen examples that use this String class, so now we will discuss it in more detail, as well as the methods that are supplied with it.

Why does Java use a class for strings instead of a built-in data type? This is because built-in data types or primitives are restricted to the few operators built into the language for math and manipulation purposes (like + and -). We spend so much of our time preparing, converting to and from, manipulating, and querying strings, that you gain significant programmer productivity from a class (versus a built-in primitive data type) given all the methods that can be supplied with it for common string operations.

For example, how many times have you written justification, trimming, and conversion code for text strings? Why not have language supplied methods to save us the drudgery. In RPG, such language-supplied functionality is given in the form of op-codes and built-in functions. In an object-oriented language, it comes in the form of methods on a simple self-contained class. Indeed, it is through string classes in object-oriented languages that we first start to appreciate the power and elegance of objects. This great ability to encapsulate useful methods or functions that are commonly needed by programmers into a class data type drives home the potential of objects and OO.

JAVA STRING BASICS AND PITFALLS

An important note about strings in Java is that the language designers relaxed slightly their strict object-oriented rules to allow strings to be concatenated directly with a built-in operator- the "plus" operator (+). They also allow an intuitive means of instantiating strings that does not force you to use formal object instantiation syntax. This underlies the importance of strings and string manipulation to every programmer and their invariable prominence in every program. The more intuitive and convenient it is to use strings in a language, the more accepted that language is by programmers. Certainly, Java's goal is to "keep it simple." If you prefer to stick to the rules, then that is acceptable, too. In other words, if you prefer to instantiate a string in the formal way and use a method call, concat(), to concatenate two strings versus the (+) operator, that is also acceptable. For example, you can use an intuitive style like this:

```
String text1 =  "George";
String text2 =  "Phil";
String finalText = text1 + " and " + text2;
System.out.println(finalText);
```

You can also use a formal style like this:

```
String text1 = new String("George");
String text2 = new String("Phil");
String finalText = new String(text1);
finalText = finalText.concat(" and ");
finalText = finalText.concat(text2);
System.out.println(finalText);
```

The output of both examples is "George and Phil," as you would expect. In these examples you see that there are two ways to initialize strings- by implicitly equating them to string literals or by explicitly allocating an instance of the String class using the **new** operator. Once you create your strings, you can manipulate them by using the many methods supplied with the String class. These samples also highlight the two means of adding strings together in Java, either via the intuitive (+) operator or via the concat method of the String class, as we described. Note that in the latter, the string passed as a parameter is appended to the string represented by the String object. However, the actual String target object is not affected. Rather, a new String object is created and returned. Thus, the method call has no side effects. Can you guess the output of the following?

```
String finalText = "George";
finalText.concat("and Phil");
System.out.println(finalText);
```

The answer is "George," not "George and Phil" as you might initially expect. Do not get caught by this common mistake. Another important consideration is string equality in Java. You cannot use the equality operator (==) to compare two string objects, as in:

```
if (text1 == text2)
```

Rather, you must use the method "equals" to do this, which returns **true** if the target string and the passed in string are equivalent, as in:

```
if (text1.equals(text2)) ...
```

This is the single, most commonly made mistake when using the String class. The problem is that the use of natural instantiation and the plus operator for concatenation tend to make you think of strings as primitive data types in Java. But they are actually objects of the String class- that is, object reference variables. Like all object reference variables, they actually contain a memory address of the class instance, and as such, the equality operator only tells you if the two variables refer to the same address, which they almost never do. The operator does not have the intelligence to make an intelligent "if all characters are the same and the strings are the same length" comparison. Rather, the code inside the equals method is required for this. Note that you are all the more prone to this pitfall as an RPG IV programmer, because RPG IV has a free-form **IF** operation code syntax that does allow you to compare two strings (alphabetic fields) using the equality operator, as in:

```
IF          STRING1  =  STRING2
```

You must take care in your Java coding to avoid this nasty bug, as you will not notice it for a while, given that the compiler will not complain about it. Equality testing of object references is legal, after all, for those cases when you want to know if two variables actually do refer to the same allocated instance in memory.

STRINGS IN RPG

RPG does not have a pure string data type similar to the String class in Java. In RPG, you can define a field as a fixed-length character field or declare an array of fixed-length character field elements:

LISTING 7-1

```
  Dmystring        S            40A    INZ('AnnaLisa')
  Dmystring2       S            10A    DIM(20)
```

In this example the first field, `mystring`, is defined as a 40-character fixed-length field, and is initialized to an initial value of `AnnaLisa` using the **INZ** keyword. The second example declares an array of 20-character elements, each 10 characters in length. This example in RPG is similar to declaring and instantiating a string object in Java. The main difference is that in Java you use methods supplied by the `String` class to manipulate the string object, compared to the RPG string operation codes and built-in functions supplied as part of the RPG language.

As you will see, Java has many more methods to facilitate string manipulation than RPG has op-codes. The following table compares all available string manipulation operation codes in RPG IV to those methods available in Java. Java offers more functionality than shown here, and we will get to that additional functionality shortly.

RPG Op-code	RPG Built-in	Description	Java Method(s)
CAT (or '+' operator)		Concatenate two strings	concat(string) OR '+' operator
SUBST	%SUBST	Extract a substring from a string	substring(int start, int end) OR substring(int start)
SCAN	%SCAN	Scan for a substring	indexOf()
	%TRIM	Trim begin, end blanks	trim()
	%LEN	Return length of string	length()
XLATE		Translate a string	Not Available
CHECK		Check for characters	Not Available
CHECKR		Check in reverse	Not Available
	%TRIML	Trim leading blanks	Not Available
	%TRIMR	Trim trailing blanks	Not Available
	%CHAR	New in V4R2. Converts various types to an outputable string.	valueOf(datatype value) method in String class
	%REPLACE	New in V4R2. Allows replacement of a substring with another.	Not Available

STRING MANIPULATION

The next few sections will examine each of the operations listed in the table and give examples of them for both RPG and Java. In the case where there is no matching method in Java, like in the case of **XLATE** and **CHECK**, we will show you how to write a method yourself to simulate the function.

Concatenation

We start with string concatenation for both RPG and Java, looking at an example to illustrate the use of this function. Let's say that you have two fields: one field that contains a person's first name and a field that contains his last name. You need to concatenate both together and print out the result. This is easy to do in both languages since both have support for concatenating strings. In RPG, we use the **CAT** operation code, as in:

LISTING 7-2

```
D  first                 S             10A    INZ('Mike')
D  last                  S             10A    INZ('Smith')
D  name                  S             20A    INZ(' ')
C          first    CAT       last:1        name
C          name     DSPLY
C                   MOVE      *ON           *INLR
```

In this example we use two fields, `first` to represent the first name and `last` to represent the last name. We declare and initialize these fields right on the D-spec. However, in more complex applications these fields may be read from the screen or from a file on disk. They can even be passed in via the command line. In the C-spec we use the **CAT** operation code to concatenate field `first` to field `last` in factors one and two. The result of the concatenation is placed in the field called `name` which is specified in the result column. Notice also that we specify `:1` in factor two in order to tell the compiler to insert one blank between the field values when concatenating them. The **DSPLY** operation code displays the value of name, which is "`Mike Smith,`" as we would expect.

The following illustrates the same example written in Java:

LISTING 7-3

```
public class Cat
{
    public static void main(String args[])
    {
        String first, last, name;
        first = "Mike ";
        last  = "Smith";
        name = first.concat(last);
        System.out.println("The name is: " + name);
    }
} // end class Cat
```

219

In this case, we use the `String` object to declare all our string variables, namely: `first`, `last`, and `name`. As we discussed earlier, by declaring the string variables and initializing them, all three string objects are created and initialized (that is, no **new** keyword is required to instantiate the object). Then we can use the `concat` method to append `last` to `first`. Notice that `first` is used as the object in the call to the `concat` method and `last` is used as the parameter to `concat`. The result of the operation is placed in the `name` variable. Then we display the result using the `println` method.

Did you notice another concatenation in the previous example? If you answered "yes", you have a sharp eye. In the `println` method we concatenated the string literal "The name is :" to the object reference variable `name` using the (**+**) operator. This is another way of concatenating two strings. In fact, this is a fast way of concatenating two strings in an expression for both RPG and Java. RPG supports the same (**+**) operator for concatenation in an expression. The following table replaces the **CAT** operation code of the previous example with the **EVAL** op-code, and the *concat* Java method with the (**+**) operator as well:

RPG IV			Java
C	EVAL	name = first + ' ' + last	name = first + " " + last;

Clearly, the use of the plus operator is a plus for programmers!

Substring

Next, let's take a look at the substring operation code in RPG and the corresponding substring method in Java. In RPG, you use the **SUBST** operation code to extract a substring from a string starting at a specified location for a specified length, as in this example:

LISTING 7-4

```
D*                                        12345678901234567890123456789
DWhyJava         S             30A    INZ('Because Java is for RPG pgmrs')
D  first         S             10A    VARYING
D  second        S             10A    VARYING
D  third         S             10A    VARYING
D  sayWhat       S             30A
D*-------------------------------------------------------------------
C     4           SUBST         WhyJava:9      first
C     6           SUBST         WhyJava:14     second
C     3           SUBST         whyJava:21     third
C                 EVAL          sayWhat = first + ' ' + second + ' ' + third
C     sayWhat     DSPLY
C                 MOVE          *ON            *INLR
```

In this example, we take a string with the value "`Because Java is for RPG pgmrs`" and retrieve different strings from it to make up the string "`Java is for RPG`". To do this, we declare three different character fields and a field to store the results. As the example illustrates, the **SUBST** operation code takes the number of characters to substring in factor one, and in factor two, the source as well as the starting position for the retrieval. For example, the first **SUBST** operation receives the value `Java` and places it in the result field first. When we retrieve all of the values, we use the concatenation operator to concatenate all fields. Finally, we display the result of the field using the **DSPLY** operation code. The result is "`Java is for RPG`."

The following example illustrates an equivalent example, written in Java, using the `substring` method of the `String` class:

LISTING 7-5

```
public class Substring
{
    public static void main(String args[])
    {
        String whyJava, first, second, third, sayWhat;
        //          01234567890123456789012345678901234
        whyJava = "Because Java is for RPG Programmers";
        first   = whyJava.substring(8,12);
        second  = whyJava.substring(13,19);
        third   = whyJava.substring(20,23);
        sayWhat = first + " " + second + " " + third;
        System.out.println(sayWhat);
    }
} // end class Substring
```

The parameters for the `substring` method have the beginning index value as the first parameter and the ending index as the second parameter. But be careful! There are two important "gotcha"s to note in regard to this method:

- The parameters are zero-based, not one-based as in RPG.
- The second parameter is one past the actual ending position you want.

Otherwise, the logic here is similar to RPG's and easy enough to follow. There is also a second version of the `substring` method, which takes as input only one parameter- the starting position (again, zero-based). This returns a string containing all characters from that starting position until the end of the target string.

In RPG IV you can also use the `%SUBST` built-in function to accomplish the same thing in expressions. The syntax of this is `%SUBST(string:start{:length})`. The parameters are the same as the op-code `SUBST`, as you see in the following example:

```
%SUBST('RPG USERS':5:5)
%SUBST('RPG USERS':5)
```

In both cases, the result is "USERS". Note the similarities to Java's `substring` method, notwithstanding the "gotcha"s mentioned. Also note that RPG's op-code and built-in require you to specify the target string to be substringed, whereas in Java that is specified as the target object variable to the left of the dot operator. Again, with objects, you start with an object and invoke methods on it, whereas in RPG all functions require the target as a parameter.

Searching For a SubString

One of the more commonly used functions in almost all languages is the ability to search one string for the occurrence of another. For example, you may have a string like "The amount paid is $100". In this case you want to find out where in the string is the amount entered. In this case, you may choose to search for the dollar sign ($) character. Once you know this, you can simply extract the characters found after it. You can determine this using the `SCAN` operation code, as the following illustrates:

LISTING 7-6

```
D*                                  12345678901234567891
Dstr            S           40A   INZ('Java is for RPG users')
Didx            S           3P 0
D*
C    'RPG'      SCAN        str              idx
C    idx        DSPLY
C               EVAL        *INLR = *ON
```

In this example, we define a string field called `str` and we initialize it to "Java is for RPG users". We find the location of the substring "RPG" in the main string, placing the desired substring in factor one, the source string in factor two, and the resulting field to contain the numeric index value in the result column. When the operation is executed, `idx` will contain the position where the substring was found, which is 13 in our example. Note that RPG allows you to specify the start location for the search in the second part of factor two. If the start location is not specified, as in this example, the default is to start at the first character.

For Java, this is a simple operation as it supplies an `indexOf` method in its `String` class:

LISTING 7-7

```
public class Scan
{
    public static void main(String args[])
    {
        //                    012345678901234567890
        String str = new String("Java is for RPG users");
        int idx = str.indexOf("RPG");
        System.out.println("RPG occurs at: " + idx);
    }
}
```

This method takes one or two parameters. The first one is the string we are looking for, and the optional second is the start location of the search (the character position). Again, this is a zero-based position, not a one-based position as it is for RPG. If we do not specify the start location, as with RPG, the default start value will be set to the first character position (that is, zero). In our example the value that is printed is 12 (zero-based, again, so 12 is the thirteenth character).

In addition to `indexOf`, Java also supplies a handy `lastIndexOf` method, which will search backwards for a given substring. Again, it has an optional second parameter for specifying where to start the search, but this time the search continues backward from that start position.

Finally, both `indexOf` and `lastIndexOf` support either a string parameter as we have seen, or a single character parameter when searching for an individual character, as in:

```
int dollarPos = myString.indexOf('$');
```

Trimming Blanks

Trimming is the process of removing leading or trailing blanks from a string, and both languages have built-in support for it. For RPG there are both op-codes and built-ins:

LISTING 7-8

```
DName++++++++++ETDsFrom+++To/L+++IDc.Keywords+++++++++++++++++++
D leftright      S              40A   INZ('      Java is for
D                                     RPG users         ')
D temp           S              45A
C*
C                   EVAL      leftright = %TRIM(leftright)
C     leftright     DSPLY
C                   MOVE      *ON           *INLR
```

The example illustrates the built-in function available in RPG for trimming. In this example, we use %TRIM on the EVAL operation code to trim both leading and trailing blanks in the field leftright. After the operation, the field contains "Java is for RPG users".

In Java this task is also easy to accomplish, using the appropriately named trim() method:

LISTING 7-9

```
public class TrimString
{
    public static void main(String args[])
    {
        String str = "    Java is for RPG users    ";
        str = str.trim();
        System.out.println("Trimmed: '" + str + "'");
    }
}
```

The result, again, is "Trimmed: 'Java is for RPG users'".

Easy stuff. However, what if you only want to remove leading blanks? Or trailing blanks? In RPG it is very easy, since the language supports two additional built-ins, %TRIML and %TRIMR for trimming left (leading) and right (trailing) blanks. However, Java has only the trim() method, and unfortunately, no triml and trimr methods. It is not brain surgery or VCR programming to write your own code to do this, however, and we will do so by the end of the chapter.

Determining String Lengths

Determining the length of a string, to decide if it is empty or needs truncation or padding, is a simple task in both languages. In RPG IV, you simply use the %LEN built-in function, specifying a field or string literal as a parameter. In Java, again with a String object, you invoke the length() method. Both return an integer indicating the length of the string.

Remember that in Java, characters are two bytes long, because they are Unicode characters. Therefore, the length returned by the length() method is the number of characters, not the number of bytes-the latter is actually two times the former. All String class methods that take or return an index number deals with the character position, not the byte offset, so you rarely need to worry about the fact that characters are two bytes long.

Translating Characters

So far we have compared RPG operation codes to *available* Java methods. As you see from the table earlier in this chapter, there are a few RPG operation codes or built-ins that are simply not available in Java. One example of this is the **XLATE** operation code in RPG, which has no apparent equivalent in Java, at least not yet. What to do in this case? Write your own method! First, let's review the RPG support. The following shows an example of the RPG **XLATE** operation code.

LISTING 7-10

```
D  from                    C                        'GPR4'
D*
D  to                      C                        'VAJA'
D*
D  string                          4A               INZ('RPG4')
D  target                          4A
D*-------------------------------------------------------------
C          from:to    XLATE        string           target
C          target     DSPLY
C                     MOVE         *ON              *INLR
```

As you know, **XLATE** translates the source string in factor two to another sequence of characters, depending on the *from* and *to* strings specified in factor one. The result of this translation is placed in the result field. In particular, all characters in the *source* string with a match in the *from* string are translated to the corresponding characters in the *to* string. The rules are that the lengths of the *from* and *to* strings must be the same, and the lengths of the string variables in factors one and two must be the same. In the example, we are translating R to a J, P to an A, G to a V, and 4 to an A respectively. We supply the value RPG4 in the source string specified in factor two and the result is JAVA after the operation.

Java has no corresponding method in its String class, but it does have a related method called replace, which takes two character parameters as input. It replaces all occurrences of the first character in the target string object with the second character. It sounds similar to RPG's **XLATE,** except that replace only replaces a single character, not a string of characters. Not to worry-what we will do is write our own Java method that emulates RPG's **XLATE** op-code by using the replace method repeatedly-once for each character in a given string of *from* characters.

What is interesting is that we cannot *extend* String (which we talk about in a later chapter) because the Java language designers made it *final,* preventing this. Thus, our String augmentation methods like this will be created as traditional "stand alone" functions-that is, they will be defined as **static**, and take as parameters whatever they need. But even **static** methods must exist in a class, so we create them in an arbitrary class.

Here, then is our Java equivalent to RPG's **XLATE** op-code (for consistency, we call our method xlate):

LISTING 7-11

```
public class RPGString
{
    public static String xlate(String source,  String fromChars,
                             String toChars, int     start)
    {
        String resultString;
        // minimal input error checking
        if (fromChars.length() != toChars.length())
          return new String("BAD INPUT!");
        if (start > source.length() || start < 0)
          return new String("BAD INPUT!");
        // first off, get the substring to be xlated...
        resultString = source.substring(start);
        // now, xlate each char in fromChars to same pos in toChars
        for (int i = 0; i < fromChars.length(); i++)
            resultString = resultString.replace(fromChars.charAt(i),
                                            toChars.charAt(i));
        // now append xlated part to non-xlated part
        resultString = source.substring(0,start) + resultString;
        return resultString;
    } // end xlate method
    public static String xlate(String source,  String fromChars,
                             String toChars)
    {
        return xlate(source, fromChars, toChars, 0);
    } // end xlate method two
} // end RPGString class
```

The required parameters are, of course, the *source* string to be translated, followed by the *from* and *to* strings, and finally the *start position,* where the translation should start. To be consistent with Java's string methods, this start position is zero-based. In order to be consistent with RPG, we want the start position value to be optional, defaulting to the first character if not passed. To support an optional parameter at the end of the parameter list in a Java method, we simply supply a second method with the same name that does not specify or accept that last parameter, which we have done, as you can see in the preceding example. This second *overloaded* method can simply call the first full version of the method and pass in the default value for the missing parameter. Recall that *overloaded* means that this method has the same name as another method in the same class, but takes a different number of parameters-that is, it has a different ***signature***. In our case, this is zero for the first character.

The code in the first and primary `xlate` method is reasonably straightforward-we first check to make sure the input is valid, then we create a substring of the source that excludes the characters before the given start position. Next, for every character in the *from* string, we use the `String` class `replace` method to replace all occurrences of that character with the character in the corresponding position of the *to* string. Finally, we append that to the substring of the source up to the *start* position and **return** this resulting string.

NOTE: In order to get an individual character out of a string, you must use the `charAt` method and supply the zero-based index of the character you want.

To test this, we write a little test case "harness" class that contains a `main` method so that we can call it from the command line and see the results. This idea of supplying test classes for each of your handwritten classes is a good idea, by the way. This way you can build up a testcase suite for regression testing purposes, but not include these classes in your shipped code. Further, they offer a good example of how to use your classes. Here then is our testcase which tests both versions of the method-first *without* specifying a start position, and then *with* specifying a start position:

LISTING 7-12

```
public class TestRPGString
{
    public static void main(String args[])
    {
        //              "012345678901234567890";
        String src  = "RPGP is for you Juys!";
        String from = "RPG";
        String to   = "JAV";
        System.out.println("Input string  : '" + src + "'");
        src = RPGString.xlate(src, from, to);
        System.out.println("Output string1: '" + src + "'");
        from = "J";
        to   = "G";
        src = RPGString.xlate(src, from, to, 16);
        System.out.println("Output string2: '" + src + "'");
    }
}
```

The example translates the characters in RPG to the corresponding characters in "JAV," then translates the character J to the character G, starting at position 16 (again, zero-based). The final result after compiling both classes and then running the test class from the command line is:

```
C:\JAVA>javac TestRPGString.java
C:\JAVA>java TestRPGString
Input string  : 'RPGP is for you Juys!'
Output string1: 'JAVA is for you Juys!'
Output string2: 'JAVA is for you Guys!'
```

Translating Case

One function in which Java has a leg up on RPG is string translation to uppercase or lowercase. There is no language-supplied function for this in RPG, but there is for Java. However, we can accomplish this task in RPG using, once again, its **XLATE** op-code, supplying to it the required upper- or lowercase characters in the *to* string parameter, as in the following example:

LISTING 7-13

```
DName+++++++++++ETDsFrom+++To/L+++IDc.Keywords++++++++++++++++++++++++
************** Beginning of data **********************************
D Lower           C                   'abcdefghijklmnopqrstuvwxyz'
D*
D Upper           C                   'ABCDEFGHIJKLMNOPQRSTUVWXYZ'
D*
D WHAT            S             30A   INZ('Java is for rpg users')
C*
C       WHAT          DSPLY
C       Lower:Upper   XLATE     WHAT            WHAT
C       WHAT          DSPLY
C                     MOVE      *ON             *INLR
**************** End of data ****************************************
```

We define two named constant strings, Lower and Upper, to contain all the lowercase characters and their matching uppercase characters. To illustrate how this works, we define a field called WHAT containing the string "Java is for rpg users". As you see, the only uppercase character in this literal is the first character J. Next we use the **XLATE** operation code with the value `Lower:Upper` in factor one and the WHAT variable in the result column. After executing this operation, the result is the whole string in upper case.

In Java, converting strings from uppercase to lowercase and vice versa is even simpler, as Java supplies us with intuitive methods to do this. The first is toUpperCase, which translates the target String object to all uppercase. The second is toLowerCase, which translates the target String object to all lowercase. For example:

LISTING 7-14

```
public class Case
{
    public static void main(String args[])
    {
        String str = new String("Java is for RPG users");
        str = str.toUpperCase();
        System.out.println("String in uppercase: " + str);
        str = str.toLowerCase();
        System.out.println("String in lowercase: " + str);
    }
}
```

Compiling and running our example results in:

```
C:\JAVA>javac Case.java
C:\JAVA>java Case
String in uppercase: JAVA IS FOR RPG USERS
String in lowercase: java is for rpg users
```

> **NOTE:** Our RPG sample does not handle international characters, such as those containing a German umlaut, while the Java methods do. That is because Java characters are Unicode based so they inherently support international characters.

Checking for Characters

As with translating characters, RPG has language support to easily handle checking for the existence of characters, while Java does not have a supplied method. RPG has two op-codes, **CHECK** and **CHECKR**. These operations verify that each character in a given *search* string specified in factor one is among the characters in the *base* string specified in factor two. Each character in the given *search* string is compared with all of the characters specified in the base string. If a match exists, the next character is verified. However, if a match does not exist, then the index value indicating the position of the unmatched character in the search string is placed in the result field and the search is stopped. If a match is found for all characters in the search string, zero is returned in the result field. In the case of **CHECK**, verification of characters begins at the leftmost character, whereas for **CHECKR,** verification starts at the rightmost character. Here are two examples, one for **CHECK** and the other one for **CHECKR:**

LISTING 7-15

```
D*
D   numbers              C                          '0123456789'
D*
D   base                          7A
D*----------------------------------------------------------------
C                       MOVE      '*22300*'    base
C           numbers     CHECK     base:2       pos       3 0
C           pos         DSPLY
C           numbers     CHECKR    base:6       pos
C           pos         DSPLY
C                       MOVE      *ON          *INLR
```

Checking characters is most commonly used to check if a numeric field contains alphanumeric characters or vice-versa. In this example, we check to see if a string of numeric digits contains any alphanumeric characters. We start by defining the set of numeric digits 0-9 and storing them in the field numbers. The first **MOVE** operation moves the string "*22300*" into the base field that we would like to check. After executing the **CHECK** operation, the value in the result field is 7. It is not 1, as you may have expected, because the second part of factor two, which is the start position, contains 2. This tells the compiler to start verification at position 2. The following **CHECKR** operation code uses similar parameters as the **CHECK** op-code except that the start position is specified to be 6. Remember that for **CHECK** or **CHECKR** the start position is relative to the start of the string. The **CHECKR** operation code, unlike the **CHECK** operation, will start verification from the right of the rightmost side of the string. The result after executing the **CHECKR** is 1 in the pos result field. Note also that the result field for both operations can be a numeric array.

As we mentioned earlier, Java does *not* have methods similar to **CHECK** and **CHECKR** for character verification. As with character translation, we need to write our own methods to take care of this. The following example contains the code to accomplish character verification. (Notice that we use the same class name RPGString as in the previous example, thus building up a number of useful static string methods in this same class):

LISTING 7-16

```
public class RPGString
{
    public static int check(String search, String base, int start)
    {
        // minimal error checking
        if (start >= base.length() || start < 0)
          return -2;
        // scan each char of base for match in search...
        for (int idx = start; idx < base.length(); idx++)
            if (search.indexOf(base.charAt(idx)) == -1)
              return idx;
        // return constant indicating match found for all
        return -1;
    } // end check method
    public static int check(String search, String base)
    {
        return check(search, base, 0);
    } // end check method two
} // end RPGString class
```

We define two check methods to simulate RPG's **CHECK** operation code, one that takes a starting position index and one that does not. The latter simply calls the former with zero for the starting position. The algorithm first checks the validity of the input parameters, then scans each character in the given base string for an occurrence in the given search string. If all characters have a match, a special constant of -1 is returned. Otherwise, the index position of the first non-matching character in the base string is returned. To be consistent with Java String class methods, we accept a zero-based starting position and return a zero-based index position. Because of this, we cannot return zero when all characters match, as RPG does, because for us zero is a valid index position. For this reason we return -1.

Now we'll define a couple more very similar methods to simulate **CHECKR** with and without a starting position parameter:

LISTING 7-17

```
    public static int checkR(String search, String base, int start)
    {
        // minimal error checking
        if (start >= base.length() || start < 0)
          return -2;
        // scan each char of base for match in search...
        for (int idx = start; idx >= 0; idx--)
            if (search.indexOf(base.charAt(idx)) == -1)
              return idx;
        // return constant indicating match found for all
        return -1;
    } // end checkR method
    public static int checkR(String search, String base)
    {
        return checkR(search, base, base.length()-1);
    } // end checkR method two
```

These are similar to the check methods; the only changed lines are shown in bold in the example. Basically, we need to loop backwards through the base string, and we need to default to the last character position when no start position parameter is passed.

A class to test these methods now looks like this:

LISTING 7-18

```
public class TestCheck
{
   public static void main(String args[])
   {
      String digits = "0123456789";
      String test   = "*22300*";
      int     result;
      result = RPGString.check(digits, test);
      System.out.println("result is: " + result);
      result = RPGString.check(digits, test, 1);
      System.out.println("result is: " + result);
      result = RPGString.checkR(digits, test);
      System.out.println("result is: " + result);
      result = RPGString.checkR(digits, test, 5);
      System.out.println("result is: " + result);
   }
} // end TestCheck class
```

Compiling and running these now gives us:

LISTING 7-19

```
c:\JAVA>javac TestCheck.java
c:\JAVA>java TestCheck
result is: 0
result is: 6
result is: 6
result is: 0
```

232

PERFORMANCE CONSIDERATIONS: STRINGBUFFER CLASS

Recall our discussion at the beginning of the chapter about the `concat` method, and how it does not affect the `String` object on which you invoke it, but rather returns a new `String` object. You have seen that this is also true of other string manipulation methods like `toUpperCase` and `replace`. This is because the `String` class is ***immutable*** — that is, you cannot change a `String` object, you can only use methods that return new `String` objects. The original string object in many cases is no longer used and is swept up later by the garbage collector.

This read-only behavior of strings can have performance implications for calculations that do a lot of string manipulating. For example, this is true of any code that builds up a string by concatenating characters inside a loop. For this reason Java supplies a second string class called `StringBuffer` that is ***mutable***-that is, it can be changed directly using supplied methods. This class is completely independent of the `String` class. That is, although some methods are common between the two, `StringBuffer` also has its own unique set of methods for altering the object directly, which we will shortly explore.

If you need to dynamically change the strings in your method, then you should use `StringBuffer` versus `String`. Both classes support methods to convert back and forth between them. For example, you can use a `StringBuffer` object to do your string manipulation, and then, once the string is complete, convert it back to a `String` object using the `toString` method supplied in `StringBuffer` for this purpose. In fact, this conversion back and forth between `String` and `StringBuffer` classes has the added advantage of allowing you to use methods available in both classes by simply converting from one class to the other. You will almost always want to accept and return `String` objects, not `StringBuffer` objects, from your methods, so this conversion is often done at the beginning and end of your method. For example, methods for significant string manipulations might follow this format:

```
public String workOnString(String input)
{
    StringBuffer workString = new StringBuffer(input);
    // do manipulation work on the workString variable
    return workString.toString();
}
```

In contrast to Java, you can use the new dynamic allocation of storage in RPG IV to allocate, de-allocate, or reallocate strings. In RPG, if you do not use pointers and dynamic allocation of storage with the three operation codes **ALLOC**, **DEALLOC**, and **REALLOC**, then the character fields you declare are fixed in length just as they are with the `String` class. Note that you can at least change the contents of an RPG character field however, if the length is not affected. This is not valid in Java's `String` class. The use of RPG IV's memory allocation op-codes has been discussed in length in the vector section in an earlier chapter, so we will not discuss it further here.

How do you declare a string using the `StringBuffer` class? You must use the formal way, with the **new** operator, optionally specifying a string literal or `String` object as input, as in:

```
StringBuffer aName = new StringBuffer("Angelica Farr");
```

There are no language extensions to allow intuitive instantiation like '= "this is a string"' as there are for `Strings`. Similarly, there are no language extensions for easy concatenation of `StringBuffer` objects using the plus sign as there are for `Strings` (mind you, usage of plus is allowed between `StringBuffer` objects inside the `System.out.println` parameter string as it is for all data types). To concatenate strings to a `StringBuffer` object, you use the `append` method:

```
StringBuffer quotedName = new StringBuffer("George");
quotedName.append(" and ").append("Phil");
```

Notice how this method does have a side effect on the object it works against, so you do not need to equate the result to another variable as you would with the `concat` method in the `String` class. This common method returns the current `StringBuffer` object so you can string together multiple method calls in one statement, as shown here. The `append` method is also convenient in that there are many overridden versions of it supporting all the primitive data types as the parameter, and conversion to a string literal is done for you. For example:

```
boolean flag = true;
StringBuffer output = new StringBuffer("flag value = ").append(flag);
System.out.println(output); // results in "flag value = true"
```

The `append` method also accepts `String` objects as input. In fact, it will accept any object as input! For objects, it simply calls the object's `toString` method to convert it to a string.

You do not always want to change your string by *appending* to it, sometimes you want to *insert* new strings into the middle of it. The `StringBuffer` class supports this with an `insert` method, with a number of overridden methods similar to `append`, allowing all manner of data types to be inserted after being converted to string format. All versions of the `insert` method take an integer insertion point index as the first parameter and the actual string or other data type to be inserted as the second parameter.

In addition to `append` and `insert`, there are `setChar` and `getChar` methods for changing a particular character value in place and retrieving the character value at a specified zero-based position. A method called `getChars` can return a substring, but in the form of a character array, not a `String`. This could, however, be converted to a `StringBuffer` by using the version of `append` or `insert` that accepts a character array as input.

234

There is also an interesting method called `reverse` that reverses the contents of the string, such that "Java" would become "avaJ." Presumably, there is a use for this somewhere!

`StringBuffer` objects support the notion of *capacity,* that is, a buffer length that is greater than or equal to the length of the string literal contained in the `StringBuffer`. Behind the scenes the `StringBuffer` class uses an array of characters to hold the string. The array is given an initial default size, and as the string grows the array often needs to be reallocated with a bigger size. This behind-the-scenes work is done for you, but there are methods to explicitly set the size (i.e., the capacity) of this buffer. You can thereby optimize performance by predicting the final size you will eventually require, minimizing the need for costly reallocations. It is by judicious use of capacity planning that you can most benefit from using a `StringBuffer` as a scratch pad to build up a computed string.

When instantiating an empty `StringBuffer`, you can specify the initial capacity by passing in an integer value, as in:

```
StringBuffer largeString = new StringBuffer(255);
```

Note that the default capacity for an empty `StringBuffer` object is 16. Aside from setting the initial capacity at instantiation time, you can also use the `ensureCapacity` method to ensure that the current buffer is at least as large as the number you pass as an argument. If it is not, the buffer size or capacity is grown to the size you specified. Despite the method name, `ensureCapacity` does not return a boolean value-in fact, it does not return anything. There is also a method for returning the current capacity, which is called `capacity`. It takes no arguments and returns an integer value.

While you have `ensureCapacity` and `capacity` methods for working with a `StringBuffer` object's buffer size, you also have `setLength` and `length` methods for working with the actual string's size. This is always less than or equal to the capacity. You can use `setLength` to grow or shrink the string's size, effectively padding it (with null characters which are hex zeros) or truncating it. Note that if you set the length of the string to be greater than the capacity, the capacity is automatically grown, just as it is when you grow a string past its capacity using `append`. On the other hand, if you truncate a string the capacity is not reduced.

To help you see the difference between capacity and length, here is an example:

LISTING 7-20

```java
public class TestStringBuffer
{
   public static void main(String args[])
   {
      StringBuffer test1 = new StringBuffer(20); // capacity
      test1.append("12345678901234567890"); // string
      System.out.println("String   = " + test1);
      System.out.println("Capacity = " + test1.capacity());
      System.out.println("Length   = " + test1.length());
      test1.setLength(50); // string length
      System.out.println("-----------------------------");
      System.out.println("String   = " + test1);
      System.out.println("Capacity = " + test1.capacity());
      System.out.println("Length   = " + test1.length());
      test1.setLength(10); // string length
      System.out.println("-----------------------------");
      System.out.println("String   = " + test1);
      System.out.println("Capacity = " + test1.capacity());
      System.out.println("Length   = " + test1.length());
   } // end main method
} // end TestStringBuffer class
```

The result of compiling and running this class is the following:

LISTING 7-21

```
C:\JAVA>javac TestStringBuffer.java
C:\JAVA>java  TestStringBuffer
String   = 12345678901234567890
Capacity = 20
Length   = 20
-----------------------------
String   = 12345678901234567890
Capacity = 50
Length   = 50
-----------------------------
String   = 1234567890
Capacity = 50
Length   = 10
```

Implementing TRIMR and TRIML in Java

Now let's go back to the trim operation and see how we can implement trim right and trim left in Java. We showed you in a previous section how both RPG and Java have built-in functions for simultaneously trimming both leading and trailing blanks. We also mentioned that RPG has built-in functions for explicitly stripping either trailing-only or leading-only blanks, using the **%TRIMR** and **%TRIML** functions. In Java, however, you must implement this functionality yourself if you need it, which we will do here. Let us first review an example of these built-in functions in RPG:

LISTING 7-22

```
DName++++++++++ETDsFrom+++To/L+++IDc.Keywords+++++++++++++++++++
D*
D input           S              16A   INZ('   Java for U   ')
D result          S              16A
C*
C                 EVAL      result = %TRIML(input) + '.'
C     result      DSPLY
C                 EVAL      result = %TRIMR(input) + '.'
C     result      DSPLY
C                 MOVE      *ON           *INLR
```

The input string is " Java for U ". Predictably, the result after **TRIML** is "Java for U .", and the result after **TRIMR** is " Java for U.". It is that easy to trim leading or trailing blanks in RPG since the language does directly support it.

Java, on the other hand, has no supplied methods in either its `String` or `StringBuffer` classes, so we must write our own. With the use of the `StringBuffer` class we previously covered, however, this is not very difficult. We will again create our two methods as **static,** we pass in as a parameter the string to operate on, and place the methods in an `RPGString` class. We call our two methods `trimr` and `triml` to be consistent with RPG. Because we will be doing a reasonable amount of manipulation on the strings, we start out in both cases by creating a `StringBuffer` temporary object from the given `String` object, and in both methods end by using the `toString` method of `StringBuffer` to convert our scratch pad object back to a `String` we can return.

The `trimr` method is the easiest, as we merely need to find that last non-blank character and truncate the `StringBuffer` at that point, using the `setLength` method to do this:

LISTING 7-23

```
public class RPGString
{
    public static String trimr(String input)
    {
        if (input.length() == 0) // error checking
          return input;
        StringBuffer temp = new StringBuffer(input);
        int idx;
        // find last non-blank character
        for (idx = temp.length()-1; temp.charAt(idx) == ' '; idx--);
        // truncate string
        temp.setLength(idx+1);
        return temp.toString();
    } // end trimr method
} // end RPGString class
```

The `triml` method is a little more complicated as it involves shifting the characters left, from the first non-blank character. This is best accomplished by brute force character-by-character copying, as we have discussed. The most efficient way to do this is to use a `StringBuffer` object that has been initialized to a sufficient capacity, as with the `temp2` variable in the following:

LISTING 7-24

```
    public static String triml(String input)
    {
        if (input.length() == 0) // error checking
          return input;
        StringBuffer temp1 = new StringBuffer(input);
        int idx, idx2;
        // find first non-blank character
        for (idx = 0; temp1.charAt(idx) == ' '; idx++);
        // copy characters to new object
        int newSize = temp1.length() - idx;
        StringBuffer temp2 = new StringBuffer(newSize);
        for (idx2 = 0; idx2 < newSize; idx2++, idx++)
           temp2.append(temp1.charAt(idx));
        return temp2.toString();
    } // end triml method
```

Once again, we write a simple little test case class to drive and demonstrate our new methods:

LISTING 7-25

```
public class TestTrim
{
   public static void main(String args[])
   {
      String test = "  Java is for RPG Programmers   ";
      String result;
      System.out.println("initially: '" + test + "'");
      result = RPGString.trimr(test);
      System.out.println("result is: '" + result + "'");
      result = RPGString.triml(result);
      System.out.println("result is: '" + result + "'");
   } // end main method
} // end TestTrim class
```

The result of compiling and running this is what we would expect:

```
initially: '  Java is for RPG Programmers   '
result is: '  Java is for RPG Programmers'
result is: 'Java is for RPG Programmers'
```

TOKENIZING STRINGS: THE STRINGTOKENIZER CLASS

Often when writing string parsing code we want to extract out individual words. Java recognizes this need and supplies a *utility* class in the java.util package, called StringTokenizer, that does this automatically. This is a good class to know about, as it can save significant coding effort in those cases where a word-by-word extraction of a given string is required. It is instantiated by specifying the String object to parse. Subsequent iteration through the words, or *tokens*, is accomplished by the two methods hasMoreTokens and nextToken, as shown here:

```
String sample = "Java for U";
StringTokenizer words = new StringTokenizer(sample);
while (words.hasMoreTokens())
   System.out.println("next word = " + words.nextToken());
```

This example results in:

```
next word = Java
next word = for
next word = U
```

What delimits or separates words or tokens? By default it is blank spaces, but this can be explicitly specified at instantiation time, by specifying all delimiting characters as a string. For example:

```
String sample = "Java, for U - and me";
StringTokenizer words = new StringTokenizer(sample, " ,-");
```

This example specifies three delimiter characters-blank, comma, and dash. You can also specify delimiters as part of the nextToken method call, in the event they are different per token.

This same functionality requires a little more work in RPG, as you have to write it yourself. However, the code is not so difficult:

LISTING 7-26

```
DName+++++++++++ETDsFrom+++To/L+++IDc.Keywords++++++++++++++++++++++
D formula         C                      'A * 2 / 3 - Num'
D tempstr         S            10A
D start           S             2P 0 INZ(1)
D end             S             2P 0 INZ(0)
C                   DOW       (start <= %LEN(formula))
C                   EVAL      end = %SCAN(' ':formula:start)
C                   IF        end = 0
C                    EVAL      end = %LEN(formula)+1
C                   ENDIF
C                   EVAL      tempstr=
C                               %SUBST(formula:start:end-start)
C     tempstr       DSPLY
C                   EVAL      start=end+1
C                   ENDDO
C                   MOVE      *ON              *INLR
```

Since you are a seasoned RPG programmer, we will not dissect this example, but rather leave that to you.

STRING CLASS: MORE METHODS

We have yet to discuss a number of remaining methods in the `String` class that offer additional functionality beyond what RPG supplies. Rather than describe them all, we leave them to your own discovery. However, here is a brief summary of some of the more interesting ones:

METHOD	DESCRIPTION
`compareTo(String)`	Compares two strings lexicographically.
`copyValueOf(char[],int,int)`	Returns a string that is equivalent to the specified character array.
`endsWith(String)`	Tests if this string ends with the specified suffix.
`equals(Object)`	Compares this string to the specified object.
`equalsIgnoreCase(String)`	Compares this string to another, ignoring case.
`getBytes()`	Convert this string into a byte array.
`getChars(int, int, char[], int)`	Copies characters from this substring into the destination character array, starting at the given offset.
`hashCode()`	Returns a hashcode for this string.
`intern()`	Returns a canonical representation for the String object, which enables very efficient string comparisons.
`regionMatches(boolean, int, String, int, int)`	Tests if two string regions are equal.
`regionMatches(int, String, int, int)`	Tests if two string regions are equal.
`startsWith(String)`	Tests if this string starts with the specified prefix.
`toCharArray()`	Converts this string to a new character array.
`toLowerCase(Locale)`	Converts all of the characters in this string to lowercase using the rules of the given locale.
`toUpperCase(Locale)`	Converts all of the w in this String to upper case using the rules of the given locale.
`valueOf(xxx)`	Takes as input a primitive data type value and converts it to a string.

We refer to the JDK documentation for the `java.lang.String` class for more detailed information.

SUMMARY

In this chapter, we strung together a number of loose strings. We hope we did not tie you in knots! We touched on the following:

- Strings are objects in Java, and instances of the String class.

- There is, however, built-in language support for defining and concatenating strings.

- To test for equality for strings, you do not use the equals operator (==) in Java. Rather, you use the equals method supplied as part of the String class.

- A number of String class methods offer similar functionality to RPG's string op-codes and built-ins. However, there is also some missing function relative to RPG, for which we have written our own code. On the other hand, strings in Java offer much new functionality.

- The StringBuffer class can be used to write efficient code for changing or manipulating strings. This is necessary because the String class is read-only, or immutable.

- The StringTokenizer class offers a quick and easy way to parse out words, or tokens, from a given string.

8

Date and Time Manipulation

INTRODUCTION

Functions that manipulate dates and times are among the most important in any application. These functions include retrieving the current date and time, and manipulations such as adding a duration to a date, subtracting a duration from a date, or formatting a date or time value. Both RPG and Java require this fundamental functionality, and both languages include "built-in" support for it.

RPG III Date and Time Review

Before RPG IV, RPG programmers had a special set of keywords to retrieve a date, day, month, or year. These are the **UDATE**, **UDAY**, **UMONTH**, and **UYEAR** keywords, respectively. In addition, to retrieve the time from the system, the **TIME** operation code was used with a variable in the result field. The specified variable (or field) could be six digits long (indicating that only the time should be retrieved), or twelve digits long (indicating that both the date and time should be retrieved).

In V2R2 of RPG III, IBM introduced a new set of keywords: ***DATE**, ***DAY**, ***MONTH**, and ***YEAR**. What did these keywords offer that the older ones did not? Have you heard of the year 2000 problem? If your answer to this question is *no*, we certainly do not want to be running your programs on January 1, 2000! (In case you're unaware of what the year 2000 problem is, it's covered later in this chapter.)

The main difference between these new keywords and their predecessors was support for four-digit *YEAR and *DATE fields. Given a four-digit field, they return the century portion of the date in addition to the year. For example, if the date is July 22, 1961, then *DATE returns 07221961, whereas UDATE returns 072261. The *DAY and *MONTH keywords are identical to UDAY and UMONTH, and were added simply to provide consistency with their predecessors. With this introduction of four-digit years to RPG, the TIME operation has also been modified to accept a field fourteen digits long. This tells the compiler that you want the century portion of the date retrieved, as well as the year.

RPG IV Date and Time Enhancements

All of the aforementioned date and time capabilities existed in the RPG language before the introduction of RPG IV. With RPG IV in V3R1, new data types were introduced, namely D, T, and Z (or Date, Time, and Timestamp, respectively). These are consistent with the same data types added to the database DDS languages in V2R1.1 of the operating system.

With this new set of data types, the language also added support for operation codes to allow the RPG programmer to easily manipulate dates and times. The ADDDUR and SUBDUR operations allow you to add and subtract a specific duration from a given date or time. The EXTRCT operation code allows you to extract a portion of a date or time from a field and place the result in the result field. In addition, the TEST operation code validates the contents of a date, time, or timestamp data type field. Further, RPG IV adds support for many known international date, time, and timestamp formats through keywords on the D (*Definition*) and H (*Header*) specifications. For example, you can tell the compiler that you want to use *DMY date format for day, month, year representation (dd/mm/yyyy). Or you can specify you want to use *USA format for month, day, and year representation (mm/dd/yyyy). We will cover this in more detail as we go.

Java Date and Time Support

What about Java? Java does supply you with some classes that are part of the JDK and that provide various methods to represent and manipulate dates and times. The main date, time, and timestamp classes are Date, SimpleDateFormat, GregorianCalendar, and Calendar. The Date, GregorianCalendar, and Calendar classes can be found in the java.util package supplied with the language, whereas the SimpleDateFormat class can be found in java.text package.

These classes come with a variety of useful methods that, in many cases, map to op-codes and function in the RPG IV language. For example, if your program calls the Date constructor with no arguments (that is, you *instantiate* an object of the Date class), the date is initialized with the current date and time. As it turns out, this is similar to using the TIME operation code in RPG IV with a result field fourteen digits long. These classes supply many other methods such as `getTime` to get the current time, or `get` to extract any part of the date or time. We will cover some of these methods in Java and show you, where appropriate, the corresponding or equivalent function supplied in RPG IV. In this chapter, we will show you some of the date and time capabilities of Java, which hint at the rich functionality it supports.

The Year 2000 Problem

Before we start discussing the differences in date and time functionality available in RPG and Java, let's briefly discuss the year 2000 problem. You must understand and avoid it before it is too late. (If you are reading this after January 1, 2000, then you can skip this section as presumably you have handled the problem already, right?)

The new millennium is approaching. It is time to ensure that all your applications are *Year 2000 ready*. What does this mean? In our environment, if you say "98" instead of "1998" to your fellow programmer or human (not to equate the two), most probably he or she would have no problem understanding what you mean. But what if you say "00"? As in: "the project will be done in 1Q00 (first quarter of the year 00)"? To many computer applications out in the industry today, it means trouble! Most applications as they are written today will interpret "00" to be the year 1900, not the year 2000.

Nearly all computer programming has taken place within the last twenty-five years. System designers, database designers, and programmers (in a shortsighted attempt to be efficient) designed many programs and databases to handle years with only two digits instead of four. Thus, it is possible a child born in the year 2000 will receive a pension check for his or her first birthday, or your grandmother or grandfather will get an invitation to join kindergarten, or your bank will suddenly make you a millionaire! (OK, so it may not be all bad.)

If you decide to move your existing applications to another language such as Java or to rewrite your existing applications in RPG IV, there are a few things you should think about. For example, do you know how to calculate a leap year? If you have not investigated this, your immediate answer might be the following algorithm: "if the year is divisible by four then it is a leap year." Guess what? This is incomplete and will cause problems. The accurate algorithm for calculating leap years is the following:

- Is the year a multiple of 400?
  If yes, it is a leap year. Just skip the following two steps.

- If not, then is the year a multiple of 100?
  If yes, then it is not a leap year. Skip the next step.

- Otherwise is the year a multiple of 4?
  If yes, then it is a leap year.

Luckily, Java provides a method in the GegorianCalendar class called isLeapYear() that returns **true** if the year passed to it as a parameter is a leap year, and returns **false** if it is not. We will show you an example of how you use this method later in this chapter. In the case of RPG, you would have to embed this list of criteria to check for in your application to ensure year 2000 compliance.

The first year in which programs may manifest a problem is the year 2000, since step one in the algorithm says that it is a multiple of 400. If your programs test the second and third conditions alone, then the year 2000 appears not to be a leap year because it is a multiple of 100. This was not a problem in the year 1600, since we did not have any programs or computers to worry about. (Ah, what *did* they do with their time back then?)

The effort to solve this problem is costing an enormous amount of money and time. While workers at IBM and other companies have tried to delay the year 2000 :-), the fact remains that time is running out. In fact, if there is one thing that may delay the widespread adoption of Java and other technologies by the AS/400 and business programming world, it is this not-so-small "diversion" that programmers are forced to deal with first.

Luckily, RPG (especially RPG IV) and, of course, Java support four-digit year variables for dates. The database added explicit support for this way back in V2R1.1. Even if you take your time adopting Java, we recommend that you accelerate plans for using RPG IV as a possible means of dealing with this problem with good programming language support.

The only warning we must add is that RPG does still have the two-digit year support through the **UDATE** and **UYEAR** keywords we mentioned earlier. Avoid using these keywords in new code, and where you have used them already, replace them with their ***DATE** and ***YEAR** equivalents.

> **NOTE:** IBM has a product to help with the AS/400 year 2000 conversion problem. The product is called BYPASS/2000, and information can be found at the IBM AS/400 software Web site **www.software.ibm.com/ad/as400**. Of course, there are numerous other tools out there that can help as well. Pick one if you have not already. But first, back to Java!

GET ME A DATE, AND GIVE ME THE TIME!

The most common way in which programs perform date and time manipulation is by getting the date and time from the system, or perhaps by reading a date from a database. How do we retrieve the date and time from the system with RPG and Java? The following illustrates this with an RPG example:

LISTING 8-1

```
C*
C          GETDATTME     BEGSR
C                        TIME                          DTTM    14 0
C                        ENDSR
```

As mentioned earlier, you use the **TIME** operation code to retrieve the time as well as the date. As you see in the above example, we create a simple subroutine that will retrieve the date and time and put them in the field DTTM. Notice the length of the field. We make the field of length fourteen so as to indicate to the system that we need not only the time, but the date as well. Also, this tells the compiler and the system that we require the date to have a four-digit year and not just two. (Recall our discussion about year 2000 problems! Get used to using four-digit years.)

On the other hand, as the following example illustrates, Java supplies you with the Date class that has many pre-written methods in it to retrieve and manipulate dates and times:

LISTING 8-2

```java
import java.util.*;
public class MyTime
{
    public static void main(String args[])
    {
        Date today = new Date();
        System.out.println("Time is: " + today);
    }
}
```

In this example, we define an object of type Date named today. After we define it, we use the object directly in the call to println, which results in something like "Time is: Tue Dec 16 16:44:52 GMT+00:00 1997." This is how you retrieve both the date and time in RPG and in Java. In the case of RPG, once you retrieve the date and time fields, you "manipulate" them by using the various supplied date- and time-specific op-codes. The same applies to Java applications, but instead of op-codes you use the supplied methods.

Next, we will examine the different techniques in both languages for manipulating and formatting date and time fields. But first, let's examine the one basic thing that all languages do to establish a base year from which all date and time manipulations are established.

BASE YEAR

Every computer contains a built-in clock as part of its hardware, which (surprise) keeps track of time. This clock is used by the CPU (*Central Processing Unit*) for hardware purposes, as well as by the operating system to establish the current date and time when you turn on your machine. In fact, if you have ever wondered how the clock stays accurate while your machine's main power supply is off, it typically uses a battery. The clock, unlike the one you have hanging on the wall, keeps track of time in milliseconds. Such precision is necessary for computers, of course, while your kitchen clock can easily live without it (depending on the precision of your recipes).

What are these milliseconds based on? If we write a little program to read the clock from your hardware you will end up with numbers such as 6874732864982. How do you interpret these numbers? These are the total number of milliseconds that have elapsed since a universally recognized time and date in history, called the *epoch*. In the case of RPG, the base year, or epoch, is Jan. 1, 1940. In the case of Java, the base year is Jan. 1, 1970.

But, back to the computer clock. What does the number returned mean to you and to your application. It really means that the clock inside your computer is continually incrementing its count of milliseconds. When your program asks for that value, the clock returns the number of milliseconds it has counted,-in the case of Java, since Jan. 1, 1970.

Why do we need a base line? It provides a standard base from which computers or programming languages do their date and time manipulation. For example, the Date class in Java actually calls a System class method that gets the number of milliseconds from the computer clock. Take a look at the following example:

LISTING 8-3

```
public class MyTimeMilliseconds
{
    public static void main(String args[])
    {
        long timeInMil;
        timeInMil = System.currentTimeMillis();
        System.out.println("Time is: " + timeInMil);
    }
}
```

In this example, we call a method currentTimeMillis() in the Java-supplied class System to retrieve the number of milliseconds elapsed from the base date. Notice that this method returns a "long" value containing the number of milliseconds. In fact, when you call certain methods in the Date class to retrieve the date for you, what really happens is a call similar to the one in the example to retrieve the milliseconds count. The method, then, calculates the number of days and determines the date or time for you. Now take a look at the calculation to determine the count. If we take our example and divide the number of milliseconds returned by 86,400,000, we will get the number of days. How did we figure that out? This is the total number of milliseconds in a day. This means if we change the previous example to the following example, we can determine the number of days between now and the base year by dividing the returned value by 86,400,000:

LISTING 8-4

```
// 1 second = 1000 milliseconds
// 1 minute = 60 seconds = 60 x 1000 = 60,000 milliseconds
// 1 hour = 60 minutes = 60,000 x 60 = 3,600,000 milliseconds
// 1 day = 24 hours = 24 x 3,600,000 = 86,400,000 milliseconds
public class MyTime2
{
    public static void main(String args[])
    {
        long timeInMil;
        timeInMil = System.currentTimeMillis();
        System.out.println("Number of days: " + (timeInMil / 86400000));
    }
}
```

Why is this important for you to know? In RPG you have specific operation codes that perform addition and subtraction for date fields. Even though Java classes Calendar and GregorianCalendar provide methods to do date/time arithmetic and formatting, sometimes you may decide to do date arithmetic using the method shown. For example, to calculate the number of days between two dates you can use the method shown in the example, or use specific methods supplied in the Calendar and GregorianCalendar classes. This is the subject of our next topic.

DATE AND TIME MANIPULATION

Date/Time Math and Duration

RPG introduced the **ADDDUR** and **SUBDUR** operation codes with the introduction of the new language definition of RPG IV in V3R1. These op-codes enable you to add a specific duration to a date or subtract it from a base date. You can add or subtract days, months, or years from a given date by specifying the second part of factor two. In addition to subtracting a number from a date by extending factor 2 to indicate the type of number being subtracted, you can subtract one date from another date, and indicate in the result field what units to give the results. Note that this saves much math on your part

(and is something Java does not have). For example, in the following sample we are subtracting the end date from the start date, and we want to know the difference in number of days as specified by the '*D' in the second part of the result:

LISTING 8-5

```
DstartD              S              D    DATFMT(*ISO) INZ(D'1998-08-18')
DendD                S              D    DATFMT(*ISO) INZ(D'1998-08-28')
C*
C      endD          SUBDUR    startD       reslt:*D          2 0
C*
```

The following table describes the different options you can specify in the second part of factor two or the result field to indicate the type of the addition or subtraction you would like to accomplish:

Date Part	Keyword	Short Form
Year	*YEARS	*Y
Month	*MONTHS	*M
Day	*DAYS	*D
Hour	*HOURS	*H
Minute	*MINUTES	*MN
Second	*SECONDS	*S
Microsecond	*MSECONDS	*MS

For example, if you want to determine the difference in number of months between two dates, you would specify *MONTHS or *M in the second part of the result field.

In order to accomplish the same thing in Java, you have a couple of options. The first one is to use the same techniques you have learned so far:

LISTING 8-6

```
import java.util.*;
public class MyDateDiff
{
    public static void main(String args[])
    {
        long timeInMil;
        Date startDate = new Date(98, 2, 18);
        Date endDate   = new Date(98, 2, 28);
        // The difference should be 10 days
        timeInMil  = endDate.getTime() - startDate.getTime();
        System.out.println("Days: " + (timeinmil / 86400000));
    }
}
```

As the example shows, you start by creating your two dates by instantiating the Date class twice. Notice that in this case, we have used a different flavor of the Date class constructor. We have supplied the constructor with three parameters consisting of the year, the month, and the day. Once we have these two objects, we use the getTime() method to retrieve the total number of milliseconds for both of these dates. Subtracting the returned values gives us the difference between these two dates in milliseconds. Again, using the same technique of dividing the result by the number of milliseconds per day (that is, the value 86,400,000) will give us the difference in days.

If you try the example shown on your own machine, you should get the result of 10 days, which is the difference between March 28, 1998, and March 18, 1998. You may wonder why we say March here instead of February because in the parameter we specify the number 2 for the month. As you may already know, array indices start in Java at zero, unlike indexing in RPG which starts at 1. So, in the case of the Date object, specifying zero for the month parameter indicates January, one indicates February, and two indicates March.

This first method is a little complicated because you are required to do the calculation yourself. However, a second and much preferred method of doing date arithmetic is using the GregorianCalendar class (and its Calendar class parent):

LISTING 8-7

```
import java.util.*;
public class TestDate
{
    public static void main(String args[])
    {
        GregorianCalendar gc = new GregorianCalendar();
        System.out.println("The date before addition: " + gc.getTime());
        gc.add(Calendar.DATE,2);
        System.out.println("The date after addition:  " + gc.getTime());
        gc.add(Calendar.YEAR,2);
        System.out.println("The date after addition:  " + gc.getTime());
    }
}
```

This example uses the GregorianCalendar class to do the date manipulation. As you see in the example, we first instantiate the GregorianCalendar class with no parameters, which gives us today's date. We next show you some date manipulation that can be done using the GregorianCalendar class. After printing the current date in the calendar, we use the add method supplied in the GregorianCalendar class to add two days to the current day. Assuming today's date is Dec. 15, 1997, the result of the first add is Dec. 17, 1997, and the result of adding 2 to the year is Dec. 17, 1999. Note that the second addition retains the day value of 17 from the first addition:

```
C:\JAVA>javac TestDate.java
C:\JAVA>java TestDate
The date before addition: Mon Dec 15 21:43:22 EST 1997
The date after addition:  Wed Dec 17 21:43:22 EST 1997
The date after addition:  Fri Dec 17 21:43:22 EST 1999
```

What, then, tells the add method what part of the date you are adding? For example, day versus year? As you can see from the example, this is the purpose of the first parameter used in the call. In the case of RPG IV, this is equivalent to the second part of factor two we entered. As you recall, RPG uses *D, *M, or *Y in the second part of factor two to distinguish the type of addition.

This example used simple manipulations, where the math of one part of the date had no impact on the others. But what if the current date is the end of the month, and we add two days to it? The month has to be increased (or reset to January) to accommodate this addition. To prove this is all handled properly, here is an example that forces this date "rolling" behavior:

```
GregorianCalendar gc = new GregorianCalendar(1997,10,30);
System.out.println("The date before addition: " + gc.getTime());
gc.add(Calendar.DATE,2);
System.out.println("The date after addition:  " + gc.getTime());
gc.add(Calendar.MONTH,2);
System.out.println("The date after addition:  " + gc.getTime());
gc.add(Calendar.DATE,26);
System.out.println("The date after addition:  " + gc.getTime());
gc.add(Calendar.DATE,1);
System.out.println("The date after addition:  " + gc.getTime());
```

This gives us exactly the results we would hope for:

```
The date before addition: Sun Nov 30 00:00:00 GMT+00:00 1997
The date after addition:  Tue Dec 02 00:00:00 GMT+00:00 1997
The date after addition:  Mon Feb 02 00:00:00 GMT+00:00 1998
The date after addition:  Sat Feb 28 00:00:00 GMT+00:00 1998
The date after addition:  Sun Mar 01 00:00:00 GMT+00:00 1998
```

As you see in these example, the first parameter in the add method uses the Calendar class to reference class constants versus the GregorianCalendar class. Why is that? As it turns out, the GregorianCalendar is a ***concrete subclass*** (covered in Chapter 9) of the Calendar class. This means all public variables and methods available in the latter are available in the former. The GregorianCalendar provides the standard calendar used by most of the world, but the Calendar class is designed to allow others to easily snap in their own. If you look up the variable index in the JDK for the `Calendar` class, you will see a lot of constants that you can reference when doing date manipulation. The following table compares the keywords available in RPG to those constants available in the `Calendar` class.

Date Part	RPG			JAVA
Year	`*Years`	`or`	`*Y`	`Calendar.YEAR`
Month	`*MONTHS`	`or`	`*M`	`Calendar.MONTH`
Day	`*DAYS`	`or`	`*D`	`Calendar.DATE`
Hour	`*HOURS`	`or`	`*H`	`Calendar.HOUR`
Minute	`*MINUTES`	`or`	`*MN`	`Calendar.MINUTE`
Second	`*SECONDS`	`or`	`*S`	`Calendar.SECOND`
Millisecond	`*MSECONDS`	`or`	`*MS`	`Calendar.MILLISECOND`

If the `add` method is equivalent to the **ADDDUR** op-code, what is equivalent to the **SUBDUR** op-code? The answer is the `add` method again! If you add a negative number, then that is equivalent to subtracting. For example, adding the following two lines of code to the previous example will result in subtracting four years from the current date (be careful-you might go back in time!):

```
gc.add(Calendar.YEAR,-4);
System.out.println("The date after deletion:  " + gc.getTime());
```

Comparing Dates

How do we compare two dates in RPG and Java? In RPG, you can simply use the comparative op-codes like **IF** to find out if a date is before, after, or equal to another date value. How is that done in Java? Again, the `GregorianCalendar` class provides you with a rich set of methods that can perform many of these arithmetic manipulations. The following example illustrates using the `before` method to determine if a date is before another date:

LISTING 8-8

```
import java.util.*;
public class TestDate2
{
    public static void main (String args[])
    {
        GregorianCalendar gc1 = new GregorianCalendar(1997, 12, 31);
        GregorianCalendar gc2 = new GregorianCalendar(1998, 1, 1);
        if (gc1.before(gc2))
            System.out.println("Yes it is");
        else
            System.out.println("No it is not");
    }
}
```

253

In this example, we create two GregorianCalendar objects, gc1 and gc2, representing Dec. 31, 1997, and Jan. 1, 1998, respectively. We then use the before method to determine if the gc1 date is before gc2. As a result, the program prints "Yes it is" as we would expect. If you substitute the after or equals methods the result would be "No it is not."

Printing Day of the Week

If you would like to print the actual name of the day instead of a number, how do you do it in RPG or Java? For example: "Oct. 22, 1997, was a Wednesday." How would you convert the number 22 to the string "Wednesday"? For RPG, as it turns out, it takes a few lines of code:

LISTING 8-9

```
D Week              S              9A    DIM(7) CTDATA PERRCD(1)
D*
D CurrentDate       S              D
D OneSunday         S              D     INZ(D'1997-08-03')
D Temp              S              7 0
D TheDay            S              1P 0
C*
C       'enter date'  DSPLY                      CurrentDate
C       CurrentDate   SubDur    OneSunday        Temp:*d
C       Temp          DIV       7                Temp
C                     MVR                        TheDay
C                     IF        TheDay = 0
C                     EVAL      TheDay = 7
C                     ENDIF
C       Week(TheDay)  DSPLY
C                     MOVE      *ON              *INLR
** CTDATA Week
Monday
Tuesday
Wednesday
Thursday
Friday
Saturday
Sunday
```

In the code you need to establish a base line to deal with the calculation. In our example, we declare the field OneSunday to represent any past Sunday. In this case, we simply pick Sunday August 3, 1997. When the user enters the date he/she wants, we simply subtract that from it to calculate the number of days elapsed. As you see, the first line prompts the user to enter the date he/she wants. Then we simply use the **SUBDUR** op-code to determine the difference in number of days between the date that was entered and our base date. Once we have the difference, we divide that by seven, which is the number of days in a week.

The following line uses the **MVR** (*Move Remainder*) operation code to move the remainder to the index that we will use later to retrieve the actual name of the day from our compile time array. For example, if the date we enter is Aug. 5,1997, then the difference between both dates is 2. Therefore, when dividing it by 7, the remainder is also 2. This means that the day we are dealing with is a Tuesday. However, what if we entered the date Aug. 10, 1997? The difference this time is 7. Dividing a 7 by a 7 will give us a remainder of 0. If we directly use this as our index to the array, we will get an "index out of range" error. This is why in the code we check for that condition. If the remainder is zero, the day is a Sunday and the index needs to be set to 7.

How can we accomplish this with Java? Java has a supplied method in the Date class that gives us the day of the week as an integer. The getDay() method returns an integer from 0 to 6 that represents the days Sunday to Saturday, respectively. This makes it much easier to do this versus RPG (actually, you will see when we cover date formatting that the GregorianCalendar class has an even simpler way to print the name of a day in text format). The same example written in Java follows:

LISTING 8-10

```
import java.util.*;
class MyDayString
{
    public static void main(String args[])
    {
        String WeekDay[] = {"Sunday",    "Monday",   "Tuesday",
                            "Wednesday", "Thursday","Friday",
                            "Saturday"};
        Date dateToday = new Date();
        System.out.println("Today is:" + WeekDay[dateToday.getDay()]);
    }
}
```

As we did in RPG, we declare a "compile time" array and initialize it to the names of the days. We then create the Date object to retrieve today's date. Once we have that, we can call the getDay() method to retrieve the number of the day. Notice that the method's return value is used as the index of the array WeekDay. Because the value returned is in the range 0-6, this maps directly to an array index. The println method prints the name of the day as a string. While this works fine, a better approach would be to use the SimpleDateFormat class described in the following section, with the 'E' special character.

FORMATTING DATE AND TIME

We will describe for you next how to format dates and, after that, times.

Formatting Date Fields

In RPG, there are many ways to format your date fields. You can simply use the new keyword `DATFMT(*format{separator})` to tell the compiler the format you want your date fields to have. You can specify this keyword in two places: on the H-spec to establish global default formatting for your date fields, or on specific fields on the D-spec to indicate specific formatting for those fields. If no keyword is specified on either, the default `*ISO` is used. The following table illustrates the different date formats available for you to use in RPG:

Date Format	Name	Format	Length	Separator
Month/Day/Year	*MDY	mm/dd/yy	8	/ - . , &
Day/Month/Year	*DMY	dd/mm/yy	8	/ - . , &
Year/Month/Day	*YMD	yy/mm/dd	8	/ - . , &
Julian	*JUL	yy/ddd	6	/ - . , &
USA Standard	*USA	mm/dd/yyyy	10	/
European Standard	*EUR	dd.mm.yyyy	10	.
International Standard Organization	*ISO	yyyy-mm-dd	10	-
Japanese Standard	*JIS	yyyy-mm-dd	10	-

For example, to tell the compiler that you want to format all your fields in the program to have the `*MDY` format, you would code this:

```
H       DATFMT(*MDY/)
```

In this example, not only are we telling the compiler the format to use ("MDY"), but we also are specifying the actual separator to use between the day, time, and year ("/"). As you see from the table, you can specify any separator you like, depending on the actual format used and whether that separator is allowed or not. We can continue in the RPG code and specify the same keyword on certain fields, but with a different format. This would indicate to the compiler that the `*MDY` format is to be used globally on all fields in your program, except for those fields that have this keyword specified on their D-spec. The rule is very simple and, in fact, it applies to both date and time formats. The following example illustrates this:

LISTING 8-11

```
H****************************************************************
H      DATFMT(*YMD/)
H****************************************************************
D EURDate          S                D          DATFMT(*EUR)
D MDYDate          S                8A
D ISODate          S                D          DATFMT(*ISO)
D DEFDate          S                D
D****************************************************************
C          *MDY          MOVE      EURDate          MDYDate
C                        MOVE      EURDate          ISODate
C                        MOVE      EURDate          DEFDate
C                        MOVE      *ON              *INLR
```

In this example, we insert the keyword **DATFMT** on the H-spec to indicate the overall date format for the program is ***YMD** with the slash separator (**/**). This format will be used if no other format is specified on the D-spec, or in factor one of a C-spec in the program. In the example, we declare three different date fields. The first uses the European format, the second uses the ISO format, and the third uses our default for the program. On the C-spec we do three moves to illustrate the date conversion from one format type to another. Assuming the field EURDate contains the value '31.07.1988', the result of each move is: MDYDate = '07/31/88', ISODate = '1988-07-31' and DEFDate = '88/07/31'.

> **NOTE:** In V4R2 of RPG IV, there are three new *external* date formats supported, but only on the **MOVE, MOVEL,** and **TEST** op-codes: ***CMDY, *CDMY,** and ***LONGJUL.** You cannot use these formats when defining new *internal* fields.

In Java it is perhaps even easier to format a date field. The JDK supplies a SimpleDateFormat class in the java.text package to accommodate it. This class is very powerful and supplies functionality superior even to RPG IV. It allows you to choose any user-defined pattern for formatting. For example:

LISTING 8-12

```
import java.text.*;
import java.util.*;
public class TestDateFormat
{
    public static void main (String args[])
    {
        Date date = new Date();
        System.out.println("Before formatting: " + date);
        String fPattern = new String("MM/dd/yy");
        SimpleDateFormat test = new SimpleDateFormat(fPattern);
        String dateString = test.format(date);
        System.out.println("After formatting:  " + dateString);
    }
}
```

We first instantiate a `Date` object with today's date. We then build the pattern, which is equivalent to the RPG IV date format of `*MDY`, by initializing it to the `String` object `fPattern`. Once we establish that, we can then instantiate a `SimpleDateFormat` object and pass to it as a parameter our pattern. This is now a date formatting machine! You can simply call its format method with any `Date` object and that date will be formatted according to the originally supplied pattern. We do so with our current `Date` object. If the current date is Dec. 24, 1998, after executing the program, the `dateString` object will contain the value `12/24/98`.

The only thing you need to change to establish a new format is the value of the pattern, either by instantiating a new object or using the `applyPattern` method. The `SimpleDateFormat` class allows you to specify various (case-sensitive) characters as part of the string to indicate different formatting patterns. These are predetermined characters for specific date parts:

Character	Meaning
G	Era designator - text
y	year - number
M	month in year - text and number
d	day in month - number
E	day in week - text
D	day in year - number
F	day of week in month - number
w	week in year - number
W	week in month - number
'	escape for text - delimiter
' '	single quotes around literals

As you have seen in the example, we have used the *M, d,* and *y* characters for the pattern. Notice that we used upper case *M* to show the month in the year, and the lower case *d* and *y* to show the day in month and year, respectively. What do you think the result would be if we used upper case *D*? As shown in the table, *D* is used to display the day's number in the year. This means that if today's date is Dec. 14, 1997, the formatted result when using the pattern "MM/DD/yy" would be "12/348/97". The following shows a few more examples:

LISTING 8-13

```
import java.text.*;
import java.util.*;
public class TestDateFormat2
{
    public static void main (String args[])
    {
        Date date = new Date();
        String fPatternA = new String("MM.DD.yyy G 'JAVA4RPG'");
        SimpleDateFormat testA = new SimpleDateFormat(fPatternA);
        String fPatternB = new String("'Day of week:' EEEE");
        SimpleDateFormat testB = new SimpleDateFormat(fPatternB);
        String dateStringA = testA.format(date);
        System.out.println("Formatted date: " + dateStringA);
        String dateStringB = testB.format(date);
        System.out.println("Formatted date: " + dateStringB);
    }
}
```

This gives us the following results:

```
C:\JAVA>javac TestDateFormat2.java
C:\JAVA>java TestDateFormat2
Formatted date: 12.349.97 AD JAVA4RPG
Formatted date: Day of week: Monday
```

Notice the use of *G* in the format to display the era, and the use of a literal 'JAVA4RPG'. Pay particular attention to the use of single quotes around the 'JAVA4RPG' literal. When specifying string literals in the format, you must enclose them in single quotes; otherwise Java assumes that each letter is meant to be one of the substitution variables. The second pattern we use is the *E* character to display the day of week. Recall that, earlier in this chapter, we showed you a technique to display the name, in text, for the day of the week.

We used the getDay method in the Date class and indexing into an array that lists the names for all seven days. As it turns out, the SimpleDateFormat class can do that using the *E* pattern as shown in the example. As a comparison, the following table lists all the date formats available in RPG and their equivalent pattern in Java.

Date Format	Name	Format	Java Pattern
Month/Day/Year	*MDY	mm/dd/yy	MM/dd/yy
Day/Month/Year	*DMY	dd/mm/yy	dd/MM/yy
Year/Month/Day	*YMD	yy/mm/dd	yy/MM/dd
Julian	*JUL	yy/ddd	yy/DDD
USA Standard	*USA	mm/dd/yyyy	MM/dd/yyyy
European Standard	*EUR	dd.mm.yyyy	dd.MM.yyyy
International Standards Organization	*ISO	yyyy-mm-dd	yyyy-MM-dd
Japanese Standard	*JIS	yyyy-mm-dd	yyyy-MM-dd

NOTE: Java allows all of the separators that you can use with RPG IV, namely: (/), (-), (.), (&), and (,) (slash, dash, period, ampersand, and comma).

Formatting Time Fields

As with date formatting, RPG has just as many optional formats for your time fields. For formatting time fields, you use a keyword similar to that for dates, namely TIMFMT(*format{seperator}). This tells the compiler the format you want your time fields to have. The possible parameters you can specify are listed in the table below:

Time Format	Name	Format	Length	Separator
Hours:minutes:seconds	*HMS	hh:mm:ss	8	: . , &
International Standards Organization	*ISO	hh.mm.ss	8	.
USA Standard	*USA	hh:mm am/pm	8	:
Europe Standard	*EUR	hh.mm.ss	8	.
Japanese	*JIS	hh:mm:ss	8	:

Again, as with date formatting, you are allowed to specify this keyword in two places: the H-spec (global default) or the D-spec (field-specific). If you like to format your times in a format similar to "hh:mm:ss" you specify the format '*HMS:' as the parameter to the TIMFMT keyword. All optional separators are indicated in the table for each specific format type. Here's an example:

LISTING 8-14

```
H     TIMFMT(*HMS,)
H*************************************************************
D EURTime                S                  D    DATFMT(*EUR)
D USATime                S                  8A
D JISTime                S                  D    DATFMT(*JIS)
D DEFTime                S                  D
D*************************************************************
C          *USA          MOVE      EURTime            USATime
C                        MOVE      EURTime            JISTime
C                        MOVE      EURTime            DEFTime
C                        MOVE      *ON                *INLR
```

In this example, we insert the keyword TIMFMT on the H-spec to indicate that the overall time format for the program is *HMS with the comma separator (,). On the C-specs, we do three moves to illustrate the time conversion from one format type to another. Assuming the field EURTime contains the value '10.25.30', after the moves the values in the fields are: USATime = '10:25 am' (assume it is morning, otherwise it will be pm), JISTime = '10:25:30', and DEFTime will contain the value '10,25,30'.

In Java, once again, it is just as easy if not easier to format a time field. Similar to formatting dates, you use the SimpleDateFormat class in the java.text package:

LISTING 8-15

```
import java.text.*;
import java.util.*;
public class TestTimeFormat
{
    public static void main(String args[])
    {
        Date date = new Date();
        System.out.println("Before formatting: " + date);
        SimpleDateFormat test = new SimpleDateFormat("hh:mm:ss");
        String timeString - test.format(date);
        System.out.println("After formatting:  " + timeString);
    }
}
```

This is identical to the previous date formatting example except that we specify "hh:mm:ss" for the format versus "MM/dd/yy". Because we specified only letters pertaining to time, we get results only showing a formatted time. Thus, if the current time is 10:25:30, after executing the program, the timeString object will contain the value 10:25:30. The letters that you can specify in the format pattern pertaining to time are:

Character	Meaning
h	hour in am / pm - number
H	hour within the day - number
m	minute within the hour - number
s	second within the minute - number
S	milliseconds - number
a	am / pm marker - text
k	hour within the day - number
K	hour in am / pm - number
z	time zone - text
'	escape for text - delimiter
' '	single quotes around literals

As with date formatting, the characters you specify in the pattern are case-sensitive. Let's look at another example:

LISTING 8-16

```java
import java.text.*;
import java.util.*;
public class TestTimeFormat2
{
    public static void main(String args[])
    {
      Date date = new Date();
      System.out.println("Before formatting: " + date);
      String fPattern = new String("'Hour in day =' hh:mm:ss:SS zz");
      SimpleDateFormat test = new SimpleDateFormat(fPattern);
      String timeString = test.format(date);
      System.out.println("After formatting:  " + timeString);
    }
}
```

This gives us the following:

```
Before formatting: Mon Dec 15 23:32:53 EST 1997
After formatting:  Hour in day = 08:32:53:92 PST
```

In this example, we use ss for milliseconds, and zz to indicate the time zone. For comparison, the following table lists the time formats available in RPG and their equivalent pattern in Java:

Time Format	Name	Format	Java Pattern
Hours:minutes:seconds	*HMS	hh:mm:ss	hh:mm:ss
International Standards Organization	*ISO	hh.mm.ss	hh.mm.ss
USA Standard	*USA	hh:mm am/pm	hh:mm aa
Europe Standard	*EUR	hh.mm.ss	hh.mm.ss
Japanese	*JIS	hh:mm:ss	hh:mm:ss

LOOK BEFORE YOU LEAP

One of the methods available in the GregorianCalendar class that is worth mentioning again is the isLeapYear() method. The following shows an example of how you use it:

LISTING 8-17

```
import java.util.*;
public class TestLeap
{
    public static void main(String args[])
    {
        GregorianCalendar date = new GregorianCalendar();
        System.out.println("1600 a leap year? " + date.isLeapYear(1600));
        System.out.println("1900 a leap year? " + date.isLeapYear(1900));
        System.out.println("1976 a leap year? " + date.isLeapYear(1976));
        System.out.println("1999 a leap year? " + date.isLeapYear(1999));
        System.out.println("2000 a leap year? " + date.isLeapYear(2000));
    }
}
```

You simply supply the method with the year as an integer parameter. This example gives us:

```
1600 a leap year? true
1900 a leap year? false
1976 a leap year? true
1999 a leap year? false
2000 a leap year? true
```

EXTRACTING DATE AND TIME

What if you have a variable that contains a date or time value and you would like to retrieve only the day portion of it, or the year portion? In RPG IV, a new operation code was introduced for this specific purpose. The new **EXTRCT** op-code allows you to specify a field of type date, time, or timestamp in factor two, followed by the duration code that specifies the specific information you want to extract or retrieve. For example, specifying a time field in factor two followed by a colon and followed by *H tells the compiler that you want to retrieve only the hour portion. The extract op-code can be used with any field of type date, time, or timestamp, and can return one of the following values depending on what you specify in the second part of factor two:

- The year, month, or day part of a date or timestamp field.
- The hours, minutes, or seconds part of a time or timestamp field.
- The microseconds part of the timestamp field.

Notice that the result field must be specified to be assigned the value returned. The type of the result field can be numeric or character. Let's take a look at an example:

LISTING 8-18

```
D*Name+++++++++++ETDsFrom+++To/L+++IDc.Keywords++++++++++++++++++++++
D CurrentDate    S              D
D OneSunday      S              D   INZ(D'1997-08-03')
D thistime       S              T   INZ(T'11.25.00')
D TStamp         S              Z
C*
C                    MOVE      OneSunday      TStamp
C                    MOVE      thistime       TStamp
C                    EXTRCT    TStamp:*H      temp1              4 0
C        temp1       DSPLY
C                    EXTRCT    OneSunday:*M   temp1
C        temp1       DSPLY
C                    EXTRCT    OneSunday:*Y   temp1
C        temp1       DSPLY
C                    MOVE      *ON            *INLR
```

In this case, we declare two fields on the D-spec. One is declared as a date field and the other as a time field. Both have an initial value so that we can illustrate the **EXTRCT** op-code. We also move both the date and time fields to a timestamp field to show you that we can extract any part of a timestamp field as well. In the first case, we extract the hour part of the timestamp field and place the value in the field temp1, specified in the result field. Next, we extract the month portion of the date field and then we extract the year portion. In this example, the **DSPLY** op-code will display the values: 11, 08, and 1997.

For Java, you can use the `get()` method of the `GregorianCalendar` class, specifying the appropriate constant for the parameter, as we have already seen:

Date Part	RPG			JAVA
Year	`*Years`	`or`	`*Y`	`Calendar.YEAR`
Month	`*MONTHS`	`or`	`*M`	`Calendar.MONTH`
Day	`*DAYS`	`or`	`*D`	`Calendar.DATE`
Hour	`*HOURS`	`or`	`*H`	`Calendar.HOUR`
Minute	`*MINUTES`	`or`	`*MN`	`Calendar.MINUTE`
Second	`*SECONDS`	`or`	`*S`	`Calendar.SECOND`
Microsecond	`*MSECONDS`	`or`	`*MS`	`Calendar.MILLISECOND`

TIME ZONES

Sometimes we require the capability to establish the current date or time in an explicit *time zone* other than the one in which the program is currently running. This functionality is not available to us in RPG, but Java does offer it. Java supports a `TimeZone` class in the `java.util` package, which can be used to instantiate an instance of a particular time zone, as in:

```
TimeZone tz_GMT = TimeZone.getTimeZone("GMT");
TimeZone tz_EST = TimeZone.getTimeZone("EST");
```

Notice how the constructor parameter is simply a string representing a valid, known time zone id, such as EST for Eastern Standard Time. To see all the supported time zones, use the static `getAvailableIDs` method:

```
String tzs[] = TimeZone.getAvailableIDs();
for (int idx = 0; idx < tzs.length; idx++)
   System.out.println(tzs[idx]);
```

In order to get the current time zone for your computer, use the `TimeZone.getDefault()` method. Finally, then, once you have a `TimeZone` object, you can use it in both your `GregorianCalendar` object to affect manipulations, and in your `DateFormat` object to affect the time displayed. In both cases, simply use the `setTimeZone` method. For example, if you have a `Date` object, say from instantiating the `Date` class explicitly or from using the `getTime()` method of a `GregorianCalendar` object, you may wish to display that object's time value for each of your offices around the world. To do this, you create a `SimpleDateFormat` object as usual, but before using its `format` method, first call the `setTimeZone` method with the `TimeZone` object you wish to use. Here is an example:

LISTING 8-19

```
import java.util.*;
import java.text.*;
public class TestTimeZones
{
    public static void main(String args[])
    {
        Date       today = new Date(); // Current date/time
        TimeZone tz1    = TimeZone.getTimeZone("PST");
        TimeZone tz2    = TimeZone.getTimeZone("EST");
        TimeZone tz3    = TimeZone.getTimeZone("GMT");
        TimeZone tz4    = TimeZone.getTimeZone("JST");
        TimeZone tz5    = TimeZone.getDefault();
        SimpleDateFormat formatter =
            new SimpleDateFormat("hh:mm:ss - 'TimeZone = ' z");
        formatter.setTimeZone(tz1);
        System.out.println( formatter.format(today) );
        formatter.setTimeZone(tz2);
        System.out.println( formatter.format(today) );
        formatter.setTimeZone(tz3);
        System.out.println( formatter.format(today) );
        formatter.setTimeZone(tz4);
        System.out.println( formatter.format(today) );
        formatter.setTimeZone(tz5);
        System.out.println( formatter.format(today) );
    } // end main method
} // end TestTimeZones class
```

This results in:

```
11:15:31 - TimeZone =  PST
02:15:31 - TimeZone =  EST
07:15:31 - TimeZone =  GMT+00:00
04:15:31 - TimeZone =  GMT+09:00
02:15:31 - TimeZone =  EST
```

Note how the displayed time is different depending on what time zone is used, which is what we wished. Here are a few final comments about this example, and using TimeZone objects:

- Some time zones, like JST (Japanese Standard Time) do not print an ID string with the *z* substitution character, but rather print their delta hour offset from Greenwich Mean Time (GMT), the base time zone. It is strange that getTimeZone recognizes the id "JST" but then loses it.

- Use the getDefault() method to return a TimeZone object representing the time zone of the machine on which the program is running at that time. In Windows 95, you may have to ensure your time zone is set properly on your machine, using the Date/Time icon in your Control Panel folder. (Use the Time Zone tab.)

SUMMARY

In this chapter, we discussed the following aspects of date and time manipulation:

- RPG IV date and time support is far superior than in its predecessor RPG III.

- The method `currentTimeMillis()` returns the total number of milliseconds since the base time or *epoch*.

- Java has a `Date` class for retrieving current dates. In comparison, you use the **TIME** op-code to retrieve the time and/or date in RPG.

- Java has another two important classes for performing date and time manipulations: `Calendar` and `GregorianCalendar`.

- To extract parts of a date in Java, use the `get()` method on a `GregorianCalendar` object.

- RPG has many supplied formatting names that can be used on the **DATFMT** and **TIMFMT** keywords on the H-spec and on the D-spec. Java has just as many and even more. You use the `SimpleDateFormat` class in Java to do the formatting for you.

- Use the `isLeapYear` method found in the `java.util.GregorianCalendar` class to test if a year is either a leap year or is not in Java. RPG IV does not have an equivalent op-code or built-in function, so you must code your own.

- Java supplies `TimeZone` and `SimpleTimeZone` classes for date formatting.

9

An Object Orientation

OO Terminology

Java is an object-oriented language. That is a good thing, but what exactly does it mean? We'll define "OO" and describe how Java implements it. We'll point out the syntax, semantic, and capability considerations. But, to make this information useful, it is important to begin to "think OO." That is quite different than "thinking procedural," as your RPG background has taught you. However, it is helpful to keep in mind that the AS/400 operating system is "object based," even if it is not object oriented. This will begin to make more sense as you gain more experience. Thinking OO when you are designing your code will feel more comfortable with time. We suggest you get in there and write some Java code right away. Don't be afraid to jump in and get your feet wet. Learning the syntax and capabilities of the language will take place as you are actually doing it. Pick a simple program you have always wanted to write to be your test case — but, please, don't ship it immediately! As you write your initial code, pick up some reading material. We suggest reference manuals and two or three books on Java. After that, read a book about object oriented design. There are hundreds on the market. Having learned the Java language will make you more familiar with the terms you will find in the books and reference manuals. You will find answers in the books to questions that will inevitably accumulate as you write your initial code. If you can, hire someone to join your team who has object oriented skills. Keep in mind that not everyone on the team needs to be proficient in OO — the initial design could be done by a different set of persons than those who do the implementation. So don't get discouraged if everything doesn't make sense right away because, believe us, your second or third project with Java or any OO language will be great! OO has many important benefits — if applied correctly.

It is generally agreed that for a computer language to be considered object oriented, it must support the following concepts:

- Encapsulation.
- Inheritance.
- Polymorphism.

What the heck are these? Read on...

Encapsulation

Java classes, like RPG IV modules, offer code reuse and packaging options through the ability to have one compiled piece of code that does a self contained set of functions, such as managing a stack. This unit is reusable "as is" by many others, especially when it is packaged as part of a Java package or a RPG IV service program. Classes are the basic building blocks of all object oriented languages. Putting variables (data) and code together into a easily reused "black box" that others can access through specifically designated interfaces ("public" in Java, "export" in RPG) is called ***encapsulation***. That is an appropriate term because you *encapsulate* the data and allow access only through related functions. Let's consider a stack example. Let's suppose that one day you decide to change the underlying data structure from an array to a dynamic linked list. No problem. You can make this change without affecting all users of the code if you have properly restricted access to the internal variables. You do this by restricting users to, say, the *push* and *pop* interfaces.

It is because of this ability to encapsulate the data (variables) from direct and unpredictable access that you often see graphics that show objects as a circle. The data or variables are in the middle, and the methods are around the outside. An example is shown in Figure 9-1:

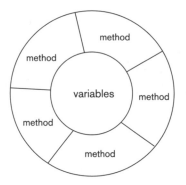

FIGURE 9-1

270

This is a way of conveying that the variables (these are class level or instance variables) in the center are protected from direct access by the methods. That is, you must use one of the methods to access the variables. This helps to ensure data integrity, as well as gives the class designer control over future changes. Keep in mind that methods in Java are like procedures in RPG IV, and class level or instance variables in Java are like global variables in RPG. It's also useful to remember that classes in Java are like modules in ILE. Because exported procedures in ILE service programs are like public methods in Java, encapsulation is possible in RPG. The trick is to create service programs that export only procedures, not variables. That forces programmer users of the service program to go through your procedures to access your variables.

Encapsulation and the AS/400

Beyond ILE modules, another good example of this on the AS/400, is the database itself. Data files on the AS/400 are typically created with very limited public access, and end users are forced to go through your programs to access the database. Typically these programs use adopted authority to gain entry to the data. It might be helpful to think of the database as being like your private variables. In contrast, your programs are like the public methods through which access to the variables is restricted.

Inheritance

Because it is possible to get encapsulation through ILE modules and service programs in RPG, why all the fuss in the industry about OO (Object Oriented)? The OO is getting so much hype because of another capability of classes — the ability to be ***extended*** (also known as ***subclassed***). This ability that classes have is unique. There is no analogy to this in RPG, at least as this book is being written. As you will see, it can offer great rewards once you get the hang of it. The examples you have seen so far of Java classes have been defined from scratch. That is a common use for Java. However, you will also often find yourself in another situation. Let's say that you want a version of an existing class that is only slightly different. You don't want to copy and maintain a second slightly altered version. This can be done! You simply define your new class and specify that it `extends` (in Java) the original class. Your new class will inherit all the variables and methods of the base class. Well, not quite. It does inherit them all, but the new code in the new class is not allowed to access any variable marked as private, or to invoke any method marked as private. Unmarked ("package") and `public` variables and methods are accessible, however

LISTING 9-1

```
// Class BaseClass
public class BaseClass
{
    private int a = 10;
    public int getA()
    {
        return a;
    }
    public void setA(int newA)
    {
        a = newA;
    }
} // end class BaseClass
// Class SubClass
public class SubClass extends BaseClass
{
} // end class SubClass
```

The example shows a new class, SubClass, that extends a base class called BaseClass. The important keyword here is **extends**. This syntax defines this new class as an extension, or subclass, of BaseClass. To users, this new class looks just like the base class. Once you instantiate an object instance of SubClass you can invoke the methods getA() and setA(...) on that object, as though you had instantiated an object of BaseClass. The new object has a variable 'a' in it, and has the same methods as the base class.

So, if objects of the new subclass look and behave just like objects of the base class, why bother? In this simple example, there is no logical reason to offer. However, your new class now has the ability to make delta revisions to the behavior of the base class as follows:

- Add new variables and methods.
- Override existing methods.
- Remove existing methods.

The process for adding new variables and methods is obvious: you just define them in the new class as usual. Overriding existing methods is done by defining a new version of the existing method in the new class. You use exactly the same name and parameters ("*signature*") as the original, but with different logic. Removing existing methods is also achieved by overriding the original method signature, but then supplying empty braces for the logic ("no operation"). You might expect a more elegant and formal method for removing methods from the class being extended. However, actually removing methods would cause a problem with the next concept we will discuss — *polymorphism* — so you are left with only this one convention. Also, in contrast to the *extended* class, the reason for *extending* classes is to add or refine functionality, not remove it.

> **NOTE:** When you override a method in a class that uses `extends`, the *signature* is important. Keep in mind that two methods with the same name are considered different if they take different parameter lists. A method's signature includes both its name and its parameter list. Therefore, to override a method, you must match both its name and its parameter list in the new class. The return type is not part of the signature. However, if you do override a method (by specifying a new method with the same name and parameter list as it has in the base class) but specify a different return type, you will receive an error from the Java compiler because of the ambiguity.

To illustrate the options of adding, overriding, and removing methods listed, we might define the new subclass to look like this:

LISTING 9-2

```
// Class SubClass
public class SubClass extends BaseClass
{
    private int b = 20; // new variable
    public int getA() // override method
    {
        return super.getA() + b;
    }
    public void setA(int newA) // remove method
    {
    }
    private void setB(int newB) // new method
    {
        b = newB;
    }
} // end class SubClass
```

Notice the use of the Java keyword `super` in the getA() method. When you override a method, you may do so by either:

- replacing the inherited implementation entirely with new logic, or
- augmenting the inherited logic with additional logic.

To do the latter, you need a mechanism for invoking the original version of the method in the inherited class. This is what **"super"** allows you to do. Like **"this"**, which is a special object variable that points to this object, **super** is a special object variable that points to the parent class. It is only valid in a class that *extends* another class.

TERMINOLOGY NOTE: The class that is extended is referred to variously as the ***superclass***, the ***parent*** class, or the ***base*** class. The class that is *extending* is referred to variously as the ***subclass,*** the ***child*** class, or the ***derived*** class. The latter is conceptually considered *lower* in the chain than the former. The concept of extending one class to make another is known as ***inheritance***. It has a lot of powers, as well as numerous design, syntax, and behavioral considerations that we have not yet discussed.

It turns out that the keyword **"super"** is always valid in Java! That is because every class inherits from some other class in Java. Even the previously introduced "base" classes, which have no explicit **"extends"** keyword, implicitly extend from the Java core class "Object". This is a powerful feature. It means that all classes have the same "super" ancestor. If you look up the class Object, in the JDK documentation for the Java supplied package java.lang, you will see it has a number of supplied methods that you may find of use. Because all classes ultimately inherit from this, every object you create or reference — regardless of the class type — will have this default set of methods. This tells us something else — there is no limit to the size of an inheritance tree. All classes implicitly extend java.lang.Object, and other classes may extend these, and so on, and so on. Pictorially, the hierarchy is usually shown (see Figure 9-2) with the class names inside square boxes and an arrow pointing from the "child" (sub) class to the "parent" (super) class. The hierarchy tree for our example follows:

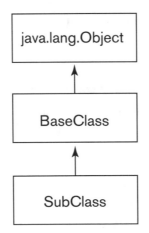

FIGURE 9-2

You can go as deep as you wish, but you will discover from experience that you will rarely require a "deep hierarchy." Although there are some situations when a deep hierarchy is warranted, most classes will not be extended much more than three or four deep. Keep in mind that **super** accesses only the immediate parent. Another important point is that two different classes can inherit from the same parent class. If there was a second subclass called SubClass2 that also "extends" the class BaseClass, the hierarchy tree would look like Figure 9-3:

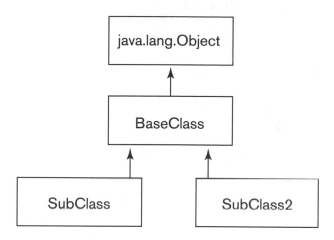

FIGURE 9-3

A "hierarchy browser" is a tool you will come to rely on when writing Java code (and any OO code). This tool shows the inheritance tree, such as the one in our example, for a selected class. All worthwhile Java development environments, including VisualAge for Java, have such a tool. In VisualAge for Java, it is incorporated into the Integrated

Development Environment (IDE) and is easily accessed by selecting the "hierarchy" tab when editing a particular class. Figure 9-4 is a snapshot from VisualAge for Java (specifically its hierarchy or browser) that shows what it looks like for the class hierarchy in our example...

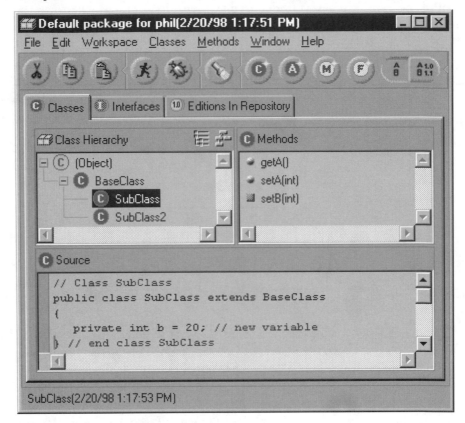

FIGURE 9-4

Inheritance is what separates "object based" from "object oriented". Notice that RPG has no equivalent to Java class inheritance. We stated that ILE RPG modules are like classes in that they offer the encapsulation capabilities of a class. But they fall down when it comes to inheritance! RPG modules, then, are closer to a particular class instance (an object) than they are to a class. In effect, they are a pre-instantiated class! The compiler and runtime have given you one instance only; you cannot have multiple instances of a module in a particular program. And, you cannot create a new module that inherits from an existing module. To refine a module for another specialized use, it is usually necessary to copy and change the code base.

Inheritance and the AS/400

There is also no equivalent to inheritance in the AS/400 operating system. There are a lot of "object types" on the AS/400 (for example, `*PGM`, `*MODULE`, `*DTAARA`), but you cannot create a new object type by extending an existing object type. All object types that IBM supplies are "siblings" to each other — there is no sense of parent/child relationships. This is why the AS/400 is referred to as an *object based* system, versus an *object oriented* system.

Well, okay, one crude AS/400 example of inheritance does perhaps exist: reference fields in DDS. If you maintain a field reference file of field definitions, this is somewhat like a base class. Each database file that you define by using or referencing your field reference file (FRF) fields is somewhat similar to a child class that "extends" its parent class (the FRF). You define new fields (simple reference), override existing fields (by redefining a reference field's length, for example), and remove (by omission) other fields.

Polymorphism

No, this is *not* a denture cream! In fact, we have already talked about this subject. When you define a class that extends another class and then override one of the inherited methods with a new implementation of that method, you are practicing ***polymorphism***. (Aren't you naughty!) Polymorphism refers to the fact that calling the same method on two objects can have different results if the objects come from different classes in the same hierarchy. There's a mouthful! (Concepts in OO that are actually very simple can be confusing to describe. And the long names that they have been given do not help!)

Often, in Java and other OO languages, you will have methods that accept an object reference as parameters. The parameter list in the method declaration must, as you know, declare the type of the object, as in:

```
void printBill(MyClass objectParm)
{
    . . .
}
```

The method, usually, invokes some method or methods in the passed-in object to perform some (presumably) useful function. Imagine, in this case, that the method's role is to print out a line with the unit cost for a service transaction. Let's say, for example, that your company performs billable services in the form of presentations, education, and programming. Because the unit cost and the unit of measurement might be different for each activity, you decide to design a class hierarchy that has at its base a class called `BillableService`. The base class has common variables such as employees involved, date range, customer, and so on. It also has common methods that each type of transaction will need to support, such as `getCustomer()`, `getCost()`, `printBill()`, and so forth.

Then you also have classes `Presentation`, `Education`, and `Programming`, each of which inherits from `BillableService` and overrides, say, the `printBill()` method to implement the unique logic required for each type of transaction. Your hierarchy might look like Figure 9-5:

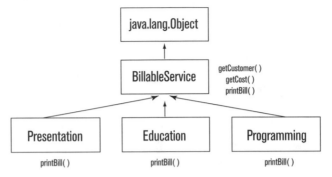

FIGURE 9-5

Now, suppose you have a class and that its job is to print out all the billable services for the month. It might have a method in it called `printBillable` that, among other things, does the following:

- Takes as a parameter an object representing an individual transaction;

- Invokes the `printBill()` method on that object.

It might look something like this:

```
public void printBillable(???? transaction)
{
    transaction.printBill();
}
```

Looks easy enough, right? But how would you define that parameter? What class type would it be? You have to expect that you will be passed objects that are of any one of the three transaction class types (`Presentation`, `Education`, `Programming`). If this were RPG or C, you might handle this one of two ways:

- Define three parameters, one for each type, as well as a numeric parameter whose value denotes which of the three types was actually passed (and pass ***OMIT** or a special null value constant for the other two). Then, do a **select** (or **switch** in C) on the type parameter, to determine which object to act on.

- Define one parameter of type pointer to the procedure. Leave it up to the caller to pass in a pointer to the appropriate procedure, then invoke that procedure via its pointer. This is known as a *callback* function (notice that there are still times when you will want to do this in Java — more will follow on this later).

In Java, life is easier because of polymorphism. You can simply define one parameter of type `BillableService`, where `BillableService` is the "base class" from our previous example. Then, you can safely invoke the "`printBill()`" method on that object, like this:

```
public void printBillable(BillableService transaction)
{
    transaction.printBill();
}
```

Then, you might have test code that instantiates and populates an object of each child type, as in:

LISTING 9-3

```
public void testPrintBillable()
{
    Presentation presObj;
    Education    educObj;
    Programming  progObj;
    // ... create and populate presObj, educObj, progObj ...
    printBillable(presObj); // call with object of type Presentation
    printBillable(educObj); // call with object of type Education
    printBillable(progObj); // call with object of type Programming
}
```

Does this look suspicious to you? If the caller of this method calls it with objects of class type `Presentation`, `Education`, or `Programming`, then how will this compile when the method is expecting an object of class type `BillableService`? And if it will compile, what will happen when the method `printBill()` is called on that object?

This is where the power of polymorphism comes in. It keeps your teeth in place, and it allows you to substitute in a parent class's object type anywhere a child class's type is expected. For example, you might expect to have to code something like this in order to handle the various possible object types as input:

```
public void printBillable(BillableService transaction)
{
    if object-type is Presentation then
      call printBill() in class Presentation;
    else if object-type is Education then
      call printBill() in class Education;
    else if object-type is Programming then
      call printBill() in class Programming;
}
```

However, all of the type-checking code of the object's runtime is done for you by the Java runtime! Thus, all those lines are replaced with one: `transaction.printBill();`

There is a fundamental concept at work here:

IMPORTANT NOTE: An object variable's declared type (*compile time*) can differ from its actual type (*runtime*). At runtime, the variable can actually refer to an object of any type *below* the declared class in its hierarchy.

The converse of this is not true. Had you declared the parameter type to be the child class `Presentation`, you could not have legally passed in an object of *parent* type `BillableService`-or an object of *sibling* type `Education` or `Programming`, for that matter. The actual type can only be the declared class type or any *child* class that directly or indirectly `extends` that declared class type. Stated another way, the actual runtime type must be at, or below, the declared compile time type.

What happens, then, on the call to method `printBill()`? This is where things get interesting. All classes in the hierarchy — the parent `BillableService` and the three children of it — define the method `printBill()` and implement it differently. Which version of the method is called? The answer is — it depends! This is a runtime decision; it depends on the runtime type of the object. The Java runtime will determine the actual object class type at runtime, and call the method of that name in that particular class. That means the appropriate version of `printBill` will be called each time! Isn't that nice? This saves you the trouble of writing hack code to determine the actual runtime type yourself and invoking the appropriate method. To help you visualize this, think of a method call on an object as being either:

- A message being sent to that object, where it is the object's responsibility to interpret how to run it (this is actually the Smalltalk model).

- A function pointer call, where each object type (class) supplies a different function address (this is close to reality, under the covers).

This, then, is ***polymorphism*** in action. You have code here which appears to be calling a particular method in a particular class — `transaction.printBill()` — yet at runtime, the actual version of the method name that gets invoked is dependent on the object's type. One method *call* statement, yet many (***poly***) possible forms (***morphs***) of output. In Greek, in fact, polymorphism means "many forms."

What if the class of the runtime object did not have an override of that method? In terms of the previous example, what if the code called method `getCost()` which only exists in the base class? The Java runtime works like this: first, it looks for the method with that exact signature in the class of which the runtime object is a type. If the runtime does not find the method there, it then looks in that class's parent class, and so on up the hierarchy. If it does not find the method, even in the universal parent class `java.lang.Object`, then you will get an error and do the Java equivalent of a "machine check." But, of course, the **JAVAC** compiler would have caught that first. If the method exists in *more* than one class, the version of the method in the lowest class in the hierarchy — starting at the object's actual runtime class type (versus compile type) — always wins.

What if the method being called only exists in one or more of the subclasses, but not in the base class? Well, if the object's compile time type is the base class, the compile will fail — the same hierarchy check is made at compile time — but from the compile time class up. In the case of our billable time example, if the method is not found in the declared parent type class of `BillableService`, that is an error. This makes sense because you are using a base class at compile time and you are certain that the method exists in *all* the subclasses — as inherited methods from a base class always do. If the method does not exist in the base class, it may not exist in the runtime classes either, as far as the compiler is concerned.

Now you can see why no formal language construct exists for a child class to remove methods from its parent class. The concept of polymorphism requires the compiler to assume that a method defined in one class is always available in its lower, or child, classes. Thus, the best you can do is override the parent's method and make it do nothing. It still exists; it just has no functionality. You also cannot restrict a method's access rights beyond what is defined at the parent level. For example, you cannot override a method in a child class and change it from a **public** method to a **private** method. The reverse, however, is permitted.

Polymorphism and the AS/400

You can find examples of polymorphism in OS/400. Consider, for example, the commands you can run against OS/400 objects — these are like methods in a class. And some of these commands are indeed polymorphic — there may be only one command, but it has different behavior depending on the type of object to which it is applied. Specifically, this applies to any of the **xxxOBJ** commands, like **RNMOBJ** (*Rename Object*) and **CRTDUPOBJ** (*Create Duplicate Object*). These actually invoke completely unique code for each object type they run against, but that difference is shielded from you as a user of these commands — it is pure polymorphic magic!

Of course, it does not happen totally by magic. You are still forced to supply the object type as a parameter in these commands. To be truly polymorphic, the AS/400 would force unique names for all objects in a library, independent of their type. Then, these generic **xxxOBJ** commands would not need to take the object type as a parameter; rather, the system would know from the name exactly which object is being referred to and, hence, its type. This is why classes in Java must have unique names within the same scope (package). In fact, you can always determine an object's class type at runtime by using the great-grandparent class `Object` — from which all classes inherit. `Object`, and, hence, all classes has a method called `getClass()`, which returns a special `java.lang.Class` object. This, in turn, has a method called `getName()` that returns a `String` with the name of the object's class, like this:

```
String classname = myObject.getClass().getName();
```

Another example of polymorphism on the AS/400 is the **Work With** or list screens in PDM (***Programming Development Manager***). In these screens, you are presented with a list of libraries, objects, or members; you can enter options beside them to invoke actions on the items in the list. These options (like option 5 to display) are polymorphic in that the resulting action is dependent on the type of object you use it against. You get a different result for each object type and, yet, you as a user always use the same simple option and let PDM take care of determining the appropriate action for the selected object's type.

Yet another example is the **WRITE** op-code in RPG. You use it the same, whether you are writing to a database, display, or printer file. The RPG runtime keeps track of which one is actually being written to, and handles each uniquely, under the covers.

INHERITING MORE

As you have seen, inheritance is the key to object orientation, which distinguishes object-*based* systems such as OS/400 from object-*oriented* systems such as Java. It is with inheritance, too, that you will need to spend a little more time learning some additional syntax and semantic rules that apply to inherited classes or objects. You'll also be introduced to a new Java construct related to inheritance.

Protected Access

You have already seen examples of the accessor modifiers that can be specified for methods, such as **public**:

```
public void myMethod()
{
  ...
}
```

There are a total of three such accessor modifiers, along with a fourth which is implicit if no modifier is specified, as shown in the following table:

Java	Description
private	Only accessible by methods in *this* class.
package (default)	Only accessible by other methods in this package. This is the implicit default.
protected	Only accessible by methods in this class *or* its subclasses.
public	Accessible by all.

Now, finally, you can see the reason for having four different access options. In Java, you can divide the world (users of your method) into:

- other methods in this class (`private`)
- other methods in other classes in this package (`package`)
- other methods in any subclass in any package (`protected`)
- other methods in any class in any package (`public`)

In order to restrict the usage of your method to one of the four categories shown above, choose the indicated modifier keyword. This restricts any method in a lower category (that is, any category below the chosen one on the list above) from your method. However, it allows access from any method in the chosen or higher bullet. That is, the access rights are cumulative:

- `private` = only code in this class can call this method
- `package` = `private` + all other classes and subclasses in this package
- `protected` = `package` + subclasses in other packages which extend this class
- `public` = `protected` + other packages (the world!)

When would you use `protected`? This is designed explicitly for cases where you want the method to be private (internal use only) to your class and any "family members" — that is, any classes that choose to extend your class into child classes. Typically, if you are defining a class to be extendible (the default, but as you will see you can prevent it), then you will use:

- `private` for all instance variables (good form *always*).
- `protected` for all helper or internal-use methods (versus `private`).

Remember that we are not talking about the ability for a child class to override a method (see the next section); rather, we are talking about the ability for a child class to simply *use* the methods in the parent class. You'll rarely encounter a need to restrict this, the way you would using `private`, instead of `protected`.

Preventing Inheritance

There are times when you will want to completely restrict the ability for another programmer to extend your class and override or replace certain methods. From a security point of view, you may have very sensitive methods that you want to ensure cannot be maliciously or unwittingly replaced. For example, the `getPay()` method for an employee object might be an example of a sensitive method. Notice the difference here between *using* and *overriding*. You do not mind child classes *using* this method — in fact, you want this, because it hides all the sensitive calculations. What you do *not* want child classes doing is *overriding* the implementation of this method. For integrity and security, it is important that all code that invokes this method get to the one and only implementation of it, and not some other implementation farther down the inheritance chain (thus preventing a *Trojan horse* kind of attack).

Final Methods

You can prevent child classes from overriding a specific method in Java by using the `final` modifier keyword on the method:

```
protected final int getPay()
{
   ...
}
```

The modifier `final` tells the compiler that no child subclass is allowed to override this method with its own implementation. The compiler will enforce this, as will the runtime. Notice, again, that in this context, `protected` indicates that child classes are allowed to *use* this method, just not *replace* it.

In addition to *security* benefits, `final` also offers *performance* benefits. It is a clue to the compiler that this method will not be participating in polymorphism, so the compiler has the option of *inlining* the method. Inlining involves turning calls to the method into static versus dynamic calls (that is, determining and recording the address of the method at compile time rather than waiting for runtime). Therefore, it is in your best interest to review your `protected` and even `public` methods for opportunities to flag them as `final`.

TERMINOLOGY NOTE: Methods that are not `final` are occasionally referred to as *virtual*.

Final Classes

Specifying `final` on each method that you want to protect or perform more efficiently (and that you are sure does not need to be overridden), is a good, fine-grained form of restriction. However, there may be classes that you decide are entirely "leaf" classes (on the hierarchy tree) that will never be overridden. So, you want to easily flag that entire class as `final`. In other words, you want to prevent others from defining new classes that extend this class (prevent others from defining child classes). You can do this in Java, too. Just use the `final` modifier at the class level and all methods inside the class are automatically designated as `final` by the compiler. In our `BillableService` example, we may be sure that no other child classes are anticipated after the `Presentation`, `Education`, and `Programming` classes, and so, for efficiency, we declare them as `final`:

```
public final class Presentation extends BillableService
{
   ...
}
```

NOTE: This concept of applying a keyword globally to a class, instead of locally to individual methods in the class, is identical to some DDS (*Data Description Specifications*) keywords on the AS/400. Many keywords, such as **CFnn** for display files, can be displayed either at the file level (apply to every record format) or at the individual record format level.

Enforcing Inheritance

The previous section discussed how to prevent child classes from overriding a particular method or prevent child classes altogether for a particular class. There are times, however, when precisely the opposite is required. You may have defined a class hierarchy in which the parent will never be instantiated directly — rather, only child classes of this class will be instantiated. This is common. In fact, you will find yourself abstracting out common behavior into parent classes whose role is to ensure the children all have common functionality. These parent classes may never be instantiated into objects themselves, as it won't make sense. Our BillableService hierarchy is such an example. We do not anticipate that a user of the class hierarchy will create an object of type BillableService; rather, users are expected to create objects of one of the child class types — Presentation, Education, or Programming. BillableService is merely an abstraction that ensures that all three child classes support a consistent set of base methods or functionality.

Abstract Methods

Consider the printBill() method in our BillableService hierarchy. It is overridden in each of the child classes. It may well be our design that nobody should ever call printBill() in the base class (BillableService) directly. Rather, we always want the appropriate child class implementation to be used at runtime. In this case, why do we have printBill() in our base class? The reason, of course, is for polymorphism, as described earlier — the ability to define a parameter as type BillableService, and invoke printBill() on that parameter, even though the runtime types will always be one of the children classes. For this to work, we must define printBill() in the base class even though we know all children will override it with their own implementations. If this is the case, why put any code inside the base class definition of printBill()? Because that code will never be invoked (by design), we might as well define the base class method as empty:

```
public void printBill()
{
}
```

This will work just fine. But it does not prevent another programmer, three years from now after you have moved on, from defining a new subclass for a new service and mistakenly not overriding `printBill` with a "concrete" implementation. The programmer will not know that he or she is expected to override this method, and so will be dumbfounded when the first tests result in no printed output.

What you really need, and what Java provides, is a way to indicate that this method is *declared but not defined* in the base class. That is, Java gives you a way to define the exact signature of the method (but not the body) and have the compiler enforce child classes to implement that method. This is achieved in Java through the use of the **abstract** modifier. This modifier identifies to the compiler that this method must be overridden and concretely implemented in each class that extends this base class. Therefore, our `printBill()` method will look like this:

```
public abstract void printBill();
```

Notice the use of the modifier **abstract**. Also make note of the semicolon at the end of the signature, versus the typical braces and method body. There is no need to define an empty body. This method has no meaning in this base class and is, in essence, merely a place-holder for child classes to indicate that they must implement this method.

Abstract Classes

The use of abstract methods in a class informs the compiler that any class extending this class must override and implement this method. It also informs the compiler that this base class cannot be instantiated directly using **new**. Rather, only child classes that extend it and implement the abstract method(s) may be instantiated. Why? Because if you were allowed to instantiate this class as an object, and you subsequently invoked the abstract method `printBill()`, you would encounter a runtime error. Therefore, when you define a method in a class as abstract (as a convenience for the programmers who will subsequently use it), you are also forced by Java's rules to specify the **abstract** modifier at the class level:

```
public abstract class BillableService
{
    ...
    public abstract void printBill();
    ...
}
```

This informs potential users of the class that it is an *abstract class* — because it has one or more abstract methods — and so cannot be used directly. Tools such as VisualAge for Java may pick up on this and display the class name with a different font or in superscript to render it visually obvious. This also alerts potential programmers who want to extend this class that there are methods in the class that must be overridden and concretely defined.

> **NOTE:** Unlike the `final` modifier, specifying `abstract` for a class does not make or require *all* methods to be abstract. Rather, it implies only that *some* of the methods will be abstract.

You can have more than one abstract class in a hierarchy. You may decide to extend one abstract class with yet another abstract class in order to further refine the abstraction. This is fine. As long as you specify the `abstract` modifier for the new subclass as well, you will not be forced to implement the abstract methods in it (although you are permitted to do so). Eventually, however, some child class must finally be defined without `abstract`.

> **TERMINOLOGY NOTE:** Classes that are not *abstract* are said to be *concrete*. Methods that are abstract are also referred to occasionally as *pure virtual*.

Finally, you can think of field reference files on the AS/400 as being similar to abstract classes. They have no "implementation" (in this case, they never hold data) but are designed explicitly to abstract out common field attributes for use in child or populated databases.

Constructors and Inheritance

As you recall, classes can have *constructors*. In fact, they usually do. These constructors are simply special methods with the same name as the class, and without any return type specified. There can be multiple constructors, each taking different numbers or types of parameters. You do not call these constructors *explicitly*; rather, the Java runtime will do this *implicitly* when you instantiate an object using the `new` operator. If you have multiple constructors, the one that is called is the one that matches exactly the number and type of parameters specified on the `new` call. For example, if you have a class called `MyClass` with two constructors-one that takes no parameters and one that takes a single integer parameter-then `new MyClass()` will call the constructor that has no parameters, while `new MyClass(10)` will call the constructor that has one parameter.

The *default constructor* takes no parameters, while other constructors can take whatever parameters are necessary to place an instance of the class in a valid initial state.

When you have a class that extends another class, *it is your responsibility* to invoke the appropriate constructor for the parent class. Suppose class Education extends class BillableService, as in the earlier example. Then suppose that BillableService has a constructor that takes in the number of hours to be billed, the customer name, and the names of the employees who provided the service:

LISTING 9-4

```
class BillableService
{
    ... // instance variables
    // Constructor:
    public BillableService(int numberHours,
                           String customerName,
                           String[] employees)
    {
      ... // do initialization using passed in values
    }
}
```

Now, consider Education, which is a subclass of BillableService. It has a constructor that also takes in a course number, which is stored in a new instance variable in class Education. This constructor must:

- Call the constructor of the parent class, with the required parameters;
- Do its own initialization, as it deems necessary.

For example, you might have:

LISTING 9-5

```
class Education extends BillableService
{
    int course; // Course number instance variable
    // Constructor:
    public Education(int numberHours,
                     String customerName,
                     String[] employees,
                     int courseNumber)
    {
        super(numberHours, customerName, employees);
        course = courseNumber;
    }
}
```

Notice the use of the Java keyword **super** to invoke the parent classes' constructor. This is, not surprisingly, the same keyword you have already seen for invoking other methods in a parent's class. When invoking a parent constructor from a child constructor, the following apply:

- The syntax is super(parms), versus super.method(parms) for regular method calls;
- The super() call must be the first line in the child's constructor.

If you neglect to make this call to the parent's constructor, Java will automatically call the parent's *default* constructor for you-that is, the constructor that takes no parameters. This may result in incorrect initialization.

Multiple Inheritance

Other object-oriented languages, such as C++, allow you to extend not only one class, but multiple classes. This can be useful in many situations where you want a class to inherit the behavior of more than one existing class. For example, you may find it useful to define a user interface window, which is both a window and an employee, so that your class inherits the methods from both. The Java language, however, does not allow this. The reason relates back to the Java designers' goal of keeping the language simple. *Multiple inheritance*, which occurs when a class extends more than one base class, has an inherit complexity: if a method or variable with exactly the same signature exists in both parent classes, which one is used in the child class? This collision problem leads to some arbitrary rules that, in other languages, make the concept of inheritance more complicated- too complicated for the Java mantra of "*Keep It Simple, Stupid.*"

If Java did support multiple inheritance, syntactically it would probably do so by allowing multiple class names after the **extends** keyword on a class definition, separated by commas:

```
public class Education extends BillableService, Printable { ... }
```

This would mean that we inherit all the methods and variables from both classes — in this case BillableService and Printable. This class would have, then, two parents.

Interfaces

While Java does not allow multiple inheritance, it does not disregard the subject totally. Multiple inheritance is too important when designing object-oriented systems. Java defines a special and simplified version of multiple inheritance that uses a new term — *interface*. Because the collision problems stem from variables and predefined methods existing in two parent classes, Java allows you to define a special type of class — an interface — that does not have any variables. It has only method signatures, not method bodies (actual code, that is). Let's look at an example:

```
public interface Printable
{
    public void print();
}
```

Note the use of the keyword **interface** rather than class. Interfaces are a specialized form of class:

- They have no variables (they do allow constants for instance variables, though);
- They have no constructors;
- They have no static methods;
- They only have method declarations, not method code;
- They can not be instantiated (that is, **new** is not valid for them).

In essence, then, they are an empty shell- an *interface* only! They are similar to an ILE RPG IV module's copy member containing its procedure prototypes. How do you use them? The idea is that the class that wants the functionality "promised" by the interface defines in the class definition that it will "implement" that interface:

```
class MyClass extends YourClass implements Printable
{
    ...
}
```

By using the Java keyword **implements**, you are declaring that your class will *implement* each of the methods declared in that interface. Your class must actually define all the methods of the interface! That is interesting. It means that a Java interface is, in fact, a ***contract***. When you declare that you will implement an interface in your class, you are agreeing to fulfill that contract by implementing *all* of the methods in that interface, using *exactly* the same signature. If you don't, the compiler will issue you a fine that will be in the form of a compile failure. Another way to look at it is that **implements** is similar to **extends**, but you are forced to override each and every method in the base class (the interface class in this case). This, then, is how Java permits a limited but still very powerful form of multiple inheritance — while a class can only extend one parent class, it *can* implement one or more interfaces, as in:

```
class MyClass extends YourClass implements Printable, anotherInterface
{
    ...
}
```

A class that implements an interface allows other code that uses objects of your class to be sure they can invoke the interface methods on your class. Typically, interfaces are quite small, with only a few method signatures. Often, in fact, there is only one. They are typically used to "mix in" specific, well-defined (via signature) functions. Interfaces are used to circumvent the single inheritance rule in Java.

The `BillableService` example shown previously had a method defined somewhere in the "user space" that was able to invoke the `printBill()` method on any object in the hierarchy by declaring the parameter as class type `BillableService`. Imagine, now, that this other method takes a collection (perhaps an array) of `BillableService` objects (or their children) and loops through them, calling `printBill()` to print out the detail record of each entry in the array; perhaps it also prints out header and footer information. Imagine that this routine became so useful that you decided to use it not only for the `BillableService` hierarchy, but for your other business objects, such as `Widgets`. After all, printing out a bill is a pretty useful function. How would you declare the parameter type to allow it to invoke a specific method — `printBill()` — on any given class? The only class common to all class hierarchies is `java.lang.Object` — but it certainly does not have a `printBill()` method in it, so using `java.lang.Object` would fail. The answer, of course, lies with interfaces.

You would define an **interface**, as we have shown, called `Printable`. Then, for every class that is to support the `print()` method (we would favor this more generic name over `printBill`) we would define the class as "**implements** `Printable`" and, of course, we would define the `print()` method in that class. This way, we could establish the expected `print` method for any class — not just classes in a specific hierarchy. Thus, we would remove `printBill()` from our class hierarchy in `BillableService`, and instead implement the `Printable` interface. We would also do the same for every class in our system that we wish to make callable by our print-looping method.

Let us examine this further. You have seen the `Printable` interface with its one method — `print()`:

```
public interface Printable
{
    public void print();
}
```

A slice of the redesigned `BillableService` hierarchy might now look like this:

LISTING 9-6

```
public abstract class BillableService implements Printable
{
  // ...
}
public final class Presentation extends BillableService
{
    public void print()
    {
        System.out.println("inside print for Presentation");
    }
}
```

> **NOTE:** These classes, of course, would be placed in separate .java source files
> that bear exactly the same name as the class.

You need not explicitly state that the child class (`Presentation`) **implements** `Printable`. This is because the parent class `BillableService` did so already. Therefore, the child class inherits this. Also, notice that the parent class `BillableService` did not define the `print()` method from the `BillableService` interface as you were told is necessary to complete the interface contract. This is only because `BillableService` is defined as **abstract** — so it is assumed by the compiler that the child classes will implement it.

> **NOTE:** This tells us that interfaces are exactly like **abstract** classes with only
> **abstract** methods in them.

Now, for illustrative purposes, let's define another completely independent class (not part of the `BillableService` hierarchy) called `Widget`:

LISTING 9-7

```
public final class Widget implements Printable
{
    public void print()
    {
        // print out meaningful report line
        System.out.println("inside print for Widget");
    }
}
```

Now we have two classes that are not part of the same hierarchy and that both implement `Printable`. Therefore, we know that we have a method called `print`. Let's imagine, now, a method somewhere called `printReport`, which takes as a parameter an array of "printable" objects and invokes the `print()` method on each of the objects. How to define this parameter? As an array of `Printable`, of course! That is, interfaces are synonymous with classes as far as declaring variables are concerned. By defining a parameter as an array of objects of type interface `Printable`, you are really telling the compiler that the array will hold objects that are of any class type that *implements* the interface `Printable`.

This, again, highlights how similar interfaces are to abstract classes. You cannot instantiate an abstract class or an interface. It is, however, common practice to define variables and parameters as being of an abstract class type or an interface type. These are then assigned objects of classes that extend the abstract class or implement the interface.

The example below shows what this `printReport` method might look like. It will probably be static, because it is not dependent on any particular instance of an object. For our purposes, then, we will stick it into the same class as our `main()` method so we can easily compile and run it to see how it works:

LISTING 9-8

```
public class TestBillable
{
  public static void main(String[] args)
  {
    Printable[] objlist = new Printable[2];
    objlist[0] = new Presentation();
    objlist[1] = new Widget();
    printReport(objlist);
  }
  public static void printReport(Printable[] objects)
  {
    System.out.println("Printing objects...");
    for (int index=0;
         index<objects.length;
         index=index+1)
      objects[index].print();
    System.out.println(objects.length + " objects printed");
  }
}
```

Basically, this class has a main method, which means that it can be invoked from the command line, and a printReport method that, given an array of objects that implement Printable, loops through the array and invokes the print() method on the objects. Main creates an array of Printable object type and populates it with an instance of a Presentation class and an instance of a Widget class. Main then calls printReport with this array. Here is the result of compiling and running this test case:

```
> javac TestBillable.java
> java TestBillable
Printing objects...
inside print for Presentation
inside print for Widget
2 objects printed
```

We see, then, that the print method for each different class was properly invoked. Note that, in main, had we tried to equate an array element to an instance of a class type that did not implement the Printable interface, the compile would have failed, as we defined the array to be of type Printable.

Callbacks

The Printable interface example of the last section is an example of a ***callback function,*** the most popular use of interfaces. These are a programming idiom, not a defined language concept. ***Callbacks*** in other languages usually invoke a utility function that requires the caller to provide an address of a function for which the utility function will need to callback to the caller. This is typically an address of a function that is unique to each caller. Classic examples of using callbacks are:

- A sort utility that will sort a given collection of items. To determine relative order, the utility must "call back" to the caller in order to do the comparisons — this is caller dependent, as it depends entirely on what you are sorting.

- Error-checking intercepts. This allows a common display, such as an "open" dialog, to permit callers to supply their own error-checking code, in the form of a function pointer, when the OK push button is pressed, for example.

To do this in RPG now, you can use the new pointer data type and **PADDR** (procedure address) keyword to define a procedure pointer. To do this in Java, which does not have pointers and hence does not have function pointers, you typically use interfaces. Instead of accepting a function pointer, your utility method accepts an object of type "**interface** I" which has a doIt() method in its contract, say. Callers then change their class to implement this interface and thus its expected method, and pass an instance of their class to the utility method. The utility method then calls back by invoking the method dictated by the interface.

Notice that, if the utility method is only designed to expect and accept objects of one class type, you do not need interfaces because you can simply define the parameter using that explicit class type. However, if you want to be able to use that method generically, passing in objects of various and not predictable class types, you will have to use an interface. There is no single class type you could possibly specify that would not preclude some other new class type from being used in the future. With callbacks, and with interfaces in general, you typically have the following pieces:

- An **interface** that defines the signature(s) of one or more methods the callback code needs or expects;
- One or more **classes** which implement that interface and uniquely implement the methods in it;
- A utility, or *callback*, method somewhere else that accepts objects of that interface type, and calls the expected interface methods in those objects;
- User code, somewhere (actually, probably in numerous places), which calls the utility method with objects of various class types — but those classes *must* all implement the interface.

So, pictorially, you have something like the arrangement shown in Figure 9-6:

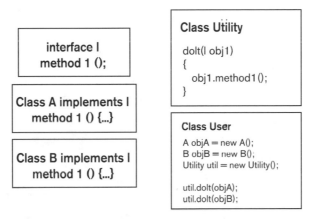

FIGURE 9-6

This is just as we did in our Printable interface example:

- Interface Printable supplied the expected method signature for print();
- Classes BillableService and Widget implemented interface Billable and method print();
- Class TestBillable supplied the utility method printReport() that accepted an array of interface Printable objects;

Class `TestBillable` also supplied the user method, `main()`, which invoked the utility method `printReport()` on objects of various class types.

Interface Summary

Let's summarize, formally, the new Java language construct we have just explored. An interface definition is a *reference* type definition, as is a class. This is in comparison to primitive data types, like integer. Interfaces exhibit much of the same behavior of an abstract class that contains only abstract methods and constant instance variables (**public static final**). The syntax for defining an interface is depicted in Figure 9-7:

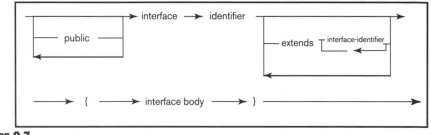

FIGURE 9-7

Some notes on defining interfaces:

- Like classes, interfaces have *package* rights by default, but can be assigned **public**. At this outer level, public versus package affects initial access rights to the type, versus the individual members (methods and fields). So, if you do not specify **public**, then only classes within this package can ***implement*** this interface.

- Like classes, interfaces can inherit from one another by using the **extends** keyword. Unlike classes, you can inherit from more than one interface at a time (comma-separate the names).

- Interface names must be unique within their scope, both for classes and interfaces. That is, you *cannot* give the same name to both a class and an interface within the same package.

- An interface body can consist of variables and methods.

- All methods in an interface are implicitly **public** and **abstract**, although these keywords can be redundantly specified. No other modifiers are permitted for interface methods.

- Interface methods, since they are abstract, have no body, just an ending semicolon.

- All variables in an interface are implicitly **public**, **static** and **final**, although these keywords can be redundantly specified. No other modifiers are permitted for interface variables.

- All variables must be explicitly initialized as part of their definition (since they are constants, after all).

Interfaces, then, allow you to inherit method signatures (via the **implements** keyword in a class definition). But, if this is all you get, versus actual code for the methods, why bother? Why not simply implement the methods directly in all the classes that need them, without bothering with the **implements** keyword and the interface at all? In the end, it seems, there has been no code sharing — the intended purpose of inheritance all along. This is a key question, and something with which you should become comfortable. The answers are:

- An interface is merely a *tag* for the compiler. It is a mechanism to inform the compiler that, yes, this class (which implements the interface) really does support the methods named in the interface. This allows you to write generic utility code that works on objects of any type — as long as they implement that interface. If you do not need such generic utility code, you do not need an interface.

- Multiple inheritance, in the end, is not that useful for fully implemented methods (versus abstract signature-only methods). If a set of fully-implemented methods is generic enough to be "mixed in" at will to any class, then clearly they are independent of the class in the first place and inheritance is not necessary. In this case, you may as well just declare an instance of the separate class inside your class and call its methods when you need to. This is why it is not a big loss that, compared to true multiple inheritance, interface methods have no body or implementation. Presumably, if you want to *inherit* these methods into many of your classes, you want to supply unique implementations anyway. If you want to inherit them into only one class hierarchy — in other words, simply define the methods in your base (parent) class — you do not need *multiple* inheritance for this.

Have you got it yet? Do not be concerned if you do not; it is a tough concept that will come with time. Some actual examples will help.

Java-Supplied Interface Examples: Cloneable and Enumeration

Java itself makes significant use of interfaces. One example of which you should be aware is the **Cloneable** interface. This interface is defined in the java.lang package, which is the one Java supplied package that is automatically imported for you. **Cloneable** is an interesting case — it is a completely empty interface! It highlights the fact that interfaces are really tags for the compiler. The java.lang package class called Object from which, as you now know, all classes inherit, has a method in it called clone(). The purpose of this base method is to create a new instance of a given object that is identical to the current instance:

```
ClassA objA = new ClassA();
ClassA objB = objA.clone();
```

It is important to have this method, because otherwise you might be tempted to use this:

```
ClassA objB = objA;
```

This does not copy `objA` at all! It simply creates a second reference to it. (Object variables, again, are merely references to allocated objects. That is, they hold object addresses, or pointers). In order to create a second copy of an object, it is up to the object itself to supply a method to do this. This is what `clone()` does. It essentially instantiates a new instance of this class (using the default constructor only) and copies bit-by-bit all the instance variables in the current class to the new class.

Sounds straightforward? Well, it is not! The problem is that you may have objects as instance variables, and as we just discussed, copying an object variable only produces a second reference to the same object — not a second copy of that object, as you would expect in this case. That is, nested objects need to be cloned too! This job is not something that the base `clone()` method inside `java.lang.Object` can take on by itself. It needs to be carefully implemented by each class — by you. So, Java makes the `clone()` method in `Object` protected — it can only be called by you in your class. Thus, `objB = objA.clone()` will always fail with a "method not accessible" error message unless you:

- Override and implement the **`clone()`** method in your class;
- In that override, change the access to **`public`**.

And that's not all. The language designers were so anxious that `clone()` only be supported by classes that really think they have implemented it properly, that they force you to also tell the compiler explicitly that you support this method. How? By defining your class as "**`implements`** `Clonable`". Only if all this has been done can a user invoke the `clone()` method on your class.

By the way, if you do decide to support this useful function, your clone method would:

- First, invoke your parent's clone method — **`super.clone();`**
- Second, invoke the clone method on all of your object instance variables (if they are not **`null`**, the value that unallocated object variables have).

This is a case where an interface is used in a unique way, as a tag to identify this class's support for a particular function. Can you do this, too? Yes, you can. There is a way to determine programmatically if the class type of a given object implements a particular interface — by first using the `java.lang.Object` method `getClass()` to return the object's `Class` object and then calling `getInterfaces()` on the `Class` object. This returns an array of `Class` objects — one for each interface implemented by this class. You can then loop through this array, invoking `getName()` on each entry looking for the interface name you are interested in.

By the way, this discussion about copying objects applies to testing for equality too. You cannot test if two objects are "equal" like this:

```
if (objA == objB) then ...
```

Since object variables are really addresses of allocated objects, this test will only test if the two variables *refer* to the same place in memory. It is really up to each class to determine equality — you may decide two instances of your class are "equal" if they have the same values for some key instance variables. The Java convention for this is to supply a method called equals:

```
public boolean equals(MyClass anotherObject)
{
    ...
}
```

A useless version of this is supplied in java.lang.Object, so you are overriding it by supplying your own. In this case, though, no "**implements** xxx" tag is required on your class.

Now for a second example of interfaces as supplied by the Java language. In the Java "utility" package called java.util, there is an interface called **Enumeration**. This is a convention that classes should use when they want to support the idea of *enumerating* or walking through a list of items. Suppose you have a class that is obviously a collection of something — say it is a Stack class that manages a stack of integers. If you want to support the ability for users to iterate through each item in the stack, you should do so by implementing the Enumeration interface. This will make it easier for users who are used to this convention from other Java supplied classes, such as Hashtable in the java.util package. Here is how it works. Enumeration contains two method signatures:

- hasMoreElements() which returns **true** if there are more elements in the collection;
- nextElement() which returns the next element in the collection.

The intended usage for these is this:

```
while (obj.hasMoreElements())
    nextObj = obj.nextElement();
```

Obviously, for you to implement these methods in your class, you will need to record some state information — namely the "current" position. For this reason, you don't implement this interface directly in your class; rather, you supply an entirely new class that implements them. This new class must take an instance of your class in the constructor, then initialize and maintain a position variable to support the implementation of the two methods. Our stack example might look like this:

LISTING 9-9

```
import java.util.*;
class EnumerateStack implements Enumeration
{
     private Stack stack;
     private int pos=0;
     // constructor
     EnumerateStack(Stack stack)
     {
          this.stack = stack;
     }
     // end-of-list test...
     public boolean hasMoreElements()
     {
          return (pos < stack.getSize());
     }
     // retrieve next element...
     public Object nextElement()
     {
          Object retobj = null;
          if (hasMoreElements())
            {
                 retobj = stack.array[pos];
                 pos = pos+1;
            }
          return retobj;
     }
} // end EnumerateStack class
```

Now, you need to supply a nice little method in your `stack` class that will return one of these:

```
public Enumeration getEnumeration()
{
     return new EnumerateStack(this);
}
```

Finally, users who want to enumerate the entries in your stack will have code that looks like this:

```
Enumeration enum = myStack.getEnumeration();
Integer nextInt;
while (enum.hasMoreElements())
    nextInt = enum.nextElement();
```

NOTE: In order for this to work, your `Stack` class would have to manage a stack of integer objects, not base types. This is because the `nextElement` method in the `Enumeration` interface is defined to return an `Object`. All primitive types, such as integer, have object versions in Java, too. For integer, this is the class `Integer`. These are "object wrappers" for the primitive types that allow you to use them as full objects as opposed to built-in base or primitive data types. This is useful in cases like this, where you want to work with objects. All of these wrappers have methods for populating the object from a primitive value, and for extracting the primitive value from the object.

You have now two examples where Java itself makes good use of interfaces — there are many more. It's your turn now to invent some!

020 — Object to Object: Casting Objects

You already know that in Java, as in RPG and in all languages, you can "cast" variables of basic data types such as integer and float from one type to another. In Java, you can cast a data type "up" to a higher precision *implicitly* — as in:

```
int a = 10;
long b = a; // cast integer (4 bytes) to long (8 bytes)
```

If you want to cast "down" to a lower precision, you must do so *explicitly* using the (type) notation, as in:

```
long b = 10;
int a = (int)b; // cast long (8 bytes) to integer (4 bytes)
```

What about object variables? Can you cast an object reference of one class type to an object reference of another class type? Would you want to? The answer, to both questions, is yes. Like casting of primitive data types, it involves rules related to loss of precision.

Why Cast?

Recall our discussion of polymorphism and interfaces, and how utility methods will often describe a parameter as a parent or interface type, yet accept object parameters of children classes at runtime. The actual parameter passed may be of a type *lower* in the hierarchy tree than was declared for the parameter type (and again, think of interfaces as purely abstract parent classes). Also common is defining an array of parent type classes and populating it with actual objects from lower in the hierarchy tree. Both cases allow common code to invoke parent-defined methods on the actual objects, and have the appropriate versions of those methods invoked, polymorphically.

What happens if there is a special case where you really do need, in this common code, to invoke a method that is only defined in the child class? At compile time, such an attempt will fail because the compiler looks in the compile-time parent class for the method. If the method does not exist there, you will not be able to compile this code.

You should strive to avoid this situation by defining the needed method in the parent class, as an empty do-nothing method if necessary. However, there are still times you will feel forced to do this. This requires an explicit cast on your part to force the compiler to treat the object as a new type. Back to our example, where `Presentation` was a subclass of `BillableService`, what if we had a new method defined only in `Presentation` called `printTitle()`:

```
public void printTitle()
{
    System.out.println("printing title of this presentation");
}
```

Now suppose we want, in our `printReport()` method, to invoke this method if, and only if, the current object is of type `Presentation`? First of all, you need to determine the type of the current object. This is done using the Java operator **instanceof**, which returns **true** or **false** at runtime if this object is actually of the class type specified. The syntax is:

```
objectVariable instanceof className
```

It is only used in expressions, since it has no side affects. So, in our case we need to use this in our loop to check if the current object in the array is of type `Presentation` and if so invoke the unique-to-`Presentation` method `printTitle`. But how do we invoke it? We need to have a variable, of type `Presentation`, to do this. We will do this by defining a local variable of this type and casting the current object to it, using the explicit object cast notation:

```
ClassType object1 = (ClassType)object2;
```

Finally, our modified `printReport` method looks like this:

LISTING 9-10

```
public static void printReport(Printable[] objects)
{
   System.out.println("Printing objects...");
   for (int index=0;
        index<objects.length;
        index=index+1)
   {
     objects[index].print();
     if (objects[index] instanceof Presentation)
        {
          Presentation pres = (Presentation)objects[index];
          pres.printTitle();
        }
   } // end for loop
   System.out.println(objects.length + " objects printed");
}
```

Now, if we run our `TestBillable` class we get:

```
Printing objects...
inside print for Presentation
printing title of this presentation
inside print for Widget
2 objects printed
```

This demonstrates that you can cast from one object type to another when necessary.

Rules of Object Casting

Here are some rules for casting objects:

- You can only cast between objects in the same hierarchy tree;
- If you cast from a parent class type to a child class type, an explicit cast is required;
- If you cast from a child class type to a parent class type, no explicit cast is required;
- If the actual object at runtime is not of the target type, you will get a runtime error. That is why you should always use the **instanceof** operator to verify this.

Common Methods to Override

You know now that all classes you create in Java implicitly extend the `java.lang.Object` class. This gives users of your class access to all the non-final, non-abstract, non-private methods in this universal class. However, there are a few methods that you should consider overriding in your new class every time. This is not to say that every class you create needs to support all of these methods, but you really should make an explicit decision in every class whether to implement these methods or not. They are:

Method	Description
finalize	This method is called by Java when an object of your class is "swept up" by the garbage collector. If you have any finalization or cleanup code to be done when the object is destroyed, put it here. For example, closing any possibly still open files.
clone	You have seen this already; it is a convention to supply this method if you want to enable object duplication.
equals	By convention, users will invoke this method to compare two objects of your class. If you want to support the idea of equality testing, you must supply this method, as the default implementation returns **false** unless you are comparing an object to itself.
hashCode	This returns a hash code, or unique key, derived from this object. If you implement the `equals` method, you probably need to override this one too, so as to return a unique hash value for different objects, usually based on instance variable values.
toString	This method is called whenever someone tries to convert an object of your class to a string, such as by specifying an object name in the `System.out.println` method. This should return a string with something useful in it.

OO Way of Life

By this time, you have seen all the language tools for object orientation as well as all the terminology. So, are you ready to design your first object oriented project? Probably not. Using these tools efficiently is a skill that comes with time. The process of designing a good object-oriented system is different than the procedural systems that you are used to. It does involve a somewhat new way of thinking — thinking in terms of objects.

Consider how you do design or development now with RPG. Everyone is different, but chances are your up-front design centers first around the functionality (subroutines, procedures, calculation specifications) that you will need to solve the "problem." The data — data structures, arrays, and so on — that you will need to support this functionality come in at a secondary stage. We are not talking about the database design here, although, for many, that design emerges from this function-centered thought process.

With OO, the design process is reversed. Rather than first thinking about the functions required to "get the job done," you are required to consider first of all about the *objects* needed. And what are objects, again? Instances of classes. And what are classes again? Data: Data (variables) and supporting functions (methods). You need to start thinking of data and functions as a single unit in order to grasp OO. Then, you start thinking about how to partition your "problem domain" into such units (objects).

Some programmers who lack actual experience writing some OO have difficulty climbing this conceptual hill. You will be surprised at some of the things that become objects in an OO world — for example, who would expect a color, like red, to be an object? Who would expect a two-dimensional point (with x and y coordinates) to be an object? But in many systems, like Java, they are. Indeed, because in Java executable code can only exist inside of objects, we find that everything is an object-well, to be precise, everything is either an object or a simple variable inside an object.

In Search of Objects

There is no magic formula to help you begin thinking in terms of OO. But there are many books that describe the up-front part of an OO project — the ***analysis and design*** (OOA, OOD). You will want to read one or two. All of these books at least discuss the following:

- How to "find" objects in your "problem domain."

- How to find and define the "roles" of your objects (that is, the methods).

- How to find and define the "relationships" between your various objects (that is, who uses what).

- How to consistently document your design. That is, most books introduce a language for writing down your object-oriented design, with conventions for depicting classes, objects, relationships and so on.

The collective approach that a book uses to describe all this is known as a ***methodology***. Such methodologies are usually named after the person or persons who have defined them. Is there a "best" methodology? Certainly there is: It is the one that you decide to use. Pick one, roll up your sleeves, and dig in. Or, ultimately, you can hire or contract-in experienced OOA/D skilled programmers and go with their recommendation.

One methodology of which you should be aware, however, is UML or Unified Modeling Language. It is a convergence of a number of leading methodologies, and it appears poised to become the industry standard. It was predominantly defined by highly regarded methodologists (Grady Booch, Ivar Jacobson, and Jim Rumbaugh) at Rational Software, the makers of the immensely popular OOA/D tool Rational Rose. For more information on UML, see Rational's Internet Web site: **www.rational.com/uml**.

In an OO project, you spend much more time at the beginning, thinking about the problem to be solved than you do in the later stages. This is a good thing, because we know from experience that the more time you spend in the "front end" of the project, the less time you have to spend in the "back end" (coding and testing) of the project. The objectives of OO are to reduce maintenance efforts and increase code reuse. By spending time analyzing the problem domain in the search for objects, we typically improve our final time-to-market and our ongoing quality, because we:

- Drive out a better problem statement (crisp list of requirements);
- Derive a system that better models the actual real-world problem, leading to end user satisfaction and higher quality.

How do you find objects? The usual trick is to start with your requirements statement, and look for nouns. These are the "low hanging fruit" — they almost always will become objects. Examples are *car, employee, manager, bank account, customer, service.* These are all examples of "problem domain" objects. Your system will also require many "implementation" objects that will be needed, in the end, to "do the job." These are "helper" objects with commonly needed functions like tax calculations, date manipulations, string manipulations, and so on. After some experience, you will get better at finding these up front, but initially you may have to "stumble" into them as you go.

How do you find roles? These affect what methods and variables your objects will have. The usual trick is, again, to start with your requirements statement, and this time look for verbs. For example, you might expect to have methods to do *printing, sorting, calculating, ordering, billing,* and so on. Establishing which roles are played by which objects is also important at this early stage.

How do you find relationships? This requires you to address design issues like class hierarchies, object parameters, object instance variables, collections of objects, and so on. How objects will use each other, including quantitative metrics ("how many"), is important to consider at this early stage. This is where you typically have to make some tough decisions, and will be affected by such real-world things as performance.

In our experience, some of the more interesting decisions that programmers have to face are centered around inheritance. The trick is to know when to inherit from another class rather than:

- Declare an instance of the parent class as an instance variable in your class. This is known as ***containment*** — your class "contains" an instance of another class.
- Pass in an instance of the parent class as a parameter to the methods that need it. This is known as ***usage*** — your class "uses" an instance of another class.

Again, there are general rules that cover inheritance. The idea in OO is to define objects that model, as closely as possible, the real world you are interested in. This means you rely on the real world to make decisions for you wherever you can. Therefore, in order to decide if a class should inherit, contain or use another class, you should ask yourself some questions about the real world relationships between the two classes:

Is the new class an example of the first class? This is the classic "is a" relationship, and if you answer yes, it implies that your new class should inherit from the first class. One classic example involves animals: if you have a class called Animal with lots of common roles like *eating, sleeping,* or *writing code* — then what would a Dog be? A dog has unique implementations of these roles, so it should be its own class, but should it contain an animal class object or inherit from one? The answer is that, in the real world, a dog is a type of animal, and therefore, the Dog class should inherit from the Animal class.

Does the new class have an example of the first class? This is the classic "has a" relationship, and if you answer yes, it implies that your new class should contain an instance variable of the first class. An example is a program for an automobile parts business. Given a Chassis class, what should its relationship be to the Car class? Is a car a chassis? No. Does a car have a chassis? Yes. Clearly, then, the Car class should contain an instance variable of a Chassis class. Furthermore, in this example, it should contain exactly one such instance variable (this is a "quantitative metric.")

Does the new class use an example of the first class? This is the classic "uses" relationship, and if you answer yes, it implies that your new class should accept as a parameter an instance of the first class. This is typically a case where you are defining a "helper" or "utility" class that performs some commonly needed function on any given object. A classic example is an *iterator*. This is a class that has functions for iterating through a collection of objects. It typically has methods for getting the next and previous items, or seeking out a particular item based on some search criteria. As we have seen, these types of classes usually lend themselves well to abstract classes and interfaces, and use a "callback" mechanism to invoke expected and required methods in the passed-in objects.

Sometimes, the notion of "has a" versus "uses" is fuzzy. This is particularly true for utility classes. One decision you will have to make when defining such a class is whether the methods will all take objects as parameters, or whether the constructor will take an object and store away its reference in an instance variable upon which the methods will then subsequently act. The answer is situation dependent, of course, but it is not always clear initially. Passing an object in the constructor means that you have a case of containment and you will need a unique instance of the class for each object on which you want it to act. You will do this usually when some state information about the object is required between method invocations (such as an iterator class that needs to remember "current location").

Passing the object in via a method is usually used when no state information is required between invocations, as in our earlier PrintReport example. Sometimes you will decide to support both for efficiency. You will allow the user to optionally pass in an object at constructor time, and to change or set the object dynamically via a setXXX() method. In this case, you are using both containment and usage. The advantage is that your caller has to undergo the overhead of instantiating an object of your class only once — and for high-use utility classes this can be a significant consideration.

Reuse Considerations

When designing your classes, be sure to think about the next project. You want, as much as possible, to define classes and interfaces that are generally reusable. This means that you should try to abstract out the general problem from the specific problem, and define parent classes and interfaces that can be reused in different hierarchies later on.

The trick is to get the abstracting right when you create class hierarchies. That is, to best define the parent class so that it is reusable in new situations by simply creating new child classes. For example, rather than defining a totally unique class for each type of widget you sell, define a parent or base class called BaseWidget with common methods all widgets need to support, like get/setPrice, get/setDescription, get/setRelatedWidgets, and so on. For each type of widget you sell, create a child class that extends this parent class, and override the inherited methods as needed. All your utility class methods will be defined to accept an object of this base class as a parameter, and through polymorphism call the real methods in the child classes. As you add new widget types later, these are simply new child classes. All your utility methods will still work as is, even with objects of the new class.

Try to use interfaces. These are the ultimate in abstraction. For example, you may have a ZipCode class, with one method verify. This is fine for US customers, but what if you expand into Canada, which has postal codes instead of zip codes? You will need to create a new PostalCode class, and rewrite the verify method. Then, your user interface code that calls it will have to figure out which class to use. And so it goes for every new country you enter. Since the verify method implementation will be totally unique per country, you should create an interface called Zip with one method signature — verify. Then implement that interface and method in each of your classes, like ZipCode and PostalCode. Thus, your user interface code remains the same — it simply defines a variable of type Zip, and equates it to an instance of the appropriate class. It can then call the verify method on that object, no matter what actual type it is. New countries are easily added by just creating a new class that implements Zip.

Also, try to avoid hardcoded values as much as possible. Rather, use parameters to methods and constructors to allow values to be passed in at runtime. For example, don't hardcode a tax rate. Rather, accept it as a parameter or, ultimately, read it from a database so you can easily change it on the fly.

This will all come with time, and you will find yourself going back with experience and changing classes and class hierarchies to be more adaptable. Rather than overwhelming you at this point with a complex example of a "good" object oriented system, we will leave that to other books. You probably are not ready for it now anyway.

Other OO Terms

Framework is another term you will hear often. This is one of those generic terms, like *groupware,* for which everyone seems to have a definition. However, framework typically refers to a collection of related classes that work together to model a generic problem or domain. Frameworks also usually exhibit the behavior of being easily tailored to your particular situation with relatively small, well-defined efforts. Further, frameworks usually exhibit the trait that your extensions are called by it (via polymorphism) versus the framework supplying APIs that your code calls.

The ultimate example of a set of frameworks in Java is the IBM SanFrancisco project, which is a large undertaking to supply a framework of business objects written in Java. The idea is that these frameworks can supply up to forty percent of a typical business application. See their Web site, **www.ibm.com/java/sanfrancisco,** for information.

Another term commonly heard in the world of OO is *object factory.* This is simply a term for a class or method that returns a *new* instance of another class. Like a factory, it spits out things — in this case, instances of a particular class.

Finally, something we find exciting is the relatively new concept of ***design patterns***. These are the result of efforts to look at many existing OO solutions to common programming or design problems, and extract from these real-world examples of OO designs for common OO programming problems. Because OO is an "experience-won" skill, the books and articles that detail design patterns that others have used to solve typical challenges offer a tremendous leg up to those starting out in OO, or starting a new OO project.

OO Design Tips

"To inherit or not to inherit, that is the question." You will soon discover that that is the question, anyway. Here are some tips about when and how to use inheritance:

Tip #1: Use the "is a" rule with a grain of salt

Despite the "is a" rule, do not inherit from an existing class unless you intend to override one or more methods. For example, the user interface class in Java — ***AWT*** (Abstract Windowing Toolkit) — has a "Frame" class that creates a frame window. Your windows will use this and add their own push buttons, entry fields, and so on. So, should your window classes inherit from Java's Frame class? Certainly your new window "is a" frame. However, with the new JDK 1.1 version of AWT there is no methods in Frame you typically need to override — so you sometimes are better off just including an instance of a `Frame` class as an instance variable in your class. This keeps you from using up your single allowance for inheriting, and is a bit better in terms of performance. However, you must supply a `getFrame` method that returns the `Frame` object so users can call its methods if they need to. There is no "answer" here, though; it depends on your situation.

Tip #2: Create child classes that add functionality

Despite the terminology, subclasses should offer a "superset" of functions compared to their parent or superclass. That is, the child class (the one with the **extends** keyword) should add methods over the parent class, not remove them. If you find yourself wanting to remove methods from your parent class because they do not apply to your child class, you probably should not be inheriting from that parent. Even if, in real life, there is an "is a" relationship, there may not be one in the actual code.

For example, a manager may not be an employee, if class `Employee` has methods dependent on hourly wages versus salary. You may have to abstract out a third common class called "HR" (Human Resource) from which `Employee` and `Manager` both inherit. (Of course, many would argue that the "is a" relationship does not apply to managers and humans!) Another option here is to have a class called `JobDescription` which `ManagerJob` extends, and then to contain an instance of `ManagerJob` in the appropriate `Employee` objects. This gives you the flexibility of defining additional employee job descriptions and supporting multiple job descriptions per employee.

Tip #3: Strive for easy and elegant user code

When designing your class hierarchies and classes, keep in mind the users of your classes. You want to minimize their effort. The "main" part of your application should be as simple and elegant as possible. This means letting your classes do as much as work as possible. For example, it might be as simple as:

```
TheApp app = new TheApp();
app.run();
```

Tip #4: Strive for small methods

If you find yourself with a very large and complicated class that has some really outrageous methods, you should look hard at it. You may need to abstract out some code into a base or helper class, and use more and smaller methods. This makes the code easier to maintain and understand.

Tip #5: Balance anticipated function versus bloat

The trick for long-lasting classes is to embellish them with as many methods as you predict might ever be needed. But don't go overboard! Do all private variables really need setXXX() methods? Will someone really want to change these variables? Do you need a particular new method, or can the result be achieved already by using a combination of other methods?

Tip #6: By wary of large numbers of instance variables

If your class has dozens of instance variables, you should look at grouping those variables into classes of their own and instantiating instances of it. Remember, classes do not have to have methods. Moving related variables into their own class will make your code more elegant, and you may then discover those helper classes have other uses too. You may also discover that some of the manipulations you were doing directly on those variables can be moved into methods of the new class!

Tip #7: Watch for static candidates

Do you have methods that do *not* act on any of your class instance variables? Maybe some utility methods you wrote that take all their information as parameters? If so, either forgo the parameters and use instance variables instead, or make the method static so it can be used by others without requiring an instantiation of your class.

SUMMARY

This has been a whirlwind "introductory" chapter to the world of object orientation. In this chapter you were briefly introduced to the following OO terminology:

- **Encapsulation**, **Inheritance**, and **Polymorphism**;
- "*Has a*," "*is a*," and "*uses*" relationships;
- ***Methodologies*** for specifying and documenting object-oriented systems. For information on the Unified Modeling Language methodology, see **www.rational.com/uml**

You were also introduced to some new specific Java constructs:

- The **extends** keyword;
- **Interfaces**, and the **implements** keyword;
- The "**instanceof**" operator;
- The "**protected**" modifier;
- The "**abstract**" modifier;
- The "**final**" modifier.

You also learned about:

- The `java.lang.Object` and `java.lang.Class` superclasses;
- The `java.lang.Cloneable` interface and the `java.lang.clone()` method;
- The `java.lang.Enumeration` interface;
- Frameworks, object factories, and design patterns.

A full introduction to, and coverage of, ***object-oriented analysis and design*** is beyond the intended scope of this chapter, but you should feel more "acclimatized" to OO now and ready to pursue it further with subsequent books. Remember, though, not everyone on the project needs to be an OO genius; only a relatively small number do. Everyone, however, should understand the basic syntax and ideas as presented here.

10

Exceptions

Finally-at long last you are going to read about an aspect of Java that you will think has been lifted right off the AS/400! You are, no doubt, plenty familiar with the concept of exceptions on the AS/400. They were part of the original architecture of the AS/400 that was a harbinger of things to come. Well, now their time has arrived! Let us begin by reviewing, ever so briefly, the AS/400 exception architecture.

AS/400 EXCEPTION MODEL OVERVIEW

On the AS/400, the idea of sending messages from one program to another is a long-established part of the programming model. All operating system APIs and functions send messages when something unexpected happens — something "exceptional." These are sent both explicitly when you code a call to these APIs, and implicitly when they are invoked by a language runtime (such as an RPG database input/output operation). Language runtimes themselves also send messages when a programming error happens, such as a "divide by zero" or an "array index out of bounds."

Messages on the AS/400 embed two important pieces of information:

- Some error message text, often with runtime substitution variables to pinpoint the problem (such as a source sequence number or error code).

- A message severity, which for program to program messages is one of: `*ESCAPE`, `*STATUS`, or `*NOTIFY`.

All error messages have a unique seven-character *message identifier* that can be explicitly monitored for.

The AS/400 message exception model is most obvious when you are writing **CL** *(Control Language)* programs and you code explicit **MONMSG** *(Monitor Message)* statements for each command call. It is possible to monitor for explicit messages (such as **MCH0601**), range of messages (such as by using 0000 for the numeric part of the message ID), or *function checks* (**CPF9999**). The function check monitors typically give sweeping "if anything at all happens, tell me about it" messages. Notice also that CL programs often send their own messages for diagnostic, status, or exceptional situations by using the **SNDPGMMSG** *(Send Program Message)* command. Programmers have learned that messages, when used properly, can be an effective way out of an troublesome situation — such as receiving unexpected input.

OPM Exception Model

In the *Original Programming Model* (**OPM** — that is, pre-ILE) days, exception messages were handled like this:

- Does the program call-stack entry that received the message handle it (monitor for it or have code waiting to receive it)?
  - **Yes**, done.
  - **No**, send a *function check* (message **CPF9999**) to that same program call-stack entry.
- Does the program call-stack entry that received the message handle **CPF9999**?
  - **Yes**, done.
  - **No**, blow away that program and send ("percolate") that **CPF9999** to the previous entry in the call-stack.
- Repeat previous step until the **CPF9999** is handled (ultimately the job ends or the interactive command line returns control).

ILE Exception Model

When writing new ILE programs, the exception model is changed in the following ways:

- The original exception message is passed all the way up the call-stack until a handler is found for it (that is, code that is willing to receive it). It is not converted to a function check right away.
- If nobody on the call-stack (to the *control boundary* — which is an activation group or an OPM program or the job boundary) handles this message, it is then converted to a function check (**CPF9999**) and the process is repeated for the function check.
- If the original message is handled by somebody on the call-stack, the entries above it are terminated.
- If nobody handles the original message, each are then given a chance to handle the function check starting at original call-stack entry that received the message.

Each entry in the call-stack that does not handle the function check is typically removed from the call-stack (depending on user answer to an inquiry message), and the next entry is given a chance to handle it.

Further, the call-stack itself is different in ILE! Not only does it contain programs, but it also contains procedures (remember, these are "grown up subroutines" that are new to RPG IV in V3R2 and V3R6, and also exist in other ILE languages). And these can have their very own unique exception handling support.

RPG III Exception Handling

We have covered the generic system support for exceptions, so now we will look closer at what is involved in RPG itself. As you recall in RPG III, RPG divides exceptions into two camps:

- *File errors*. These can occur when processing files, such as "record not found."

- *Program errors*. These are programming errors, such as "divide by zero."

RPG III offers three ways to handle exceptions:

- Error indicators ("*Resulting Error Indicator*") on many op-codes. These are set on by the language at runtime if the op-code fails

- INFSR error subroutine for file errors.

- *PSSR error subroutine for program errors.

You can also code special data structures (INFDS and PSDS) that the language at runtime will update to indicate the error that occurred (in the *STATUS subfield).

When returning from an error subroutine the value of factor two on the ENDSR (*End Subroutine*) op-code can be used to determine where control returns to.

We will not bore you with further details because we are assuming that you are already intimately familiar with this process and architecture.

ILE RPG (RPG IV) Exception Handling

How have things changed for RPG IV? That is a good question, but the answer could easily fill an entire chapter on its own. For more detailed information, we suggest that you consult **ILE RPG/400 Programmer's Guide** (SC09 2074 01). However, in a nutshell, the basics follow:

- You still have error indicators, INFSR and *PSSR subroutines, INFDS and PSDS data structures!

- INFSR subroutine and INFDS data structures are identified on the F-spec with the new INFSR(xxx) and INFDS(xxx) keywords.

- **INFSR** subroutines apply only to the mainline code, *not* to procedures. You will have to rely on error indicators for file processing in a procedure.

- ***PSSR** subroutines are local to the procedure they are declared in (yes, you can define subroutines inside procedures). This means you need one for *every* procedure (they could all call a common subprocedure) *and* one for the mainline code.

- ***PSSR** subroutines inside procedures must have a blank factor two on the **ENDSR** statement — and if control reaches that far the procedure will end there. Unfortunately, you have to rely on **GOTO** prior to **ENDSR** in order to continue processing.

- **INFDS** and **PSDS** data structures are global in scope. That means that they are accessible by all procedures.

- There is an entirely new option — an ILE exception handling bindable API (**CEEHDLR**). This registers an ILE exception handler for this procedure, and its undo cousin (**CEEHDLU**) unregisters an ILE exception handler. Using these APIs gives you a language-neutral way of dealing with exceptions in ILE. Typically, then, you will code a call to **CEEHDLR** at the beginning of your procedure and a call to **CEEHDLU** at the end of your procedure.

EXCEPTIONS IN JAVA

The AS/400 and RPG exception model has taught us to be disciplined when it comes to proactively designing in support for error situations. If we don't follow this practice, we risk exposing those ugly function checks to our customers. So, doing more work up front prevents problems in the long run. We produce more robust, fault tolerant code that is cheaper to maintain. (So, it is safe to say that RPG programmers are *exceptional*!!) These noble goals have been taken to heart by the Java designers. (Actually, they are a reasonably standard OO thing.)

Java also provides the feature of ***exceptions*** for unexpected situations, and it has language constructs for sending and monitoring them. The consequences of ignoring them are even more frightening than on the AS/400. In fact, Java goes a step further than simply ending your program at *runtime* if you fail to monitor for an exception that happens. It actually tries to catch, at *compile time*, where you missed coding in monitors for potential exceptions. To accomplish this, it has further language syntax for defining for each method what exceptions callers of this method need to monitor for.

Exception Objects in Java

In contrast to RPG, Java does not have "error indicators." It provides only the concept of "exception messages," such as the AS/400 exception model. What are these "messages?" They are Java objects of course! There is a Java defined class called **Throwable**, which all Java exceptions inherit from. This class is in the Java supplied package **java.lang**, which all Java code implicitly imports. Any Java class that directly or indirectly extends Throwable is an "exception" in Java, whether that class is Java-supplied or written by you. You use unique language syntax to send these exceptions back up the method call-stack, and to monitor for them in code you call.

Objects of the Throwable class contain a string describing the exception, which is retrievable with the **getMessage()** method. Another useful method in this class is **printStackTrace()**, which prints out a method call-stack trace from the point where this exception was sent. Java programmers are particularly fond of this latter method because it is very useful in debugging.

AS/400 exceptions have a severity associated with them, as well as a unique message ID. Java exceptions (or Throwable objects) have this information too. The severity and unique ID is implicit with the particular class of the exception object. In other words, there are many exception classes (they extend the Throwable class), so the exact error can be determined by the exact exception object that was used. That means that the class itself is equivalent to a message ID because it uniquely identifies the error. It also often implies a severity. Java supplies a number of subclasses of Throwable for many specific errors and groups of errors.

The primary subclasses of Throwable are Error and Exception. Error exceptions are typically non-recoverable system errors, such as "out of memory." Exception errors are further subclassed by RunTimeException and other classes (see Figure 10-1). RunTimeException errors are programming errors you make, such as an array index out of bounds (hey, it happens). The other subclasses of Exception are, typically, related to preventable user-input errors.

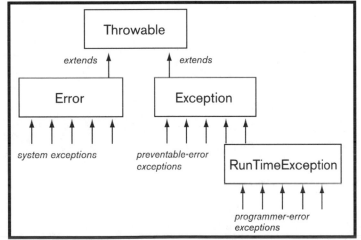

FIGURE 10-1

You typically do not monitor for Error exceptions or subclasses of them in Java. For one thing, you usually can't do much about them. What's more, you will never send one of these exceptions yourself. These exceptions are sent only by the system. What you need to be concerned with are Exception exceptions (good name, is it not?) and their subclasses. When sending your own exceptions, you have our permission to ignore RunTimeException and its subclasses. These are used by Java to tell *you* that you made a programming error, not for you to tell *others* that you made a programming error. There is little point in listing all of the subclasses here because, as you will see, every class you use clearly documents the Exception subclass objects it might send. So you will learn them as you need them. (After all, it's probably safe to say that you don't know all the AS/400 system and language runtime exception message IDs by heart.) We have no doubt that you will need them!

The last point to make about Throwable objects (it is only Exception objects that you really care about) is that you can define your own. You will probably need to do this in Java *if* you are writing robust code or, more precisely, *when* you are writing robust code. If you discover an unexpected error situation in your error checking code, such as bad input or expected resource not found, you should send an exception versus using a return code. Return codes, such as an integer value, should be used to identify valid possible results, not to identify exceptional situations. For example, an end of file is a valid possible result. File not found is an exceptional situation. The first will almost always happen; with good input, the latter should almost never happen. It, in other words, is a frequency call.

Having decided that you should send an exception, your next step is to peruse the Java documentation for an existing Exception subclass that applies to your situation.

Searching Java Documentation for Classes

To find an existing class, search the Java Development Kit documentation. You are looking for an HTML file called `tree.html`, which conveniently shows all the classes in the Java supplied class hierarchy.

Searching Local Documentation

If you have downloaded the documentation to your workstation computer, open a Windows explorer view on the directory where you placed the JDK (probably something like `c:\jdk1.1.5`), and then open the `docs` subdirectory. Next open the `index.html` file. This is always where you begin your Java documentation search. When you "open" the file, you bring up your registered Web browser for that file.

Searching JavaSoft Online Documentation

If you prefer to use the documentation from the JavaSoft Web site, point your Web browser to:

`http://www.javasoft.com/products/jdk/1.1/docs/index.html`

This puts you at the main documentation page for JDK version 1.1. (We assume that part of the URL will read 1.2 or 2.0 for the next version.)

Drilling Down to the Tree View

- Find the heading **Java API Documentation**, and click on the link under it: **Java Platform Core API**.
- At the top of the page that appears, click on the **Class Hierarchy** link.
- Use *Ctrl+F (Find)* to search for the appropriate parent class. For example, when you search for "`java.lang.Exception`," at the second hit you will see all the Java-defined exceptions that inherit from this class.

If you find an existing exception that meets your needs, such as IOException, use it and send an object of that class for your exception. (Instructions on performing this procedure follow.) If you cannot find one that will work in your situation, create a new class that extends Exception or one of its children (see Figure 10-2). Just as you would never send your own instance of Error or RunTimeException exceptions, you would never create your own child subclasses of these.

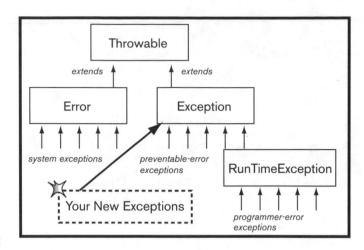

FIGURE 10-2

For example, you might define

```
public class BadZipCode extends Exception
{
    . . .
}
```

Because it is your own class, you might define constructors that take additional useful information, such as the method name, where the error occurred. This information could be beneficial to the code that receives such an exception if you also supply a getMethod() method. You might also decide to record the bad zipcode number as follows:

LISTING 10-1

```
public class BadZipCode extends Exception
{
    private String badzip;
    private String method;

    public BadZipCode(String badzip, String method)
    {
        super("Bad zipcode '" + badzip + "' given.");
        this.badzip = badzip;
        this.method = method;
    }
    public String getBadZip()
    {
        return badzip;
    }
    public String getMethod()
    {
        return method;
    }
} // end class BadZipCode
```

Keep in mind that when one class extends another, the child class inherits all the methods of the parent class (Exception, in this case). This means your new class will have the getMessage() and printStackTrace() methods of the grandparent Throwable class.

Sending Java Exceptions — throw Statement

Having decided that you will send an exception in your error checking code, how do you do it? First, you have to instantiate an instance of the particular Exception child class, of course. Then you use the Java operator called **throw**. (These steps can be combined into one statement.) In the following example, we have detected an error in our input and have decided to "throw" an instance of our new BadZipCode exception class:

```
public void myMethod(ZipCode zipcode)
{
  if (zipcode.isbad())
    {
        BadZipCode exc = new BadZipCode(zipcode.toString(),"myMethod");
        throw(exc);
        //or just: throw(new BadZipCode(zipcode.toString(),"myMethod"));
    }
  ...
}
```

The **throw** operator is similar to CL's **SNDPGMMSG** command on the AS/400. As our example shows, you can either send an instance of one of Java's predefined exception classes (such as IOException), or you can send an instance of your own exception class (such as BadZipCode) . Typically, you will try to use an existing class that matches your error situation. Don't create your own unless you can't find an existing one that meets your needs. You may, however, choose to create your own class so that you can supply as much information in it as you want. This choice is comparable to deciding whether to use a supplied CPF or MCH message on the AS/400, or to create your own new message in your own message file. By the way, the generic message **CPF9898** ("&1") that many of us use on the AS/400 is similar to using the generic Exception class in Java. On the AS/400, we substitute in our own message text in **CPF9898**. We can do the same in the constructor of Exception, as shown below:

```
throw (new Exception("You made a big mistake there pal!"));
```

It is important to remember that you never throw exceptions that are of type Error. You use Exception because Error exceptions are for dramatic system errors and are thrown only by the system.

What does using **throw** do? It ends your method, that is what! Any code following the **throw** statement is *not* executed. You have done the equivalent of sending an escape message in a CL program. The current method is removed from the stack and the exception is sent back to the line of code that called this method. If that code does not monitor for this exception, the method it is in is also terminated. The exception is sent back to the caller of the method, just as in RPG function check percolation. It continues until it finds an entry in the call-stack that monitors for this exact exception (or one of the parents of this particular exception class, as we will see).

Monitoring for Java Exceptions — try/catch Blocks

Now that you know how to send or throw an exception to the callers of your code when you have detected an error, let's discuss what those callers do to monitor for it or to process it. To monitor for an exception, there is additional Java language syntax. Keep in mind that in Java you can place multiple lines of code in its own "block" (with its own variable scope) using braces, as follows:

```
{
    // one or more statements of code
}
```

The Java syntax for monitoring for messages builds on this, which allows you to specify a "*try/catch*" combination, as follows:

```
try
{
    // try-block: one or more statements of code
}
catch (Exception exc)
{
    // catch-block: code to handle the exception
}
```

The idea is this: place any method call statement that may *throw* exceptions inside a *try-block*. Because it is a block, you can actually place one or more statements inside the block. If any of the statements inside the *try-block* do throw an exception, the *catch-block* will get control. Any code inside the *try-block*, after the exception-throwing call, is not executed. Control flows immediately to the *catch-block* upon receipt of a thrown exception.

The *catch-block* defines a parameter, which is the exception it will handle. Java passes that exception object at *runtime* if an exception is thrown. Your *catch-block* code can use methods on the object to display information to the end-user, if desired. For example, you may do something like the following inside your *catch-block*:

```
System.out.println(exc.getMessage());
```

Recalling our zipcode example, here is what caller code may look like:

```
  try
{
   ...
   myObject.myMethod(zipcode);
   ...
}
catch (BadZipCode exc)
{
   System.out.println(exc.getMessage());
   System.out.println("... in method " + exc.getMethod());
}
```

Java is similar to RPG in this respect. You have code, user-defined or system supplied, that may possibly send (that is, *throw*) exceptions. If the caller of that code doesn't monitor for that exception, its call-stack entry will be removed and the next call-stack entry will be given the exception. The call-stack is peeled back until a handler is found, or the whole application ends.

Monitoring for Multiple Java Exceptions

The **catch** statement we showed is actually the part that is equivalent to CL's **MONMSG**, not the **try** statement. Although both **try** and **catch** are necessary syntactically, it is the **catch** statement that tells Java which exception type you are monitoring for. If your *try-block* gets an exception that the catch statement did not identify in it's parameter (for example: catch (MyException exc)), then it is as though you never had the *try-catch* block. Your method is ended and the exception is sent back to the previous call-stack entry.

What if you call a method that throws more than one possible exception? How do you define the **catch** statement when you need to monitor for multiple possible exceptions? For instance, in our example, what if myMethod could throw either a BadZipCode exception or an IOException. In the latter case, your *catch-block* will not get control because you told it to monitor only for BadZipCode exceptions. The following two options exist:

1. Suppose it does not matter to you *which* exception happened. It only matters that *some* exception happened. You can define a parent exception class type on the catch. The catch will actually get control of any exception that is of the defined type *or lower* on the hierarchy chain. This is similar to specifying **MCH0000** on the CL **MONMSG** command. Or, to catch *all* exceptions, specify the root parent of all catchable exceptions — Exception. This is equivalent to specifying **CPF9999** on the CL **MONMSG** command.

2. Define *multiple* catch-blocks after the ***try-block***. This is perfectly legal. The exception object received will be compared to each catch statement's parameter, in turn, until a match on type is found (or the catch defines a child of the thrown exception class type). Use this technique when it is important to your error recovery code to know *exactly* what exception was thrown. The need for unique error handling code is also a good criteria to use when deciding whether or not you need to define your own exception classes.

Here is an example:

LISTING 10-2

```
try
{
    ...
    myObject.myMethod(zipcode);
    ...
}
catch (BadZipCode exc)
{
    System.out.println(exc.getMessage());
    System.out.println("... in method " + exc.getMethod());
}
catch (IOException exc)
{
    System.out.println(exc.getMessage());
    System.out.println("Bad input—naughty, naughty!");
}
```

Finally, there is **finally**. This is an optional block you can define at the end of all your catch statements:

```
try
   block
catch (exception-type-1 identifier)
   block
catch (exception-type-2 identifier)
   block
finally
   block
```

You might think this is what will get control in an exception situation if none of the catch statements handled that particular exception type. This is only partly correct, however. The ***finally-block***, if present, is *always* executed. That is, it is executed whether or not an exception was received in the ***try-block***, and whether or not a ***catch-block*** processed it. For example, if a BadZipCode exception is thrown by code in the ***try-block***, the code inside the BadZipCode ***catch-block*** will be executed as well as the code inside the ***finally-block***.

Finally is typically used to do code that has to be done *no matter what*, such as closing any open files. Notice that no statement inside a *try-block*, not even a `return` statement, can circumvent the *finally-block* if it is present. If the *try-block* does do a `return` statement, then the *finally-block* will be run and the *try-block*'s return statement will be honored. (It is, however, possible to override the *try-block*'s return value in the `finally` statement by coding another `return` statement.)

We should also point out that you can throw exceptions in your class constructor code. This has the effect of cancelling the instantiation or `new` attempt. In this case, users of your class must place the `new` operator inside a *try-block*..

Who Throws What

If you have done any CL programming on the AS/400, you know how painful it can be to get those **MONMSG** statements just right. You typically have to examine the CL reference manual for each CL command you call to see what messages that command might send. And you can only hope that the list includes any messages that its nested command or program calls might send. How many times have you wished for an automated way to determine this list? For example, it would be nice to have a tool that, given a CL command as input, returns a list of all the possible messages that particular CL command might send. This is a similar problem OO language programmers face when trying to determine the exceptions any particular method call might result in. Java designers thought about this problem. They knew that if they didn't come up with a solution, the exception architecture in Java would suffer two real-use problems:

- Programmers would not use it enough, which would lead to too much error prone code (human nature being what it is).

- Programmers who did decide to place sensitive method calls inside *try/catch-blocks* would find it painful to determine what exceptions each method could possibly throw.

They would be dependent on those methods having the proper and up-to-date documentation that is available to them (much as you are dependent on this for AS/400 commands).

So, Java designers decided to force method designers to specify up front — in the method signature — what exceptions are thrown by that method. This is done by specifying a **throws** clause on your method signature:

```
public void myMethod(ZipCode zipcode) throws BadZipCode
{
  ...
}
```

You *must* specify this if you *explicitly* throw an exception, or your compile (**JAVAC**) will fail. Furthermore, your compile will fail if you call a method that throws an exception and you do not have a ***try/catch-block*** for that explicit exception (or one of its parents). The compiler is able to catch this because it knows all the methods you call. It also knows, via the "`throws`" clause, what exceptions those methods throw. Isn't that nice? You have compiler help to write robust code. You are *forced* to handle any exceptions produced by code that you invoke, either with an explicit ***try/catch-block***, or by listing the exceptions in your method's `throws` clause. What's more, you are *forced* to tell the world what exceptions you throw yourself. The `throws` clause then is a form of *forced documentation* for your code that makes it easier for callers to handle your exceptions. In fact, it forces the callers to handle your exceptions. It is possible to list multiple exception classes after the `throws` keyword by separating them with a comma:

```
public void myMethod(ZipCode zipcode) throws BadZipCode, IOException
{
    . . .
}
```

Actually, it is not exactly true that you have to define in the `throws` clause *every* exception that called-code may produce. You only need to document the exceptions you do not explicitly handle with a ***try/catch-block***. Keep in mind that if you call a method and it throws an exception you do not handle, it is percolated up to the caller of your method. You may very well choose to do this in cases where there is no reasonable action you can take to recover from the exception.

Sometimes you may decide to handle the exception, but then throw it again anyway. This is legal, and can be done with a simple "`throw exc;`" statement in your ***catch-block***. In this case, because you are throwing this exception (albeit, again), you must define it in your method's `throw` clause. If your method code does not monitor for an exception it might receive, you must specify that exception in your method's `throws` clause in addition to any exceptions your code explicitly throws.

User Error Messages Versus Exceptions

Exceptions are not necessarily meant to be user error messages! In RPG code we often use an AS/400 message file to define error messages. They are then sent to the job log when something unexpected happens or when something is in progress or completes. These messages (often of type *diagnostic, status,* or *completion*) provide the end-user of your application with information. They are not necessarily something to be monitored by other programs on the stack. In fact, programs cannot even monitor for diagnostic or completion messages.

You could try to accomplish the same thing in Java by printing a receiving exception object's message text (`getMessage()`) to standard out, or to an information line on your window. However, you will be asking for trouble. The method that is doing the throwing will be terminated after your user message is thrown. These messages are not meant for this kind of passive user information. Instead, simply write the error message text to the appropriate place. Java does not have externally defined message files, but it does have ***resource bundles*** that define strings outside of your executable code. They make translation and reuse easy. We will discuss resource bundles in a later chapter. Be forewarned, however, that one feature you will sorely miss is ***substitution*** values. Java provides no easy way to define a string with '&1', '&2', and so on in the text, and then substitute these values with runtime specific values. You have to write your own code to do this because the `String` class in Java does not supply this rudimentary function. Consult the User Interface chapter for information about resource bundles and options for string substitution.

SUMMARY

In this chapter we covered:

- A review of the AS/400 and RPG exception model.
- An introduction to the Java exception model.
- The Java Exception class hierarchy.
- The Java **throw** statement, which is like CL's **SNDPGMMSG**.
- The Java **try/catch/finally** statement, which is like CL's **MONMSG**.
- The finally **block**, if present is always executed.
- The Java **throws** clause for method signatures.
- The two popular methods all exceptions have are printStackTrace and getMessage.
- That in addition to Java's supplied exception classes, you can write your own by extending the Exception class or one of its children.
- That Java supplied exceptions are divided into two hierarchies: those that extend Error and do not need to be monitored, and those that extend Exception, and do need to be monitored.

11

Threads

THREADS — SOMETHING NEW

Threads, in contrast to the "exceptions" that were covered in the last chapter, are something absolutely foreign to an RPG program. This means you need to be prepared for a chapter that mainly focuses on Java without providing many RPG comparisons. However, we predict that you will find this utterly new concept interesting. In fact, we predict that there will be increasingly more discussions of threads on the AS/400, especially since they have been introduced to the operating system starting with V4R2.

Synchronous Versus Asynchronous

In RPG you call subroutines, procedures, and programs "synchronously." Your code that makes the call does not get control back until the called code has completed. For example, let's say that program P1 calls program P2 using the **CALL** op-code. Execution of P1 will stop at the **CALL** op-code to wait for the execution of P2 to end and return before the code *after* the **CALL** statement is executed. A similar situation exists with the **EXSR** and **CALLP** op-codes for subroutines and procedures. This is also true of Java method calls, such as myObject.myMethod(), as you have seen. But Java also has built-in support for "asynchronous" calls. They are calls that *spawn* a second *thread of execution* and return immediately. Both the *calling* code and the *called* code run at the same time (concurrently). Imagine that, with enough threads of execution, you could have a whole *suit* of execution. Spun by the *collar*. (Sorry, bad joke. Really, it's a *knit*.)

In order to distinguish between a traditional *synchronous* call and a threaded *asynchronous* call, the latter is often referred to as "spawning" versus "calling." A time-graph that shows which method is currently executing would look something like Figure 11-1:

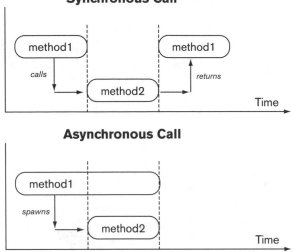

FIGURE 11-1

It is important to note that when a method is invoked as a thread (we will discuss the syntax of doing this shortly) it runs at the same time as the code after the "call" statement. Which one ends first is not predictable, and your calling code does not get the "return" value from the thread. This is because the "call" statement returns immediately — before the callee has even run. This is quite similar to submitting a program call to batch in RPG via the **SBMJOB** command, and is in contrast to using the **CALL** op-code.

Threads Versus Jobs

Asynchronous execution (no, it is not a new form of capital punishment!) is not totally foreign to AS/400 programmers. In fact, it is done quite often. Many interactive applications have a print function key or menu option that submits a job to batch, instead of performing it interactively. This allows the user to get control immediately while the print job runs quietly in the background. This is a disconnected job in that the application does not care when it ends. It merely submits it and forgets about it. Some applications that involve numerous screens of input for a single transaction will run a job in the background, "gathering information" from the database, so they can be shown to the user by the time they reach the final screen. This is a connected job because the main interactive job must "synch up" with the background batch job by the final screen. This is something usually done using data areas, data queues, or some other form of "inter-job" communication.

"Jobs" on the AS/400 are synonymous with "processes" on other platforms. How do they differ from threads in Java? Overhead. To start a new job requires a significant amount of system resources, as you well know. Calling another program in the same job is expensive enough. That is why ILE significantly reduces the need to do this. Starting another job altogether is considerably more expensive. There is overhead in allocating storage, setting up library lists, setting up job attributes, loading system resources, and so on. You would not do this without due consideration, and certainly not for frequently repeated application functions. In Java, the equivalent of starting another job would be starting another Java Virtual Machine. Via the system's command analyzer, you would invoke another Java program (via `Java MySecondClass`, for example). For more on how to invoke another job from within Java, see the final chapter of this book.

Threads, on the other hand, have relatively very little overhead because they share everything with the other threads in that job or process. This includes all global (that is, instance) variable data. No new memory is allocated for the "secondary" threads. Even if you do not spawn a thread, your main code is considered to be running in a thread (the "primary" or "main" thread). Methods invoked in another thread each get their own copy of local variables and parameters, as you would expect for a method. But instance variables, which are defined at the class level and are equivalent to RPG global fields, are shared. If you spawn two methods for the same instance of a class, they both have the same copies of the global variables in that class. Figure 11-2 depicts this sharing:

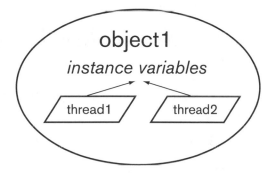

FIGURE 11-2

We will have more to say about this sharing of instance variables and its implications later in the chapter.

To do threads efficiently, of course, the underlying operating system must have true built-in support for "threads" of execution versus just jobs or processes. Java cannot do this on its own. All major operating systems today support "native" threads (as opposed to simulated threads or lightweight jobs). This includes OS/400 as of V4R2, as part of its new built-in robust Java support. Typical operating system thread support includes the ability to start, stop, suspend, query, and set the priority of the thread. You might give a print job low priority so that it gets only idle CPU cycles versus the user-interactive threads, for example. The Java language has built-in support for all of this in its thread architecture.

Questions arising at this point might include the following:

- How do I call a method asynchronously (that is, spawn a thread)?
- How do I stop a thread?
- How do I get back information from that thread?
- If necessary, how do I wait for that thread to end?
- How do I temporarily suspend a thread?
- How do I change a thread's priority?
- How do threads exchange information with each other?

All of these questions will be answered in due course. Don't worry. We won't leave you hanging by a thread!

How to Call a Method Asynchronously: Spawning Threads

Let us imagine we have some code: a method that we want to run asynchronously so as to improve response time for the end user. For convenience, we will use the `printReport` method from Chapter 9. That is potentially a long running method and something well suited to a "background thread." The method follows:

```
public static void printReport(Printable[] objects)
{
    System.out.println("Printing objects...");
    for (int index=0;
         index<objects.length;
         index=index+1)
      objects[index].print();
    System.out.println(objects.length + " objects printed");
}
```

There are exactly two ways to run a method asynchronously in Java. The one you choose depends on whether the class containing the method to be run asynchronously is free to inherit from another class or not. If it already inherits from one, then it cannot inherit from another.

Spawning Option One — Extend Thread

The method you wish to run asynchronously may be part of a class that is not already extending another class. Or it may not be written yet, which leaves you free to put it in a new class definition. In these cases you may choose to extend the Java-supplied class Thread. The instructions follow:

- Add **extends** Thread to your class definition.
- Define a method with signature public void run(). Because it takes no parameters, the input to it should be passed in through class instance variables.

To **run** the code, create an instance of the class and invoke the start() method on it. This method is inherited from the Thread parent class. It merely invokes the run() method. Why not just invoke run() directly? Because, that would be a synchronous call! The start() method Java supplies in the Thread class does the work of creating the asynchronous thread. You have to call it before it calls your run() method in turn. Figure 11-3 depicts this process:

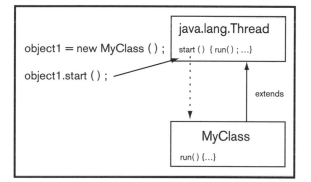

FIGURE 11-3

Referring back to our TestBillable class from the OO chapter, we might have:

LISTING 11-1

```java
public class TestBillableThread extends Thread
{
  Printable[] objects; // array to be printed
  // constructor
  public TestBillableThread(Printable[] objects)
  {
      this.objects = objects; // store array in instance var
  }
  public static void main(String[] args) // cmdline entry
  {
    Printable[] objlist = new Printable[2];
    objlist[0] = new Presentation();
    objlist[1] = new Widget();
    // create instance of this class, run it
    TestBillableThread object1 = new TestBillableThread(objlist);
    Object1.start();
    System.out.println("Printing job spawned");
  }
  public void printReport()
  {
     System.out.println("Printing objects...");
     for (int index=0;
          index<objects.length;
          index=index+1)
       objects[index].print();
     System.out.println(objects.length + " objects printed");
  }
  public void run()
  {
      printReport();
  }
}
```

The changes we made to this class to have it run the printReport() method asynchronously were:

- Changed the class to **extend** Thread. (We do not have to explicitly use java.lang.Thread because the java.lang package is always implicitly imported by Java.)

- Changed the class name to TestBillableThread so we do not clobber our sample from the OO chapter. (We subsequently put this class in a file called TestBillableThread.java.)

- Defined an "objects" array variable as an instance variable, so the printReport() method would have access to it.

- Added a *constructor* that takes an existing array as a parameter, and sets the instance variable to it.

- Changed the `main` method to instantiate an instance of this class. It passes in the local array that it creates as a parameter and then immediately runs the `start()` method on the new class instance. This is inherited from our parent class `Thread`, and will implicitly invoke the `run()` method. We also added another `println` statement after spawning the thread, so we can see if it gets written before, during, or after the printing done in the `printReport` method.

- Changed `printReport` to use the instance variable versus taking in a parameter, and therefore removed the **static** modifier. (**Static** methods *cannot* access instance variables.)

- Added the "public void run()" method because it is required for a class that extends `Thread`. This simply calls the `printReport()` method in our example. We could have just renamed `printReport` to `run`, but we prefer to keep the `run` method very small.

Now, if we compile and run this sample program (`JAVA TestBillableThread`), we get:

```
Printing job spawned
Printing objects...
inside print for Presentation
Inside print for Widget
2 objects printed
```

In this case, the calling code executed before ("Printing job spawned") the threaded method. This is not guaranteed, though. The thread code could run after or during the running of the main code. It is dependent on the operating system's *time-slicing* algorithm for assigning CPU cycles to each running thread. The main code that spawned the thread is referred to by convention as the *"main thread of execution."*

Spawning Option Two — Implement Runnable

It is possible that you will not have the option of changing your class to **extend** Thread. This could happen because your class already extends another class. (The Java single-inheritance rule is that you can extend only one parent class.) You can choose to **implement** the Java-supplied interface `Runnable` (also defined in the `java.lang` package). This option is just as easy to implement (pardon the pun) as the "extend Thread" option:

- Add **implements** Runnable to your class definition.

- Define a method with signature "public void run()".

To "run" the code, create an instance of the class `Thread` passing in an instance of your class to the constructor, and invoke the `start()` method on that `Thread` instance. Figure 11-4 depicts this architecture:

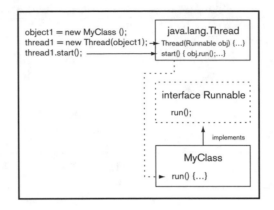

FIGURE 11-4

Referring back to our previous `TestBillableThread` class, to use this option we might have:

LISTING 11-2

```
public class TestBillableRunnable implements Runnable
{
  Printable[] objects; // array to be printed
  // constructor
  public TestBillableRunnable(Printable[] objects)
  {
      this.objects = objects; // store array in instance var
  }
  public static void main(String[] args) // cmdline entry
  {
    Printable[] objlist = new Printable[2];
    objlist[0] = new Presentation();
    objlist[1] = new Widget();
    // create instance of this class, run it
    TestBillableRunnable object1 = new TestBillableRunnable(objlist);
    Thread thread1 = new Thread(object1); // create thread object
    thread1.start(); // implicitly invoke the run method of object1
    System.out.println("Printing job spawned");
  }
  public void printReport()
  {
      System.out.println("Printing objects...");
      for (int index=0;
           index<objects.length;
           index=index+1)
        objects[index].print();
      System.out.println(objects.length + " objects printed");
  }
  public void run()
  {
      printReport();
  }
}
```

If we run this, we get the same output as with the "**extends** Thread" version:

```
Printing job spawned
Printing objects...
inside print for Presentation
inside print for Widget
2 objects printed
```

The changes we made to the original TestBillable class this time were:

- Changed the class to **implement** Runnable (different than previous example).

- Changed the class name to TestBillableRunnable so we do not clobber our previous sample. We subsequently put this class in a file called TestBillableRunnable.java to distinguish it from the previous example.

- Defined an "objects" array variable as an instance variable so that the printReport() method would have access to it (same as previous example).

- Added a *constructor* that takes an existing array as a parameter, and sets the instance variable to it (same as previous example).

- Changed the main method to instantiate an instance of this class, passing in the local array it creates as a parameter; instantiate an instance of the Thread class, passing in our class object as a parameter; and invoke the start() method on that Thread class object (different than previous example).

- Changed printReport to use the instance variable versus taking in a parameter, and therefore removed the **static** modifier (same as previous example).

- Added the "public void run()" method because it is required for a class that **implements** Runnable (same as previous example, but for different reason).

Note that relative to our "**extends** Thread" version earlier, all we had to do was:

- Change the class to **implement** Runnable instead of **extend** Thread.

- Change the main method to also instantiate a Thread object with our object as a parameter, and invoke start() on that.

This shows that the two options are extremely similar. It also shows that, if you first choose to **extend** Thread, changing it later (if you decide you now need to extend another class) to **implement** Runnable is very straightforward.

Stopping a Thread

You will find that your first and primary use of threads will be for putting long running jobs in "the background." This will improve the response time to your end users. You will also find that, in most such cases, you will want to give the user the option of canceling that long running job. This is good user-in-control design, and your users will expect that kind of control. How many times have you decided to kill a compile job because you discovered an obvious bug in the source while waiting for the job to complete?

Let's say that you want to allow a long running thread to be stopped. The typical mechanism is to use an instance variable that both the running threaded method and the controlling thread (usually just the main or default thread) have access to. The controlling thread waits for a user indication that the running thread should be killed, and then sets the common instance variable to indicate this. Meanwhile, the method running in the thread periodically checks that variable and, if it is set, voluntarily ends itself by returning.

Let's look at an example. Suppose we have admittedly contrived code that loops for a given number of seconds and displays the elapsed seconds during each iteration. This code will be in a method called `longRun()`, say. We will code this to allow the number of seconds to be passed in on the command line, and then allow the user to cancel the loop by pressing the **Enter** key on the command line.

What follows is part 1 of a two-part stoppable thread code example:

LISTING 11-3

```java
public class TestThreads extends Thread
{
  long seconds; // how long to run
  boolean stop = false;
  // constructor
  public TestThreads(long seconds)
  {
      this.seconds = seconds; // store time limit in inst var
  } // end TestThreads constructor
  // Mainline
  public static void main(String[] args) // cmdline entry
  {
    TestThreads thisObject;
    long        longValue;
    // verify a parameter passed
    if (args.length != 1)
      {
       System.out.println("Please supply number of seconds");
       return;
      }
    // verify parameter is numeric:
    try
    {
      Long longObject = Long.valueOf(args[0]);
      longValue = longObject.longValue();
    }
    catch (NumberFormatException exc)
    {
      System.out.println("Sorry— " + args[0] + " is not valid");
      return;
    }
    // create new instance of this class, passing in parameter
    thisObject = new TestThreads( longValue );
    System.out.print("Running... ");
    // start the thread running...
    thisObject.start();
    System.out.println("... press <Enter> to stop");
    // watch for <Enter> key
    try
    {
      System.in.read();
    }
    catch (java.io.IOException exc) {}
    // <Enter> pressed—turn on "stop" flag
    thisObject.stop = true;
  } // end main method
```

Here is the second and last part of the stoppable thread code example:

LISTING 11-4

```
// Potentially long running method
public void runLong()
{
   for (int secs=0;
        (secs < seconds) && !stop;
        secs++)
   {
       try
       {
         sleep(1000); // sleep for one second
         System.out.println(secs + " seconds");
       }
       catch (InterruptedException exc) { }
   } // end for-loop
   if (stop)
     System.out.println("... thread stopped");
} // end runLong method
// Required "run" method that will call the long-running method
public void run()
{
    runLong();
} // end run method
} // end TestThreads class
```

If you run this program from the command line and pass in a maximum number of seconds parameter, you will see that it prints out the current seconds count every second, and is stoppable by pressing the <**Enter**> key...

```
>java TestThreads 30
Running... ... press <Enter> to stop
0 seconds
1 seconds
2 seconds
3 seconds
... thread stopped
```

The breakdown of the class is this:

- The class inherits from Thread so that it can run one of its methods as a thread.

- There is a *constructor* that takes in, and stores in a class instance variable, a given number representing the maximum number of seconds to loop.

- There is a **static** main method that, of course, is what gets control from the command line. It validates the input and creates an instance of this class, which passes in the user supplied number.

- The `main` method then spawns the thread by invoking the `start()` method on the object instance, and does a "`read()`" to wait for the user to press **<Enter>**. When this happens, the object's instance variable "`stop`" is set to **true**. Keep in mind that you can try this example as non-threaded by swapping the `start()` method call with a direct call to `longRun()`. You will see that, without the use of threads, the loop cannot be interrupted and canceled.

- There is a `longRun` method, called by the required `run()` method, that loops for a given number of seconds. In each iteration it "sleeps" for one second. `Sleep` is a method inherited from the `Thread` class. If we chose to `implement Runnable` instead of inheriting from `Thread`, we would code `Thread.sleep(1000)` because we would not inherit this method. `Sleep` is a static method. Note that this method throws an exception, so it must be called in a ***try/catch-block***. The parameter to `sleep` is the number of milliseconds to sleep for. This is a *friendly* way to kill time because it gives other threads a chance to run.

- The `runLong` loop will stop either when the maximum seconds is reached or the "`stop`" instance variable gets set to **true**.

This convention of using a mutually accessible variable to control the stopping of the thread works well in most situations. There are times, however, when it will cause a problem:

- You have no convenient mutually accessible variable to use for communications.

- You have no easy way in the long running code to check a variable in a timely manner.

These are examples of cases in which you may find it necessary to forcefully "kill" a running thread. This is possible with the method `stop()` we inherit from the `Thread` class. We will try using this now in our example instead of the mutual variable method. We change the `main` method line of code...

```
thisObject.stop = true;
```

... to instead be

```
thisObject.stop();
```

... and then recompile and run. After a few seconds of running, we press **<Enter>** and get the expected results:

```
>java TestThreads 30
Running... ... press <Enter> to stop
0 seconds
1 seconds
2 seconds
```

In fact, this time it was even more responsive. Pressing `<Enter>` resulted in an immediate end to the program. Previously, it took up to a second to respond while the runLong method waited to wake up from its "sleep."

The one potential downside of using stop() is that our thread method did not get a chance to do any cleanup that it may require (in our case, to simply print out "thread stopped"). The need for this is rare. For example, you may need to close an open file as part of your post pardum. There is a way to get control when you die. The stop method works by sending an exception of class type ThreadDeath to the thread object it was invoked on ("thisObject" in our example). Because this exception extends Error versus Exception, we do not normally monitor for it. However, if you do want to know when your code is being "killed" by the stop method, you can put the entire body inside a *try/catch-block*, catching ThreadDeath. You must put the whole body inside the **try** because you do not know which instruction will be running when the death knell comes. So, in our example, we place the body of the runLong() method in a *try/catch-block*...

LISTING 11-5

```
// Potentially long running method
public void runLong()
{
   try
   {
     for (int secs=0; (secs < seconds); secs++)
       {
          try
          {
            sleep(1000L); // sleep for one second
            System.out.println(secs + " seconds");
          }
          catch (InterruptedException exc) {}
       } // end for-loop
   } // end try
   catch (ThreadDeath exc)
   {
     System.out.println("... thread stopped");
     throw(exc);
   }
} // end runLong method
```

Now, when we run and cancel, we see:

```
>java TestThreads 30
Running... ... press <Enter> to stop
0 seconds
1 seconds
2 seconds
... thread stopped
```

Notice in our code that we re-**throw** the ThreadDeath exception after catching it. This is important so the thread continues to die as expected (with dignity!). You might say, then, that you should *try* to *catch* your *body* before it dies!

If we implemented Runnable instead of extending Thread, we would invoke stop on the Thread instance *instead* of our class instance: threadObject.stop(). This is because stop() is a member of the Thread class.

Stopping Multiple Threads — ThreadGroups

This example is "easy" in that we have only a single thread running. But, what if we instead started multiple threads running and wanted to stop all of them at the same time? We could, of course, invoke stop on each of them in turn. In real life, however, this can get messy when we may not know how many threads are running and do not have a convenient way of enumerating all of them. This is common enough, especially in Internet programming where, for example, you may have numerous threads downloading numerous images and resources. In fact, Java designed in support for "***thread groups***". This is a mechanism for partitioning threads into a uniquely named group, and allowing individual actions such as stop to be easily applied to *all* threads in the group.

To create a thread group, you create an instance of the ThreadGroup class and pass in any unique name you want for the group:

```
ThreadGroup groupObject = new ThreadGroup("longRunning");
```

To identify that new threads are to be created as part of a particular thread group, you pass in the ThreadGroup object as a parameter to the Thread constructor:

```
Thread threadObject = new Thread(groupObject, thisObject);
```

Note that this is only permitted for the **implements** Runnable option, not the **extends** Thread option. There is no Thread constructor that takes a ThreadGroup object parameter and does *not* take a Runnable object parameter.

To test this in our example, we change our code to use **implements** Runnable instead of **extends** Thread, and we change only our main method as follows:

- Create a ThreadGroup object, and create two Thread objects.
  ```
  thisObject = new TestThreads( longValue );
  ThreadGroup groupObject = new ThreadGroup("longRunning");
  Thread threadObject1 = new Thread(groupObject, thisObject );
  Thread threadObject2 = new Thread(groupObject, thisObject );
  ```

- Start both threads.

```
threadObject1.start();
threadObject2.start();
```

- Stop the ThreadGroup object, versus the Thread object.

```
groupObject.stop();
```

Running this now gives the following result:

```
>java TestThreads 30
Running... ... press <Enter> to stop
0 seconds
0 seconds
1 seconds
1 seconds
2 seconds
2 seconds
```

You see each line twice because we have two threads running. This ability to control multiple threads as a group is a welcome addition that Java offers above the typical operating system support for threads. You will find it can save much ugly code. Note that we use the same object (thisObject) in this example and spawn two threads on it. This is quite legal and quite common.

NOTE: The example shown here only catches ThreadDeath so it only runs cleanup code when threads are stopped — not when they die for other reasons or run cleanly. If cleanup really is important regardless of how the thread ends, you should put it in a **finally** clause, as discussed in the previous chapter.

Ending Programs with Java Running Threads

You may be wondering at this point what happens when the main method ends and threads are still running. You saw that, after spawning the threads, the main method regained control immediately. The threads then started running asynchronously in the background. What happens when the end of the main method is reached and there are still background threads running? When execution reaches the *very end* of the main method, the Java Virtual Machine will queue up its 'exit' until all active threads have finished running. That is, the program will remain running until those background threads have all finished. You will notice this because you will not get control back at the command line where you issued "Java xxx," and you will see Java listed as one of the programs still running in the call stack.

There are times when you simply want to force an exit. That may involve *killing* any rogue threads still running. You can do that by exiting your program with **System.exit(0);**. Unlike an implicit or explicit `return` statement, this does not wait for running threads to end. Sometimes this is necessary for idle background threads, as you will see when using the AS/400 Toolbox for Java classes, for example.

Daemon Threads

The statement about programs not ending until all threads have finished does have a corollary. When you create a `Thread` object, you can invoke the `setDaemon(true)` method on it to identify this thread as a "*daemon*". What does that mean? You've sold your soul! Well, independent of that, it means this thread is a "*service thread*" that never ends. At program end time, Java will *not* wait for daemon threads before exiting. Instead, it will just kill those threads! An example of a daemon thread is a timer thread. That is something that just runs in the background and sends out "tick" events, say. Another example might be a thread that watches a data queue or phone line. Marking these types of threads as "daemons" saves you the trouble of explicitly killing them yourself when you are ready to exit your program.

Java's Own Threads

Even if you do not use threads yourself, Java considers your non-threaded code to be part of a "main thread." There are other default threads in any Java program, notably the "*garbage collector*" thread. This a daemon thread that always lurks in the background waiting for an opportunity to vacuum up an unused object. Using a graphical user interface causes another daemon thread to run as well to "watch" for user **events** like mouse movements.

THINKING ASYNCHRONOUS — DANGER LURKS...

In our examples of threads so far, we have used a thread to allow long running code to be interrupted. In a real world application you will use threads in other ways. For example, you will use them for any potentially long running operation to ensure overall system efficiency and higher throughput. Just as a bank has multiple tellers and a grocery store has multiple checkout counters, your programs will often have multiple asynchronous *transaction* threads. Often this design will involve one common repository class — such as a bank or store class — and a separate transaction class that is threaded. You will spawn multiple transaction threads, each taking as input an object in the repository, and acting on that object. The transaction thread class will take an instance of the repository class as a constructor parameter, and its `run()` method will invoke one or more of the methods on that repository object. This is illustrated in Figure 11-5:

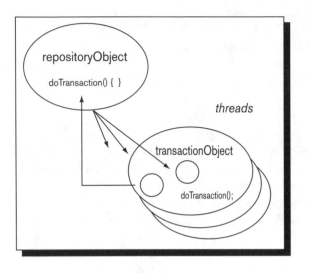

FIGURE 11-5

In this design, you will end up with many simultaneous threads using a single instance of an object. The implication is that they will be attempting to view and change the variables in that object simultaneously. Consider an RPG IV module that is used in a ***PGM** object. It has global variables, just as a Java class has instance variables. Like threads, you can have multiple users running your program simultaneously. However, they each get their own copies of those global variables. With threads, they all share the same copy! This can be dangerous, of course. The threads may 'step on each other' — one changing a variable under the foot of another.

As application programmers, you are used to this. You already have to deal with the problems of simultaneous access to your database and you religiously use locking mechanisms to ensure the integrity of the database. Thus, to build "thread safe" Java programs, you have to learn the Java syntax and idioms necessary to do with instance variables what you do today with database records.

We will mention the following two points before moving on to thread-safety: The design of a complex Java multiple user application, and the role of threads in that application; and how single objects can have multiple threads of execution.

First, the design of a complex Java multiple-user application: Will you have to worry about these complex multithreaded applications? Perhaps not, if all you are doing initially is adding a Java graphical user interface onto your host RPG application. In this case, your Java user interface will run on the client, and each concurrent user will invoke

346

independent instances (jobs) of your RPG *backend* code as needed. Your existing database logic in the RPG code will be as robust as always. However, as you delve deeper into writing and running Java server code on the AS/400 itself, you may come to a design like the one shown in Figure 11-6:

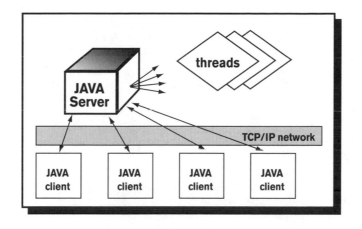

FIGURE 11-6

In this scenario, rather than having separate AS/400 jobs servicing each client, you have but one server job running, with one or more threads per client. This scales better (although admittedly the AS/400 does an exceptional job of handling many thousands of jobs) because threads have less overhead than separate jobs. Combined with **RMI** (*Remote Method Invocation* — Java's built-in support for distributing a Java class between a client and a server) or CORBA (*Common Ojbect Request Broker Architecture* — an "enterprise" level industry standard for distributing objects) this can offer an effective new way to design your large scale applications with thousands of concurrent users. To do this, however, you will have to delve deep into threads and thread safety.

Second, how single objects can have multiple threads of execution: You may be a tad unclear as to how one object can have multiple threads of execution. Think of a bank object. At any one time it may have thousands of individual threads all calling its "transferFunds" method. It may seem confusing to have so many executing threads, perhaps all on the same method. Do not mix up objects with executing threads. One is about memory, and the other is about instruction pointers. It may help to think of the object as a database file, and the methods as RPG programs that use that database. You have only one database file but, at any one time, you have numerous users running your RPG program or programs that manipulate that database.

Multi-Threaded Danger — Inventory Example

The following example shows how multiple threads using a shared object can be dangerous. Consider a system where orders of an item are accepted and fulfilled. The in-stock inventory of the item is also monitored. You may have a class called `Inventory` that manages this:

LISTING 11-6

```java
public class Inventory
{
  private static final int AMOUNT_INCREMENT = 2000;
  private int onHand = 5000; // amount in inventory
  public boolean stop = false; // stop whole thing
  // method to fulfill an order
  public void takeOrder(int howMany)
  {
      int old = onHand;
      String error = "";
      if (stop) // have we been stopped?
        return; //  exit now
      if (howMany > onHand)
        {
         // increase inventory
         addToInventory(howMany);
         error = "Order: " + howMany + ", old: " + old + ", new: " + onHand;
        }
      // actually take order
      onHand = onHand—howMany;
      // inventory should never be negative, but still...
      if (onHand < 0)
        {
         System.out.println("Error—onHand less than zero! " + onHand);
         System.out.println(error);
         stop = true;
        }
  } // end takeOrder method
  // method to increase inventory stock, taking into
  // account the size of the current order
  private void addToInventory(int howMany)
  {
      if (howMany > AMOUNT_INCREMENT)
        onHand +=(howMany-onHand)+1;
      else
        onHand += AMOUNT_INCREMENT;
  } // end addToInventory method
} // end Inventory class
```

This is a very simple class. It starts with an initial amount of inventory *onHand* (5000) and each order taken (`takeOrder` method) decrements the amount of the order from the inventory. First, however, a check is made to ensure the size of the order will not deplete the current inventory. If this would be the case, the inventory is increased before the order is filled (`addToInventory` method). Note that we check the `stop` instance variable before even bothering to enter the body of the method. You will see where `stop` is set at the end of the method.

This is very basic stuff — what could go wrong? Look at the `takeOrder` method. Because we bump up the inventory to cover the current order whenever necessary (admittedly non-robust algorithm), it seems ludicrous to have the "`if (onHand < 0)`" check. How can it get below zero if the lines of code just above it ensure that it does not? In a synchronized world, of course, it cannot. But in a threaded world, it can. To see this, we need another class — a thread class — whose `run` method will call the "`takeOrder`" method on an instance of `Inventory`. This is a typical "transaction" type of thread class:

LISTING 11-7

```
public class OrderThread implements Runnable
{
  Inventory inventoryObject; // passed in to us
  int       howMany; // how many items to order
  // constructor
  public OrderThread(Inventory inventoryObject, int howMany)
  {
      this.inventoryObject = inventoryObject;
      this.howMany = howMany;
  }
  // "run" method, called by using Start()
  // This method places the order for the given amount
  public void run()
  {
      // place the order
      inventoryObject.takeOrder(howMany);
  } // end run() method
} // end OrderThread class
```

An instance of this class will be created for every order, and it will be run as a thread. However, there will be only a single instance of our `Inventory` class. That instance will be passed in via the constructor to every instance of this `OrderThread` class. This makes sense — while we get many orders, there should never be more than one inventory. To test our little "system," we need a final class that contains the needed `main` method to get control from the command line. This will create a single `Inventory` object, but there will be many sample "`OrderThread`" objects to really stress test this thing:

LISTING 11-8

```
public class TestInventory
{
  public static void main(String[] args) // cmdline entry
  {
    Inventory inv = new Inventory();
    java.util.Random random = new java.util.Random();
    int idx;
    System.out.println("Running... ");
    for (idx = 0; (idx <= 1000) && !inv.stop; idx++)
    {
      int nextRandom = java.lang.Math.abs(random.nextInt());
      nextRandom = (nextRandom % 10000) + 1;
      OrderThread newOrder = new OrderThread(inv, nextRandom);
      Thread newThread = new Thread(newOrder);
      newThread.start();
    }
    if (inv.stop)
      System.out.println("...stopped at: " + idx);
    else
      System.out.println("...all orders placed.");
  } // end main method
} // end TestInventory class
```

This test creates 1,000 order-taking threads, each one asking for a random number of items that ranges up to 10,000. Potentially, all of these threads will run simultaneously, really testing our logic that is designed to never let the inventory fall below zero. This code creates a single instance of the Inventory class and passes it into every instance of OrderThread, so all threads are operating on a single object. We use a Random object from the java.util package to generate our random numbers for the simulated orders. If the inventory ever does fall below zero (seemingly impossible, but still....) we notice this and stop creating new threads because the system has obviously degenerated and is now unstable. If we compile and run these classes, we get the following output:

LISTING 11-9

```
>java TestInventory
Running...
Error—onHand less than zero! -921
Order: 5820, old: 2001, new: 4899
Error—onHand less than zero! -1695
Error—onHand less than zero! -7353
Order: 5658, old: -921, new: -1695
Error—onHand less than zero! -7582
Order: 229, old: 1, new: 2001
...stopped at: 104
Order: 7354, old: 5821, new: 5659
```

There are a number of very interesting (scary?) things about this output:

- The inventory fell below zero — despite explicit code to check and prevent that!
- Even after we "stopped" new threads from executing the `takeOrder` thread by setting the `stop` variable, we still got numerous "error" outputs, indicating these threads were already past the `if (stop) return;` code at the beginning of the method.
- The `Error` and `Order` lines are not always synchronized in the output, even though these were issued one line after another in the code.

The `Error` and `Order` lines both print out the value of the `onHand` variable (look at the *"new"* value for the `Order` lines), just at different points in the `takeOrder` method. However, while no changes are made to the variable in the intervening code, the variable value has still changed between the two.

All of this clearly indicates one thing: computers cannot be trusted! Well, actually, it demonstrates that there are multiple threads of execution running inside this `takeOrder` method simultaneously. The switching from one thread to another can, and does, happen quickly (from one line to the next) and arbitrarily. This causes a problem for us because of the common variable (`onHand`) these lines of code are sharing and manipulating.

What is happening is this: between the line of code that checks the `onHand` balance...

```
if (howMany > onHand)
```

... and the line of code which decrements the balance...

```
onHand = onHand—howMany;
```

... another thread is gaining control, and running the same decrementing line of code. This means the check is passing for a particular thread but, by the time it actually does the `onHand` variable decrement another thread has already decremented the variable (see Figure 11-7):

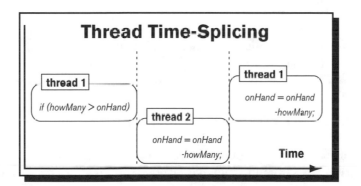

FIGURE 11-7

This causes the variable to be decremented twice without the check, letting it go below zero. Threads work by *preemptive time-slicing* — that is, each thread is given a small amount of CPU time to perform a few *atomic* instructions. Then it is preempted and another thread is given a similar amount of CPU time to perform a few of its instructions. This continues until each thread is complete (by reaching the end of the run() method). An *atomic* instruction is essentially one line of bytecode. Generally a single line of Java source code compiles into numerous Java bytecode instructions. This is not unlike RPG where a single C-spec statement can compile into multiple underlying machine code instructions. This means you cannot guarantee even that an entire line of source code will run before the next thread is given control.

Solution — Synchronizing Asynchronous Execution

This may sound hopeless. If you cannot guarantee order of execution, how can you possibly guard against these unexpected *concurrency* errors? The answer to providing this *thread safety* is elegantly simple. It involves merely adding one Java keyword to one line of code! What you need to be able to do is to guard against this unexpected *interruption* whenever you have code that is dependent on a common variable remaining stable from one line of code to the next. The magic keyword in Java to do this is `synchronized`. When specified as a *method modifier*, it tells Java that this entire method needs to be executed without interruption by other threads. Effectively, it allows only one thread to execute this method at a time. All waiting threads get queued up "at the door." As each thread finishes executing the method, the next thread that is waiting is let in.

We change our takeOrder method definition to include the keyword `synchronized`:

```
public synchronized void takeOrder(int howMany)
```

Now, after compiling, we run the test again and get no unexpected errors:

```
>java TestInventory
Running...
...all orders placed.
```

This code will run *slower*. After all, we have reduced the amount of asynchronous execution considerably — but it will run *correctly*, and that, after all, is the *primary* fundamental requirement!

Fine-Grained Synchronization

We have synchronized the entire takeOrder method, but we could actually synchronize just the lines of code we need to "guard" instead. Java defines a `synchronized` block — a block of code that can be placed inside a "`synchronized`" statement so only that block is protected from interruptions by other threads. To use this "fine grained synchronizing" you have to think carefully about what code is "exposed" by multiple concurrent threads of execution. At a minimum, it is any code that changes a common (instance) variable. However, if you have code that tests the current value of the variable and then does work based on that current variable value, you will need to synchronize the entire block. You need to always be thinking "what if the value of the variable changed right now" for each line of code. In our case, we need to treat the onHand variable check and the onHand variable decrement as a single unit of operation so we can guarantee that no other thread can decrement the variable in-between and, hence, cause an underflow. So, we remove **synchronized** from the takeOrder method declaration and instead place it around this sensitive block of code:

LISTING 11-10

```
synchronized(this)
{
  if (howMany > onHand)
    {
     // increase inventory
     addToInventory(howMany);
     error = "Order: " + howMany + ", old: " + old + ", new: " + onHand;
    }
  // actually take order
  onHand = onHand-howMany;
} // end syncrhonized(this)
```

In our case, there will be no appreciable difference in total execution time. This is true only because we ended up having to put almost the entire method's code into the **synchronized** statement anyway. However, if there was a significant amount of other code outside of the synchronized block, we would see overall throughput improvements.

In general, you should simply use **synchronized** at the *method level* (as a modifier) on any methods that manipulate common variables, *unless*:

- You are very sure about the minimum set of code that needs to be synchronized. In our case, moving the line that decrements onHand out of the synchronized block causes the unexpected error situations to happen again. If we were not checking for this in the code, we would have ended up with a very serious bug that could have gone undetected for a long time, or until our suppliers received a negative-amount order!

The **synchronized** versus unsynchronized code ratio is worth the extra risk.

Was it even worth using threads in this example? Maybe not. We ended up having to synchronize the majority of the code. However, threads are *usually* a good idea because your code per transaction is *usually* complex and the synchronized part — even if it is an entire method — is relatively small. That is, usually the thread will involve more code than a single method call. The use of threads can give very busy applications at least the "chance" for individual transactions to be completed in a shorter time than if they all had to wait for the previously submitted transactions to complete. Further, by spawning threads, you give control back to the end user immediately, rather than forcing him to wait an indefinite amount of time for the transaction to complete. This reason alone dictates that threads should be used more often than not for user-initiated transactions. "Leave the customer in control" is a maxim to live and code by.

Threaded Application Design Alternatives

We put each transaction in our example in its own thread. This is not the only possible design, of course. Another option would be to give each user his own thread instead, and let it perform the transactions synchronously *within* the thread. This is a reasonable alternative because users will expect their own transactions to be performed in the order they are submitted anyway. It may, thus, reduce the overall number of threads running and improve response time. If you have too many threads competing for processor time, you may run into ***thrashing*** — a situation where so many threads are running each one gets only enough time to do a minuscule amount of work each slice. Another option would be to create a fixed-size ***thread-pool*** of *transaction* or *service* threads. In this design, a predetermined number of threads — say a dozen or so — are spawned at application start time and each transaction or thread-qualifying request is fed to the next available thread. If no thread is available the request is queued up and the next transaction thread to become available reads it from the queue and executes it. Or the thread-pool grows by one thread to a pre-set maximum. Again, this can reduce the amount of thread-switching and improve performance for *very* heavy use applications.

MORE ON THE SYNCHRONIZED KEYWORD

You have now seen the basics of threads in Java. The remainder of this chapter goes into more detail and can be safely skipped if you are only looking for an introduction to Java or to threads. If you are ready for more detailed information on threads, however, read on.

The `synchronized` keyword, as you have seen, can be specified as a method modifier, or as a code-block keyword. In the latter case, you saw in the example that it requires a parameter. For the example we specified, the keyword `this` represented the current object. This `synchronized` keyword is actually equivalent to the AS/400 command `ALCOBJ` (*Allocate Object*) with the `*EXCL` (*Exclusive, no read*) parameter. That is, it *locks* an object so that you have exclusive access to it. It always locks some class *instance* — a Java "object". When used as a method modifier, it is locking the object the method is part of. When used as a code-block keyword, it is locking the object you specify as a parameter. In both cases, it is the entire object that is locked, not just the method or code-block. Thus, at runtime when a thread (including the main thread) calls a synchronized method or tries to enter a synchronized block, the algorithm is this:

- Is the specified object locked? (Is another thread running any synchronized code for this object right now?)
  - **Yes** — wait in this object's queue.
  - **No** — lock this object, run the code.

When the code is done running (execution reaches the end of the method or block) the object is unlocked and the next thread in the queue is allowed in. Just as with **ALCOBJ**, nested synchronized methods or blocks on the same object bump up the lock count for the object. It is not until the current thread that has the lock reduces the lock to zero that the object is finally unlocked for others to use (see Figure 11-8).

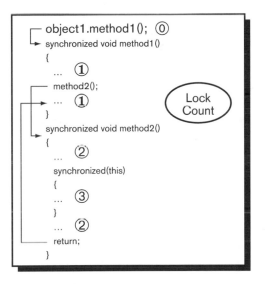

FIGURE 11-8

The use of **synchronized** as a method modifier is actually equivalent to putting the entire method body in a synchronized(this) block. It is, to be sure, the safest and easiest way to synchronize sensitive code that changes common variables *in this object.*. However, there will also be times when code in one method changes variables in *another* object (either directly or through setxxx methods). In these cases, you will have to use synchronized(object) blocks around the sensitive code, where "object" is the object reference variable that will be changed.

When you "lock" an object via the use of **synchronized** (either as a method modifier or a code-block keyword) it is important to know that you do not block other un-synchronized methods from running in that same object. This means you can have one thread running an un-synchronized method that reads the common variables at the same time another thread is running inside a synchronized method that perhaps changes those variables. Locking an object only affects other threads that attempt to run synchronized code on that object. Normally code that reads only a common variable is OK to leave un-synchronized, unless it is doing multiple lines of code that depend on the variable not changing from one line to the next. For example, if you have something like:

```
if (account < 0)
   sendNotice("You have an outstanding account of " + account);
```

you will clearly have to be careful that the `account` value does not go above zero by the time the `sendNotice` method is called in the second line. These two lines should be placed inside a **synchronized**(this) block to ensure the common variable does not change from one line to the next.

Synchronizing Producer/Consumer Relationships: wait / notify

There are times when you will have one synchronized thread that needs to wait on another thread. Java supplies two methods, each one part of the base `java.lang.Object` class, which are available to all. They are called **wait()** and **notifyAll().** These methods can only be used inside synchronized methods or blocks. `Wait` will wait indefinitely, or goptionally a specified number of milliseconds, until another thread calls `notifyAll`. Wait is always used inside a loop checking for some condition the thread is dependent on. After waiting, the condition is rechecked:

```
while (variable < threshold)
   wait();
```

The thread that calls `wait` gets put on a "***wait queue***" for the current object, until the object is *unlocked.* That allows another thread to get in for this object. The threads on a wait queue are only *released* when `notifyAll` is called by some other thread for this same object. There is actually a method called `notify` as well, which explicitly *releases* the thread that has been waiting the longest. `NotifyAll` will *release* all waiting threads. What does it mean to be *released?* It means this thread is back in the queue waiting to get into the synchronized object. Another thread may have gotten in, because `wait` resets the lock count to zero in the meantime. When it does finally get back in, it starts executing again where it left off at the `wait()` method call. The lock count is then restored to the value it had when the thread call originally called `wait`. This is illustrated in Figure 11-9:

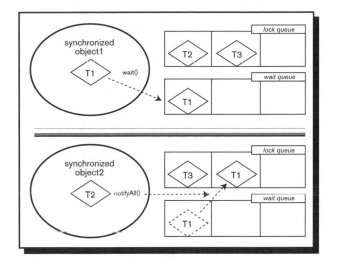

FIGURE 11-9

In the picture, *Tn* represents ***Thread n***. If there were more threads in the wait queue, notifyAll would move them all to the lock queue, while notify would move only the first one (*T1* in this case). Note that a thread will also move from the wait queue to the lock queue if it specified a number of milliseconds in the call to wait(mmmm) and that time limit has expired.

You will use the **wait/notify** pair in situations where there is one section of code that produces some output, which another section of code (perhaps the same method, perhaps a different method) is dependent on. For example, you may have a queue object with synchronized methods for reading and writing the queue. The read method would wait until the queue is non-empty...

```
// inside read method
while (isEmpty())
  wait();
```

... and the write method would notify or notifyAll after adding the entry to the queue:

```
// inside write method
addEntry(newItem);
notify();
```

When to use `notify` and when to use `notifyAll`? Good question. If only there was a good answer. In this case, we added only one item to the queue. Because we know only one thread will be able to use it, using `notifyAll` is not appropriate. If there was an "append" method that added numerous items to the queue, we would use `notifyAll` so all waiting threads would get a chance. The worst that will happen is that one or more threads will return to life only to find their condition still is not met. They will redo their `wait` call.

A thread calling the `read` method in this case would be a good candidate for a ***daemon*** thread. You would typically not want the application to be prevented from exiting if that `read` method was still waiting for an entry on the queue.

Deadly Embrace — Deadlock!

Synchronization is a great tool to ensure correctness in your multi-threaded applications. However, it is dangerous tool as well! You can, very easily, arrive at a situation where all running threads are "blocked" because they are waiting for each other. This is like the law that is still on the books somewhere that states, "When two trains meet at an intersection, neither can leave until the other is gone." Consider the following situation:

Thread T1 runs synchronized method `obj1.method1()`, locking `obj1`. Thread T2 runs synchronized method `obj2.method2()`, locking `obj2`. Now, `obj1.method1` tries to call `obj2.method2`, and so thread T1 is put in the lock queue for `obj2` while it waits for thread T2 to finish. But `obj2.method2` calls `obj1.method1`, and so thread T2 gets put in the lock queue for `obj1` while it waits for thread T1 to finish (see Figure 11-10). Each is blocked now, waiting on the other, and will wait forever. No other threads needing these objects will ever run either and, unless these are daemon threads or `System.exit` is used, the program will not end unless forcefully killed.

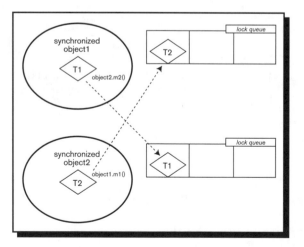

FIGURE 11-10

This is a deadly embrace known as *deadlock*. There is nothing that Java can do to help you here! If you hit this problem, it will manifest itself intermittently (timing dependent) and be a complete bear to debug. You need to avoid the problem outright by careful design — that is, by avoiding mutual calls from one object's synchronized method to another's and back again. If necessary, you will have to use a third object with a synchronized method that makes the necessary calls to the other two objects via *un-synchronized* calls.

Wait and **notify** do not help or hinder the deadlock possibilities, but they do add the risk of a thread "waiting" forever if another thread does not someday notify it. However, because the waiting thread unlocks the object, at least other threads have a chance to run. If it is important for the waiting thread to eventually run (say if it is waiting on resources in order to place a customer order), then this will still be a serious problem. You may want to specify a time-out limit, even if it is 10 minutes, on the **wait** method to indicate when something appears to be stuck! Of course, there is a risk that it is waiting on itself:

```
public synchronized void waitOnMe()
{
    while (variable < threshHold)
      wait();
    variable += threshHold;
    notify();
}
```

In this case, the code that notifies waiting threads is clearly unreachable. There is no point in waiting on a situation your subsequent code will address. Just go ahead and address it!

THREAD PRIORITIES

In our diagrams and discussion about synchronization, we used the terms "lock queue" and "wait queue." They are a misnomer in that they imply that the threads are put into and taken off the queues in a deterministic manner — say first in, first out. This is not the case. They are, in fact, randomly chosen by the *thread scheduler*. The algorithm used to choose them is not programmatically predictable. It may vary from platform to platform, depending on the underlying operating system's scheduling support for threads. Better terms for us to use would be "lock set" and "wait set." These, however, create their own aura of confusion.

One of the criteria Java tries to enforce in the scheduling of threads (and all multi-threaded operating systems support) is that of ***thread priority.*** By default, your threads will all have "normal" priority and, thus, the same relative weighting for this criteria. However, by using the `Thread` method `setPriority`, you can set the priority to any number between 1 (lowest) and 10 (highest). The default is 5 (normal) for convenience, there are predefined constants in the `Thread` class for `MIN_PRIORITY` (1), `NORM_PRIORITY` (5), and `MAX_PRIORITY`(10).

New threads inherit the priority of their parent threads (the main thread has normal priority), or that of their `ThreadGroup` if one is specified. Using `ThreadGroups` is a convenient way to set the priorities of all similar-role threads.

When the thread scheduler needs to pick another thread for its turn to run, get off the locked queue, or get off the wait queue, it will use an algorithm involving both the thread's priority and its time "waiting" so far. Higher priority threads, all things being equal, will get more CPU time than lower priority threads. It is a general rule of thumb that user interface threads run as a high priority to improve response time, and daemon "background" threads run as a low priority to take whatever cycles they can steal.

LOOSE THREADS

We conclude this chapter by discussing some other aspects and functions available to you as a threaded programmer:

Named Threads. When you create a new `Thread` object, you can specify a new unique name for that thread, and query it at any time. This may be helpful for debugging or logging purposes.

Yield. This is a friendly `static` method in `Thread` that you can use in your code to voluntarily give up your current CPU slice. That lets another thread run. If all your threads consist of the same `synchronized` method, there is no point to invoking `yield` in that method because no other thread can run anyway. Until you finish the method and, hence, relinquish the lock, the other threads remain stuck on the lock queue. Unlike `wait`, `yield` does *not* unlock the object and does *not* put your thread on the wait queue.

Suspend and Resume. One thread can *suspend* another thread by calling its `suspend` method (good choice of method name, no?), and subsequently bring it back to life by invoking its `resume` method. This could be useful when you want to confirm a user's cancel request, for example. While asking the user to confirm, you would *suspend* the thread (or `ThreadGroup`!) and if the decision is not to cancel after all, you would *resume* it. These also make a "Pause" push button easy to implement.

Join. This is an interesting method! It is easy to wait for a thread to finish. You simply call join() on its Thread object. This will *not return* until that thread has finished (by returning from its run() method). An example of where this is very useful follows shortly.

Checking the Pulse. You may occasionally need to determine if a given Thread object has "finished" running or not. The Thread method isAlive() will return **true** if the thread has not yet finished (not returned from its run method). Be careful though — if you have not yet called start() on this thread, you will get **false** from this query.

Timing Threaded Applications

When writing applications, we often want to measure the elapsed time to gauge the performance impacts of changes we make. This is especially true in a multiple thread application, where we want to ensure adding a **wait** here, a **yield** there, a **synchronized** statement over there, does not seriously degrade the overall "throughput" of the application.

To measure an application's time, an easy trick is to change the main entry point to record the current time in milliseconds at the very beginning, and record it again at the very end. Then, take the difference and spit it out to standard-out (that is, console) or a log file. We then make a number of test runs through the application and average the total elapsed time. Now, if we change something, we can rerun the testcases and compare the average elapsed time. Of course, this will be very dependent on the current load of the system. It has to be taken with a grain of salt. For code running on the workstation, the usual trick is to run the testcases after a fresh reboot so memory is in as consistent a state as possible between runs.

To measure the elapsed time in our inventory example, we will change the `main` method in the `TestInventory` class to print out the elapsed time — in milliseconds — that the entire process takes. We will use the `Date` class in the `java.util` package to record the current time in milliseconds twice — once before all the threads are spawned, and once after, and display the difference:

LISTING 11-11

```
// Mainline
public static void main(String[] args) // cmdline entry
{
  Inventory inv = new Inventory();
  java.util.Random random = new java.util.Random();
  int idx;
  java.util.Date startTime = new java.util.Date();
  System.out.println("Running... ");
  for (idx = 0; (idx <= 1000) && !inv.stop; idx++)
  {
     int nextRandom = java.lang.Math.abs(random.nextInt());
     nextRandom = (nextRandom % 10000) + 1;
     OrderThread newOrder = new OrderThread(inv, nextRandom);
     Thread newThread = new Thread(newOrder);
     newThread.start();
  }
  if (inv.stop)
    System.out.println("...stopped at: " + idx);
  else
    System.out.println("...all orders placed.");
  java.util.Date endTime = new java.util.Date();
  long elapsed = endTime.getTime()-startTime.getTime();
  System.out.println("Elapsed time: " + elapsed);
} // end main method
```

Actually, this is not quite the correct way to do this. Why? Because when we get the current time at the end of the `main` method, we cannot be sure the threads have finished running. Remember, the `start()` calls return immediately, so we will be taking the second time-reading potentially before the threads have even started to execute. What we need is a way to wait for all the spawned threads to complete and then check the time. We will do this by creating all the threads in a single `ThreadGroup` and then waiting for them all to finish. This is a good strategy anyway, because it also gives us an easy way to `stop` all these threads when something untoward happens or is detected: just use `object.stop()` on the `ThreadGroup` object.

How do we wait for all the threads in the group to finish? Painfully, as it turns out! You have to *enumerate* (list) all the threads in the group, then invoke the `Thread` method `join` on each of them. The method `join` "waits" on the thread to finish, and only then do you get control back. (If it is already finished you get control back immediately.) What is missing from Java is a `join` method for the `ThreadGroup` itself — but the code is not that intellectually taxing, and so we add it in before the final time reading is taken. Note that `join()` may throw an `InterruptedException` exception, so we have to "catch" it:

LISTING 11-12

```
// Mainline
public static void main(String[] args) // cmdline entry
{
  Inventory inv = new Inventory();
  java.util.Random random = new java.util.Random();
  int idx;
  java.util.Date startTime = new java.util.Date();
  ThreadGroup orderGroup = new ThreadGroup("Orders");
  System.out.println("Running... ");
  for (idx = 0; (idx <= 1000) && !inv.stop; idx++)
  {
     int nextRandom = java.lang.Math.abs(random.nextInt());
     nextRandom = (nextRandom % 10000) + 1;
     OrderThread newOrder = new OrderThread(inv, nextRandom);
     Thread newThread = new Thread(orderGroup, newOrder);
     newThread.start();
  }
  if (inv.stop)
    System.out.println("...stopped at: " + idx);
  else
    System.out.println("...all orders placed.");
  // wait for all threads to end...
  Thread allThreads[] = new Thread[orderGroup.activeCount() + 10];
  orderGroup.enumerate(allThreads);
  for (int j = 0; j < allThreads.length; j++)
  {
     if (allThreads[j] != null)
       try
       {
         allThreads[j].join();
       }
       catch (InterruptedException exc) {}
  } // end for-loop
  java.util.Date endTime = new java.util.Date();
  long elapsed = endTime.getTime()-startTime.getTime();
  System.out.println("Elapsed time: " + elapsed);
} // end main method
```

Now, with our accurate elapsed-time checking in place, we can make a few sample runs and record the average time:

LISTING 11-13

```
>java TestInventory
Running...
...all orders placed.
Elapsed time: 6210
>java TestInventory
Running...
...all orders placed.
Elapsed time: 6150
>java TestInventory
Running...
...all orders placed.
Elapsed time: 7090
```

We see then that our average time is 6483 milliseconds (mileage may vary!).

Note here that our TestInventory class can be kept as a separate test case we can easily rerun at will without affecting the "real" application code that we ship. You may, in fact, write multiples of these little test "main" classes to test various inputs, outputs, and timings. By keeping these as separate classes, you do not have to worry about shipping them with the production version of the application.

SUMMARY

In this chapter we covered the topic of threads in Java:

- The two methods for defining threads: `extends Thread` and `implements Runnable.`
- The `ThreadGroup` class for grouping similar-function threads.
- The use of the `Thread` class `stop` method to stop threads or entire thread groups.
- The definition of a **daemon** "background" thread.
- How to create **synchronized** methods and code to avoid common variable corruption.
- How to use `Thread`'s **wait** and **notify** methods as a means of waiting and triggering codependent synchronized threads.
- The definition of **deadlock** and its potential to happen in synchronized threads.
- The concept of thread priorities, as set by `Thread`'s **setPriority** method, and their effect on thread CPU share.
- The use of `Thread` class methods **sleep**, **yield**, **suspend**, **resume,** and **isAlive** for managing non-synchronized thread state.
- The use of `Thread` class method **join** to wait on a running thread to finish.

12

User Interface

USER INTERFACES: AN INTRODUCTION

All of the Java examples you have seen so far that have involved user input or output have interacted with the user by means of command-line parameters and System.in and System.out. This, of course, is not the real world of application programming. Just as your RPG interactive programs use display files (or WORKSTN files) to present and query information to and from the user, Java programs use Graphical User Interfaces (or GUIs) to present and query information to and from the user. Your introduction to Java would be woefully short if it did not include a discussion on how to code these GUIs in Java. (Because these are actually object-oriented user interfaces, you might say they are OOUI GUI!) Before we delve into the GUI guts, let us briefly review what you already do with RPG.

USER INTERFACES WITH RPG

AS/400 Display Files

Like database files, you create display files on the AS/400 using Data Definition Specifications, or DDS. For display files, of course, you use DSPF source versus PF or LF, but the idea is similar. Display file DDS is a rich language that allows you to define record formats that contain entry fields, text constants, and more.

You already know this. You know also that you can use Screen Design Aid (SDA) to design your display file DDS in a *WYSIWYG* (What You See Is What You Get) manner. You use Source Entry Utility (SEU) to edit the DDS directly. Or you use the follow-on Windows-based versions of these products — CODE Designer and CODE Editor — in the CODE/400 product.

What is important to note about display files as a preparation for our Java User Interface discussion, is that their hierarchy involves the display file *FILE object itself, inside of which are record formats. Inside of record formats, in turn, are fields. The named and reference fields are designated as input, output, or both (or possibly hidden, program, or message). This is important to the RPG program, which will read-from and write-to these fields.

The other important thing to note about display files is that they are rich in function, supporting datatype-aware fields, default field values, reference fields, display attributes, built-in validity checking and, not to forget our favorite, subfiles. Furthermore, they are described and compiled independent of all the RPG programs that subsequently use them, making for true reuse. As you will see, all this is lost in the brave new world of Java (as it is for any GUI product, including VisualBasic). You will miss display files, except for the fact that they are so darned green!

RPG Display File Processing

Display file processing in RPG is actually modeled after database file processing, making it convenient and relatively easy to learn. Basic aspects of RPG Display File processing include:

- *Declaring* the externally described **WORKSTN** file with an **F**-spec, indicating typically that the file is combined (input/output), full procedural (no cycle processing!), and externally described. The RPG compiler then automatically defines field variables in your program from all the record formats of the display file. Of course, this often leads to name collisions, given the many record formats inside a typical display file, so the **F**-spec often includes use of the keywords **IGNORE** or **INCLUDE** in order to limit which record formats are declared in the program. Also, the keyword **PREFIX** is often used to insert characters to the beginning of each included field name to ensure its uniqueness.

- For subfiles, declaring the subfile name and the program variable to hold the subfile's current relative record name, using the **F**-spec keyword **SFILE**.

- Initializing the display file record format's indicators and output fields.

- For subfiles, loading a page worth of records using **WRITE** to populate the subfile.

- For each "screen," **WRITE** background record formats and write/read via **EXFMT** (execute format) the final record format containing the input-capable fields and/or function keys. For subfiles, this will be the subfile control record format, with the appropriate indicator turned on to allow for display of the actual subfile on the display. **EXFMT** will block until the user presses Enter or a function key.

- Processing the screen's input, depending on whether Enter or a function key was pressed.

- For subfiles, processing each user changed record in the subfile, using the **READC** (Read Changed) op-code.

- Typically, exiting the program if F3 was pressed, or else looping around to the **WRITE/EXFMT** operations again.

USER INTERFACES IN JAVA, NOW AND THEN: AWT AND JFC

In Java, there is no externally described language for defining your user interface independent of your code. This is in contrast to what AS/400 display files allow. Rather, your user interface is built up dynamically with Java code, as you will see. This programmatic approach to the user interface offers some advantages (for example, use of conditional logic versus hard-to-maintain indicator conditions) but also some disadvantages relative to reuse and code size. However, the reuse disadvantages can easily be overcome through the use of good object-oriented principles. For example, if you have common window and dialog styles, and common window parts such as a customer number prompt, these can be encapsulated in classes that can be easily reused and extended as needed, leading to code savings and to consistent standards.

There are a number of fundamental differences between the display file programming model and Java's dynamic event-driven programming model for user interfaces:

Display File	Java
Enter or Fkey-driven input	Event-driven input
Modal display of records (processing waits on user)	Modeless display of windows (processing does not wait on user)
24x80 or 27x132 screen sizes	Programmer-defined screen sizes, by pixels
Row, column field addressing	Relative field addressing, depending on window's "layout manager"
Built-in support for online help	No built-in support for online help

We will cover each of these differences in this chapter. This discussion is based on the Java 1.1 AWT (Abstract Windowing Toolkit) version, where AWT is the package supplied by the Java language for doing user interface work. (Keep in mind that the current release of the JDK, as of this writing, was 1.1.5; 1.2 was in beta.) This is changed quite significantly from the previous Java 1.0 version of AWT. We are expecting another significant change in the Java 1.2 version even as we speak. The goal of Java is to provide you with a set of Java classes and interfaces to which you can code that are independent of the operating system it is running on. In this AWT package, this is done by doing the actual implementation of each AWT class using the underlying runtime operating system's user interface APIs. This has led to some minor differences in behavior between operating systems because of the different behaviors of the underlying system APIs.

Another reality is that the AWT, even in Java 1.1, is lacking some very key user interface pieces, such as notebooks, multiple column list boxes (a.k.a., "subfiles"), tree-view containers, and more. All of the very basic pieces are there but, for modern compelling user interfaces, there are holes. Of course, there are tons of shareware and commercial Java classes on the Web that you can download to plug these holes. But, in our opinion, it would be better for Java to have these functions built-in because they are now fundamental. The good news is, it will be. All this will be done in the next major release of the Java JDK (1.2), which will include a Java AWT "follow on" package called JFC (Java Foundation Classes). These will be written completely in Java, rather than using operating system APIs, and will be much richer in function. As of this writing, a beta version of JFC was available. But our crystal ball tells us that, as you read this, JFC is available already. Further, it is available to be used as with JDK 1.1 as well as 1.2. The part of JFC in which you will be most interested is called Swing, which contains the user interface classes. These classes are "way cool", and you must be sure to look at them.

However, our discussion will remain focused on Java at the JDK 1.1 level using AWT. So, let us turn our attention to this ubiquitous AWT package. Your time learning these will not be wasted because they will provide you with a good footing that will allow you to step into the Java Foundation Classes in the future. It also allows you to get going immediately by using Java 1.1 capable browsers such as HotJava, Netscape Communicator, and Microsoft Internet Explorer 4.0.

Let us pause for a final message on this subject. You probably learned display file DDS first by using SDA. However, over time you realized the importance of knowing the underlying DDS statements and source. This is also true of Java. While there is no externally described language for Java UI, there are lots of Java *WYSIWYG* design tools that use drag-and-drop ease-of-use to lay out your design, such as the Visual Composition Editor in IBM's VisualAge for Java. These design tools subsequently generate the Java code for you. The use of these tools is, of course, encouraged. As with SDA, the very minimum that you will get out of them is an excellent teaching device as you look at the generated code. So keep this in mind (as well as the wealth of information available on Java UI programming and the fact that the release of JFC is imminent) when we tell you that we will not spend an overwhelming amount of time on the "guts" of Java UI programming. Rather, we will give you the fundamentals that will get you going, based on the belief that even with great GUI tools you are always a better programmer for having learned the underlying code.

NOTE: In all our following examples, we will import the `java.awt` and `java.awt.event` packages so you can easily access all the classes and interfaces within them, as shown below:

```
import java.awt.*;
import java.awt.event.*;
```

Overview of Java AWT

The basis of Java's user interface support is the classes in the `java.awt` package. Again, AWT stands for ***Abstract Windowing Toolkit***. These are a hierarchy of classes that all extend, or inherit from, `java.awt.Component`. The classes can be categorized as follows:

- ***Basic components***, such as `Button` and `Checkbox`, that implement individual GUI parts as you would see in a typical GUI application. You instantiate instances of these, optionally use methods to tailor them, then finally "add" them to your "containers."

- ***Containers***, such as a `Frame`, `Dialog`, or `Panel`, that contain basic components. A frame is a main window. A `Dialog` is a modal "secondary" window (*modal* means that it has a `Frame` window parent, and that parent is locked until the `Dialog` child is closed). A `Panel` is an interesting thing. It is a sub-window "square" for grouping basic components together into a composite component.

- ***Layout managers***, which define how "added" components to a container are to be displayed, or "laid out.".

- ***Events***, from the `java.awt.event` package, which are used to process input from each of the components.

The idea is to create an instance of a container object, such as a `Frame` window, and "add" to it instances of the basic components, such as a `Checkbox` object. This is done using the "add" method of the container object. Let us quickly look at an example:

```
Frame window = new Frame(); // Main window
Button okButton = new Button("OK"); // push button
window.add(okButton);
window.show(); // show it!
```

This will display a main window (see Figure 12-1) with an OK push button...

FIGURE 12-1

Any questions? More details are presented in the following section.

Basic Components: Buttons, Lists, Text, and More

Let us start by enumerating the basic components that Java supports:

Component	Description
Button	push buttons
Checkbox	check boxes (multiple selection) or radio buttons (single selection)
Choice	drop-down list box. Use this instead of radio buttons when there are many choices
Label	text constant
List	selection list (poor man's subfile)
TextField	entry field (a.k.a. named field in DDS)
TextArea	Multiple-line entry field (a.k.a. named field with **CNTFLD** keyword in DDS)

These classes and their usage are well covered in plenty of books, as well as in the JDK documentation itself, so we will not linger too long on well-trodden paths. But we will give you the information that you need to get going while referencing your display file background.

Here is a quick summary of the typical way to instantiate and initialize objects of these classes:

Instantiation	Parameters
`button1 = new Button("Cancel");`	Text to display on the push button. Use `setLabel` to change the text later.
`cbFish = new Checkbox("Fish",true);`	Text to display on the check box, initial enabled state. Use `setLabel` and `setState` to change later.

`cbg = new CheckboxGroup();`
`rb1 = new Checkbox("Option 1", cbg, false);`
`rb2 = new Checkbox("Option 2", cbg, false);`
`cbg.setSelectedCheckbox(rb1);`
	For radio buttons (single-choice), first create a CheckboxGroup, then specify it when creating all radio buttons in the same group. Finally, use CheckboxGroup's `setSelectedCheckbox` method to identify the radio button to be pre-selected.

`dropdown = new Choice();`
`dropdown.addItem("choice 1");`
`dropdown.addItem("choice 2");`
`dropdown.select(0);`
	For drop-down lists, create the drop-down and add items to it. Finally, use `select` to choose the relative item number to be initially selected.

`prompt1 = new Label("Enter name");`	Text to display as the constant. Use `setText` to change later on. Use `setAlignment` to set alignment to LEFT, CENTER or RIGHT.

Instantiation	Parameters

```listbox = new List(2,false);```
```listbox.addItem("item 1");```
```listbox.addItem("item 2", 0);```
```listbox.select(0);```
	Number of items to display in the list box per page, and whether or not multiple selection is allowed. Items can be appended (```addItem```) or inserted. Items can be selected (```select```) and removed (```remove```).

```entryName = new TextField("yourname", 10);```	Default text to display and the number of characters to allow as input. Use ```setText``` and ```setColumns``` to change later on.
```entryComments = new TextArea("comments", 5,``` ```1, TextArea.SCROLLBARS_BOTH);```	Default text to display, and the number of rows and columns. Also which scroll bars to show (```_NONE```, ```_BOTH```, ```_HORIZONTAL_ONLY```, or ```_VERTICAL_ONLY```).

Figure 12-2 shows what these components look like:

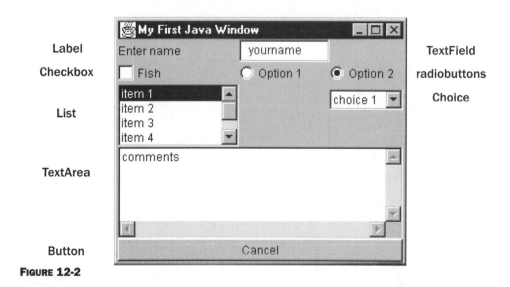

FIGURE 12-2

373

All these classes inherit from the class `java.awt.Component`, so they pick up some important methods from this parent class. Specifically, you get methods for:

Description	Method
Enabling/disabling("graying out")	`setEnabled(true/false), isEnabled()`
Showing/hiding	`setVisible(true/false), isVisible()`
Setting focus to this component	`requestFocus()`
Setting focus to the next component	`transferFocus()`
Setting background color	`setBackground(java.awt.Color)`
Setting foreground (text) color	`setForeground(java.awt.Color)`
Setting the font	`setFont(java.awt.Font)`

The colors you are allowed to use are defined in `java.awt.Color`, and are self explanatory:

Colors
`java.awt.Color.black`
`java.awt.Color.blue`
`java.awt.Color.cyan`
`java.awt.Color.darkGray`
`java.awt.Color.gray`
`java.awt.Color.green`
`java.awt.Color.lightGray`
`java.awt.Color.magenta`
`java.awt.Color.orange`
`java.awt.Color.pink`
`java.awt.Color.red`
`java.awt.Color.white`
`java.awt.Color.yellow`

For example, to change a text constant's (`java.awt.Label`) colors you might code:

```
Label constant = new Label("**overdraft**");
constant.setBackground(java.awt.Color.red);
constant.setForeground(java.awt.Color.white);
```

By default, the user-specified system settings colors are used, and you can query these as well by using the `java.awt.SystemColor` class. Because this class extends `java.awt.Color`, you can substitute these colors anywhere a `Color` is allowed. If you are artistically inclined, you can create your own unique colors by specifying the red-green-blue components on the constructor of a `Color` object, or by using the `brighter()` and `darker()` methods.

For fonts, you have to create a new `Font` object by specifying a font name, style, and size. For example:

```
constant.setFont(new Font("sansSerif",java.awt.Font.BOLD,12));
```

See the `java.awt.Font` class documentation for more detail on creating fonts.

These are the base "building block" classes that you will use repeatedly throughout your AWT programming.

> **NOTE:** All of these basic components (there a few less frequently used components as well, such as `Scrollbar`) are valid, both in applications (command-line invoked) and applets (embedded in Web browser pages).

Containers: Windows, Frames, and Panels

In order to see the basic components you created in the previous section, you need a window of some kind. This will usually be an instance of the `Frame` class (remember, frames are considered *containers* as they *contain* other components). This `Frame` class provides a main window with all the usual pieces — border, title bar, minimize, maximize, and close buttons, and a system menu in the upper left-hand corner. You create a frame, or "main" window, easily enough:

```
Frame myWindow = new Frame("My First Java Window");
```

This creates an actual window. However, it is not too useful yet, because you cannot see it!

```
myWindow.show();
```

This displays it (note some people prefer to use `setVisible(true)`. However, it will display as a tiny little thing. Prior to calling `show`, you need to do some typical tailoring:

- *Set the window's size.* This is done using the `setSize` method, specifying the width and height of the window in "pixels" (a graphical unit of measurement, *very* small). Finding the exact size is a matter of trial-and-error, but the following will get you going (later, after adding components to the window, you can use the `pack()` method to resize the window to match the contents):

  ```
  myWindow.setSize(300,200);
  ```

- *Set the window's position.* This is done using the `setLocation` method, specifying the *x* and *y* pixel address relative to the upper left-hand corner of the screen (*x* pixels across, *y* pixels down). Notice that the address is of your window's upper left corner. This, too, is trial and error, but this will get you going:

```
myWindow.setLocation(200, 100);
```

- **_Set the window's title._** If you do not specify it in the constructor to `Frame`, you can specify it later using `setTitle(String)`.

- **_Optionally, set the window's font, background color, and foreground color._** These will be inherited by all the components you add to the window (but can be overridden by individual components). Use `setFont`, `setBackground`, and `setForeground` for these, as described in the basic component section earlier in this chapter. By default, your system's current settings for these are used.

- Finally, "add" all the components you wish to display in the "client area" or middle part of the window. These will include the basic components described previously, such as push buttons. We will cover this crucial step shortly.

Before our first sample code, let us pause for a word on programming style. We suggest that, for each window in your application, you have a new class that "extends" the `Frame` class, and initializes and populates it in the constructor. Define all of the component and container objects as private instance variables of the class, and instantiate them in the constructor. You will need these variables to be available to your other methods when it comes time to process input; hence, the need to make them instance variables.

Why define the class to "**extend** `Frame`"? Good question. Recall our OO discussion in Chapter 9, where we stated that the rule of thumb is to extend a class, rather than containing an instance variable of it, when your new class "is a" flavor of that class. In our case, our new class "is a" frame window; therefore, we extend the `Frame` window class. This gives all users of our class instant access to all of the methods inside the `Frame` class, too. Mind you, there are many who prefer to "contain" a `Frame` class object inside their class, as it leaves them free to extend another class (in Java, you can only extend one class, remember). It is up to you. If you choose this route, you should include a `getFrame()` method, though, in order to return a reference to that variable so callers can manipulate the `Frame` object directly. At any rate, in our case you might have a new class with code that looks like this:

LISTING 12-1

```
import java.awt.*;
import java.awt.event.*;
class TestFrame extends Frame
{
    TestFrame()
    {
        super(); // call Frame's constructor
        setTitle("My First Java Window");
        setSize(300,200);
        setLocation(200,100);
        setBackground(java.awt.Color.lightGray);
        // add components here
        show(); // make window visible
    }
} // end TestFrame class
```

Note the use of **super** — we have to call the constructor of the class we **extend**, in this case Frame. This actually creates our frame window. Note also that we do not make the class "**public.**" This is, again, a style choice. We leave the default access of package, typically, for window classes, because it is usually only "our" code inside our package that will be using this window. If, however, you create a generically useful window that you want the programming public at large to be able to instantiate and use, by all means make your window classes **public.**

Finally, you need a little test code to instantiate your window. We will do this by including the following method in our little class as well. All you have to do is instantiate an instance of your class, as our constructor method TestFrame() does all the work to prepare and show it:

```
public static void main(String args[])
{
    TestFrame test = new TestFrame(); // instantiate ourself
}
```

Compiling this class with both these methods, and then invoking "java TestFrame" produces the window shown in Figure 12-3, roughly in the center of your screen:

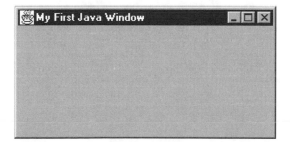

FIGURE 12-3

If you code and run this, you will notice that you cannot close this window! You must kill it using Ctrl+Alt+Delete (on Windows95 or WindowsNT). That is because we have no code for "close" as yet; we will cover it later in the user input section of this chapter.

An alternative to a Frame window is a Dialog window. This is used when you want to prompt the user for information and "block" while waiting for his or her response (this is called *modal* behavior). Typically, dialogs are used to display error messages or prompt for information needed to complete an action, such as prompting for a user ID and password. Coding a Dialog class is very similar to coding a Frame class:

LISTING 12-2

```
import java.awt.*;
import java.awt.event.*;
class TestDialog extends Dialog
{
    TestDialog(Frame parent)
    {
        super(parent, true); // true => modal
        setTitle("My First Java Dialog");
        setSize(200,100);
        setLocation(250,150);
        setBackground(java.awt.Color.lightGray);
        // add components here
    }
    public static void main(String args[])
    {
        TestFrame test = new TestFrame(); // parent frame
        TestDialog test2 = new TestDialog(test); // us
        test2.show(); // show the modal dialog
    }
} // end TestDialog class
```

Notice that we must accept a parameter in our constructor now, namely a "parent" Frame object. This is because Dialog windows are always "secondary" or children to a main window or Frame — the parent window. Thus, the Dialog class constructor requires a reference to the parent window, as our Dialog window will be "modal" to that. Modal, in this context, means that the parent frame window will be locked, preventing user interaction until our child dialog window is closed by the user. Frame windows do not have this modal behavior. So, we pass to our "super" class constructor this parent reference, via the call to super(parent) . (Now, tell us, how often do you call your "super" parents? Would it hurt to call them more often?)

We also specify `true` in this super class constructor call. This indicates that we want the `Dialog` to be modal to the parent. Because modality implies the call to `show` will block until the `Dialog` is closed, we removed the call to `show` from the constructor, and instead leave that up to the caller to invoke when he or she is ready.

Notice also that we changed the size and location values for this example so it would not overlap our previous example's window (the one shown in Figure 12-3). Notice that we also changed our `main` method to instantiate our new class, using our first `Frame` class as the parent.

Finally, this gives us the window arrangement shown in Figure 12-4:

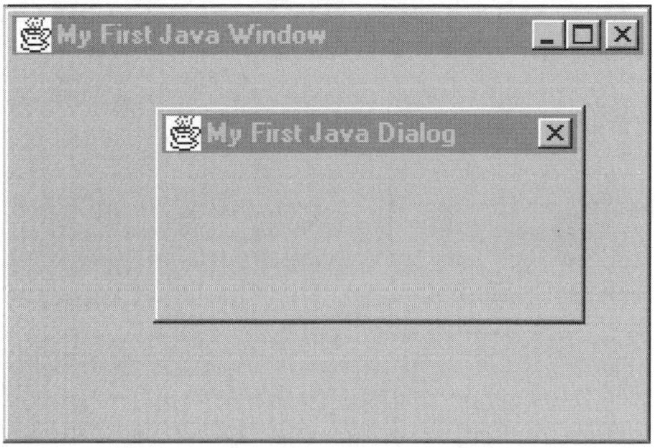

FIGURE 12-4

The `Dialog` class allows you to specify, and query-via set and get methods-whether the dialog is modal and also resizable by the user. Dialogs, however, are not minimizable or maximizable by the end user, as you can see by the fact that they lack minimize and maximize buttons in the upper right-hand corner.

NOTE: Both `Frame` and `Dialog` extend `java.awt.Window`, which extends `java.awt.Container`, which in turn extends `java.awt.Component`. So, in the end, many methods like `show` are common to both. Furthermore, many methods like `setBackground` are shared with the basic components.

Adding Components to Containers: Layout Managers

Now the really fun part begins: populating our windows with **components** like push buttons, entry fields, and others. If you think about display files, you'll realize that frame and dialog containers are like record formats, and components are like the fields and constants in your record formats. The record formats "contain" fields. How do you "lay out" your fields in display file DDS? You do it by specifying row and column addresses, and the display file compiler (**CRTDSPF**) determines the "display length" for each field. You must be careful not to overlap fields. In Java, you "layout" your components by adding them to your container (frame or dialog). That is, you first instantiate instances of component objects, as in:

```
Button okButton = new Button("OK");
```

Then, you "add" that object to your container, like this:

```
add(okButton);
```

But, what does this mean? Where does it go? Notice that we do not specify anything equivalent to a row and column address. The answer is: it depends! It depends on what *layout manager* you specify for your object. Prior to adding objects to a container, you need to specify a layout manager for that container. These are classes, which define rules about where "added" components will be placed. In order to specify a particular layout manager, you would code the container method setLayout:

```
setLayout(new xxxLayout());
```

Having done this with a desired xxxLayout class, your components are then added according to the rules of that *layout manager* class. This class ensures the components will not overlap each other. The layout manager options are:

Layout Manager	Description
BorderLayout	You can only add 5 components. The window is divided into 5 regions: North (top), South (bottom), West (left), East (right), and Center (middle). When adding components, you must specify which region to place it in. Great for simple windows.
FlowLayout	Each component inserted after the previous one, with some padding. If it fits horizontally, it will go there; otherwise it starts on the next line. Great for push buttons.
GridLayout	Divides the window into evenly sized "cells". You must specify in the constructor how many rows and columns to allocate. Each "add" then takes the next sequential cell. Cell size is the largest "display size" of all the added components. Great for "property sheet" style windows.
GridBagLayout	The most complex, and the most flexible. The window is divided into cells, again, but each is sized to be as big as it needs to be for the component in it. Requires use of the GridBagConstraints helper class to define the attributes of each populated cell. Great for everything, if you can handle the coding.
CardLayout	One component per "card" and only one card can be displayed at a time. Methods exist for cycling through the cards. Great for "wizards" and poor man's notebooks, and any other rotating page design.

NOTE: There is yet another option — specifying a *layout manager* of `null` as in:

```
setLayout(null);
```

This layout mode indicates that you will hard code the pixel *x* and *y* address of every component you add. This is not a recommended option, however, because it means you will produce a screen resolution-dependent window, one that does not gracefully allow for resizing by the user.

Let us now have a look at the layout options. We will not cover `CardLayout` here, though, but rather leave that to your research for the rare cases when you need it. Besides, the upcoming JFC packages have better options than `CardLayout` for designing paged notebooks. Aside from `CardLayout` however, all the following layout managers are still used in the new JFC packages so your time and skills will not be wasted.

Using BorderLayout

NOTE: This example and all the subsequent ones use only main `Frame` windows, not secondary `Dialog` windows. The code that follows for frames is identical for dialogs. However, for dialogs you would extend `Dialog` instead of `Frame`, and would require the parent main window as a parameter in the constructor. Most of your windows will be `Frame` windows, while dialogs will be reserved mostly for error messages or other actions that require a user response before continuing.

Here is the code for our example `Frame` window class extension, using the `BorderLayout` manager to show five components (instruction line, entry field prompt, entry field, list push button, and an OK push button):

LISTING 12-3

```java
import java.awt.*;
import java.awt.event.*;
class TestBorder extends Frame
{
    // define GUI components
    private Label      instruction;
    private Label      prompt;
    private TextField entry;
    private Button     listButton;
    private Button     okButton;
    // Constructor
    TestBorder()
    {
        super();
        setTitle("My First Java Window");
        setSize(300,200);
        setLocation(200,100);
        setBackground(java.awt.Color.lightGray);
        // instantiate components
        instruction = new Label("Enter company number");
        prompt      = new Label("Number");
        entry       = new TextField(5);
        listButton  = new Button("List...");
        okButton    = new Button("Ok");
        // set window layout manager
        setLayout(new BorderLayout());
        // add components to window
        add(instruction,"North");
        add(prompt,      "West");
        add(entry,       "Center");
        add(listButton,  "East");
        add(okButton,    "South");
        // show the window
        pack();
        show();
    } // end constructor
    public static void main(String args[])
    {
        TestBorder test = new TestBorder();
    }
} // end TestBorder class
```

Notice the call to the `pack()` method at the end of the constructor, which is before to the call to `show()`. The `pack` method will pack your fields and window automatically, removing extra space. This is handy because otherwise you are dependent on setting your window size properly. Whether you use `pack()` or not is up to you, but we will show all examples both with and without it so you can see its effects.

Figure 12-5 shows the result of compiling and testing this class, first *without* the call to `pack()`, then *with* the call to `pack()`:

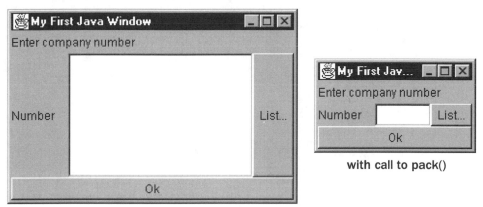

without call to pack()

with call to pack()

FIGURE 12-5

Notice that the call to `pack()` does not take into account the width required by the title. However, that is a small price to pay for the much improved look of the window! Notice also that this example of a border layout turned out so well because we happen to have exactly five components, one for each of the five regions that `BorderLayout` defines. If we had more, what would we do? The answer involves "nested containers" and will be discussed in the upcoming section on the `Panel` container.

Using FlowLayout

With a `FlowLayout` manager, you simply add each component, one after another, and they are appended to the screen. If they fit on the current row, they go there. If not, they wrap to the next line. If there simply is not enough space left to show the component, it is not shown. Here is a sample class that shows this layout manager (**NOTE:** We use ** SAME ** to represent code that is the same as in the previous example code):

LISTING 12-4

```
class TestFlow extends Frame
{
    // define GUI components
    ** SAME **
    // Constructor
    TestFlow()
    {
        ** SAME **
        // instantiate components
        ** SAME **
        // set window layout manager
        setLayout(new FlowLayout());
        // add components to window
        add(instruction);
        add(prompt);
        add(entry);
        add(listButton);
        add(okButton);
        // show the window
        ** SAME **
    } // end constructor
    public static void main(String args[])
    {
        TestFlow test = new TestFlow();
    }
} // end TestFlow class
```

Figure 12-6 shows the results-again, first without `pack`, and then with `pack`:

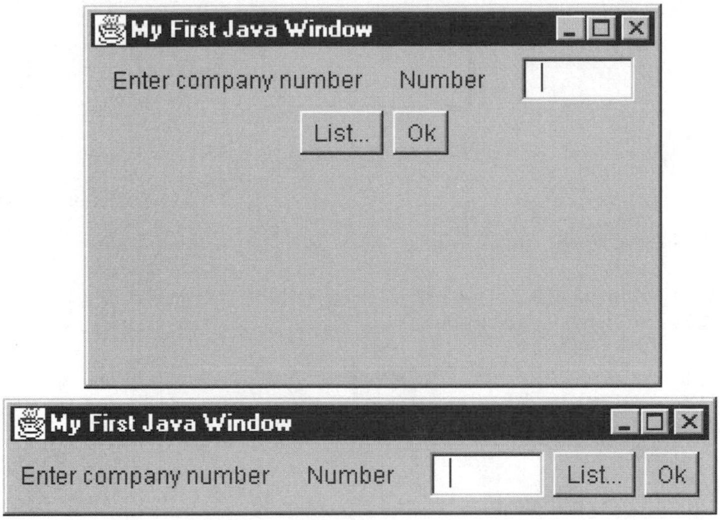

FIGURE 12-6

Sizing the window moves the components around automatically to fit the new window size. That is, they "flow" as required.

Using GridLayout

The GridLayout manager divides the screen into the specified number of rows and columns. After that, the components are added to the next cell, moving left-to-right. Each cell will be as big as the biggest one necessary to hold the largest-sized component. This is a tricky one to use in our example case. Why? Because we do not have an even number of components per row. We have one on the first row (the instruction Label), three on the second row (the number Label, the entry TextField, and the list Button), and finally one on the third row (the OK Button). What we will do is to specify 3 rows and 3 columns, then add a dummy Label object to the empty cells so they have something (otherwise all of the components would be shifted inappropriately):

LISTING 12-5

```
class TestGrid extends Frame
{
    // define GUI components
    ** SAME **
    // Constructor
    TestGrid()
    {
        ** SAME **
        // instantiate components
        ** SAME **
        // set window layout manager. 3 rows, 3 cols
        setLayout(new GridLayout(3,3));
        // add components to window
        add(instruction);     // row 1, col 1
        add(new Label(" ")); // row 1, col 2
        add(new Label(" ")); // row 1, col 3
        add(prompt);          // row 2, col 1
        add(entry);           // row 2, col 2
        add(listButton);      // row 2, col 3
        add(new Label(" ")); // row 3, col 1
        add(okButton);        // row 3, col 2
        // show the window
        ** SAME **
    } // end constructor
    public static void main(String args[])
    {
        TestGrid test = new TestGrid();
    }
} // end TestGrid class
```

Figure 12-7 shows the result:

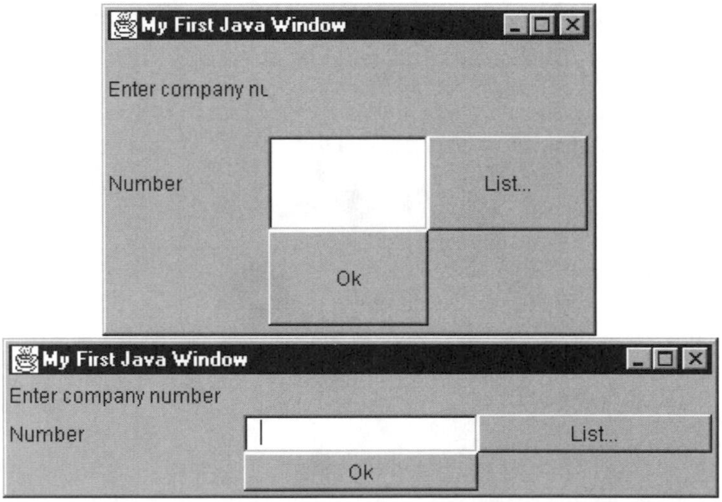

FIGURE 12-7

Notice how the version without packing truncates the "Enter company number" text. This is because the hard-coded window size is insufficient to hold the widths required for each cell. However, the pack option nicely resizes everything to fit. You see here that the GridLayout manager is useful only in certain situations (well, more than you may think, as we will see in the Panel section). Here is an example (Figure 12-8) of a very useful fit for the grid layout manager — one that can be used to list "name, value" pairs of information:

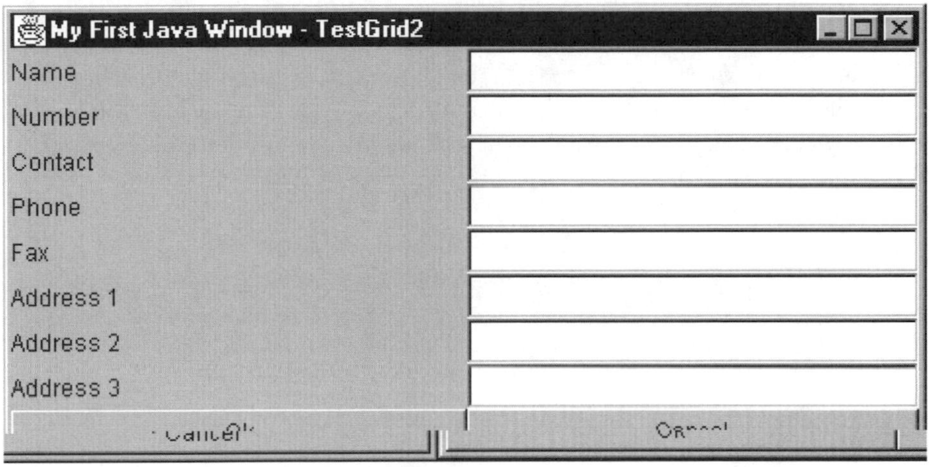

FIGURE 12-8

Another good use for the GridLayout manager is for evenly sized push buttons (see Figure 12-9), if that is a style you prefer over buttons that are sized to fit their text:

FIGURE 12-9

Using GridBagLayout

The GridBagLayout manager is far and away the most complex of all the layout managers to which you can code. However, when all the previously mentioned layout managers fail to meet your purposes, you can be sure that this one will work — always! Like GridLayout, it divides the screen into cells. However, you do not specify the rows and columns for the cells when you instantiate the layout object. Rather, it is done implicitly as you add each component. For each component you add, you specify the row and column coordinates (0,0 based), and the number of rows and columns this component is to span. You can also specify information such as whether the component is allowed to grow and shrink with the sizing of the window (horizontally and/or vertically), whether it is to be stretched to fit the cell(s) it is in, or whether and how it is to be aligned in the cell(s).

There is potentially a lot of extra information to be specified with each component as it is added, which is why there is relative complexity. How is all this extra information specified? Not via parameters to the add method, as you might expect. That would make this method too complicated and would require numerous parameters. Rather, in true object-oriented fashion, there is another class you need to instantiate that will contain all this information, which is called GridBagConstraints. With this approach, you can specify all your defaults once initially. Then you change only the defaults you need to for each component that you add. The non-object-oriented part of this class, however, is that all this information is specified by explicitly changing variables in the object, versus the better approach of using "set" methods.

Here, then, is a rundown of the steps needed to use a GridBagLayout for a layout manager:

1. Instantiate an instance of GridBagLayout, no parameters.

2. Instantiate an instance of GridBagConstraints, no parameters.

3. Specify the GridBagLayout object as the layout manager, via setLayout, as usual.

4. Set all your preferred default values in the GridBagConstraints class.

5. For each component to be added:

   - Set the required values of the GridBagConstraints object uniquely for this component (such as the row, column address — or "gridy, gridx" variables).
   - Call the GridBagLayout method setConstraints, passing your component and the GridBagConstraints object.
   - Call the "add" method of the window to add the component, as usual.

Here are the important variables that need to be set in GridBagConstraints:

Variable	Description
gridy, gridx	The row and column position (0-based) for this component, where 0,0 is the upper lef-hand corner.
gridheight, gridwidth	The numbers of rows and the number of columns this component will occupy. Default is one each.
weighty, weightx	Does this component grow in either direction when the window is sized? If yes, specify 1.0, otherwise specify 0. The default is 0. Typically, specify 1.0 for weightx for TextFields, 1.0 for weightx and weighty for Lists and TextAreas. At least one component should have a non-zero value.

Variable	Description
`fill, anchor`	What to do when the cell(s) are larger than the component? • *Stretch the component: set fill to* HORIZONTAL, VERTICAL *or* BOTH. *Default is* NONE; *do not stretch in either direction.* • *Align the component: set anchor to* CENTER, NORTH, SOUTH, WEST, *or* EAST. *Or* NORTHEAST/WEST, SOUTHEAST/WEST. *Default is* CENTER.

The tricky part, (one that will eventually come very easy to you), is determining the `gridy/x` and `gridheight/width` to specify for each component. Here is a little algorithm you can follow to get you going:

1. Lay out the intended screen in your mind or on paper.

2. Determine how many unique rows there are (three in our running example). If you have a list box with three push buttons beside it, vertically aligned, then you would count three rows for that. Draw a line horizontally across the bottom of each component.

3. Determine how many unique columns there are (three in our running example). Draw a line vertically at the start of each component.

4. Determine, for each component:

   • In which row and column it should start.
   • If there are no components beside it, its width is the number of remaining columns. Our first instruction line, for example, will span all three columns. If there are components beside it, the width is the difference between this component's starting column and the one beside it.
   • If there are no components beside it, its height is one. If there are components beside it, its height is the number of components, vertically, beside it. For example, the list box with three push buttons vertically beside it will have a height of three (or more, if you want padding).

Looking at our running example, Figure 12-10 shows how we would divide it up:

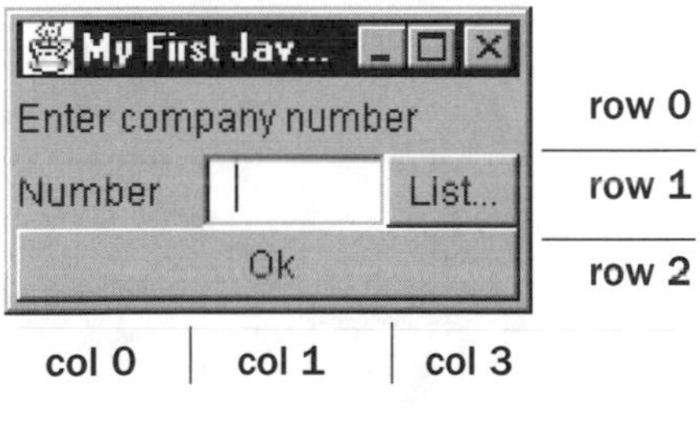

FIGURE 12-10

All right, then, let us see the code!

LISTING 12-6

```
class TestGridBag extends Frame
{
    // define GUI components
    ** SAME **
    // Constructor
    TestGridBag()
    {
        ** SAME **
        // instantiate components
        ** SAME **
        // set window layout manager
        GridBagLayout       gbl = new GridBagLayout();
        GridBagConstraints gbc = new GridBagConstraints();
        setLayout(gbl);
        gbc.fill   = GridBagConstraints.HORIZONTAL; // stretch hor'ly
        gbc.anchor= GridBagConstraints.SOUTH;       // bottom justify
        // add components to window
        gbc.gridy=0; gbc.gridx=0; gbc.gridheight=1; gbc.gridwidth=3;
        gbl.setConstraints(instruction,gbc);
        add(instruction);      // row 1, cols 1-3
        gbc.gridy=1; gbc.gridx=0; gbc.gridheight=1; gbc.gridwidth=1;
        gbl.setConstraints(prompt,gbc);
        add(prompt);           // row 2, col 1
        gbc.gridy=1; gbc.gridx=1; gbc.gridheight=1; gbc.gridwidth=1;
        gbl.setConstraints(entry,gbc);
        add(entry);            // row 2, col 2
        gbc.gridy=1; gbc.gridx=2; gbc.gridheight=1; gbc.gridwidth=1;
        gbl.setConstraints(listButton,gbc);
        add(listButton);       // row 2, col 3
        gbc.gridy=2; gbc.gridx=0; gbc.gridheight=1; gbc.gridwidth=3;
        gbl.setConstraints(okButton,gbc);
        add(okButton);         // row 3, cols 1-3
        // show the window
        pack(); // try it with and without
        show();
    } // end constructor
    public static void main(String args[])
    {
        TestGridBag test = new TestGridBag();
    }
} // end TestGridBag class
```

And what does this produce? See Figure 12-11:

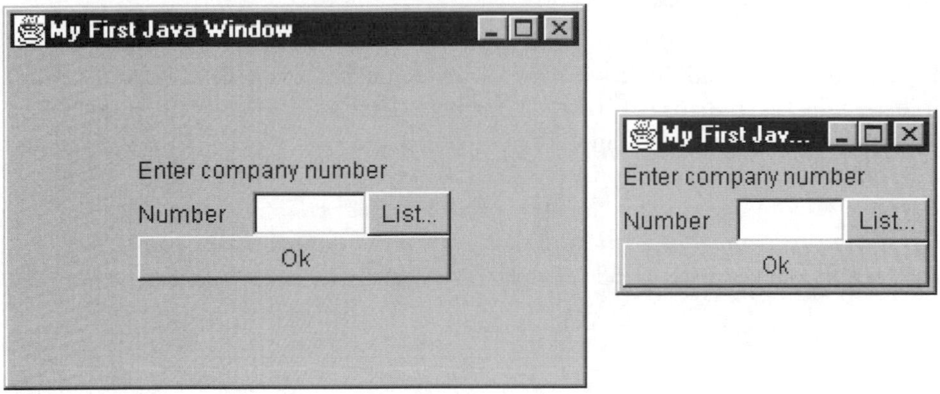

FIGURE 12-11

Again, these are shown first without packing, then with packing. Why, without packing, do they clump into the center? Because we did not specify a `weighty` or `weightx` nonzero value for any component, so the "extra space" is simply given to the edges. Otherwise, it would be distributed among the weighted components.

Figure 12-12 shows what it looks like if we decide to give the OK push button a weighty, weightx of 1.0 each (and specify a `fill` value of `GridBagConstraints.BOTH`):

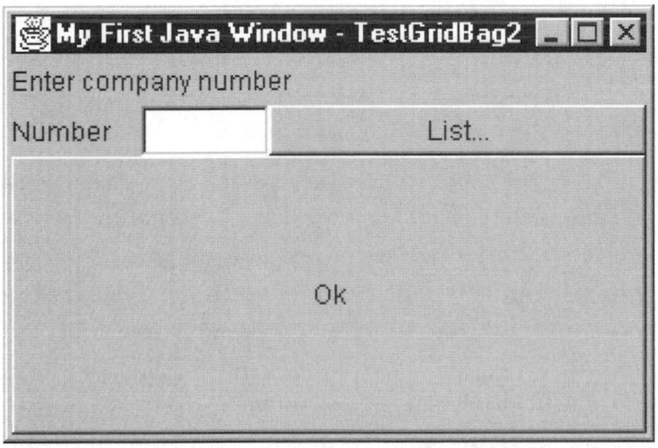

FIGURE 12-12

Remember, users can resize your windows, even if you pack them so that they look good initially, so it is important to identify those components you would like to grow when the window is sized, by specifying nonzero values for `weightx` and `weighty`.

Specifying Padding between Components

When you start to fine-tune your user interfaces, you may be interested in changing the Java-supplied default padding between the components that you add. This can be done with each of the layout managers by specifying horizontal and vertical "gap" values on the constructors. Alternatively, you can use the `setHgap` and `setVgap` methods supplied by each layout manager class, except for the `GridBagLayout` class, which requires you to specify the `ipadx` and `ipady` variables in the `GridBagConstraints` object. The values you specify are in pixels, and you might find that 5 is a good number if you do not like a "tight" look. In our `BorderLayout` example, if we change the `setLayout` line to look like this:

```
setLayout(new BorderLayout(5,5));
```

We would get this (Figure 12-13):

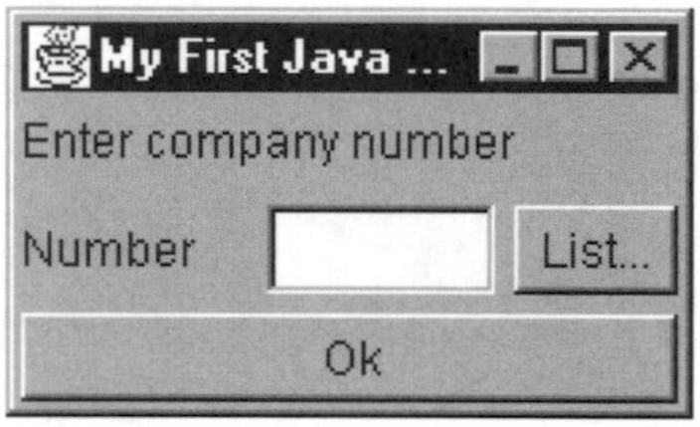

FIGURE 12-13

Notice the padding between the components: this is a 5-pixel padding.

Nesting Layout Managers: Panels

You have seen, so far, how you can add components to your `Frame` or `Dialog` window object directly, using one of the layout manager classes to define how the added components will be placed. Earlier, we stated that `Frame` and `Dialog` classes were like display file record formats. But this is not exactly accurate. That is because rarely do our applications' "screens" consist of a single-record format. Rather, we typically combine multiple formats to produce a single screen. For example, the function key descriptions at the bottom ("F3=Exit F5=Refresh F12=Cancel") are often separate-record formats that we reuse in many screens. Also, for subfiles, we always use one record format for the column headings (subfile control) and another for the subfile details (subfile). Thus, it is not totally accurate to equate a display file record format to a `Frame` window. A record format is really just a "part" of a `Frame` window or "screen."

In Java, you can also define subparts of a window, accumulate them to produce a single whole window, and reuse them in many different windows. This is done using a `Panel` class. This, like a `Frame` and a `Dialog`, allows components to be added to it, and requires a layout manager class to define how the components will be arranged. However, `Panel` has no visible borders or other frame pieces, as it is meant to be used as *part* of a frame window. By using panels, you can greatly increase your flexibility in choosing a layout manager, because you can add *panels* to a Frame window instead of adding *components* directly. This way, one area of your screen can use a panel with one layout manager that is appropriate for it, and another can use another panel with another layout manager that is appropriate for *it*. Think about the BorderLayout layout manager — it can only allow five components to be added, one each in the North, South, West, East, and Center regions. This is very restrictive, except that each of those "components" could, in fact, be a panel that contains numerous "nested" components.

Consider our OK push button at the bottom of our running example so far. Next, imagine we wanted to have a Cancel push button there as well. With the BorderLayout manager, which was one of our best options so far, we would be in trouble, since our South region already has the OK button included. How can we add the new Cancel button? The answer is this: put both the OK and the Cancel buttons into a separate Panel object, and add that to the South region. Because Panel inherits from the class Component, just as Button and the other basic components do, we can add a Panel object anywhere we can add a Component object.

Here is an example: First, we will create a new class that extends Panel, much as we extended Frame, and we will define the push buttons in this class and add them to the panel, after specifying the layout manager:

LISTING 12-7

```java
import java.awt.*;
import java.awt.event.*;
class TestPanel extends Panel
{
    // define GUI components
    private Button okButton;
    private Button cancelButton;
    // Constructor
    TestPanel()
    {
        super();
        // instantiate components
        okButton    = new Button("Ok");
        cancelButton= new Button("Cancel");
        // set window layout manager
        setLayout(new FlowLayout());
        // add components to window
        add(okButton);
        add(cancelButton);
    } // end constructor
} // end TestPanel class
```

Now, we will modify our earlier sample program that used a BorderLayout layout manager. Instead of defining, instantiating, and adding an OK Button object to the South region, we will define, instantiate, and add a "buttons" TestPanel (the class we just defined) object to the South region:

LISTING 12-8

```java
import java.awt.*;
import java.awt.event.*;
class TestBorderWithPanel extends Frame
{
    // define GUI components
    private Label      instruction;
    private Label      prompt;
    private TextField entry;
    private Button     listButton;
    private TestPanel buttons; // OK and Cancel button panel
    // Constructor
    TestBorderWithPanel()
    {
        super();
        setTitle("My First Java Window");
        setSize(300,200);
        setLocation(200,100);
        setBackground(java.awt.Color.lightGray);
        // instantiate components
        instruction = new Label("Enter company number");
        prompt      = new Label("Number");
        entry       = new TextField(5);
        listButton  = new Button("List...");
        buttons     = new TestPanel();
        // set window layout manager
        setLayout(new BorderLayout(5,5));
        // add components to window
        add(instruction,"North");
        add(prompt,      "West");
        add(entry,       "Center");
        add(listButton, "East");
        add(buttons,     "South");
        // show the window
        pack();
        show();
    } // end constructor
    public static void main(String args[])
    {
        TestBorderWithPanel test = new TestBorderWithPanel();
    }
} // end TestBorderWithPanel class
```

This gives us the layout shown in Figure 12-14:

FIGURE 12-14

We now have a completely reusable class that defines our common buttons (much like our common function keys record formats), offering not only increased flexibility in choosing a `Frame` layout manager, but overall code reduction and that all-important "encapsulation" idea. Our company design standards can be "encapsulated" by these common `Panel` classes, and easily changed if desired. For example, we may choose to have all our buttons the same size, in which case we simply change our `TestPanel` class to use a `GridLayout`; then all users of it get the benefit, as shown in Figure 12-15:

FIGURE 12-15

Panels offer tremendous flexibility and options. You should exploit that power. In fact, panels can be nested inside other panels to maximize your options. Suppose this entire little "customer number" prompt became a commonly required element in many other windows, perhaps even more complex than this one. You can make this entire class, which currently extends `Frame`, a completely reusable "panel" by changing it to extend `Panel` instead. In such a case, you would remove the size and location settings, since that will probably by done by the parent window. However, they are still valid if you choose to leave them. In fact, another advantage of panels is that they allow you to give "sub sections" of your window unique attributes such as colors and fonts. Here is what our new version of our class might look like (note that it is almost identical to the previous example, only slightly smaller due to the loss of the `Frame` tailoring code)

LISTING 12-9

```
import java.awt.*;
import java.awt.event.*;
class CompanyPrompt extends Panel
{
    // define GUI components
    private Label      instruction;
    private Label      prompt;
    private TextField entry;
    private Button     listButton;
    private TestPanel buttons;
    // Constructor
    CompanyPrompt()
    {
        super();
        // instantiate components
        instruction = new Label("Enter company number");
        prompt      = new Label("Number");
        entry       = new TextField(5);
        listButton  = new Button("List...");
        buttons     = new TestPanel();
        // set window layout manager
        setLayout(new BorderLayout(5,5));
        // add components to window
        add(instruction,"North");
        add(prompt,     "West");
        add(entry,      "Center");
        add(listButton, "East");
        add(buttons,    "South");
    } // end constructor
} // end CompanyPrompt class
```

Now, our main window class code becomes very simple, since this sub-panel is the only part we are adding to it. We will simply use a BorderLayout and add an instance of this new CompanyPrompt panel to it, in the "Center" region:

LISTING 12-10

```
import java.awt.*;
import java.awt.event.*;
class TestNestedPanels extends Frame
{
    // define GUI components
    private CompanyPrompt companyprompt;
    // Constructor
    TestNestedPanels()
    {
        super();
        setTitle("My First Java Window");
        setSize(300,200);
        setLocation(200,100);
        setBackground(java.awt.Color.lightGray);
        // instantiate components
        companyprompt = new CompanyPrompt();
        // set window layout manager
        setLayout(new BorderLayout(5,5));
        // add components to window
        add(companyprompt, "Center");
        // show the window
        pack();
        show();
    } // end constructor
    public static void main(String args[])
    {
        TestNestedPanels test = new TestNestedPanels();
    }
} // end TestNestedPanels class
```

As shown in Figure 12-16, this gives us our now familiar results:

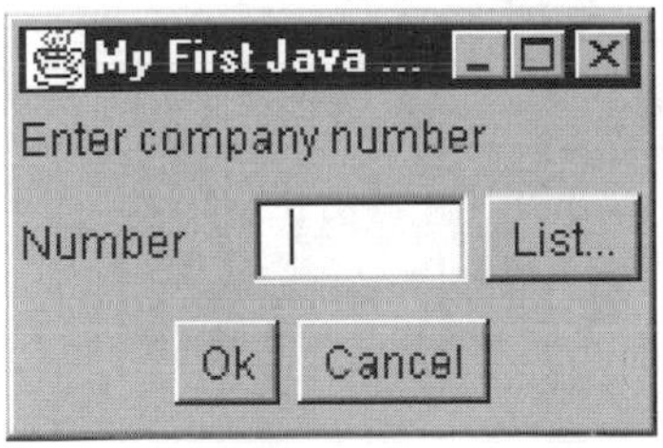

FIGURE 12-16

While it appears that we are only back where we started, we are in fact much further ahead. We now have a completely reusable self-contained "prompt" that we can embed anywhere we may need it. Actually, it is not totally self-contained yet — it does not process user input in any way. But we will deal with that later.

Advanced Components: Menu Bars, Pull-Downs, and Popups

In our RPG applications, we typically start with a "menu" that allows the user to choose an application "area" to go into. For example, a typical menu might allow the user to work with customers, enter data into customer accounts, keep track of inventory, and so on. Once the menu option is chosen by the user, the appropriate RPG program is launched (in ILE RPG, of course, this is likely to be an appropriate RPG module inside the master program).

In fact, display file DDS now supports more modern user interfaces because Version 2 added menu bars, pull-downs, windows, radio buttons, check boxes, push buttons, and so on. However, for whatever reason, these are not widely used. Perhaps it is because of the complexity in coding them. This is too bad. Using them can provide a more compelling and usable interface, and can make it easier to switch to graphical user interfaces such as Java offers. In fact, the AS/400 functionality added to VisualAge for Java includes a display file-to-Java conversion utility that does a great job of converting these new constructs. (It also converts the traditional display file constructs, but it is especially adept at these new ones, given their affinity to GUIs.)

Menu Bars and Pull-Down Menus

You will be hard-pressed to find a 5250-style traditional "menu" in a graphical user interface application. Rather, these user interfaces have "menu bars", such as the the one shown in Figure 12-17:

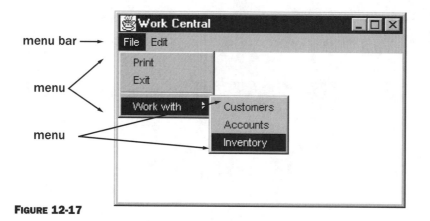

FIGURE 12-17

398

This example is comprised of the following:

- A menu bar object of class `MenuBar`;
- Two menu objects of class `Menu`, for the "File" and "Edit" menus;
- Another menu object for the "Work with" nested cascading menu;
- A number of "menu items" objects of class `MenuItem` for the items like "Print", "Exit", and "Customers."

The steps to take to define these menus inside a Java `Frame` class object are:

1. Create the `MenuBar` object.

2. Create the `Menu` objects for the pull-down menus and nested menus.

3. Add the `Menu` objects to the `MenuBar` object.

4. Create the `MenuItem` objects.

5. Add the `MenuItem` objects and nested `Menu` objects to the `Menu` objects.

6. Add the `MenuBar` object to the `Frame` window, using `setMenuBar`.

Here is the code to produce the previous example:

LISTING 12-11

```java
class TestMenu extends Frame
{
    private MenuBar    menubar;
    private Menu       fileMenu, editMenu, appMenu;
    private MenuItem   printMI, exitMI;
    private MenuItem   customersMI, accountsMI, inventoryMI;
    // Constructor
    TestMenu()
    {
        super();
        setTitle("Work Central");
        setSize(300,200);
        setLocation(200,100);
        // instantiate menu bar and menus
        menubar  = new MenuBar();
        fileMenu = new Menu("File");
        editMenu = new Menu("Edit");
        appMenu  = new Menu("Work with");
        menubar.add(fileMenu);
        menubar.add(editMenu);
        // instantiate menu items
        printMI = new MenuItem("Print");
        exitMI  = new MenuItem("Exit");
        // instantiate "Edit" menu items—not shown
        customersMI = new MenuItem("Customers");
        accountsMI  = new MenuItem("Accounts");
        inventoryMI = new MenuItem("Inventory");
        // populate menus with menu items
        fileMenu.add(printMI);
        fileMenu.add(exitMI);
        fileMenu.addSeparator();
        fileMenu.add(appMenu);
        // populate "Edit" menu—not shown
        appMenu.add(customersMI);
        appMenu.add(accountsMI);
        appMenu.add(inventoryMI);
        // add menubar to window
        setMenuBar(menubar);
        show();
    } // end constructor
    public static void main(String args[])
    {
        TestMenu test = new TestMenu();
    }
} // end TestMenu class
```

Before too long, we will cover the important topic of how you are notified when a menu item is selected. Keep in mind that you can also include "toggle-able" choices in your menu items. We are referring to items the user can turn on or off that have a visible check mark beside those items currently selected. An example is shown in Figure 12-18:

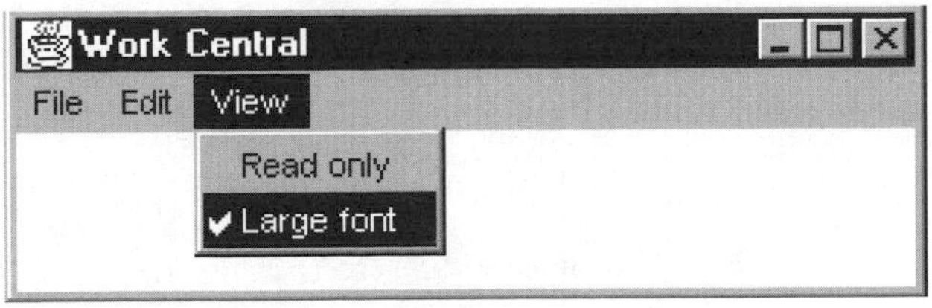

FIGURE 12-18

These items are created using `CheckboxMenuItem` instead of `MenuItem`. You can set their initial "checked" state to "on" in the constructor. Here is the code we added to our example to achieve this effect:

LISTING 12-12

```
private Menu        viewMenu;
    private CheckboxMenuItem editModeMI, fontModeMI;
        viewMenu  = new Menu("View");
        menubar.add(viewMenu);
        editModeMI  = new CheckboxMenuItem("Read only");
        fontModeMI  = new CheckboxMenuItem("Large font", true);
        viewMenu.add(editModeMI);
        viewMenu.add(fontModeMI);
```

Notice that you can also set a `CheckboxMenuItem`'s state by calling its `setState` method and specifying **true** (show check mark) or **false**. You can query its state by calling its `getState` method, which returns **true** or **false**.

Popup Menus

In the world of GUI applications, a now common part of the user interface landscape is the type of menu that "pops up" when you click the mouse. For example, you might have a list box that shows a popup menu with the options "insert," "remove," and "change," when the user clicks on that box. These menus, which are often referred to as ***context menus,*** have become popular because they offer a way to support additional functionality without taking up screen real estate. For example, you do not have to find room in your window for "Insert," "Remove," and "Change" push buttons. These popups, when used with lists, replace the display file practice of including an input-capable entry field in front of each item in the list where users can type arcane one- or two-digit "options." Java supports popup menus beginning with version 1.1. They are coded using the `PopupMenu` class, which extends the Menu class discussed previously. To code a popup menu you do the following:

1. Declare a variable of class type PopupMenu, and instantiate it, optionally specifying a name for the popup, like this:

```
PopupMenu popup = new PopupMenu("Work with");
```

2. Declare and instantiate instances of MenuItem to contain the popup values, as in:

```
MenuItem insertMI = new MenuItem("Insert...");
MenuItem removeMI = new MenuItem("Remove");
MenuItem changeMI = new MenuItem("Change...");
```

NOTE: The ellipses ("...") are a convention for menu items that display another dialog, which presumably "insert" and "change" would have to do.

3. Add the popup menu to the Frame, Dialog, or Panel:

```
add(popup);
```

4. Enable the part you want to support popups to get the mouseReleased event:

```
myListBox.addMouseListener(this);
```

You also have to change your class to add "implements MouseListener"

5. Define empty methods required by the MouseListener interface but not of interest to us:

```
public void mouseClicked(MouseEvent event) {}
public void mousePressed(MouseEvent event) {}
```

Define the method mouseRelease that we are interested in. It will be called by Java when mouse button 2 is clicked and released while the cursor is in the target part—in our case in part myListBox:

```
public void mouseReleased(MouseEvent event)
{
        Component part=3D event.getComponent();
        if (event.isPopupTrigger() && (part == myListBox))
            popup.show(part, event.getX(), event.getY());
}
```

Note the use of isPopuptrigger which returns true if mouse button two was used on Windows, or mouse button one was use on other systems which use button one for popups. Also, note that use of getX and getY which return the x and y pixel addresss of the cursor, which the popup.show method requires.

6. a method `processMouseEvent` that the system will call when mouse button two is clicked in the `Frame`, `Dialog`, or `Panel`. Add code in the method to check if this is a "popup trigger" (that is, a mouse button two click) and, optionally, to check if the mouse is over the appropriate component such as a list box. Finally, if satisfied, call the `show` method of the `PopupMenu` class specifying the component, and its *x* and *y* pixel address (using `getX` and `getY` method calls):

```
public void processMouseEvent(MouseEvent event)
{
    Component part = event.getComponent();
    if (event.isPopupTrigger() && part == myListBox)
      popup.show(part, event.getX(), event.getY());
    super.processMouseEvent(event); // pass event up the chain
}
```

Getting notified when a menu item is selected from a popup menu is identical to getting notified when a menu item is selected from a pull-down menu. We will discuss this in more detail soon.

Menu Item Shortcuts

You will frequently want to supply keyboard *shortcuts* for menu bar and popup menu items. These are key combinations, such as Ctrl+R or Ctrl+Shift+A, that will act as alternatives to selecting the item from the menu. These can be specified when creating your menu items, as the second parameter on the new `MenuItem(...)` or new `CheckboxMenuItem(...)` calls. They are specified by creating an instance of the `MenuShortcut` class. You simply specify a character to use as the shortcut. On Windows, Java will automatically assign the shortcut to be "Ctrl" plus the specified character. Notice that Ctrl is the standard for shortcut keys on Windows. You can also optionally specify that the Shift key is required by specifying **true** for the second parameter. For example, in the following code we changed our menu example to supply shortcuts of Ctrl+P for print, and Ctrl+Shift+E for exit:

```
MenuShortcut printSC = new MenuShortcut('p');
MenuShortcut exitSC  = new MenuShortcut('e',true);
printMI = new MenuItem("Print", printSC);
exitMI  = new MenuItem("Exit", exitSC);
```

This allows the user to specify these key combinations instead of selecting the menu item (it looks the same to your program). It also visually changes the menu items to reflect these shortcuts, as shown in Figure 12-19:

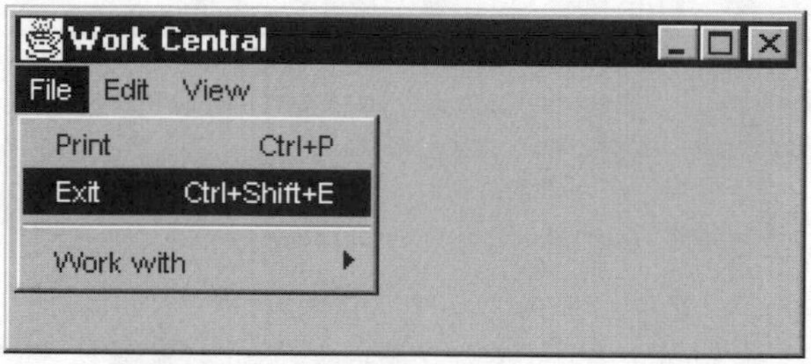

FIGURE 12-19

Unfortunately, there is no way to assign a function key as a shortcut. This is not that uncommon, especially for migrated AS/400 applications. For these, you will have to insert the unique code yourself to trap the keyboard input and check for the function keys that you want to enable.

Processing User Input — Events

Congratulations on having created some great looking user interfaces. Now what? How do you process input from them? In RPG programs, you simply perform an **EXFMT** operation (or a **WRITE** and a **READ**), which waits to read the user input from the input fields. It is a synchronous, or *modal*, operation. Your processing code occurs sequentially after your screen input operation.

In Java, your input processing code will not be sequential after your show method call. This is because the show method, except for modal dialogs, returns control to you immediately. This happens before the user has entered any input. It is an asynchronous, or *modeless*, operation. For modal dialogs, it returns only after the dialog has been dismissed via the dispose method call. In RPG, you really have only two forms of input information: the text entered by the user, and the key that was pressed by the user (such as Enter or a function key). In essence, then, the pressing of a key is the only user *event* with which you are concerned. You process the screen values after that event. In Java and in all graphical user interfaces, by contrast, you have many more *events* to be concerned with. For example:

- Pressing a push button
- Selecting an item in the list
- Selecting a menu item
- Checking a radio button or check box
- Typing of text
- Clicking a mouse button
- ... many more

You do not have to be concerned with all the possible events that a user can trigger, but you will frequently want to "monitor" a few of them. This will provide immediate error checking and visual feedback. For example, you may want to prevent users from typing alphabetic characters in a numeric entry field (this is your job, unfortunately, as Java supplies no built-in entry field validity checking support, the way DDS does). You may want to "gray out" or disable certain components when a radio button is selected, re-enable them when the button is deselected, and so on.

NOTE: Most of your windows will have an OK push button that will be the closest functional thing to the Enter key "event" in display file processing. Most of your function keys will also end up becoming push buttons in a Java GUI screen. For example, F12 becomes a Cancel push button, F5 becomes a Refresh push button, F4 becomes a List... or Browse... push button, and so on.

If the call to show is roughly equivalent to RPG's **EXFMT**, but it returns control to us immediately, how do we get control when an "event" happens? In Java, these "events" are Java objects (of course!) that are sent to your own class *if you tell Java to do that*. Notice that the Java "event model" we will describe here for Java 1.1 AWT is identical in the new Java Foundation Classes in Java 1.2, so your time is well spent learning them. Furthermore, as we will discuss in the final chapter, this event model also applies to something called Java beans.

What Are These Java Objects?

These event objects are instances of various classes (depending on the event that happened) that inherit from, or **extend**, the Java class java.awt.AWTEvent — the root event class. Each unique event, such as ActionEvent for push button presses, sends to your program an object of the appropriate event class. From this object you can query (via method calls on the object) information such as the GUI component that triggered the event (using the event.getSource() method call).

How do you tell Java to send these event objects to your class? You have to do three things:

1. Indicate that your class is capable of responding to these events by including implements xxxListener on your class definition, where xxx is different for each type of event in which you are interested. For example, implements ActionListener will cause the system to send you action events, much as what happens when a push button is pressed (versus, say, text events when text is typed).

2. Supply a method in your class that will be called by the Java runtime for specific events. These methods have to use the exact names and parameter types (that is, "signature") that Java defines for each type. These are all defined in the `xxxListener` interfaces, which is defined in the `java.awt.event` package. For example, for action events you are required to supply the method "`public void actionPerformed(ActionEvent event).`" It is in these methods that you will process the event and query inputs and states as required.

3. After creating each GUI component, such as a push button, you must "register" that it is to send its events to your class. Do this using the `addxxxListener(your-class-object);` method that all input-capable Java components support. For example, if you implement the `ActionListener` interface in your actual window class, then for a push button you might code:

```
okButton.addActionListener(this);.
```

Before going into more details about all the event types and their associated listeners, let us examine an example. We will use the version of our running example where all of the components were moved to a separate `CompanyPrompt` class that extended `Panel`. We will change our window class that added this prompt to the "Center" region of a border layout. Our first change will be to add a "message line" at the bottom of the window where we can display output messages for debugging and learning purposes. We suggest this anyway as a general addition to all your windows because it is a great way to display messages to the user. It is just like the message subfile line we are used to in display files. We have chosen to implement the message line as a `TextArea` component, made read-only, so that we will get a horizontal scroll bar for large text. Another option is to use a `Choice` component so that multiple messages could be displayed at once, but we want to keep it simple. Here is the revised class with this new message line added:

LISTING 12-13

```
import java.awt.*;
import java.awt.event.*;
class TestEvents extends Frame
{
    // define GUI components
    private CompanyPromptWithEvents companyprompt;
    private TextArea        msgLine;
    // Constructor
    TestEvents()
    {
        super();
        setTitle("TestEvents");
        setSize(300,200);
        setLocation(200,100);
        setBackground(java.awt.Color.lightGray);
        // instantiate components
        msgLine         = new TextArea("msg line",1,1,
```

LISTING 12-13

```
        java.awt.TextArea.SCROLLBARS_HORIZONTAL_ONLY);
    msgLine.setEditable(false); // read-only
    msgLine.setForeground(java.awt.Color.red);
    companyprompt = new CompanyPromptWithEvents(msgLine);
    // set window layout manager
    setLayout(new BorderLayout(5,5));
    // add components to window
    add(companyprompt, "Center");
    add(msgLine,       "South");
    // show the window
    pack();
    show();
  } // end constructor
  public static void main(String args[])
  {
      TestEvents test = new TestEvents();
  }
} // end TestEvents class
```

Notice that we changed the line that instantiates new CompanyPrompt to pass in msgLine as a parameter to the CompanyPrompt constructor. We changed the CompanyPrompt class to accept a TextArea component reference as a parameter to the constructor, so that this class can write to that TextArea when processing events. Here is the revised CompanyPrompt class, renamed to CompanyPromptWithEvents, with code added to process the "List..." push button being pressed:

LISTING 12-14

```
import java.awt.*;
import java.awt.event.*;
class CompanyPromptWithEvents extends Panel
                             implements ActionListener
{
    private TextArea  msgLine;
    // define GUI components
    private Label     instruction;
    private Label     prompt;
    private TextField entry;
    private Button    listButton;
    private TestPanel buttons;
    // Constructor
    CompanyPromptWithEvents(TextArea msgLine)
    {
        super();
        this.msgLine = msgLine;
        // instantiate components
        instruction = new Label("Enter company number");
        prompt      = new Label("Number");
        entry       = new TextField(5);
```

LISTING 12-14

```
        listButton   = new Button("List...");
        listButton.addActionListener(this);
        buttons      = new TestPanel();
        // set window layout manager
        setLayout(new BorderLayout(5,5));
        // add components to window
        add(instruction,"North");
        add(prompt,      "West");
        add(entry,       "Center");
        add(listButton,  "East");
        add(buttons,     "South");
    } // end constructor
    // Process button actions
    public void actionPerformed(ActionEvent event)
    {
        if (event.getSource() == listButton)
          msgLine.setText("List button pressed!");
    }
} // end CompanyPromptWithEvents class
```

The result of running this now and pressing the "List..." push button is shown in Figure 12-20:

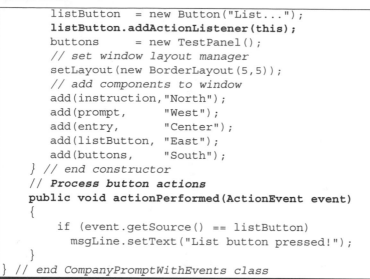

FIGURE 12-20

You see how easy it is to get control when user initiated events occur. Now that we have seen the Java infrastructure for event processing, let us solve that thorny little problem that our examples so far have shared: you cannot close the windows except by killing them!

The event that we are interested in is the WindowEvent, which is sent for any interesting window-related user actions such as closing, maximizing, minimizing, and restoring the window. Closing the window is the one activity that Java does not handle on its own, so we are forced to handle it. Because handling this event is likely to be commonly required, we have decided to create a separate new class that processes only this event by implementing the WindowListener interface. We can then create an instance of it to use in any window class we have. Here is the code:

LISTING 12-15

```
import java.awt.*;
import java.awt.event.*;
public class FrameListener implements WindowListener
{
    private Window owner;        // window we are monitoring
    private boolean mainWindow;  // is this a main window?
    // constructor
    public FrameListener(Window owner, boolean mainWindow)
    {
        this.owner = owner;
        this.mainWindow = mainWindow;
    }
    // called when user closes window...
    public void windowClosing(WindowEvent e)
    {
        owner.dispose();
        if (mainWindow)
          System.exit(0);
        return;
    }
    public void windowOpened(WindowEvent e) {}
    public void windowClosed(WindowEvent e) {}
    public void windowIconified(WindowEvent e) {}
    public void windowDeiconified(WindowEvent e) {}
    public void windowActivated(WindowEvent e) {}
    public void windowDeactivated(WindowEvent e) {}
} // end FrameListener class
```

It may be helpful to talk about some things here in more detail. First of all, notice that the constructor takes in two parameters, a Window object and a boolean variable. The former is simply the window we are monitoring; we will need this to close that window. The latter tells us whether this is the main window in our application. We decided to ask for this because, when closing the main window, we have to do something special — we have to call System.exit to exit the entire application. (This is like setting on indicator LR in RPG.)

409

Nobody else will do this for us. If we do not do this, the window will disappear but the Java virtual machine will keep running along in the background. Look now at the windowClosing method. This is what Java will call when the user closes the window by using the *x* in the upper right-hand corner on Windows or selecting Close from the system menu of the window. All we have to do is call the dispose() method on the window that we are monitoring, and that window will be destroyed. We also call System.exit, as discussed for main windows.

What are all those other empty methods? If you look at the WindowListener interface in the java.awt.event package, you will see that it defines all these method signatures. Recall that to implement an interface in your own class, you must implement every one of the methods defined in the interface. That is what we have done, but since we are not interested in monitoring for any of these other window events, we just leave the methods empty. In fact, for those xxxListener interfaces that have multiple methods in them, Java supplies some helper classes. They are called xxxAdaptor and they "implement" the xxxListener class and supply empty versions of the methods, as we have done here. The advantage is that you can choose to extend these classes and only code the methods you want to override, versus having to define all the empty methods as we did. However, because you can only extend one class in Java, you cannot use these if your class is already extending another class — or some day might. You are better off, in our opinion, typing in the empty methods.

Now, finally, let us see how to put this common new class to use. We would need only to change our last TestEvents class to use this class by changing its constructor to:

- Instantiate an object of the class (notice that the parameters match what the class's constructor expects):

```
FrameListener closer = new FrameListener(this, true);
```

- Register to the system that we want this new object to handle Window events for us (we code this anywhere prior to the show() line of code):

```
addWindowListener(closer);
```

Notice here that because our class extends Frame, when we call addWindowListener we are actually calling this method in the Frame class. We are a Frame, because we inherit from one!

That is it — we can now finally close our windows. That is always a great feature to support in production-level applications (a little humor here).

Here are all the typically used xxxListener interfaces:

Listener	Description
ActionListener	An action occurs, such as a button being pressed, a mouse double-click on a list entry, or a menu bar item or popup menu item selected.
WindowListener	A window event occurs, such as a window closing.
FocusListener	A component gains or loses focus.
ItemListener	Something is selected, such as a check box, radio button, item in a list, or a CheckboxMenuItem is toggled.
KeyListener	A key on the keyboard has been typed. Use this to capture function keys, for example, or verify characters as they are typed.
MouseListener	The mouse has been clicked or enters/exits a component's visual area.
MouseMotionListener	A mouse is being dragged or moved over a component.
TextListener	The text in a TextField or TextArea has been changed.

See the JDK documentation for these java.awt.event interfaces for details about the methods they require you to implement if you want to monitor for these events. Each of these methods will be passed an appropriate xxxEvent object as its first parameter, so you should also see the JDK documentation for these java.awt.event classes for a description of the information you can retrieve from these event objects.

One thing most of your event methods will need to do is to determine exactly which component triggered this event. For example, your screen will often have multiple push buttons and multiple menu-bar items, but only one ActionPerformed method to process all of them. All event objects support the getSource() method that returns an Object reference to the specific component or menu item that is responsible for triggering the event. By comparing this value to your component reference variables (which is why we made them instance variables versus local to the constructor, so you could refer to them in these other event processing methods) you can determine what to do:

```
Object component = event.getSource();
if (component == okButton)
    . . .
else if (component == openMenuItem)
    . . .
```

411

Processing Input

To write the code that "implements" the appropriate listener interface, you will have to put in code in your event processing methods in order to retrieve information from the screen. This is done using appropriate "get" methods on your components. As part of your processing of input, you may also find yourself needing to change the state of something, for which there is usually an equivalent "set" method defined in the component class. Here is a summary of some of the more frequently used methods in each component for querying and setting values:

Comp't	Query Methods	Set Methods
Button	getLabel to return button text.	setLabel to set button text.
Checkbox	getLabel to return button text. getState to return selected state. getCheckboxGroup for radio buttons.	setLabel to set button text. setState to change selected state.
Checkbox-Group	getSelectedCheckbox to return selected radio button.	setSelectedCheckbox to set the selected radio button.
Checkbox-MenuItem	getLabel to return item text. getState to return selected state.	setLabel to set item text. setState to set selected state.
Choice	getSelectedIndex to return integer index of the selected choice. getSelectedItem to return String.	select to select the item with the specifed position, or the specified string.
Label	getText to return displayed text.	setText to set displayed text.
List	getSelectedIndex to return integer position of selected item. getSelectedItem to return string value of selected item. getItem to return string in given position.	addItem to append or insert item to list. remove to remove item from the list (or use RemoveAll). ReplaceItem to change item. select to select an item.
MenuItem	getLabel to return item text.	setLabel to set item text.
TextArea / TextField	getText to return user entered text. getSelectedText to return selected text.	setText to change all text. select to select text subset. selectAll to select all text. setCaretPosition to position cursor. setEditable for read mode.
TextArea		append to add text. insert to insert text. replaceRange to replace text.

NOTE: Remember that all item and text position numbers are zero-based in Java!

As a quick example, here is a sample code that reads an entry field, where the entry field is an object reference variable of type TextField called myEntry:

412

```
String theText = myEntry.getText();
```

NOTE: You will often want to strip off the leading and trailing blanks, using the String class method trim():

```
String theText = myEntry.getText().trim();
```

Finally, when processing your OK push button in your actionPerformed method, you will be querying all the user-specified information on the screen to validate it. If it is all valid, and you want to exit your window, call the dispose() method that you inherited from Frame. Otherwise, display an error message and just "return" from that method so the window remains displayed.

Error Checking

When working with display file entry fields, we have the luxury of simply defining the data type and some validity checking keywords (using the **CHECK** DDS keyword), and we can let the system take care of most input data error checking for us. In Java AWT, the TextField component is far more basic — it accepts any string as input, period. It is up to us, then, to verify what the user has typed in. You will have to write all this code yourself, unfortunately. We suggest you create a new class that extends TextField, and perhaps call it AS400TextField. You can place all your validity checking code in here and then use objects of this field instead of TextField directly. You have the choice of:

- Verifying input as the user types it, using the KeyListener interface
- Supplying a "verify" method that verifies the input when called by the programmer (for example, when the "OK" button is pressed)

We prefer the latter option because it is less disruptive to end users and does not impede performance (checking every keystroke can be slow). Your new class might have methods, such as setDataType, setMaxLength, that supply information to help your verify method check for errors.

Your verify method will read the contents of the entry field; left- or right-justify it with or without padding, as desired; then ensure that the contents are valid for the data type, length, decimals, and so on, as specified via the setXXX methods. The justified output should be resent to the screen for visual update. If there is an error, you should display it in an error message box or on the `TextArea` message line if there is one (you should supply a `setMsgLine` method for identifying this). To help do your verifying of input, you could look at the `DecimalFormat` class in the `java.text` package, or simply write your own. For example, to pad and justify an integer data type, you might have a method like:

LISTING 12-16

```
public static final String padInteger(int intnum, int finalLen)
{
    String paddedString;
    paddedString = Integer.toString(intnum);
    int curLen = paddedString.length();
    if (curLen < finalLen)
      {
        StringBuffer temp = new StringBuffer(finalLen);
        int padAmount = finalLen—curLen;
        int i,j;
        for (i=0; i < padAmount; i++)
            temp.append('0');
        for (j=0; i < finalLen; i++,j++)
            temp.append(paddedString.charAt(j));
        paddedString = temp.toString();
      }
    return paddedString;
}
```

To verify the padded and justified number, you might have:

LISTING 12-17

```
public static final int verifyInteger(String stringInt, int min, int max)
{
    int returnVal = -1;
    try
    {
      Integer intObj = Integer.valueOf(stringInt);
      returnVal = intObj.intValue();
      if ((returnVal < min) || (returnVal > max))
        returnVal = -2;
    }
    catch (NumberFormatException e) {}
    return returnVal;
}
```

If you do detect an error, you may want to change the foreground and background colors of the entry field, which you know how to do; just be sure to reset them again as the first thing you do in the verify method. You should also do a `component.requestFocus()` call to set the focus on the entry field being verified if there is an error. With this, you will have coded the equivalent to **DSPATR(RI PC)** in DDS. You might put these methods in their own class, such as `StringMethods`.

Error Messages

Having written your code to verify the user's entry field input, you now must display an error message if it is wrong. On the AS/400, of course, we use messages defined in a message file, with substitution values supported. In Java, you work with `String` objects. Your first decision must be how to deal with substitution variables. Presumably you want to create a number of "generic" error messages like you do on the AS/400, and substitute the particular values in on the fly. The `String` class, unfortunately, does not support replacing substrings with other substrings, so you have two choices here:

1. Use the `MessageFormat` class in the `java.text` package. This allows you to specify in the constructor a string message with substitution variables defined between curly braces, as in "File {0} not found." The substitution values are supplied as an array of Java objects (usually strings), and the number between the curly braces is used as the index into that array.

2. Write your own substring substitution static method class.

Here is how you might do the latter (another candidate for a `StringMethods` helper class):

LISTING 12-18

```
public static String sub(String msg, String subOld, String subNew)
{
    StringBuffer temp = new StringBuffer();
    int lastHit = 0;
    int newHit = 0;
    for (newHit = msg.indexOf(subOld,lastHit); newHit != -1;
        lastHit = newHit, newHit = msg.indexOf(subOld,lastHit))
      {
        if (newHit >= 0)
          temp.append(msg.substring(lastHit,newHit));
        temp.append(subNew);
        newHit += subOld.length();
      }
    if (lastHit >= 0)
      temp.append(msg.substring(lastHit));
    return temp.toString();
}
```

This will substitute all occurrences of a given substring with a replacement string, returning the resulting "final" string. For example, you may define error message string constants of the form:

```
public static final String MSG_FILENOTFOUND = "File &1 not found.";
```

You could then call the method `sub` with the contents of an entry field with the code:

```
msg = sub(MSG_FILENOTFOUND, "&1", filenameEntry.getText().trim());
```

In either case, you finally have a `String` object with the required substitution performed. How, then, do you display that to the end user? If it is not a question requiring a user response, such as "File &1 already exists. Replace it?", then we recommend you display it in a `TextArea` component on the bottom of your window, as we already discussed. You may wish to change the colors of that area to be white characters on a red background when displaying an error message, in order to attract the user's attention.

However, what if you need to ask the user a yes/no question, or what if you want to just force the user to read the message? You will need to define a new class for popup error messages. It will have to use a `Dialog` class, because you do not want your program to regain control after showing it until the user has answered the error (via Yes, No, or OK buttons). Thus, you want the modal support offered by the `Dialog` class. You should supply a constructor that takes as input the `Frame` parent, the message to show, and whether or not to show Yes/No buttons (boolean). You could then easily show the message in a `TextArea` read-only component in the "Center" of a flowed layout panel, and the Yes/No or OK buttons in the South area. The `actionPerformed` method should set an instance variable `buttonPressed` to an integer constant and then dispose the dialog, and you should supply a `getButtonPressed()` method as well so as to retrieve that value. This sequence of steps is too big to show you in one shot. So we'll show the class without the constructor first, and then show the constructor code:

LISTING 12-19

```java
import java.awt.*;
import java.awt.event.*;
public class MsgBox extends Dialog implements ActionListener
{
    public static final int MSG_OK  =0; // for a response of OK
    public static final int MSG_YES =1; // for a response of YES
    public static final int MSG_NO  =2; // for a response of NO
    private int      buttonPressed = 0;
    private Button okButton, yesButton, noButton;
    // constructor
    public MsgBox(Frame parent, boolean showYESNO, String msg)
    {
        // SHOWN IN NEXT SAMPLE
    }
    // return what button was pressed
    public int getButtonPressed()
    {
        return buttonPressed;
    }
    // process user input
    public void actionPerformed(ActionEvent e)
    {
        Object obj = e.getSource();
        if (obj == okButton)
          buttonPressed = MSG_OK;
        else if (obj == yesButton)
          buttonPressed = MSG_YES;
        else if (obj == noButton)
          buttonPressed = MSG_NO;
        dispose(); // we are done!
    } // end actionPerformed method
} // end MsgBox class
```

Now for the constructor code:

LISTING 12-20

```
// constructor code...
super(parent,true); // call Dialog constructor
setTitle("Error Message"); // Set default title
setSize(270,200); // width, height
setLocation(300,150); // x, y
setBackground(java.awt.Color.gray);
setForeground(java.awt.Color.black);
setLayout(new BorderLayout());
TextArea text = new
  TextArea(msg,4,1,java.awt.TextArea.SCROLLBARS_NONE);
text.setEditable(false); // readonly
text.setBackground(java.awt.Color.lightGray);
Label iconLabel = new Label("", Label.CENTER);
iconLabel.setFont(new Font("Serif",Font.BOLD,48));
add(new Label(""),java.awt.BorderLayout.NORTH);
add(iconLabel,java.awt.BorderLayout.WEST);
add(text,java.awt.BorderLayout.CENTER);
if (showYESNO) // yes and no buttons
  {
    yesButton = new Button("Yes");
    yesButton.addActionListener(this);
    noButton  = new Button("No");
    noButton.addActionListener(this);
    Panel yesnoButtonPanel = new Panel();
    yesnoButtonPanel.setLayout(new FlowLayout());
    yesnoButtonPanel.add(yesButton);
    yesnoButtonPanel.add(noButton);
    add(yesnoButtonPanel,java.awt.BorderLayout.SOUTH);
    iconLabel.setText("?");
              iconLabel.setForeground(java.awt.Color.orange);
  }
else // ok only button
  {
    okButton = new Button("OK");
    okButton.addActionListener(this);
    add(okButton,java.awt.BorderLayout.SOUTH);
    iconLabel.setText("!");
    iconLabel.setForeground(java.awt.Color.red);
  }
```

This is a fully-developed example, so you can use it in your own code if you wish. Do not strain your eyes too much now trying to read it all — but it is a good exercise for you. Using this class, then, would be as simple as the following for an OK button:

```
MsgBox msg = new MsgBox(parent,false,"List pressed!");
msg.show();
```

And as simple as this for yes / no buttons:

```
msg = new MsgBox(parent,true,"Continue?");
msg.show();
if (msg.getButtonPressed() == MsgBox.MSG_NO)
  // do something
```

This would give you message dialogs such as the ones showed in Figure 12-21:

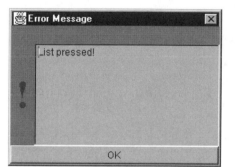
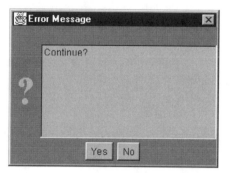

FIGURE 12-21

Applets Versus Applications

Recall from Chapter 2 our discussion on Java applets versus Java applications:

- Applications can be invoked from a command line, using `java MyClass`. This first class requires the existence of a `public static void main(String args[]) {...}` method, which the Java runtime looks for.

- Applets cannot be invoked from the command line. They must be imbedded inside an HTML (*HyperText Markup Language*) Web page, using an **APPLET** tag to refer to them. The Web browser, on encountering an **APPLET** tag, will retrieve the applet from the host server where the Web page came from, and "run" it.

All of our examples to this point have used an application-style "main" method and have been invoked from the command line for "testing" purposes. However, all of the "non main" code is still valid for applets; applets use the same Java language and Java-supplied packages as Java applications do. However, there are some restrictions related to security. Java applets are by default restricted to a **sandbox** that prevents them from accessing in any way the workstation or personal computer the Web browser is running on, or any server other than the one they came from. Applets, then, cannot:

- Access local files in any way, including running local programs.
- Access or change local properties, like the current working directory.

- Access any server except the one they came from, via any form of communications, including JDBC or the AS/400 Toolbox for Java classes.

These restrictions are enforced by the Web browsers, although most allow these to be configured. Further, Java 1.1 includes the capability now of digitally "signing" your applets using the JDK supplied JAVAKEY tool. We will not discuss this tool here but, briefly, it allows for mutually consented use of a Java applet that has full access rights. It ensures:

- The user of the applet that the applet came from you and has not been tampered with since.

- The programmer of the applet that only those people or "entities" identified are allowed to run the applet.

Applets and AWT

If Java applications require the existence of a "`main`" method to be invoked from the command line, what do applets require to be invoked from a Web browser? The answer is:

Applets, by definition, are classes that "extend" the java.applet.Applet class

That is how you create an applet — you create a new class that extends `Applet`. Simple, no? What is so special about this `Applet` class? Actually, not too much. The `java.applet.Applet` class itself extends the `java.awt.Panel` class. We have already seen the `Panel` class — we used it to produce self-contained and easily reusable (*encapsulated*) window "parts" containing components and a layout manager to manage their appearance. It makes sense that an applet would extend, or "be a" panel then, because the Web browser already supplies the `Frame` window, and the applet is simply staking out a part of the real estate of that window. This is what panels do as well. What the `Applet` class does beyond that of the `Panel` class is manage the interaction between your applet and the Web browser "host."

To create an applet, start with a fresh new class:

```
public class MyFirstApplet extends java.applet.Applet
{
  ...
} // end class MyFirstApplet
```
NOTE: Applet classes must be public!

You will also supply method overrides to four key methods from the `Applet` class, which the Java runtime will call automatically at the appropriate times in an applet's life:

Method	Description
`public void init() {...}`	Called once when the applet is first loaded. Does initialization of variables and state. Equivalent to a constructor, or RPG's `*INZSR`.
`public void start() {...}`	Called after init at applet load time, but also called to "restart" a resting applet after the user "surfs away" and subsequently returns to this Web page. Equivalent to an RPG program's "main line" code. Typically, this restarts threads and possibly restores state.
`public void stop() {...}`	Called when the user "surfs" away to another Web page. Typically, this suspends threads.
`public void destroy() {...}`	Called just before the browser exits, to give you a chance to clean up anything, like canceling any threads and closing any files or JDBC connections, for example.

NOTE: You do not have to override all of these methods with your own, but most robust applets will. The minimum you need, however, is simply init. Let us now take our previous TestEvents example, convert it from an application Frame window class to an applet, and have a look! Notice the commented out lines of code are those that are not applicable to an applet, or have been changed in the subsequent line of code:

LISTING 12-21

```java
import java.awt.*;
import java.awt.event.*;
//class TestEvents extends Frame
public class TestMyApplet extends java.applet.Applet
{
    private CompanyPromptWithEvents companyprompt;
    private TextArea        msgLine;
    //TestEvents()
    public void init()
    {
        //super();
        //setTitle("My First Java Window");
        //setSize(300,200);
        //setLocation(200,100);
        setBackground(java.awt.Color.lightGray);
        msgLine       = new TextArea("msg line",1,1,
            java.awt.TextArea.SCROLLBARS_HORIZONTAL_ONLY);
        msgLine.setEditable(false); // read-only
        msgLine.setForeground(java.awt.Color.red);
        companyprompt = new CompanyPromptWithEvents(msgLine);
        setLayout(new BorderLayout(5,5));
        add(companyprompt, "Center");
        add(msgLine,       "South");
        //pack();
        //show();
    }
}
```

421

Was that simple enough? We just changed the class definition to be **public**, extended Applet instead of Frame, changed the constructor method to the init() method, and commented out any Frame window-related method calls. Not bad. Plus, we reused our CompanyPrompt class verbatim! You see that all the input processing applies as is to applets. Note that pack() is not allowed for applets. Figure 12-22 shows what this looks like now in Microsoft Internet Explorer 4.0:

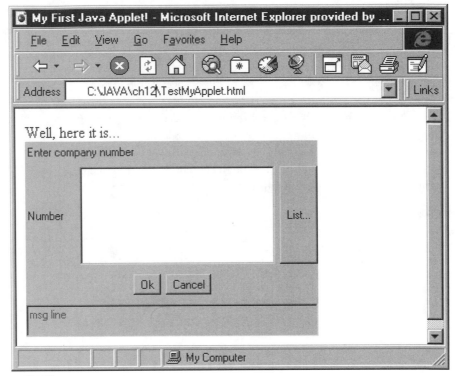

FIGURE 12-22

How did we get this to show up in a Web page? With the following snippet of HTML source:

LISTING 12-22

```
<html>
<head>
<title> My First Java Applet! </title>
</head>
<body>
<p> Well, here it is...
<br>
<APPLET CODE="TestMyApplet.class" WIDTH=300 HEIGHT=200>
</APPLET>
</body>
</html>
```

The **APPLET** tag is what is important here. With it you identify your applet class via the **CODE**= parameter, and the size of your applet's panel via the **WIDTH** and **HEIGHT** parameters (these are equivalent to `java.awt.Frame`'s `setSize` method). There are many more possible parameters to the **APPLET** tag, such as **CODEBASE** to identify a subdirectory where your applet class files live, relative to the Web page's HTML files. For information on this tag, consult any *other* Java book, or the documentation for the Sun JDK, in the file `docs/guide/misc/applet.html` off your JDK subdirectory.

Graphics

Java includes graphics support that is quite rich in the `java.awt.Graphics` and `java.awt.Canvas` classes. However, these are not often used in business applications such as yours, and are also well-covered in many other books. So, we will not cover them here. If you need to draw a polygon, however, rest assured that you can! More likely, you will wish to display an image, and the `java.awt.Image` class is intended to do just that. The `Applet` class method `getImage` makes retrieving the image from your server relatively simple.

AS/400 Display Files Versus Java AWT

Here are some comparisons between AS/400 Display Files and Java AWT.

What about online help? You will have to use `Dialog` classes with a `TextArea` for now, or wait for JFC. That will allow you to use HTML as your online help, with a component for displaying HTML within your application.

What about message files and messages? See the next section on resource bundles.

What about subfiles? Try the multi-column container control from Taligent (`www.taligent.ibm.com`), or wait for JFC. Alternatively, the Data Access Builder tool in the VisualAge for Java Enterprise edition generates a multiple-column list control for your database. Further, the AS/400 feature of this product includes a Java subfile class, and even a display file to Java translation tool. See `www.software.ibm.com/ad/as400/vajava` for details. There are also many Java multiple-column list components available on the Web for download or purchase. For example, see the vendors listed at the `www.software.ibm.com/ad/vajava website`, which are part of the IBM "Object Connection" program for third-party Java beans (Java beans are discussed in Chapter 14).

What about edit codes? You are on your own, except for the `java.text.NumberFormat` class. However, the AS/400 feature of the VisualAge for Java Enterprise edition does include Java `editcode` and `editword` classes.

What about the **CHECK** keyword? You have to write it all. See the previous section on Error Checking.

What about the **DSPATR** keyword? Use the methods like `requestFocus` (**PC**), `setForeground` and `setBackground` (**RI**), and `setFont` (**UL**). Blinking is out, however, unless you want to start a thread that alternates your foreground color between black and the background color!

What about the **COLOR** keyword? Use the `setForeground` and `setBackground` methods.

TRANSLATION-READY USING RESOURCE BUNDLES

Do you support translating your products into different languages, such as German, French, or Japanese? If you do not, yet, you probably will someday. So, you should always plan your code to allow for this. Preparing for international support usually involves keeping our string constants outside of our program. That means that the translators can access them, and we can ship only one program object that can display different languages dynamically.

On the AS/400, this is done by use of display file objects (we usually let the translators directly edit the text constants in them) and message files. We can then simply change our library list to have our programs pick up the different versions of these translated objects. In Java, there are no message files and, as we discussed, no external user interface objects. Up to this point, we have hard-coded all of our user interfaces strings (for example, text constants, titles, button labels, and so on) and error message strings. The downside of this, of course, is that we'll need to produce redundant copies of our Java programs for each language we want to support. That will create a maintenance nightmare.

Java 1.1 tackled the whole area of internationalization support, including not only translated strings but also the wider topics of currency, collating sequences, and the formatting of numbers, dates, times, and so on. This "internationalization framework" was actually based on code supplied by IBM's Taligent subsidiary at the time. There is a good tutorial on the whole subject in Sun's online and book format tutorial on Java. See `http://java.sun.com/docs/books/tutorial/intl/index.html`.

Locales

The main idea behind international support is to allow your program to work in different languages automatically. The trick is to define all your language-sensitive and country-sensitive information (for example, currency is different per country while language may not be) in a class that is somehow "tagged" as being for a particular language and/or country. Then, for each language and/or country in which you wish your program to operate "correctly," you simply supply a unique version of this "class." For Internet applets this is especially important, given the international access your applet will have.

At runtime, then, you need to identify somehow the language and/or country in which your user wishes to work. This can be by asking him directly via the user interface (for example, through language and country `Choice` drop downs), or by simply using the Java system default, which is set up to be the same as the computer, Web browser or other "host" in which the Java application or applet is running. Having determined the language and country pair (or optionally, either a language or country, using defaults for the other) then your program will choose the appropriate class we described earlier, containing language/country-specific information such as translatable strings. How does it do this? Let us look just a little deeper...

In Java, the current operating language/country "mode" is captured by a class called `Locale` (pronounced "low cal") in the `java.util` package. You create a new `Locale` object by specifying in the constructor the language and the country, as strings. One of these strings can be null, if you are not interested in country-specific languages or language-specific countries. The string values are two-character codes that are predefined by an ISO (International Standards Organization) standard. However, you need not worry about them; rather than instantiating locales, you will probably just use the predefined "constant" locales supplied as helpers in the `Locale` class, such as `Locale.US`, `Locale.GERMANY`, `Local.GERMAN`, and so on.

What are these mysterious locales and why do you need them? There are a number of classes in the `java.text` package for message/date/number formatting, and so on that allow you to pass in one of these locale objects so the formatting is done correctly for that locale. For example, the appropriate date format and decimal point symbol are used. If no locale is specified, the system default locale is used, which you can always query by calling `Locale.getDefault()`. These methods are called *locale sensitive*. They are intended to work "correctly" for any given locale, or at least the locales they claim to officially support.

To warm up your fingers for more coding to come, here is a simple little locale program:

```
import java.util.*;
public class TestLocale
{
    public static void main(String args[])
    {
        Locale defloc = Locale.getDefault();
        System.out.println("name is     : " + defloc.getDisplayName());
        System.out.println("language is: " + defloc.getLanguage());
        System.out.println("country  is: " + defloc.getCountry());
    }
}
```

On our Windows95 system, this provides the result:

```
name is     : English (United States)
language is: en
country  is: US
```

Translated Strings — Resource Bundles

What we want to do is design our own *locale-sensitive* classes! The tricky thing to realize here is that these `Locale` objects are quite useless on their own — they hold no "real" information. They are simply objects that your code (and the Java-supplied code in `java.text`) can use as an indication or key as to which language to display, or language/country to support. We are going to write a locale-sensitive version of our first version of our running sample, the simple `BorderLayout` version of "My First Java Window." We will change the class constructor to take an optional `Locale` object, and display the window in the language for that locale. If it is a locale into which we have not translated our strings, then we'll simply show it in English. Because we will only translate into one other language — German — this will often be the case.

The first thing we need to do is "extract" all the strings from the program and put them in their own class. We want to put them in a two string array, where the first string is merely a "key" or identifier for finding the second, translated string. This way, our program will extract the strings by reading them from the array using that index. In fact, Java has built-in support for this in the form of a `ListResourceBundle` class that we **extend** to create our own class:

LISTING 12-23

```
import java.util.*;
public class MyStrings extends ListResourceBundle
{
    public Object[][] getContents()
    {
        return contents;
    }
    static final Object[][] contents =
    {
        {"TITLE",  "My First Java Window"},
        {"INSTR",  "Enter company number"},
        {"NUMBER","Number"},
        {"LISTPB","List..."},
        {"OKPB",   "Ok"}
    }; // end contents array
}
```

The getContents method is required to be overridden from the base
ListResourceBundle class, as it is defined as **abstract**. It returns the array of
translatable strings, an array we call contents in our example. Now, let's create a German
version of this class. We will translate all the strings to German. But we will also change
the name of the class slightly, so as to indicate that it is for German locales ("Deutsch" is
the German word for German, hence, the "-de" suffix)...

LISTING 12-24

```
import java.util.*;
public class MyStrings_de extends ListResourceBundle
{
    public Object[][] getContents()
    {
        return contents;
    }
    static final Object[][] contents =
    {
        {"TITLE",  "Mein Erstes Java Fenster"},
        {"INSTR",  "Firm nummer eingeben"},
        {"NUMBER","Nummer"},
        {"LISTPB","Liste..."},
        {"OKPB",   "Ja, Das ist Gut!"}
    }; // end contents array
}
```

Now, we need to change our code to use these strings, and the appropriate version, as
opposed to hard-coding the strings. We do this by using the getBundle static method in
the ResourceBundle class to return the appropriate version of our class. We give this
method the "base" name of our ListResourceBundle class extension ("MyStrings") and a
locale object, and it loads the appropriate class for that locale. Once we have this

427

ResourceBundle reference (a grandparent class of our MyStrings class, so by polymorphism it can point to a MyStrings object at runtime) we can extract strings from it using the method getString, which takes that string "key" we defined for each string. Let us have a look:

LISTING 12-25

```
import java.awt.*;
import java.awt.event.*;
import java.util.*;
class TestTranslated extends Frame
{
    // define GUI components
    private Label       instruction, prompt;
    private TextField entry;
    private Button      listButton, okButton;
    private ResourceBundle strings;
    // Constructor
    TestTranslated(Locale locale)
    {
        super();
        strings = ResourceBundle.getBundle("MyStrings",locale);
        setTitle(strings.getString("TITLE"));
        setSize(300,200);
        setLocation(200,100);
        setBackground(java.awt.Color.lightGray);
        // instantiate components
        instruction = new Label(strings.getString("INSTR"));
        prompt      = new Label(strings.getString("NUMBER"));
        entry       = new TextField(5);
        listButton  = new Button(strings.getString("LISTPB"));
        okButton    = new Button(strings.getString("OKPB"));
        // set window layout manager
        setLayout(new BorderLayout(5,5));
        // add components to window
        add(instruction,"North");
        add(prompt,      "West");
        add(entry,       "Center");
        add(listButton, "East");
        add(okButton,    "South");
        // show the window
        pack();
        show();
    } // end constructor
} // end TestTranslated class
```

That is it; we are now "locale sensitive". It would be good form to also supply a second constructor, such as:

```
// Constructor 2
TestTranslated()
{
    this(Locale.getDefault());
}
```

We can now invoke this class with a German locale, as in:

```
TestTranslated test = new TestTranslated(java.util.Locale.GERMAN);
```

This will produce the expected German results (see Figure 12-23):

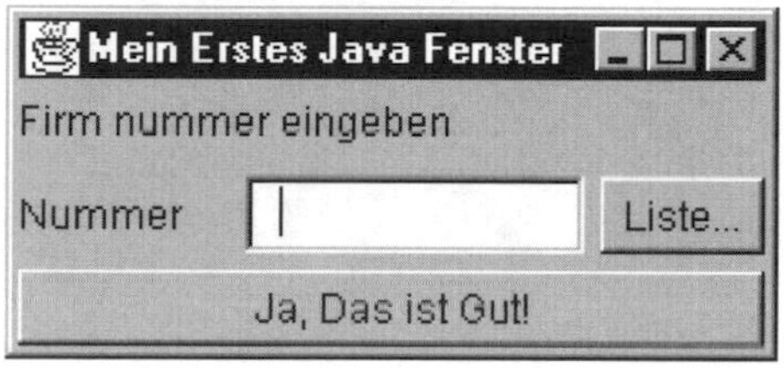

FIGURE 12-23

If we call it with any other locale, or none at all (if we code in that second constructor) we get the default English version. We can add new languages by simply copying and renaming our `MyStrings` class to `MyStrings_xx`, where xx is the appropriate two-character ISO language code (for example: `fr` for French, `es` for Spanish, `it` for Italian, `ja` for Japanese, and `pt` for Portuguese). You can get these codes from your `Locale` class documentation. The name is important. The `getBundle` method we call to find the correct class tacks on the appropriate suffix, to the given base name, for the given locale. Thus, supplying it with a `MyStrings` base name and a German locale sent it looking for a class `MyStrings_de`, which it found. If it does not find the class (after trying a couple of other variations involving the country code of the locale) it looks for the base class, `MyStrings`. This, then, is your default for unsupported locales.

We recommend that you always put all of your potentially translatable strings inside `ListResourceBundles` like this, rather than hard-coding them as you go. It is much more difficult to go in after the fact and find all the strings than it is to start out correctly in the first place.

There is more to supporting internationalization than simply factoring out your translatable strings, as you probably know — small details like date formats, postal codes, currency, and so on. You can learn about all of this in your JDK documentation as you need to, especially in the classes in the `java.text` package.

SUMMARY

In this chapter, you learned:

- About the Java **Abstract Windowing Toolkit** package (`java.awt`), and what it offers in terms of components and layout managers.

- That AWT, at the time of writing, was due to be superseded by JFC. Don't worry, however; most of everything learned here applies to JFC — it is a superset of AWT functionality, for the most part.

- About processing input (events) in Java.

- How to write Java applets versus applications.

- How to write translatable user interfaces in Java.

- That we will miss display file DDS.

13

Database Access

ACCESSING DATA WITH RPG

By this point in your reading you have been exposed to much of the Java language, and should be getting comfortable with, at the very least, the Java syntax and capabilities. However, as you think about existing AS/400 RPG applications, it is important to realize that the primary activity in all of your RPG code is accessing your data. Almost all AS/400 RPG applications revolve around database access. They are "based" on "data." Of course, "momma" is important too, but it is our "data" that we hold most dear! Clearly, then, in order to put Java to use — either on the client or on the server — you will need to know how Java programs can access DB2/400 data.

The AS/400 Database — DB2 for OS/400

The AS/400 operating system comes with its own built-in database called DB2 for AS/400 (well, that is what it is called today), or (affectionately) **DB2/400**. You create database files using an externally described source language — DDS (*Data Definition Specifications*). Typically, you create physical files that will contain data using **PF** (*Physical File*) DDS source that you compile with the **CRTPF** (*Create Physical File*) command. You can also create logical views over one or more physical files using **LF** (*Logical File*) DDS source that you compile with the **CRTLF** (*Create Logical File*) command. Logical files do not contain data; they simply provide an easy mechanism for "viewing" that data differently than it was defined in the physical file(s). Logical files can be simple (one record), multiple record, or join logical files (data from multiple databases joined into a single record).

DDS is used to describe the record formats of a database, each of which contains field definitions.

RPG Database Access

We have been spoiled in RPG with respect to database access. It is just too easy! RPG programs typically use the built-in RPG database "record level" access (that is, record input/output via op-codes like **READ**, **WRITE,** and **SETLL**), versus embedded SQL (*Structured Query Language*). Database access then involves:

- *Declaring* the externally described **DISK** file with an **F**-spec, indicating at that time if the file is to be input, output, update, input-with-add, or output-with-add. The RPG compiler then automatically defines a structure of field variables in your program from the record format of the file. Of course, there is still the option of program-described files, but these are rarely used and no longer recommended.

- *Opening* the file, either by letting it be *implicitly* opened when this module is first called (unless it is already open and using a shared **ODP** (*Open Data Path*)), or by specifying **USROPN** on the **F**-spec and *explicitly* opening it using the **OPEN** operation code.

- *Positioning*, if necessary, the file *cursor* at the required record position, using **SETLL** (*Set Lower Limit*), **SETGT** (*Set Greater Than*) or **CHAIN**.

- Using the appropriate record-level operation codes to *read* (**READ**, **READP**, **READE**, **READPE**, **CHAIN**), *write* (**WRITE**), *update* (**UPDATE**), or *delete* (**DELETE**) the specified record or current record.

- *Locking* the current record, if required, using **LOCK.**

- *Unlocking* any leftover record locks, if required, using **UNLOCK**.

- *Closing* the file, either by letting it be *implicitly* closed when the program exits with **LR** set to **ON**, or by using the **CLOSE** operation code so as to *explicitly* close it.

Of course, many RPG programs today still use the RPG cycle to process files. However, this is generally considered an unstructured and, hence, obsolete form of database access. If you are writing ILE RPG IV modules in which you specify the new (as of V3R2 and V3R6) **NOMAIN** keyword on the **H**-spec, then you do not even have the option of using the RPG cycle because it is not permitted. When writing service programs for general reuse, for example, you might often write self-contained procedures that open, process, and close the files entirely within the body of the procedure (if the files are subsequently used in other places, of course, it will still be more efficient to leave them open, as is common practice, by using **RETURN** without setting **LR** to **ON**). Note that VisualAge for RPG does not support the RPG cycle at all.

This RPG built-in database support is sometimes called *direct database access.* It is noteworthy in the database industry because most relational database access is done through some form of Structured Query Language or SQL statements, as we will discuss.

RPG Database Access Under Commitment Control

If you are conducting sensitive multiple-database transactions, which consist of multiple database updates each, you also use ***commitment control***:

- Prepare for commitment control using the CL commands **CRTJRN** (*Create Journal*), **CRTJRNRCV** (*Create Journal Receiver*) and **STRJRNPF** (*Start Journal Physical File*).

- Start commitment control for your application using the CL command **STRCMTCTL** (*Start Commitment Control*).

- Declare the files on the **F**-spec as being under commitment control, using the **COMMIT** keyword. Note that an optional runtime flag can be specified for *dynamically* controlling the use of commitment control.

- Open the files, either letting them be opened automatically or by specifying the new **USROPN** keyword on the **F**-spec and using the **OPEN** operation code.

NOTE: If using dynamic commitment control via the **COMMIT** keyword, you can specify a program parameter for the flag. The runtime will then open the file with or without commitment control based on this flag, which means that the use of **OPEN** is not essential for dynamic commitment control decisions.

- Work with the files' records using the usual RPG operation codes.

- Commit the files' changes using the **COMMIT** operation code, or...

- Cancel the files' changes if any error occurs, using the **ROLBK** (*Roll Back*) operation code.

- End commitment control using the CL command **ENDCMTCTL** (*End Commitment Control*).

NOTE: Commitment control can be scoped to either the job or an ILE activation group. Commitment control allows you to treat multiple database operations as a single atomic unit of work — either they all succeed or none of them succeed. This is the fundamental way in which complex transactions ensure database integrity: you do not want "partial" transactions to corrupt the state of your data.

ACCESSING DATA WITH STRUCTURED QUERY LANGUAGE

SQL (*Structured Query Language*) is a database industry standard method of accessing a *relational* database (containing records and fields). The current standard is ANSI SQL92. While not extraordinarily popular *yet* among the AS/400 RPG crowd, more and more users are looking at it as a portable way to access the database (and recent gains in the performance and functionality of SQL on the AS/400 has helped). Your SQL code and your SQL skills are transferable to other databases and other systems. As you will see, your SQL skills are also directly portable to Java.

SQL is a language that has a well-defined syntax for creating and manipulating databases. It is comprised of SQL statements with well-defined syntax. If you use it to create databases on the AS/400, those databases are identical and interchangeable with database files created with **DDS**. If you have an existing database created with traditional DDS, you can still access that database with SQL's database manipulation statements, as though the database was created with SQL statements and vice versa. (Note, though, that there are *some* differences.) One restriction, however, is that SQL cannot be used to access multiple-record-format logical files: SQL assumes one format per file (file = ***table*** in SQL) and has no syntax for qualifying format names when reading or writing a database.

When using SQL, you do not use the RPG record-oriented style to access your data. Rather, you use statements where you specify record ***filter criteria*** to retrieve, update, or delete all ***rows*** (records) meeting that criteria. By contrast, in RPG you would code a loop to read through all records (hence record-level access) you wish to view or update, while in SQL you first retrieve all rows using a filter. You then iterate through each row. An example of a filter is:

```
SELECT * FROM CUSTOMER WHERE STATE='PA'
```

In this case, we are retrieving all records from the CUSTOMER ***table*** (database file) where the STATE field is equal to 'PA'. Note that for each row we have specified that we want all (*) the ***columns*** (fields) returned. Alternatively, we could have specified an explicit list of comma-separated field names. The **WHERE** clause in this statement is called the ***predicate***. It can get extremely complex and use boolean logic and numerous operators to explicitly identify the exact records we are looking for. There is support for retrieving from multiple tables, for doing "total" type calculations, and more. As you explore SQL, you will be amazed at the extreme power of this statement (see Paul Conte's book, which is referenced at the end of this chapter, for a good introduction to the power of SQL). The result of this query will be a temporary ***result set*** containing all of the returned records, and there are SQL statements for iterating through each record in the result set (for example, in RPG **FETCH** moves you to the next record and places the field values for that row into specified variables). To update records there is no need for iteration — you simply specify the filter criteria for the affected records and the new value for the field or fields you want to change. For example:

```
UPDATE CUSTOMER SET RATE=2 WHERE STATE='PA'
```

In this case, all records in the CUSTOMER database file where the STATE field is 'PA' have their RATE field changed to the number 2. Easier than writing loops? You can also use a version of this that updates only the current row of the iterating loop. To delete records is similar:

```
DELETE FROM CUSTOMER WHERE STATE='WY' AND RATE=2
```

This will delete all records from the CUSTOMER database where the STATE is equal to 'WY' and the RATE field has a value of 2. For these type of "apply to all records of this criteria" operations, SQL can offer some coding advantages. In fact, you will notice that it is similar to creating a logical file "view" over the database on the fly. To insert records into a database, you use the INSERT INTO statement, as in:

```
INSERT INTO CUSTOMER (CUSTOMER, STATE, RATE) VALUES('Bobs Bait', 'MA', 1)
```

In this case, we are inserting into the CUSTOMER *table* (file) a single *row* (record) with values specified for the *columns* (fields) CUSTOMER, STATE, and RATE. There is also syntax to insert multiple rows into the database in a single statement.

Interactive SQL versus Embedded SQL

SQL consists of *statements* such as SELECT, UPDATE, DELETE, and INSERT. On the AS/400, these statements can be run *interactively* with the result shown immediately, via the STRSQL (*Start SQL*) CL command. This places you in a shell for submitting SQL statements. Also, you can code your SQL statements into a source member and run them from there via the RUNSQLCMD (*Run SQL Command*) CL command. In both cases, you are *interactively* executing a subset of the SQL statement language called *dynamic SQL* (we'll discuss this soon).

Another option is to *embed* SQL statements directly into your RPG, COBOL, C, PL/I, and FORTRAN source (and as of V4R3, C++). Even REXX supports embedded SQL. In these cases, you use special syntax to distinguish between your "native" source and your SQL source. All SQL source is bracketed by EXEC SQL and END-EXEC. For RPG, then, you might have:

```
C/Exec SQL
C+ UPDATE CUSTOMER
C+    SET RATE=2
C+    WHERE STATE='PA'
C/End-Exec
```

All SQL statements are coded on C-specs. To continue an SQL statement over multiple lines, you use a plus sign in position 7, as shown above with "C+". Note that the SQL statements entered are free-format and case insensitive.

One thing to note about embedded SQL is that you do not use a SELECT statement directly to retrieve a set of *rows* (records). Rather, you have to declare a *cursor* by using the DECLARE CURSOR statement, and specify SELECT there as a statement clause. Then, you can OPEN the cursor (this reads the records from the database that meet the SELECT criteria, effectively placing them in temporary storage, although this may actually just involve creating an access path), FETCH the individual records from the *result set* (one at a time), process the *columns* (fields) of the currently fetched record, and CLOSE the cursor.

Rather than declaring a file and processing file records as you do in native RPG code, with SQL you declare a cursor on the file and process the resulting set of records produced by the cursor.

When you embed SQL source in your RPG source, you no longer use the RPG compiler command. Rather, the compilation is done using the appropriate SQL *preprocessor* command. For ILE RPG, this is CRTSQLRPGI. This preprocessor works in two steps:

- Preprocess the SQL source into *processed SQL statements* and native RPG source code, which are placed into a temporary source member (the processed SQL statements go into the associated space of the temporary source member).

- Invoke the appropriate traditional RPG IV compiler to compile the intermediate RPG source member into a module, program, or service program (depending on the OBJTYPE parameter of the CRTSQLRPGI command). This step also compiles the *processed SQL statements* into an *access plan* that is placed in the associated space of the final object. Note that the preprocessor does this step for you.

See the **DB2 for OS/400 SQL Programming** manual (SC41-4611-00) for more details on using embedded SQL.

Static SQL versus Dynamic SQL

SQL statements can be either *static* or *dynamic*. SQL embedded in a programming language such as RPG can be either of these. Static statements can *only* be embedded in another language and precompiled. Dynamic statements, on the other hand, can *also* be issued in numerous other ways (interactively, in their own source member, or via *CLI APIs,* as we will see). Dynamic statements can be *prepared* and *executed* dynamically (depending, say, on runtime information the program has) while static statements are "hard-coded" into the source program.

Although the statements themselves are hard-coded for static SQL, you still can use program variables to define the parameter values to the statement dynamically. To do this, you specify your program variable name right in the SQL statement, but prefix it with a colon. However, the boolean logic for the filter is still hard-coded. For example, while you can specify a variable for 'PA' in our examples (e.g., WHERE STATE=:MYVAR), you cannot turn 'STATE=' into a variable. For this you can use embedded *dynamic* SQL. There are some SQL statements that are both static and dynamic, and there are some that are only one or the other. Static SQL typically offers better performance over dynamic SQL, because the pre-compiler has more information available for optimizations (such as caching the compiled version of the statements). However, that difference can often be minimized through the judicious use of performance enhancing techniques, such as "preparing" often-repeated statements.

Why Use Embedded Dynamic SQL versus Embedded Static SQL? Flexibility. As we have discussed, dynamic statements allow you to decide at runtime *which* SQL statement to run. **HERE'S AN EXAMPLE:** If your program operates on a *specific* file, but allows the user or caller to decide *what the query, update, delete, or insert action will be*, you would choose dynamic over static.

Embedded SQL versus SQL CLI APIs

To use SQL in your programs, you have two choices:

- Embed SQL statements (static or dynamic) inside your RPG code, as we have discussed, and use the RPG SQL preprocessor to translate those statements to native RPG and invoke the RPG compiler on that intermediate output.

- Call SQL system APIs (Application Programming Interfaces) from your program. These APIs are based on the standard X/Open SQL CLI (*Call Level Interface*) specification. These APIs are similar to Microsoft's **ODBC**, which is also based on (and extends) the evolving X/Open standard. Basically, these APIs allow you to pass in SQL statements to be executed, although there are a few other APIs that perform functions besides just "submitting" SQL statements to the database manager — for example, there are APIs for "connecting" and "disconnecting" from a remote database.

Almost all RPG programs that use SQL use embedded SQL because it is both easier to use and more efficient. However, the CLI APIs do offer some additional advanced functions beyond embedded SQL. Furthermore, SQL preprocessors are typically supplied by each database vendor for their own database (the precompiler binds your programs to those of the database), while CLI APIs are far more database vendor independent (a more *standard* standard). A CLI program can potentially be written to easily target multiple vendor databases by dynamically connecting to the database, querying database "support" information, and passing in SQL statements on the fly.

CLI APIs are mainly used to execute passed-in SQL statements by submitting them to the database. When using CLI APIs, you can usually execute only dynamic SQL statements. However, some static-only statements have equivalent CLI APIs (for example, the **FETCH** SQL statement is not dynamic, but there is an **SQLFetch** API in CLI).

Why Use SQL CLI APIs versus Embedded Dynamic SQL? Even more flexibility. While dynamic statements allow you to decide at runtime which *SQL statement* to run, CLI APIs go further and allow you to decide at run-time which *file* to operate against. These APIs provide the ultimate control at runtime, and offer the most functionality and flexibility. Furthermore, with CLI APIs you can query information about the database itself— such as DB2/400 — and what SQL constructs it supports.

Here's an example: If your program allows the user to decide the *file and the query* or manipulation statements to run, you would choose CLI over dynamic SQL. Furthermore, if your program is designed to operate against multiple databases (such as DB2, Oracle, Sybase, Microsoft, etc.) via end-user control, you will need to use CLI.

Here is a summary of the various flavors of SQL:

SQL Statement Type	Run Interactively?	Embed in RPG Source?	Invoke via CLI API?
Static	No	Yes	No
Dynamic	Yes	Yes	Yes

Embedded Static	Embedded Dynamic	CLI APIs
• Best performance. • Easiest to code. • Hard-coded file and field names.	• Need to use prepared statements to get performance. • Hard-coded file names, but dynamic field names.	• Hardest to program. • Similar to embedded dynamic in performance. • Total flexability in choice of file and field names.

Local SQL Versus Distributed SQL

SQL can be used by a program to access a database either locally (on the same system) or remotely (on a system other than where the program resides). The latter is called "distributed SQL." Note that these are the same set of SQL statements we have been discussing, plus a few more that are unique for accessing remote data — such as the **CONNECT** statement for *connecting* to the remote database (something you must do before processing SQL statements for that database).

Distributed SQL can be embedded or can be executed through CLI APIs:

- RPG programs on the host use *local embedded* SQL (*static* or *dynamic*) to access their local database.

- RPG programs on the host can also use *distributed embedded* SQL (*static* or *dynamic*) to access a remote database on another system.

- VisualAge for RPG programs on Windows can use *embedded, local, or distributed* DB2/NT *SQL* (*static* or *dynamic*) and accesses DB2/400 data via a gateway like DB2 Common Server. Of course, VARPG also supports direct RPG-style DB2/400 database access with the familiar op-codes such as READ, WRITE, SETLL, CHAIN, and so on, versus SQL.

- VisualBasic programs on Windows use CLI *APIs* (that is, ODBC) that execute *dynamic* SQL statements to access DB2/400 data. These are typically not distributed SQL statements, but can be if you wish to access databases across multiple systems.

- Java programs running on the client use dynamic SQL, too, via CLI APIs, as we will discuss.

Note that ODBC programs and Java programs running on the client accessing a DB2/400 database on a single AS/400 server do not *need* to use *distributed* SQL, as you might expect because the database is on a different system than the program. Rather, these support direct database access as though the database were local, using a database server program that runs on the AS/400 accepting these remote (client) database requests. You only need to use distributed SQL from the client if you want to access databases across *multiple* AS/400 servers, or you want to access DB2/400 data by going through another database such as DB2/NT.

Confused? It *is* confusing! But there's even more! When using distributed SQL that is, for instance, embedded in your RPG program, the compiled SQL statements are not stored locally by the precompiler as they are for non-distributed SQL. Rather, they are stored on the remote system where the database exists. How are they stored? By using a ***package*** object. You identify to the database that your embedded-SQL RPG source is using *distributed* SQL by specifying a remote or local database name on the RDB (*Relational DataBase*) parameter of the **CRTSQLRPGI** preprocessor command. At that time, you also name the package you wish to create from your embedded SQL statements on the SQLPKG (*SQL Package*) parameter. This package object is merely a persistent way to store the processed SQL statements (the access plan) from your RPG source.

SQL Terminology

As you have seen, SQL uses its own set of terminology that differs from the native AS/400 terminology:

AS/400 Term	RPG Term	SQL Term
DB2/400	n/a	Database
Library	n/a	Collection
Library + objects	n/a	Schema
Physical File	DISK File	Table
Logical File (no key)	DISK File	View
Logical File (with key)	Keyed DISK File	Index
Record Format	Format	MetaData
Record	Data Structure	Row
Field	Field	Column

Why the new terms? Because this is a database- and operating system-independent standard language. In SQL, you have one or more *databases*, each with one or more *collections*. Each collection has one or more *tables*, and each table has one or more *columns*. On the AS/400, there is just one database (DB2/400), while in the rest of the world there are many databases, which makes common terminology important. Using this terminology, DB2/400 has collections (*libraries*) of tables (*physical files*), and has views (*logical files*) as well as indexes (*keyed logical files*). Each table contains one or more columns (*fields*). When you read from the database, you read rows (*records*) of data.

Figure 13-1 illustrates these terms:

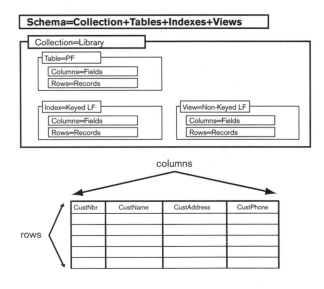

FIGURE 13-1

Views are like traditional logical files (and they are implemented as logical files) that allow you to define a filtered view of one or more files. You can then access that view from your program as though it were a physical file. However, views provide significantly more filtering capability than logical file DDS can offer.

Indexes are also implemented as logical files but, unlike views, you cannot access them from your program as though they were physical files. Rather, they are tools that you can use to define a permanent access path to your database file for performance reasons. Your code still refers to the original file, but the system recognizes when it is appropriate for an existing index to be used. This saves the overhead of creating a temporary access path on the fly. Mind you, indexes do require some additional system overhead in terms of maintenance, so there is a tradeoff to be considered.

SQL Languages: DDL Versus DML

We have discussed the various flavors of SQL statements, but we have not covered what SQL statements actually *do*. SQL statements are divided into two different sub-languages: DDL (*Data Definition Language*) and DML (*Data Manipulation Language*). DDL statements are used to create and alter entire tables or files. They are equivalent to DDS for defining your database *definitions* versus your *data*. DML statements, in contrast, are for manipulating actual data — for example, reading, updating, inserting, and deleting rows or records of data.

DDL "Common" Statements

Statement	Description
CREATE SCHEMA / COLLECTION	*Create a new schema/collection (library)*
CREATE TABLE	*Create a new table (file)*
CREATE INDEX	*Create a new index (keyed logical file)*
CREATE VIEW	*Create a new view (non-keyed logical file)*
ALTER TABLE	*Add/Delete/Change a column (field definition), add constraints, add/delete a key*
DROP XXX	*Deletes COLLECTION / SCHEMA, TABLE, INDEX, VIEW or PACKAGE*

DML "Common" Statements

Statement	Description
DECLARE CURSOR	*Declares a cursor (embedded SQL only)*
OPEN	*Opens a cursor (embedded SQL only)*
FETCH	*Reads the next row of an opened cursor (embedded SQL only)*
SELECT	*Reads one or more rows (records) (CLI only)*
INSERT	*Inserts one or more rows*
UPDATE	*Updates one or more rows*
DELETE	*Deletes one or more rows*
CLOSE	*Closes a cursor (embedded SQL only)*
COMMIT	*Commit previous transactions (e.g.* **INSERT**, **UPDATE**, **DELETE**), *commitment control*
ROLLBACK	*Undo previous transactions, commitment control*

As you get into Java and its database support you will be using these concepts, so they are important to know.

What You Need for SQL on the AS/400

To use SQL on the AS/400, including high-level languages like RPG, you must have the IBM product DB2 Query Manager and SQL Development Kit for OS/400, Program Number **5716-ST1**. You do not require this product to *run* SQL applications, only to *develop* them. It includes a Query Manager, the SQL preprocessors, the interactive SQL utility, and the SQL statement processor. This product is not required to use CLI APIs, either; they come free with the operating system. Nor do you need this product for Java database access, although you may find the interactive SQL command very handy for learning SQL.

ACCESSING DATA WITH JAVA

Java has built-in support for *relational* database access. Its support is patterned after Microsoft's ubiquitous ODBC (*Open DataBase Connectivity*) standard. ODBC is a C language set of APIs that abstracts out database access. That allows you to write database accessing code once and easily target multiple database vendors.

While SQL and CLI are standards, like many standards they are open to interpretation and extension. All database vendors supply "unique" flavors of them. For example, the ANSI SQL92 standard is evolving quickly, and vendors are at various stages of implementing the new additions to the standard, such as database triggers and stored procedures. ODBC is a successful attempt by Microsoft to design a standard set of APIs to which programs can code, independent of the database vendor. It is based on the CLI API standard, not embedded SQL. Why? Embedded SQL requires a precompiler to parse out and "compile" the SQL statements. These preprocessors are supplied by the database vendors, and each accepts the vendor's own flavor of SQL. To write vendor-neutral code with embedded SQL would be difficult.

Java's database support is patterned after ODBC, but is written entirely in Java (rather than C). It is, like ODBC, a "framework" for database access in which:

- Developers write their database vendor-neutral code using language-supplied syntax and support.

- The database vendor supplies a piece to be "plugged in" to the infrastructure (see Figure 13-2), allowing the database-neutral code to access that particular vendor's product. An example follows:

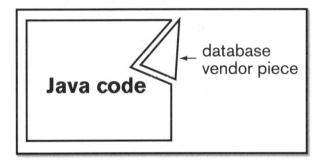

FIGURE 13-2

This framework is called, not surprisingly, JDBC (a trademarked name, but it is often referred to as *Java DataBase Connectivity*). JDBC involves:

- A Java package (**java.sql**) with classes and methods for database connectivity, manipulation, queries, and more.

- A Java "core language" JDBC *database driver manager*, similar to ODBC's driver manager, that comes with the language.

- Database vendor-supplied JDBC *database drivers*, which is unique to each database vendor. These "snap in" to allow a single JDBC application to access multiple databases with minimal code changes. The Java-supplied driver manager essentially passes on all SQL statements to the snapped-in database driver supplied by the vendor. While JDBC is database-neutral, you can still exploit unique database vendor functions, if desired.

- A Java language-supplied ***JDBC/ODBC*** bridge to allow, in the short term, Java access to any database via its ODBC database driver. You will only need and want to use this, however, if your database vendor is one of the few left on the planet that does not yet supply a pure Java JDBC driver. This bridge will often be slower, and may only be as portable, as the ODBC DLLs it requires.

The key is that you need to write your Java code to the `Java.sql` package, not the database vendor APIs. The classes and interfaces in this package pass on the requests to the underlying database on your behalf (see Figure 13-3). This way, you can easily swap in the particular database with minimal impact to your code.

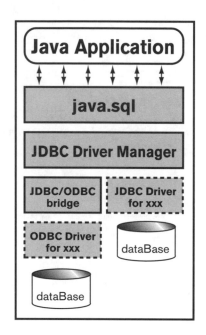

FIGURE 13-3

Does DB2/400 have a "pure Java" implementation for JDBC? Yes, it does. It is part of the AS/400 Toolbox for Java product, which was in public beta at the time of this writing (to find it, go to **http://www.as400.ibm.com** and search for "java" or follow the links from "software"). It also comes with IBM's VisualAge for Java enterprise edition, and Borland's JBuilder/400. There are a number of very useful classes in this product, but only the JDBC driver is an industry standard. The remainder are unique to the AS/400 and will require you to decide between platform portability and ease-of-use programming (in our experience, most AS/400 programmers will opt for the latter). The JDBC driver, as well as all the non-visual classes in the toolbox, can be used either on the client connecting to an AS/400 (V3R2 or above) or on the server with the new Java virtual machine (V4R2 or above). While the packaging of the toolbox is not finalized as of this writing, it is expected to come in the form of a self-expanding .CLASS file that you can install on your client operating system by simply running Java against it. (Be sure to read the supplied README.HTML file.) This will put a file called JT400.ZIP in the directory \JT400\LIB. Add this to your CLASSPATH statement (for example, c:\jt400\lib\jt400.zip) in your AUTOEXEC.BAT file on Windows95, for instance:

```
SET CLASSPATH = .;c:\jt400\lib\jt400.zip;c:\myJavaDir
```

Once the toolbox has been installed, it is time to start writing your Java database code.

Java JDBC Programming

The java.sql package that comprises JDBC is a Java equivalent to CLI. Recall our earlier discussion about CLI APIs — they are a set of APIs for executing dynamic SQL statements. For JDBC, these are a set of classes for executing SQL statements. Figure 13-4 depicts in table form the use of CLI APIs in a language like ILE C versus the use of JDBC in Java (admittedly, this is only of interest to ILE C programmers who have used these APIs):

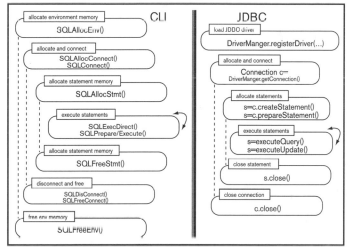

FIGURE 13-4

The `java.sql` package consists of a number of **public** "**interfaces**" (recall that these are like abstract classes — only method signatures are supplied, not method implementations). Your code, however, uses these as though they were fully implemented classes. This is because each database-vendor-supplied JDBC driver simply implements each of these interfaces. The interfaces include:

java.sql Interface	Description
Driver	This is the main interface, supplying the connection method for accessing a database.
Connection	This represents a specific session with a specific database.
Statement	Used to execute explicit SQL statements
PreparedStatement	Used to prepare repeatedly executed SQL statements and execute them. **Extends** Statement
ResultSet	Returned from an SQL query or stored procedure call, this contains the list of returned rows (records) and methods for traversing them and extracting columns (fields).
CallableStatement	Used to call stored procedures. **Extends** PreparedStatement
ResultSetMetaData	Used to dynamically determine the column (field) definitions for a ResultSet. Saves hard-coding field attributes.
DatabaseMetaData	Used to dynamically determine information about the database itself. That is, information about conventions and limits of the database (DB2/400 in our case) as well as information stored in the database's catalog — such as a list of "registered" stored procedures.

Using JDBC involves, typically, the following steps:

1. Importing of the java.sql package:

```
import java.sql.*;
```

2. Loading the JDBC driver you wish to use (DB2/400 in our case):

```
DriverManager.registerDriver(new com.ibm.as400.access.AS400JDBCDriver() );
```

3. Connecting to the database:

```
Connection conn  = DriverManager.getConnection("jdbc:as400://mySystem");
```

4. Preparing the SQL statements you wish to execute:

```
Statement stmt = conn.createStatement(); // OR
PreparedStatement pstmt = conn.prepareStatement("... ? ... ?");
```

5. Running the SQL statements (note applies to `Statement` and `PreparedStatement` objects):

```
stmt.execute(String sql); // execute any SQL statement
stmt.executeQuery(String sql); // execute SQL query, like SELECT
stmt.executeUpdate(String sql); // execute SQL INSERT, UPDATE or DELETE
```

6. Retrieving the information returned by the SQL statements:

```
ResultSet rs = stmt.executeQuery(String sql);
while (rs.next ())
   String column1 = rs.getString(1); // get column 1 as a string
rs.close();
```

7. Handling any errors resulting from the SQL statements - wrap every JDBC call in a try/catch-block, for `SQLException`:

```
try{...}
catch(SQLException exc)
{
   System.out.println( "SQL error: " + exc.getMessage() );
}
```

8. Closing the statements, when done:

```
stmt.close(); // stmt is a Statement object from step 4
pstmt.close(); // pstmt is a PreparedStatement object from step 4
```

9. Closing the database connection, when done:

```
conn.close(); // conn is a Connection object from step 3
```

OK, ready to code? Let's examine these steps in more detail.

1. Import the java.sql Package

To use the classes and methods in the `java.sql` package, your source files must include the `import java.sql.*;` statement at the top of the .java file. To help us follow along, let's assume we are creating a new class to test our new JDBC skills, which is called `TestJDBC1`. So now, in the early days, it might simply look like:

LISTING 13-1

```
// file TestJDBC1.java
import java.sql.*;
public class TestJDBC1
{
    public static void main(String args[])
    {
        System.out.println("Inside TestJDBC");
    }
}
```

2. Load the JDBC Driver

You must tell Java which database drivers you wish to work with. In our case, we wish to use the DB2/400 JDBC driver. To "load" a driver, you simply instruct the JDBC `DriverManager` class to "load" that particular class. How do you do this? You simply code:

`DriverManager.registerDriver(new com.ibm.as400.access.AS400JDBCDriver());`
This searches the CLASSPATH statement's directories, JAR files, and ZIP files for the named class.

This line of code needs only to be executed once per session, prior to any subsequent JDBC calls. Notice that this method throws the exception `SQLException` if it cannot find the class. So, now, our evolving test program might look like this:

```
import java.sql.*;
public class TestJDBC2
{
    public static void main(String args[])
    {
        System.out.println("Inside TestJDBC");
        try
        {
          DriverManager.registerDriver(new
              com.ibm.as400.access.AS400JDBCDriver());
        }
        catch(SQLException exc)
        {
          System.out.println("DB2/400 JDBC driver not found!");
          System.exit(1);
        }
        System.out.println("Class found OK");
        System.exit(0);
    }
}
```

NOTE: Notice the use of **"System.exit(0)"** or **"System.exit(1)"** to end our program. Because all the classes in the AS/400 Toolbox for Java product, including the JDBC driver, spawn non-daemon threads in the background, you are forced to end your application with this so that those background threads are killed. Otherwise, you will find the process "Java" running forever! By convention, you pass this zero for a successful end and non-zero for not-so-successful end. You can think of `System.exit` as being equivalent to **SETON LR** in RPG.

3. Connect to the Database

When using JDBC, you must "connect" to a database before using it. Typically, this will involve supplying a user name and password because the database is usually protected (data represents your company's "crown jewels," after all). To make this connection, use the `java.sql` class `DriverManager` and its static method `getConnection`. This method returns an instance of a `Connection` class from the `java.sql` package (a method that returns an instance of a class is called an ***object factory***).

In SQL terms, remember, the "database" we are interested in is DB2/400. There is exactly one per AS/400 system. Note that in Step 2 you could have loaded multiple database drivers to allow simultaneous access to more than one database (say, to DB2/400 and DB2/NT) at a time. When you create a `Connection` object, you must uniquely identify the "driver" with which you wish to connect, as well as the actual database. In our case, for DB2/400, the former is specified as "`jdbc:as400`" while the latter is specified as the "name" of the AS/400 to which you need to connect. For example, we might have:

```
Connection conn = DriverManager.getConnection("jdbc:as400://mySystem");
```

What you are specifying for the `getConnection` parameter is actually a **URL** (Universal Resource Locator, just like Web browsers use). This is Java standard for database drivers. Each driver determines which URL syntax it will "accept"; and in our case, it will accept anything starting with "**jdbc:as400.**" The ***DriverManager*** will actually loop through each loaded driver, asking it if it accepts the specified URL. The first driver to respond positively is given ownership of this connection.

The actual syntax for the JDBC connection to DB2/400 is:

```
"jdbc:as400://systemName</defaultSchema<;list-Of-Properties>>"
```

The system name identifies which AS/400 you are going to connect to. The optional `defaultSchema` is the default AS/400 library to access in subsequent operations that do not specify a qualified file name. If no default is specified here, the default library list of your user ID is used to find the file. Yes, "*schema*" equals "library" in the JDBC terminology for the AS/400. The optional "list of properties" is a semicolon separated list of **property=value** specifications. A long list of properties is supported by the DB2/400 JDBC driver, and you are referred to the toolbox documentation for a complete list. However, here is a short list of the more interesting properties:

Property	Values	Defaults
user	User name to use in the signon	none
password	Password to use in the signon	none
naming	"**sql**" or "**system**": lib.file or library/file	"**sql**"
access	"**all**" (all SQL statements allowed), "**read call**" (**SELECT** and **CALL** allowed) and "**read only**" (only **SELECT** allowed).	"**all**"
errors	"**basic**" (normal as/400 server error messages) or "**full**" (detailed as/400 server error messages).	"**basic**"

You can specify the user ID and password for the AS/400 connection in one of three ways:

1. Specify it in the connection URL as ";user=uuuuuuuu;password=pppppppp".

2. Specify it in the getConnection method call as the second and third parameters:

getConnection("jdbc:as400://mySystem","uuuuuuuu","pppppppp");

3. Do not specify it at all, in which case the user will automatically be prompted for it.

In addition to these "interesting" properties, there are a number of others that deal with performance tuning, international support, and transaction commitment control. You are well-advised to read up on them (the properties documentation table can be reached from the AS/400 Toolbox for Java's *Table of Contents*, under *JDBC*).

Here's more information on naming: The default naming convention used for a *JDBC/400* (we'll use this term for short when referring to the JDBC driver for DB2/400) connection is "**naming=sql.**" You can also specify "**naming=system.**" This means that, in order to qualify a table reference on an SQL **SELECT** statement, for instance, you would specify COLLECTION/TABLE, as in MYLIB/MYFILE. It also means that an unqualified table name reference, as in TABLE, is equivalent to *LIBL/TABLE.

As you know already, your library list is used to find the table (that is, the default library list of the *user ID* that is specified for the connection). If you are not concerned with portability, this is fine. However, if you are thinking about portability to other databases, you may want to leave the default of "**naming=sql.**" This makes your qualified name syntax consistent with all other databases. This convention is COLLECTION.TABLE, as in MYLIB.MYFILE. Sounds like a painless enough change — just use a dot instead of a slash. However, be careful! This also changes where the system looks for unqualified table names. Now, for TABLE, the system will not look in the library list for file TABLE. Rather, it will only look in the library with the same name as the user ID that is specified in the connection. Therefore, obviously, using "naming=sql" implies that you will fully qualify all your table references. If this is not possible because you are dependent on library list searches, specify this:

naming=system

What might our sample program look like now? Let's create a new, non-static method to do the database connection in, called testConnect. We will also define an instance variable for this Connection object. Now that we have instance data and a non-static method, we will need to instantiate an instance of ourselves as well. Then we can call the new testConnect method on that instance (object), and test out this connection stuff. We will pass in the system name to connect to as a parameter, and we will also let the JDBC driver prompt for user ID and password.

LISTING 13-2

```
import java.sql.*;
public class TestJDBC3
{
    Connection conn;
    public static void main(String args[])
    {
        System.out.println("Inside TestJDBC");
        try
        {
          DriverManager.registerDriver(new
              com.ibm.as400.access.AS400JDBCDriver ());
        }
        catch(SQLException exc)
        {
          System.out.println("DB2/400 JDBC driver not found!");
          System.exit(1);
        }
        System.out.println("Class found OK");
        TestJDBC3 test = new TestJDBC3(); // create instance of us
        test.testConnect("mySystem"); // SUPPLY YOUR SYSTEM NAME!
        System.exit(0);
    } // end main method
    public boolean testConnect(String sys)
    {
        System.out.println("Connecting to system " + sys + "...");
        try
        {
          conn = DriverManager.getConnection("jdbc:as400://"+sys);
        }
        catch (SQLException exc)
        {
          System.out.println("connect failed with: '" +
                            exc.getMessage() + "'");
          return false;
        }
        System.out.println("connected ok");
        return true;
    } // end testConnect method
} // end class TestJDBC3
```

NOTE: You need to specify your AS/400 system name, not leave it as "mySystem"! Also notice that no user ID or password are specified; as a result, the AS/400 JDBC driver will automatically prompt you at runtime for these values, as shown in Figure 13-5:

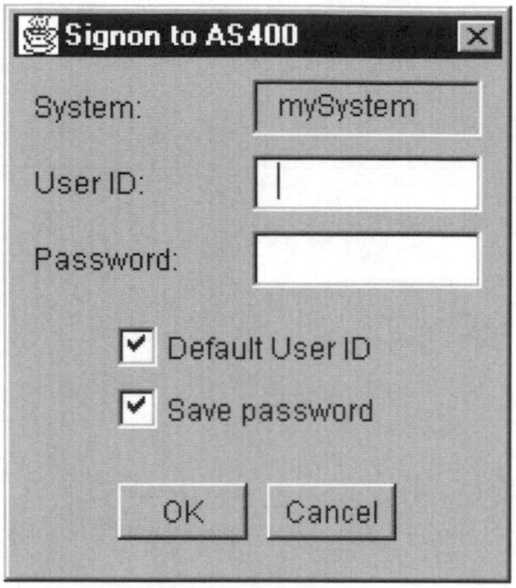

FIGURE 13-5

This is a great time-saver. It means that you do not have to write any code to prompt for a user ID and password. What happens if the user ID or password is invalid? You automatically get a message (Figure 13-6) informing you:

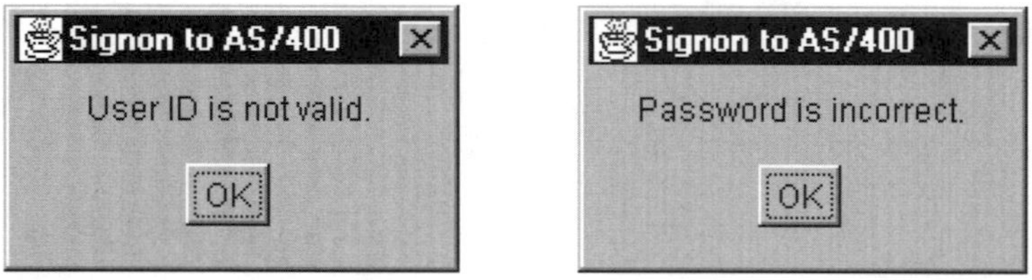

FIGURE 13-6

In addition, there is built-in support to handle the "password expired" problem. This is a safe prompt as well — the password is not echoed to the screen, and it is sent across the wire encrypted. What's more, it is never stored anywhere persistently.

NOTE: If your connection still fails even after specifying a valid system name, user ID, and password, then ensure that your host server jobs are started by using the AS/400 command **STRHOSTSVR *ALL** (Start Host Servers). Also, ensure that your QUSER user ID is still valid and its password has not expired! The AS/400 JDBC driver uses this user ID behind the covers, just as ODBC does.

What is the system name? This is either the TCP/IP address of your AS/400 (JDBC uses only TCP/IP for communications) or a "host name" that you have equated to that address. Your system must be configured for TCP/IP to connect to it from Java clients. Configuring this is beyond the scope of this book, but it is not too difficult of a task to accomplish. Once configured, you can use **CFGTCP** (*Configure TCP*) to find the system's TCP/IP address. If your company has set up a *Domain Name Server* (DNS), you probably also have an actual "name" for your system that is simply mapped by the DNS to the TCP/IP address. Alternatively, if you are writing Java applications versus applets, you may have a mapping statement for this in your "hosts" file on your workstation hard drive. Products such as Client Access and Personal Communications will set this for you as part of their configuration support.

4. Prepare the SQL Statements

To use JDBC, you must use SQL statements. The `java.sql` package includes two classes that you use to create instances to represent SQL statements. When you execute an SQL statement, the database performs two steps:

1. "Prepare the statement" by effectively compiling it;

2. "Running" the prepared statement.

The first step can be reserved for multiple-use statements, which saves time in the second and subsequent execution of the statement. Thus, the two flavors of SQL statement classes in JDBC are:

- *Statement.* Use this class to execute statements on the fly. If you have an SQL statement that is to be run only once, this is the class to use. Its `executeXXX` methods take any `String` object assumed to contain a valid dynamic SQL statement. If, however, you expect to execute the same statement more than once, it is more efficient to use `PreparedStatement`.

- *PreparedStatement.* Use this class to prepare a statement that will be executed multiple times. Note that it allows substitution variables, or "*markers*", in the form of question marks (?) so that the same statement can be reused multiple times with different values. See the SQL documentation for where you are allowed to use these "markers," but essentially they can be used in **SELECT** statements for the value of a column name (as in WHERE STATE=?), in the **SET** clause of an **UPDATE** statement, and the **VALUES** clause in an **INSERT** statement. They cannot be used to substitute in the table names or column names themselves, however. That would change the access path of the statement, so it cannot be turned into a variable. You must use separate statements for this. If you cannot hard-code these values, you will have to use a Statement object instead of a `PreparedStatement` object.

To instantiate instances of these classes, you do not use the **new** operator. Instead, you use the `createStatement()` or `prepareStatement(...)` methods of your previously allocated Connection object to create these statements for you. For example:

```
Statement          stmt  = conn.createStatement();
PreparedStatement pstmt =
   conn.prepareStatement("SELECT * FROM CUSTOMER WHERE CUSTNO=?");
```

Notice how `Statement` objects do not specify the statement-to-execute at allocation time, whereas prepared statements do. This is an indication of the longevity of prepared statements. At the time prepared statements are created, as shown in the example, they are verified and "compiled" at the DB2/400 server. You must couch your `prepareStatement` method call in a ***try/catch-block*** for `SQLException`, and pay attention to the exception — it usually implies that you have specified an improper SQL statement (or that you have not yet "connected" to the database as in the previous step).

Having created an instance of `Statement` or `PreparedStatement`, you can subsequently "execute" that statement.

5. Running the SQL Statements

Prior to running your prepared statements (`PreparedStatement` class objects), you have to specify the values for all the "markers" (question marks) you supplied in your statement when preparing it. To do this, use the appropriate `setXXX(int, value)` method in the `PreparedStatement` class. The exact method to use depends on the type of the value you want to substitute which, in turn, depends on the type of the database field or column whose value you are supplying. For example, if you are specifying a value for a decimal field, you would use `setBigDecimal`. For character database field values, you would use `setString`. All of the `setXXX` variables take two parameters: the first is the relative 1-based position of the marker to substitute; the second is the value to be substituted. These methods are the functional opposite of the `getXXX` methods you will see in the next section ("Retrieving the Information in Result Sets"). For example, to set the substitution value for the previous section's example (`"SELECT * FROM CUSTOMER WHERE CUSTNO=?"`) you might specify:

```
pstmt.setString(1, "PA");
```

The number 1 for the first parameter indicates you are substituting for the first question mark. You must substitute for all the question marks before executing the prepared statement. These substitutions stay in effect for the life of the `PreparedStatement` object, or until reset or until cleared (via the `clearParameters()` method). The `setXXX` methods include:

Method	SQL Type	DDS Type
setBigDecimal	NUMERIC	decimal
setBoolean	SMALLINT	binary(4,0)
setByte	SMALLINT	binary(4,0)
setBytes	VARBINARY	character, **CCSID(65535)**
setDate	DATE	date
setDouble	DOUBLE	float, **FLTPCN(*DOUBLE)**
setFloat	FLOAT	float, precision depending on value
setInt	INTEGER	binary(9,0)
setLong	INTEGER	binary(9,0)
setNull	NULL	sets the value to "null" for null-capable fields (**ALWNULL** DDS keyword)
setShort	SMALLINT	binary(4,0)
setString	CHAR, VARCHAR	character, **VARLEN** character
setTime	TIME	time
setTimestamp	TIMESTAMP	timestamp

To actually run or execute an SQL statement, you call one of two methods on the object:

- **executeQuery** if you are running an SQL SELECT statement. This method call sends the statement to the database and returns a `ResultSet` object. A result set is an instance of the `ResultSet` class, and there are methods for traversing it (these are covered in the next step).

```
ResultSet rs = stmt.executeQuery(String sqlStmt): // for Statement
ResultSet rs = pstmt.executeQuery(); // for PreparedStatement
```

- **executeUpdate** if you are running an SQL INSERT, UPDATE, DELETE statement, or SQL DDL (*Data Definition Language*) statements like CREATE TABLE. This method call sends the statement to the database, where it is run. It then returns a count of the affected rows or zero for DDL statements.

```
int result = stmt.executeUpdate(String sqlStmt): // for Statement
int result = pstmt.executeUpdate(); // for PreparedStatement
```

There is also a generic **execute** method that can return multiple-result sets. This is pretty much exclusive to stored procedure calls, however, and will be covered later in this chapter.

NOTE: You will use the **SELECT** statement with the executeQuery method whether you are retrieving *one row* or *multiple rows*. The former is just a special case of the latter. For example:

```
SELECT * FROM MYFILE
```

retrieves all the rows (and all the columns because of *) from file MYFILE, whereas

```
SELECT * FROM MYFILE WHERE KEYFIELD = 'A'
```

retrieves a single row from file MYFILE — one where the unique key field has a value of 'A'. This, then, is equivalent to RPG's **CHAIN** op-code.

What SQL Statements?

What SQL statements can you execute in your execute and executeUpdate methods? Basically, any dynamic ***SQL statement***. We cannot possibly cover the extremely large topic of SQL in one section of one chapter. Instead, we refer you to the hundreds of books on the subject, including the SQL manuals for DB2/400. Keep in mind, however, that you will primarily be using a **SELECT** statement via executeQuery to read data, and **INSERT**, **UPDATE**, and **DELETE** to manipulate data. One popular question is: "can I create on the fly tables, views, indexes, etc.?" The answer, again, is yes. You use the appropriate **SQL CREATE** statement for these, which is submitted via the executeUpdate statement.

6. Retrieving the Information in Result Sets

After executing a SQL **SELECT** statement by using the executeQuery method, you will have a populated ResultSet object. This contains all the rows that met the criteria specified in the **SELECT** statement. You iterate sequentially through the result set by using the next() method, which bumps the implicit ***cursor*** ahead by one row.

It is important to note that, initially, the cursor is positioned before the first row; you must do one next() call to read the first row. Next() will return **true** as long as there is another row to advance to. When it returns **false**, then you have reached the end of the rows (that is, the end of the file). For example, to iterate through a multiple-row **SELECT** statement's result set, you code the following:

```
ResultSet rs = stmt.executeQuery("SELECT * FROM MYFILE");
while ( rs.next() )  // while more
    // do processing
```

For single-row **SELECT** statements, you are expecting exactly one returned row. So, your logic might look like this:

456

```
ResultSet rs = stmt.executeQuery("SELECT * FROM MYFILE WHERE KEYFIELD='A');

  if ( !rs.next() ) // no rows?
    // issue error message
  else
    // do processing
```

So what is the "do processing" part of these examples? That is, how do you extract the values for each *column* (field) of the current row? The trick is to know the following:

- The relative *position* of the column (e.g., first column is position 1) or the explicit *name* of the column (the field's DDS name).

- The data type of that column, and its equivalent Java data type.

With this information, you can declare a variable of the appropriate Java data type by using the appropriate getXXXX() method of the ResultSet class. There is one *get* method for each data type, and it returns the specified column's value of the current row as that data type. Note that all methods support two versions: one in which the first parameter is an integer representing the column position to retrieve, and the other in which the first parameter is a string representing the name of the *column* (i.e., field name) to retrieve. These are the functional opposite of the PreparedStatement class's setXXX methods discussed previously.

getXXX method	SQL DataTypes	Description
getBigDecimal(int,int) or (String, int)	DECIMAL, NUMERIC[1]	Second parameter is the *scale* — the number of digits after the decimal. Returns a **java.math.BigDecimal** object.
getBoolean	NUMERIC[1]	Returns a Java **boolean** basic type. **true** for non-zero, **false** otherwise or if **NULL**.
getByte	SMALLINT[1]	Returns a Java **byte** basic type (one byte, signed).
getBytes	BINARY, VARBINARY	Returns a Java **byte array** basic type: byte[]
getBinaryStream	BINARY, VARBINARY	Returns a **java.io.InputStream** object.
getAsciiStream	CHAR, VARCHAR, BINARY, VARBINARY	Returns a **java.io.InputStream** object.
getUnicodeStream	CHAR, VARCHAR, BINARY, VARBINARY	Returns a **java.io.InputStream** object.
getDate	CHAR, VARCHAR, DATE, TIMESTAMP	Returns a **java.sql.Date** object.
getDouble	FLOAT, DOUBLE[1]	Returns a Java **double** basic type.
getFloat	REAL[1]	Returns a Java **float** basic type.
getInt	INTEGER[1]	Returns a Java **int** (integer) basic type.
getLong	INTEGER[1]	Returns a Java **long** basic type.
getShort	SMALLINT[1]	Returns a Java **short** basic type.
getString	any	Returns a **java.lang.String** object.

getXXX method	SQL DataTypes	Description
getTime	CHAR, VARCHAR, TIME, TIMESTAMP	Returns a **java.sql.Time** object.
getTimeStamp	CHAR, VARCHAR, DATE, TIMESTAMP	Returns a **java.sql.Timestamp** object.

NOTE: For types with superscript 1, the recommended type(s) are shown, but this method can actually be used for SQL types SMALLINT, INTEGER, REAL, FLOAT, DOUBLE, DECIMAL, NUMERIC, CHAR, VARCHAR (and TINYINT, BIGINT, BIT, and LONGVARCHAR, although DB2/400 does not support these SQL types). For more information on data types, see the following section ("More on Data Types").

As previously mentioned, you can either specify the name or the 1-based position of the column. It is recommended that if your SELECT statement uniquely identifies the columns — as in SELECT COL1, COL2 FROM TABLE — then you use the name again on the getXXX method call. If you specify that you want all columns — as in SELECT * FROM TABLE — then you use the column numbers because the names are probably not known. If you know the column name but want to specify the column number, you can use the ResultSet method findColumn(String).

Notice that there are three getXXXStream methods (Binary, ASCII, Unicode). They are intended for very large fields, such as bitmap images. They are alternative methods that allow you to retrieve these values in smaller, fixed-size blocks, rather than as a single blob with the getBytes or getString methods. To use them, you must access the returned java.io.InputStream objects immediately. Otherwise, you face losing them on the next rs.getXXX or rs.next call. The following example is from the **"JDBC Guide: Getting Started"** document included in the JDK documentation:

```
java.sql.Statement stmt = con.createStatement();
ResultSet r = stmt.executeQuery("SELECT x FROM Table2");
// Now retrieve the column 1 results in 4 K chunks:
byte buff = new byte[4096];
while (r.next()) {
  Java.io.InputStream fin = r.getAsciiStream(1);
  for (;;) {
    int size = fin.read(buff);
    if (size == -1) { // at end of stream
        break;
    }
    // Send the newly-filled buffer to some ASCII output stream:
    output.write(buff, 0, size);
  }
}
```

If your database uses **NULL** values for unset fields (for instance, DDS keyword **ALWNULL**) then your code processing the result set may deem it important to know if the value for a retrieved column is indeed **NULL** or not. To test this, use the ResultSet method wasNull() — it returns **true** if the last column read via a getXXX method call has a **NULL** value.

Recall that when using SQL in RPG programs, your processing for SELECT involves using **DECLARE CURSOR** and specifying the select statement as a clause of this declaration (using the FOR clause). Thus, in RPG, you name your *cursor* whereas in JDBC it is implicit. The ResultSet class and its next and getXXX methods are equivalent to RPG SQL's **FETCH NEXT** and **FETCH NEXT INTO** statements. There may be times when using JDBC when you want to process an UPDATE or DELETE on the *current* row, instead of specifying a row selection criteria. This is called *positioned update and delete* in SQL parlance. To do this, you need some way in your subsequent UPDATE or DELETE statement to specify the result set, and the current row-position within it.

Keep in mind that the result sets are actually implemented and stored in the database. They are given names by the database, even when we do not do so in JDBC. To get this name so you can specify it on your **UPDATE** or **DELETE** statement, use the ResultSet method getCursorName. Here is an example:

```
while ( !rs.next() )
{
   ...
   String sql = "DELETE FROM MYFILE WHERE CURRENT OF ";
   sql += rs.getCursorName();
   stmt.executeUpdate(sql);
   ...
}
```

There is also a setCursorName method if you choose to explicitly name the result set. This method is part of the statement object class, however, not the ResultSet class.

NOTE: When you do a positioned update or delete as shown here, you must use a different statement object than the one used to produce the result set!

Reading Rows a Few At a Time

A popular question is: "Can I read the database *xx* rows at a time, as I am used to with my subfile processing?" This answer is yes. You simply code your result set processing to process only the next *n* records at a time. For example, you might have a method called readNextNRows:

```
public short readNextNRows(ResultSet rs, short n) throws SQLException
{
    short readRows = 0; // return how many rows actually read
    for (boolean more = rs.next();
```

```
                        more && readRows < n;
                        readRows++, more = rs.next())
          {
              // process the current row
          }
          return readRows;
    }
```

Of course, this requires some coding on your part. It is not absolutely necessary to bother with this, though. Instead, you may take a shortcut by placing the result set processing in a separate thread so that it runs in the background and can be interrupted by the user. In most cases, this effectively removes the need to only retrieve *n* records at a time because the user is not forced to wait for all records to be read before continuing. The earlier chapter on threads should make this easy for you to code. Simply place the database retrieval code in a class that **implements** Runnable, and have the run method do your database retrieval. Also, include a private stopped boolean variable, and stopReading() method that sets it to **true**. Then check if stopped == true in your record processing loop. This way, your code that uses this class to retrieve records in the background can stop that retrieval by simply calling the stopReading() method:

LISTING 13-3

```
import java.sql.*;
public class ReadRowsInBackground implements Runnable
{
    private ResultSet rs;
    private boolean   stopped = false;
    public ReadRowsInBackground(ResultSet rs)
    {
        this.rs = rs;
    }
    public void stopReading()
    {
        stopped = true;
    }
    public void run()
    {
        try
        {
          while (!stopped && rs.next())
          {
            // process the current row
          }
          rs.close();
        }
        catch (SQLException exc)
        {
            // handle exception
        }
    } // end run method
} // end class ReadRowsInBackground
```

To use this class, then, you would code the following:

```
ReadRowsInBackground readThread = new ReadRowsInBackground(rs);
readThread.start();
```

Of course, if you are populating a list box, you will have to change the constructor to also accept a list box object so your `run` method can put the retrieved rows directly into it. You should also include a "*Stop*" push button in your user interface and, when pressed, stop the database retrieval with `readThread.stopReading();`. You may also call this when the user has chosen the record with which he or she wishes to work.

If you do decide to process your queries in a thread (and we do suggest it!), you should look at two methods in the `Statement`, `PreparedStatement`, and `CallableStatement` (for stored procedures; this will be covered shortly) classes that will be of use in this scenario:

- **cancel().** This can be called by another thread to cancel a long running query prior to `executeQuery` returning.
- **setMaxTimeout(int seconds).** This can set an upper limit in seconds for how long to wait for the SQL query to end. The default is 0, no time limit.

Another potentially useful method is `setMaxRows(int max)` to set an upper limit on how many records to be retrieved in a result set. Again, the default is 0, no limit.

> **NOTE:** You might still decide to retrieve only a page or two of records at a time if memory is a concern. That is, if your list involves, say, tens of thousands of records or more, it would clearly be reasonable to load only on demand. This could be easily coded into our example, by specifying in the constructor the number of records to retrieve each time, and changing the loop to only retrieve that many "next" records.

One last note on result sets: They do not take up memory in your Java program equivalent to the number of rows selected by the SELECT statement. This is simply database memory that is taken. Your Java program contains memory at any given time only for the current row. This will not be true if you specify the "blocking" property on the connection (and it applies), in which case there will be Java memory allocated for the block of rows retrieved.

7. Handling Any Errors

You have see this already — wrap any of your JDBC methods in *try/catch-blocks* for `SQLException`. Alternatively, include "**throws** `SQLException`" in your method definition and let the caller of the method handle it.

You should be aware, though, that there are cases where JDBC (actually SQL) will issue warnings, not errors. This may be due to data truncation, implicit commits, and so on. To be thorough, or for SQL statements that you know could result in SQL warnings, you can check for any warnings after executing an SQL statement (view execute, executeQuery, or executeUpdate) by using the method getWarnings in the Statement class. This returns the first warning in the form of an instance of the SQLWarning exception class. This object, then, supports the getNextWarning() method for retrieving additional warning messages if there are more than one of them. Keep in mind that you should always call your Statement object's clearWarnings() method before executing a statement to be sure that any subsequent warnings are actually used for that statement execution:

```
stmt.clearWarnings(); // stmt == Statement object
stmt.execute(sqlString); // execute sqlString SQL statement
SQLWarning warning = stmt.getWarnings();
while (warning != null)
{
  warning = warning.getNextWarning();
  System.out.println("Warning: " + warning.getMessage());
}
```

Finally, rather than checking the warnings at the statement object level, you can check them at the Connection level itself, to retrieve all the warnings posted for a number of statement executions. Note that the method names and usage are identical:

```
conn.clearWarnings(); // conn == Connection object
// execute one or more statements
SQLWarning warning = conn.getWarnings();
while (warning != null)
  warning = warning.getNextWarning();
```

Indeed, if this is not enough flexibility, you can even check them on the ResultSet object, again using the identical methods.

One last word on truncation warnings: These actually have their own Java exception class, DataTruncation, which inherits from the SQLWarning class. In fact, SQLWarning also inherits from SQLException, so you get access to all the methods in all these classes for DataTruncation exceptions. The DataTruncation class includes methods, such as getDataSize() to return how many bytes should have been processed and getTransferSize() to return how much data actually was processed (on a read or a write). Another useful method is getIndex(), which returns the column number of the truncated field. If you suspect a truncation warning, you can use the inherited getSQLState() method of your SQLWarning object to check for truncation state "01004" and then cast your object to a DataTruncation object in order to access the unique methods in that class:

```
if (warning.getSQLState().equals("01004"))
  {
    DataTruncation t = (DataTruncation)warning;
    int colIdx = t.getIndex();
    int truncd = t.getTransferSize();
    System.out.println("Column " + colIdx + " truncated at " +
        truncd + "bytes");
  }
```

Normally, you will never get this exception. However, it can happen if you use the setMaxFieldSize(int) method on a Statement or PreparedStatement object. This method places an upper limit on how many bytes will be read or written to the database for any column.

8. Closing the Statements

If you do not close your Statement and PreparedStatement objects, it will be done for you when these objects are garbage collected. However, because they typically involve some database resources as well, it is good form to explicitly close them via their close method as soon as you have established that you are finished with them. The same practices apply to ResultSet objects and, as you'll see later, CallableStatement objects.

> **NOTE:** Any currently open ResultSet for a statement is closed implicitly when you execute another statement with the same Statement object.

9. Closing the Database Connection

Just as with Statement objects, it is a good practice (though not essential) to close your database connection (the Connection object) when you have determined programmatically that you are finished with it.

A Database Query Example

Let us evolve our example to include a database query. We will modify our sample to include a new instance variable for the Statement object, and a new testQueryAll method. We will read all the records from the PDM user-defined-options database in QGPL (we choose this database because it is both small, and it is likely to exist on your system, too).

LISTING 13-4

```
import java.sql.*;
public class TestJDBC4
{
    Connection conn;
    PreparedStatement pstmt;
    public static void main(String args[])
    {
        ... same ...
        TestJDBC4 test = new TestJDBC4(); // create instance of us
        if ( test.testConnect("mySystem") )
          test.testQueryAll();
        System.exit(0);
    } // end main method
    public boolean testConnect(String sys)
    {
        ... same ...
    }
    public boolean testQueryAll()
    {
        System.out.println("querying all...");
        try
        {
          if (pstmt == null) // only create once
            pstmt = conn.prepareStatement("SELECT * FROM QGPL.QAUOOPT");
          ResultSet rs = pstmt.executeQuery();
          System.out.println("query results:");
          while (rs.next())
            System.out.println(rs.getString(1) + " " +
                               rs.getString(2).trim());
          rs.close();
          pstmt.close();
        } // end try
        catch (SQLException exc)
        {
            System.out.println("query all failed with: '" +
                               exc.getMessage() + "'");
            return false;
        }
        System.out.println("query done");
        return true;
    } // end testQueryAll method
} // end class TestJDBC4
```

Here are the results of running the program:

LISTING 13-5

```
Inside TestJDBC
Class found OK
Connecting to system mySystem...
connected ok
querying all...
query results:
 C CALL &O/&N
CC CHGCURLIB CURLIB(&L)
CD STRDFU OPTION(2)
. . .
TD STRSDA OPTION(3) TSTFILE(&L/&N)
WS WRKSBMJOB
query done
```

At this point, you have seen the introductory tour to Java's JDBC (and its SQL base), and we will now dig deeper into the details of data types, database constructs, metadata, and more. If you are merely looking for an introductory level of information, you may safely skip directly to the next chapter if you wish. If you are ready for more details, come along...

More on Data Types

When using SQL, whether it is embedded in RPG code through CLI APIs or through JDBC, you use predefined SQL datatypes. This is to ensure consistency and portability from one database vendor to another. When using SQL in RPG, these datatypes are mapped to and from RPG-native data type variables by the database.

The operation is similar for JDBC. You have seen how the getXXX methods in the ResultSet class allow you to equate an SQL column's data type to a Java basic data type or a Java object data type (like java.math.BigDecimal). And you have seen how the setXXX methods in the PreparedStatement class allow you to equate a Java basic data type or Java object. The conversion to/from the AS/400 EBCDIC values from/to Java's ASCII values happens automatically for you, including codepage conversions. The following is a summary table of the SQL datatypes and their AS/400 DDS and RPG equivalents. (The data type mapping is merely the preferred or most common mapping, but you can easily map to and from various types — as you saw, for example, in the setXXX methods)

SQL Type	DDS Type (Len)	Default	Java Type
BIGINT[1]	B=Binary (9,0)	B (9,0)	`int`
BINARY[2] (n)	A=Character (n) CCSID(65535)	A (1) CCSID (65535)	`String`
BIT[1]	B=Binary (4,0)	B (4,0)	`short`
CHAR (n)	A=Character (n)	A (1)	`String`
DATE	L=Date (10)	L	`java.sql.Date`
DECIMAL (n, m)	P=Packed (n,m)	P (5,0)	`java.math.BigDecimal`
DOUBLE (n)	F=Float FLTPCN(*DOUBLE) (x,x-1)	F (17,16) *DOUBLE	`double`
FLOAT (n) n=1-14	F=Float FLTPCN(*SINGLE) (x,x-1)	F (17,16) *DOUBLE	`float`
FLOAT (n) n=25-53	F=Float FLTPCN(*DOUBLE) (x,x-1)	F (17,16) *DOUBLE	`double`
INTEGER	B=Binary (9,0)	B (9,0)	`int`
LONGVARBINARY[1]	A (n=max size) VARLEN CCSID(65535)	A (n=max size) VARLEN CCSID(65535)	`String`
LONGVARCHAR[1]	A (n=max size) VARLEN	A (n=max size) VARLEN	`String`
NUMERIC (n, m)	S=Zoned (n,m)	S (5, 0)	`java.math.BigDecimal`
REAL	F=Float FLTPCN(*SINGLE) (8, 7)	F (8,7) *SINGLE	`float`
SMALLINT	B=Binary (4,0)	B (4,0)	`short`
TIME	T=Time (8)	T	`java.sql.Time`
TIMESTAMP	Z=Timestamp (26)	Z	`java.sql.Timestamp`
TINYINT[1]	B=Binary (4,0)	B (4,0)	`short`
VARBINARY[2] (n) ALLOCATE (m)	A=Character(n) CCSID(655635) VARLEN(m)	A (1) CCSID(65535) VARLEN	`String`
VARCHAR (n) ALLOCATE (m)	A=Character (n) VARLEN(m)	A (1) VARLEN	`String`

The datatypes listed with the (1) superscript are not actually supported by JDBC for DB2/400 (as you will see by perusing the `JdbcSQLTypes.html` documentation file in the Toolbox). However, they are mapped to reasonably equivalent SQL types, which is reflected here.

For the datatypes listed with the (2) superscript, note that DB2 for AS/400 does not actually support BINARY and VARBINARY SQL types; however, the JDBC for DB2/400 driver does support them simply by equating them to DB2/400's CHAR/VCHAR CCSID(65535) values, which is perfectly reasonable. When should you use them? When you need to store bitmaps! If you decide to include images in your parts database, for example, use a VARBINARY field (other databases support BLOB — binary large object — datatypes for these, but VARBINARY will work just as well). Another common technique for storing bitmaps is to include them in the Integrated File System (IFS) as a stream file, then include a character field in the database that contains the name of the file. This, of course, requires more programming effort to "retrieve" them — specifically, it requires the use of other non-portable classes in the AS/400 Toolbox for Java product.

In addition to these, DB2/400 supports three SQL types that JDBC does not explicitly support: GRAPHIC, VARGRAPHIC, and LONGVARGRAPHIC for "pure DBCS" fields. These map to the G (Graphic) data type in DDS, with **VARLEN** where appropriate. For Java, you should map to Java's String class type. For really long fields of these types, you could also use the getUnicodeStream() method in ResultSet to return the values in chunks.

The SQL datatypes are specified on the SQL statements CREATE TABLE and ALTER TABLE when specifying the datatypes for the new columns. The matching java.sql.Types integer constants are used in JDBC on the getObject() methods in the ResultSet class, and on the setObject() method of the PreparedStatement class. These methods allow you to set and read database values with Java objects rather than specific Java type variables. These are also used on the CallableStatement class's registerOutParameter() methods, as you'll see soon. Further, these constants are returned from the metadata classes when dynamically querying field type information, as we'll soon discuss.

You will notice that some SQL datatypes map to non-primitive Java datatypes — that is, to Java classes. For example, the **DATE, TIME**, and **TIMESTAMP** SQL datatypes map to the classes Date, Time, and Timestamp in the java.sql package. Furthermore, and most dear to your heart, the **DECIMAL** SQL data type (packed decimal to you) is mapped to the BigDecimal class in the java.math package. These classes were created to handle the datatypes that SQL databases support but that Java, prior to JDBC, did not. You need to look at the Java documentation for these classes to see how to create, query, test, manipulate, and convert objects of these classes. There are methods for all of these.

Variable Length Field Considerations in JDBC

In V2R1.1 of OS/400, support for variable length fields was added to the database via SQL and the **VARLEN** DDS keyword. They allow you to specify a maximum length in the usual way for *potentially* long values, plus an *allocate* value for the typical length (ALLOCATE in SQL, **VARLEN** keyword parameter in DDS). The allocated length is reserved in each record of the database, while each individual record can have a different *actual* length for the value of these fields. If the actual length is greater than the allocated length, then the "extra" space is carved out of a part of the database that can vary in size.

The key is that not *every* record has to allocate the *maximum* value, only those records that need it. This is great for fields that rarely take up their potential size. For example, you may allow the user to enter comments in your user interface. To preserve database size, you would allocate only 100 bytes per record for the typical comment, but allow up to, say, 2000 bytes to be typed in and stored in the database. Also, as mentioned earlier, you may decide to store bitmaps with your records. Because not every bitmap is the same size, and perhaps not every record may have a bitmap, you can use a variable-length character field, with **CCSID** 65535 specified, so no codepage mapping occurs.

Notes:

- If you do not specify an allocation length value for variable-length fields (for example, no parameter specified for the **VARLEN** DDS keyword), then the entire field is stored in the variable portion of the database, which might be appropriate for bitmap fields where a reasonable allocation length is difficult to guess.

- Variable-length fields reserve two bytes in the allocated area to store the actual size of the variable part of the field.

- RPG IV does not have built-in language support for variable length fields, until V4R2.

The new V4R2 support in RPG IV for variable-length character fields includes a new definition specification keyword, **VARYING**, for declaring variable length standalone fields, and a new ***VAR** data attribute for externally described formats. There is also special support added for converting to and from a variable length field. See the **ILE RPG for AS/400 Reference** manual for V4R2 (**SC09-2508-00**) for details, or the "*What's New*" item in the *Help* pull-down of the CODE/400 editor (when editing RPG IV source).

NULL Value Considerations in JDBC

In V2R1.1 of OS/400, support for null-capable fields was added to the database via SQL and the **ALWNULL** DDS keyword. This important feature allows you to identify that certain non-key fields in your record can remain "unset". Traditionally, to indicate that a field in a particular data record has not been set to any value, we "mark it" with our own special value for which we then test in our code. This poses problems, not the least of which is finding a "special value" that it is not possible to use for a valid value. Since this "unspecified" setting for data record field values is so common, you can now let the database tag it.

For null-capable fields you can specify a default value of "null" using the DDS keyword **DFT(*NULL)**. For SQL **CREATE TABLE** statements, the default for non-**PRIMARY KEY** fields is null-capable, and the default value for such fields is **NULL**. To override this, you must specify **NOT NULL**. For SQL **INSERT** statements, the **NULL** value is the default for *null-capable* columns when no column value is specified. Notice that the database actually reserves one bit for each null-capable field (and, hence, needs one byte per eight null-capable fields from your maximum record length). This bit is set to 1 for null fields, 0 for non-null fields.

NOTE: Date, time, and timestamp fields cannot be null-capable. Their default value for new records is always the current date, time, and timestamp.

To use null-capable fields in your database effectively, the language you use must support testing and setting the null value. This was added to RPG IV as of V3R7. The new RPG IV support includes a new **ALWNULL(*USRCTL)** value on the **CRTRPGMOD** and **CRTBNDRPG** commands, a new **%NULLIND** built-in function for querying and setting the "null-ness" of a field, and the ability to read and position to null-key-value records using an indicator in factor two of the **KFLD**.

SQL, including embedded SQL inside RPG, has had this support since V2R1.1, however. There is syntax in the **CREATE TABLE** and **INSERT** statements, among others. The ability to query whether a field read from the database is null or not is dependent on the language "hosting" SQL. In RPG with SQL, you specify a variable to contain the null-ness of an SQL-read row. In Java's JDBC, you can call the ResultSet method wasNull() for the previous read column (via getXXX method) of the current row. Another important capability of SQL is the ability to specify "WHERE column-name NOT NULL" or "WHERE column-name NULL" on a **SELECT** statement. This restricts retrieved rows to exclude or only includes those with null values in the specified column. These options can also be specified in the optional **WHERE** clause of the **UPDATE** and **DELETE** statements.

Commitment Control in JDBC

JDBC supports commitment control, of course, because it is a major part of the SQL standard. To use commitment control with JDBC, you first must specify a *transaction isolation* level. By default, this is "none," but you can specify it either as a property on the connect() statement, or later via a call to the connection object's setTransactionIsolation(...) method. The property values correspond to the **COMMIT** parameter on the **CRTSQLxxx** preprocessor commands, while the setTransactionIsolation parameter is a constant integer defined in the `java.sql.Connection` class. The former is a DB2/400 friendly way to do it, the latter a database-portable way. The transaction isolation affects how affected database objects, like selected rows, are locked for the life of a "transaction" relative to other concurrent transactions. A transaction is one or more SQL statements. The transaction isolation options are:

"transaction isolation" Property	setTransactionIsolation() method	CRTSQLxxx COMMIT parameter
"none"	TRANSACTION_NONE	*NONE or *NC
"read committed"	TRANSACTION_READ_COMMITTED	*CS
"read uncommitted"	TRANSACTION_READ_UNCOMMITTED	*CHG or *UR
"repeatable read"	TRANSACTION_REPEATABLE_READ	*RS
"serializable"	TRANSACTION_SERIALIZABLE	*RR

See the DB2/400 SQL reference documentation for information on these isolation levels.

Once you choose and specify a transaction isolation level, you must next decide whether to do explicit `commit/rollback` calls, or use the default setting of `autoCommit`. In this default mode, all SQL statements are automatically committed after their last result set row has been read (for `executeQuery`) or the statement has been executed (for `executeUpdate`). It is also implicitly committed when you execute another statement, if it has not been already. You can, and probably will, turn off **autoCommit** mode by calling `setAutoCommit(false)` on your connection object. In this case, you explicitly code your own calls to the `commit()` or `rollback()` methods on your connection object (see `Connection` class documentation).

Retrieving Database MetaData in JDBC

One thing you are sure to miss in Java is the lack of *externally described* files. That is, you cannot simply code the equivalent of an **F**-spec and have all the file's field names automatically defined in your program for you. In terms of this function, we go back a number of years in usability and are thrust into a world where we have to hard-code field names, types, lengths, and so on into our program, and manually keep those in synch with the database. We have no comforting level-check support to ensure that we have done that job properly. And we cannot rely on clever "impact analysis" tools to identify programs affected by a field definition change. Furthermore, because there is no externally described language for user interfaces like display files offer, we lose the benefits of reference fields as well. This is not Java's fault! It is just that this exceptional productivity and quality advantage is unique to the AS/400 and DB2/400 — so what's a poor portable language to do?

Don't despair. There is *something* Java can do, and it *has* done it. JDBC, and in fact SQL in general, provide a way to at least query this information at run time, so you do not have to hard-code it. This information is known as **metadata** and includes everything you need to know about a field or column definition. Of course, using this dynamic approach will result in a performance hit but, if you are really concerned about maintenance and integrity, you may decide that it is worth the sacrifice. Actually, if you are writing a truly dynamic application where you cannot predict the file or fields that will be used, then you will *have* to use this technique.

What you need to use is the `ResultSet` class's `getMetaData()` method, which returns information about the columns for this result set. This information includes the number of columns and, for each column, the name, label, type (as an integer mapping to one of the `java.sql.Types` values), type name (as a string), precision (total length), scale (number of decimals), and even something called the display size. These are all retrieved using the appropriate `getXXX()` method in the `ResultSetMetaData` class.

The following is a sample Java class designed to test the retrieval and display of metadata information for the file `QCUSDATA` in library `QPDA`, which all AS/400 development boxes have. This example builds on the previous one. We have simply defined a new method and, while we do not show it, we changed the code that called `testQueryAll` to instead call `testMetaData` (our new method). First, we show a couple of small helper methods that are needed to pad strings out to a given width, followed by the actual `testMetaData` method (you will find the full sample in a file called `TestMetaData.java` — note the uppercase T)...

LISTING 13-6

```
public static final String padString(String padString, int finalLen)
{
    StringBuffer temp = new StringBuffer(padString);
    int curLen = padString.length();
    int padAmount = finalLen-curLen;
    for (int idx = 0; idx < padAmount; idx++)
       temp.append(' '); // append blank
    return temp.toString();
}
public static final String padString(int padInt, int finalLen)
{
    return padString(Integer.toString(padInt),finalLen);
}
```

Here is the actual `testMetaData` method that uses the above helper methods...

```
public boolean testMetaData()
{
    System.out.println("querying metadata...");
    try
    {
      Statement stmt = conn.createStatement();
      ResultSet rs = stmt.executeQuery("SELECT * FROM
            QPDA.QCUSDATA");
      ResultSetMetaData rsmd = rs.getMetaData();
      int nbrColumns = rsmd.getColumnCount();
      int colIdx;
      System.out.println("Column Information");
      System.out.println("==================");
    System.out.println("Name       " + "Label      " + "TypeName   " +
"Digits " + "Decs " + "DispSize ");
    System.out.println("-----------" + "-----------" + "-----------" +
"-------" + "-----" + "---------");
        for (colIdx=1; colIdx<nbrColumns; colIdx++) // loop through
columns
        {
            System.out.print(padString(rsmd.getColumnName(colIdx),11));
           System.out.print(padString(rsmd.getColumnLabel(colIdx),11));
            System.out.print(padString(
                    rsmd.getColumnTypeName(colIdx),11));
            System.out.print(padString(rsmd.getPrecision(colIdx),8));
            System.out.print(padString(rsmd.getScale(colIdx),5));
            System.out.println(padString(
                    rsmd.getColumnDisplaySize(colIdx),9));
        } // end column for-loop
        rs.close();
        stmt.close();
    } // end try
    catch (SQLException exc)
    {
        System.out.println("Failed with: '" + exc.getMessage() +
            "'");
        return false;
    }
    return true;
} // end testMetaData method
```

The result of running this sample follows:

LISTING 13-7

```
querying metadata...
Column Information
==================
Name        Label      TypeName   Digits Decs DispSize
-------------------------------------------------------
CUST        CUST       CHAR       5      0    5
NAME        NAME       CHAR       20     0    20
ADDRESS     ADDRESS    CHAR       20     0    20
CITY        CITY       CHAR       20     0    20
STATE       STATE      CHAR       2      0    2
ZIP         ZIP        DECIMAL    5      0    7
SEARCH      SEARCH     CHAR       6      0    6
CUTYPE      CUTYPE     CHAR       1      0    1
ARBAL       ARBAL      DECIMAL    8      2    10
ORDBAL      ORDBAL     DECIMAL    8      2    10
LSTAMT      LSTAMT     DECIMAL    8      2    10
LSTDAT      LSTDAT     DECIMAL    6      0    8
CRDLMT      CRDLMT     DECIMAL    8      2    10
SLSYR       SLSYR      DECIMAL    10     2    12
```

Other methods are available that you may find useful (although the brief documentation supplied for some of them may cause frustration). Some of these methods include:

Method	Description
isAutoIncrement	always **false** for JDBC/400
isCaseSensitive	always **true** for text types such as CHAR, and always **false** for numeric types like DECIMAL
isCurrency	always **false** for JDBC/400
isDefinitelyWritable	always **true**
isWritable	always **true**
isNullable	**true** if null-capable (**ALWNULL**)
isReadOnly	always **false**
getColumnCount	number of columns
getColumnDisplaySize	display size needed to show this column's value. For example, for decimal columns it is the total length plus 2 for the decimal point and a sign
getColumnName	column name (DDS field name)
getColumnType	column data type. One of the java.sql.Types integer constants
getColumnTypeName	same as above, but as readable string
getPrecision	total length (including decimals)
getScale	decimal positions

The idea behind the metadata is that you can query this information rather than hard-coding it. That will allow your Java code to automatically handle any changes in your database definition. In many cases this is feasible, while in other cases it is not. For example, if your field names are not meaningful, you see that the returned information does not include DDS `TEXT` values and you will probably decide to hard-code this information. In fact, it is true the `getLabel` method in the `ResultSetMetaData` class is totally redundant with `getName` and, hence, not of any value. This decision was made by the JDBC/400 team because of the performance overhead of retrieving a column's label (that is, a field's `TEXT` value) on the AS/400. If this information is needed, there is a workaround, though, which we will discuss next.

There is also a class called `java.sql.DatabaseMetaData`, which offers a vast amount of information about the database itself (that is, DB2/400) and can provide even more dynamic information if it is needed for truly user-driven applications. An instance of this is returned using the `Connection` object's `getMetaData()` method. The information returned in the large number of methods in this class can be categorized as follows:

Category	Example	Description
Database support information	`supportsFullOuterJoins()`, `getDateTimeFunctions()`	Describes what SQL functionality this database (DB2/400 in our case) supports.
Database terminology information	`getCatalogTerm()`, `getProcedureTerm()`	What terminology this DB uses for common items.
Database name and version information	`getDatabaseProductVersion()`, `getDriverVersion()`	What version is this DB or JDBC driver at.
Cataloged information	`getProcedures()`,`getTables()`, `getSchemas()`	Get lists of database-related objects from the system.
Specific information	`getColumns()`, `getProcedureColumns()`, `getCrossReference()`, `getExported/ImportedKeys()`, `getIndexInfo()`	Get explicit information about a given database object .

The last two categories are the two that you may need to use. The other categories are only needed for completely portable, database-neutral, and dynamic applications, such as a generic database query tool.

As mentioned before, the one method you may really need to use is `getColumns`, if you do want to retrieve the "label" or field description for a column. This method returns a `ResultSet` class object containing the metadata for every column (by default) in the specified table (file) in the specified schema (library).

For every column in the file, you will get one row in the result set, and it will contain 17 pieces of information (one piece in each column of the result set), much of it useful: (1) *catalog name,* (2) *schema name,* (3) *table name,* (4) *column name,* (5) *data type,* (6) *type name,* (7) *column size,* (8) *buffer length,* (9) *decimal digits,* (10) *numeric precision radix,* (11) *nullable,* (12) *remarks,* (13) *column definition,* (14) *SQL data type,* (15) *SQL date/time substitution,* (16) *character octet length,* and (17) *ordinal position.* Phew! This information is not documented in the AS/400 Toolbox for Java documentation. At least not at the time of this writing, but is documented in the JDBC specifications documentation and in a number of JDBC books. In our case, we just retrieved the `ResultSetMetaData` and used `getColumnName()` to figure it out. As you see, you are interested in column 12, the "REMARKS" column. This will give you the label:

```
DatabaseMetaData dbmd = conn.getMetaData();
rs = dbmd.getColumns(null, "QPDA", "QCUSDATA", null);
while (rs.next())
   String label = rs.getString(12);
```

NOTE: The label is the **TEXT** value, not the **COLHDG** value. There is no metadata method for retrieving this, as **COLHDG** is an AS/400 unique value. However, the **CRTPF** DDS compiler will default the **TEXT** value to the **COLHDG** value if **TEXT** is not specified.

See the AS/400 Toolbox for Java documentation for another example of using database and result set metadata (search for the file `JDBCQueryExample.html` in the `doc` subdirectory into which the toolbox was installed).

One last comment: If you really did want to code your own level-checks to ensure that hard-coded attributes are not obsolete, you could do so by calling a stored procedure and having it return the level-check value for the given database file's record format. Then, you could store the compile-time level check value as a constant in your Java program and compare it at runtime to the current level-check value. The system API your stored procedure needs to use to retrieve this is `QDFRTVFD` — but beware, this is a nasty API to code to.

GOOD STUFF: STORED PROCEDURES, TRIGGERS, AND RI

As part of the evolving SQL standard, new database constructs have been defined. These include

- **Constraints.** (These are rules about key validation, often called **Referential Integrity** or **RI**);

- **Triggers.** (These are user-supplied programs called when records are added, changed or deleted);

- **Stored procedures.** (These are user-supplied programs called directly via SQL statements).

These are all part of an effort to allow you to move your database rules out of each of your programs and into the database itself. This is a very important concept. It means that you can increase the number of ways in which your users can access your data, without compromising the data integrity. Currently, much of the input validation for a database is done by your RPG program logic. This logic is often duplicated across multiple programs (ILE can help here by allowing you to code one reusable ***MODULE** or ***SRVPGM** object that all your programs can share) and is subject to multiple maintenance problems. It also means that, to allow access to the data from, say, a Java client or even a Java server program, you will have to again duplicate that logic or else code your Java programs to call your RPG programs in order to manipulate the data. By centralizing all these validation rules into the database itself (see Figure 13-7), you can ensure that, no matter how your data is accessed, it will remain valid.

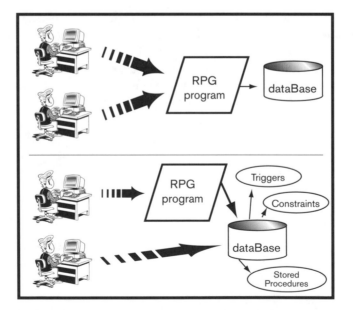

FIGURE 13-7

With DB2/400 (and the rest of the DB2 family) stored procedures and triggers can be written in any high-level language, and can include embedded SQL if desired.

NOTE: Because they must be a program object, you cannot use Java to create stored procedures or triggers on the AS/400 server. Java does not compile into *PGM objects on the AS/400; rather, they remain .class objects in the Integrated File System (IFS). However, it would be nice if Java could be used to create these!

We will next cover the considerations involved in using these exciting and *relatively* new database constructs from Java applications using JDBC.

Stored Procedure Calls in JDBC

What are *stored procedures*? They are simply programs on your server that you can call via SQL statements. This means, ultimately, that the database itself actually calls the program. Stored procedures can be passed parameters, and those parameters can be updated and the new value made available to the calling program. They can also be coded to return an SQL result set to the calling program. They are often used by enterprising programmers for two reasons:

- They provide a standard (that is, portable) means of calling existing programs on the server.

- They provide a terrific way to improve database access performance versus multiple remote SQL statements.

You have already seen the SQL statement classes Statement and PreparedStatement, of which you acquire object instances via the Connection class's createStatement() and prepareStatement() methods. To call an AS/400 program object as a stored procedure, you use another statement class — CallableStatement. You acquire an object instance of this via the Connection class's prepareCall() method. It is important to note that CallableStatement extends PreparedStatement, so it inherits all of its methods, and PreparedStatement extends Statement so inherits all of its methods.

When you call an AS/400 program object as a stored procedure, you can pass in parameters to the program as:

- *Input-only* (read by, but not updated by, the called program).
- *Output-only* (updated by, but not read by, the called program).
- *Input-output* (read by, and updated by, the called program).

Further, your stored procedure program can optionally return a result set if it is used to retrieve a list of rows from the database. Some databases support a return code from a stored procedure call, but DB2/400 does not. Instead, simply update one of the output or input/output parameters.

To invoke a stored procedure program from JDBC, then, you follow these steps:

- Create a `CallableStatement` object by using your connection object's `prepareCall` method, specifying an SQL **CALL** statement as the parameter, and specifying a question mark "marker" for each parameter (whether input, output, or both). This is done only once, and the resulting object can be used (*executed*) multiple times after:

```
CallableStatement proc1 = conn.prepareCall("CALL MYLIB/MYPROG(?, ?, ?)");
```
(Note the syntax of the program name is lib/program for system naming, or lib.program for SQL naming.)

- Specify the parameter data types *and values* for each *input-capable* (input or input-output) parameter using the `setXXX` methods that your `CallableStatement` object inherits from the `PreparedStatement` class:

```
proc1.setInt(1, 1);
proc1.setString(2, parm2String);
```

(Note that the first parameter is a relative number of the marker you are setting, and the second parameter is the value to set it to. These values remain until you change them or clear them via `proc1.clearParameters();`)

- Specify the parameter data types for each *output-capable* (output or input-output) parameter using the `registerOutParameter` method of your `CallableStatement` object:

```
proc1.registerOutParameter(2, java.sql.Types.CHAR);
```

(Note the first parameter is the relative number of the marker you are registering, and the second parameter is the SQL type of the parameter. See our previous table in the *More on DataTypes* section of this chapter. For input and output parameters, you must do this step *and* the previous step, and the types specified for both must be consistent.)

- Call the stored procedure program using the `execute` or `executeQuery` methods that your `CallableStatement` object inherits from the `Statement` class. Use the former only if your stored procedure returns *multiple* result sets. Use the latter if it returns one result set or no result set (in this case the result set will simply be empty):

```
ResultSet rs = proc1.executeQuery();
```

- Retrieve the values of each *output-capable* parameter using the appropriate `getXXX` method of your `CallableStatement` object (see `CallableStatement` class methods in this case) if the stored procedure program *does not* return a result set:

```
String returnedValue = proc1.getString(2);
```

- Loop through each result set row, using `rs.next()`, and for each row use the appropriate `getXXX` method of your `ResultSet` object (see `ResultSet` class methods in this case) if the stored procedure program *does* return a result set:

```
while (rs.next())
{
    System.out.println("Returned value: " + rs.getString(2));
}
```

One last thing to note: You cannot just call any program object this way without first registering the program in the DB2/400 SQL *catalog*. This is done using the SQL statement **CREATE PROCEDURE**. This need only ever be done once, either from your Java program by executing a `Statement` object with this command, or through interactive SQL on the AS/400 itself.

There is a good example of using stored procedures, including a sample RPG stored procedure program, in the IBM redbook **Accessing the AS/400 with Java, SG24-2152-00**. One common question, however, is how to code the AS/400 stored procedure program so as to return a result set. The answer is elegantly simple. Use embedded SQL: use **DECLARE CURSOR** with a **SELECT** clause to define the result set, then use SQL's **OPEN** to open the cursor and SQL's "**SET RESULT SETS CURSOR** *cursor-name*." That's it. Your RPG program's cursor is now returned to your Java program as a JDBC result set. It is not difficult stuff. Your program can both return a result set and update parameters for maximum flexibility. In fact, your program can return multiple result sets! This is handled in JDBC by using the `execute` method and iterating through the result sets via the methods `getResultSet()` and `getMoreResults()` that the `CallableStatement` class inherits from the `Statement` class.

Triggers in JDBC

What are database *triggers*? They are programs that you write, and which you tell the database to call when records are inserted, updated, or deleted (your choice). They can be called just before, or just after, the record is affected (again, your choice). Triggers are a popular means of keeping multiple-database files in synch with each other, without hard-coding this logic into the application itself. You can "register" trigger programs in DB2/400, for a particular file, using the CL command **ADDPFTRG** (*Add Physical File Trigger*). They are removed using **RMVPFTRG** (*Remove Physical File Trigger*).

What do these have to do with Java and JDBC? Well, nothing directly. However, we are often asked if triggers are honored for database files that are accessed through Java, and the answer is absolutely yes! The point of triggers is to ensure that database integrity and business rules are enforced no matter how the database is accessed. They would not fulfill that mandate if you could circumvent them somehow, and so of course you cannot. They are always executed, even when data is manipulated via JDBC in Java. Thus, while there is no specific JDBC syntax for triggers (none is needed), triggers are still often a key part of a Java application, simply because they are a key part of an application's database.

Referential Integrity in JDBC

What is *referential integrity*? It is a well-defined database way of doing something you have always done in your business logic. That is, you can ensure that a record inserted, updated, or deleted in one file (*dependent file*) has a matching record in another file (*parent file*). For example, if you have a class list database for a school course, you must ensure that the student numbers for each record always have corresponding entries in the master student database. The latter is the parent file, and the former is the dependent file, in this case. That is, one field in the dependent file is actually a key field in the parent file, something known in SQL parlance as a *foreign key*. The typical "rules," then, that you code into your logic involve the following checks to ensure the *integrity* of your data, between the parent file and the dependent or *referring* file:

- *Inserting a class-list record*: ensure that the student number of the new record exists in the student (master) file.

- *Updating a class-list record's student number*: ensure that the new number exists in the student file.

- *Updating a student file record's student number*: ensure that that number does not also exist the class list file.

- *Deleting a student file record*: ensure that that student's number does not also exist in the class list file (possibly delete it there, too, as part of the transaction).

There are relatively new CL commands that allow you to define these rules (*constraints*) in the database itself (the dependent database) rather than using error-prone, circumventable program logic. These commands include **xxxPFCST** (*xxx Physical File Constraint*) for **ADD, RMV, CHG,** and **WRK**. To see the full list, use **GO CMDCST** (*Constraint Command Menu*).

In addition to the CL commands, the SQL statements **CREATE TABLE** and **ALTER TABLE**, when used to create or update columns (that is, field definitions) have explicit syntactical support for defining constraints. This is done by tagging the appropriate key field in the parent file as **UNIQUE** (null and duplicate records allowed) or **PRIMARY** (null and duplicate records not allowed), and using the **CONSTRAINT** clause when defining or altering the dependent file.

Other than the ability to execute SQL DDL statements like these from JDBC, there are no unique considerations when using constraints within Java applications that use JDBC. Like triggers, the important thing to remember is that these constraints, if they exist in the database, will be fully honored by your JDBC database manipulation code. Your data will continue to be referred to as having integrity, constraining orders aside!

PORTABILITY CONSIDERATIONS

If you are going to be writing Java code to be portable to other databases (heaven forbid), then there are some things you can keep in mind as you go. First, rather than specifying JDBC/400 unique properties on the `DriverManager.getConnection()` statement you should use, where possible, the JDBC-driver-independent methods on the `Connection` class. Here are the properties that can alternatively be specified via `Connection` methods:

Property	Equivalent Method	Comments
"access=read only"	setReadOnly / getReadOnly	When specifying that you do not intend to do update the database
"transaction isolation"	setTransactionIsolation / getTransactionIsolation	Note that the property sets the default, whereas the methods can change and query the setting dynamically

Also recall that you can specify the user ID and password on the `getConnection` method as parameters, versus using the JDBC/400 properties (although you will typically let the JDBC driver prompt for this information anyway). Also, use the default property value `naming=sql` so that your subsequent SQL statements are not AS/400 unique.

To port the database itself, you will have to write equivalent SQL Data Definition Language statements to produce the database, versus the AS/400 specific DDS. You might want to use JDBC's metadata classes to write a Java program that does this for you! That would be an interesting project.

If you are writing new Java code and find yourself rewriting some RPG code in Java in order to achieve database integrity, consider moving that code into the database itself. That is, really look closely at using triggers, constraints, and even stored procedures. This will be of benefit not only to your new Java code, but also your existing RPG code. Plus, it will keep your Java code smaller and less error prone. The problem, of course, is that you cannot write trigger programs or stored procedures in Java, so they have their own portability concerns. There are a few things to consider here:

- As of V4R2, you are able to author your triggers in SQL itself.
- You could always write a *small* RPG, C, C++, or COBOL program for the trigger or stored procedure, and just have it invoke a Java program.

481

- You could also consider writing your triggers and stored procedures in RPG IV with embedded SQL. Then, you could port this to at least Windows 95 and WindowsNT using IBM's VisualAge for RPG and DB2/NT (or by its new name Universal DataBase for Windows NT). It should port with only very minimal change.

- There is always REXX, which is available practically everywhere. For example, it is available on Windows 95 and NT as part of CODE/400.

- Ultimately, C or C++ offer reasonable platform portability, but they are yet another language to learn.

PERFORMANCE CONSIDERATIONS

Do you care about database access performance? Have you met anyone who does not? This is a huge topic, and covers significant ground — from the AS/400 ODBC server that JDBC uses, to database models and good SQL programming standards, to JDBC driver properties you can tweak. JDBC is like ODBC, not only from the point of view of programming but performance as well. The upshot is that you need to pay attention to the details in order to get the performance you want and need — but if you do, good performance is attainable. Although this extensive subject is beyond the scope of this book, we can still point you in the right direction.

First of all, the JDBC/400 driver uses the same server-side program that ODBC/400 uses. That means any performance tuning suggestions for the latter apply to the former. There is an IBM redbook that, although written for an ODBC audience, will apply to a large degree to JDBC programmers as well: **AS/400 Client/Server Performance Using the Windows Clients**, SG24-4526-01. Further, there is some mention of performance tips in both the AS/400 Toolbox for Java documentation, and in the redbook **Accessing the AS/400 System with Java**, SG24-2152-00. We also anticipate that someday a redbook will be explicitly dedicated to Java database performance tips for AS/400 programmers as well. Check the redbook Web site at **www.redbooks.ibm.com**.

Briefly, though, here are some things you need to consider:

- Using stored procedures!

- Using prepared statements (PreparedStatement) for any SQL statement that may be executed more than once.

- When querying data, only ask for those columns that you actually intend to use (on the SELECT statement). Every column you retrieve carries the overhead of network transmission and codepage conversions. If you do not need all of them, do not ask for all of them.

- Read carefully the performance properties supported by the JDBC/400 connection class (these are specified on the getConnection URL parameter and documented in the toolbox documentation). Especially, look at *extended dynamic support* and *blocking* (for read-only queries). The former allows you to cache access paths in named packages for frequently run queries; the latter allows you to retrieve the result set rows blocks at a time.

- Read up on SQL. The semantics of your SELECT and WHERE statements can affect the database performance in fulfilling these requests. This is much literature on SQL performance considerations.

Finally, if you are looking to truly optimize your DB2/400 database access, even at the expense of database portability, consider the direct record i/o classes supplied in the AS/400 Toolbox for Java. These offer direct database access versus JDBC's SQL interface. But be forewarned that they are unique to DB2/400.

OBJECT-ORIENTED DATABASE ACCESS

We leave you with a suggestion for designing your database access Java code. For each database you will access, define two Java classes — one for representing a single record in the database, and one for representing multiple records in the database (such as the result of a query). The first class-let's call it OneRecordXXX where XXX is the name of the database file-will contain at least:

- A private instance variable for each field in the database, with getXXX() methods for each that simply return the values of these variables, and setXXX() methods for each that set the values of the instance variables to the given values. (Note that XXX represents the field name.)

- A private instance variable for the Connection object.

- Private instance variables for PreparedStatements for doing individual record read, update, delete, and insert.

- Methods open() and close() that connect to the database (set Connection object) and close the connection, respectively.

- A read() method that reads a single record from the database, populating the field instance variables after. It should only be valid if all the *key* field setXXX() methods have been called. This will use the appropriate PreparedStatement object to execute an SQL SELECT statement.

- An update() method that updates a record in the database. This should only be valid if *all* of the field instance variables have been set with setXXX() . This will use the appropriate PreparedStatement object to execute an SQL UPDATE statement.

- A delete() method that deletes a record in the database. This should only be valid if all the key field setXXX() methods have been called.

- An `insert()` method that inserts a new record into the database. This should only be valid if all the field `setXXX()` methods have been called.

The second class will be used for multiple-record queries. Let's call it `MultiRecordXXX`, where XXX is the name of the database file. This class, then, might have:

- A private instance variable for the `Connection` object.
- A private `ResultSet` instance variable to contain the result of the query.
- A private `PreparedStatement` instance variable to contain the SQL select statement.
- A method `open()` that does the connection to the database, and prepares the statement.
- A method `getList()` that executes the **SELECT** prepared statement. This may be done based on passed-in variables.
- Methods `closeList()` and `close()` that close the result set and the `Connection` object.
- A method `getNext()` that does an `rs.next()` call to position the cursor at the next result set item, and returns an instance of `OneRecordXXX`. This will populate each of the fields in the returned object with the values from the current row of the result set.

Of course, you will likely add many more methods and probably choose a different design than we have suggested here, but the point is to have your programmers come to think of these classes as *being* the database file. That way, you will have isolated all database interactions for that file to but a few classes that are easily changed if the database changes. You can also tweak the code internally all you want for performance without affecting the users of the code. You should even consider defining interfaces or abstract classes, called `OneRecord` and `MultiRecord`, with the minimum set of methods that you want all specific database classes to support. The specific database classes for each database file will then implement or extend these to define the concrete implementations and if desired add unique-to-this-database methods. However, you will be able to write generic code that accepts or uses `OneRecord` or `MultiRecord` objects without worrying about which particular database file is currently involved.

The Data Access Builder tool in the Enterprise version of VisualAge for Java generates code similar to this for you, given a specific database table. However, writing your own code to do this is not beyond your new Java capabilities!

SUMMARY

This chapter, admittedly, covered lots of different topics, including:

- A brief introduction/review of RPG and SQL database access, and commitment control.

- The architecture of **JDBC** for database access in Java: Java supplies a **driver manager**, and each database vendor supplies their own JDBC **database driver**. You code the Java supplied JDBC classes only; the database drivers "snap in" underneath these.

- An overview of the steps needed to use JDBC classes in Java programs to access and manipulate DB2/400 data: *load* the driver, *connect* to the database, *create* statement objects, *execute* the statements, *process* the results, and finally *close* the necessary objects.

- A brief introduction to the database constructs **stored procedures**, **triggers,** and **constraints**, and how they are utilized through JDBC.

- How to use **commitment control** through JDBC.

- Some considerations for portability and performance.

- Most importantly, a number of references to additional information.

You may not be an expert yet at programming database access in Java, but you are certainly on your way!

REFERENCES

This was a very brief introduction to the large topic of SQL and database programming, as well as that of JDBC programming. It is not intended to be all-encompassing, but rather a primer. To find out more, you are referred to one of the many competent references on the subject:

- DB2 for AS/400 home page — `http://www.as400.ibm.com/db2/db_m.htm`
- DB2 Product Family home page — `http://www.software.ibm.com/data/db2/index.html`
- AS/400 database and SQL programming information — **Database Design and Programming for DB2/400** by Paul Conte, Duke Press, April 1997, ISBN 1882419065
- IBM SQL reference manual — **DB2 for OS/400 SQL Reference**, SC41-4612-00
- IBM SQL user guide manual — **DB2 for OS/400 SQL Programming**, SC41-4611-00
- IBM SQL CLI manual — **DB2 for OS/400 SQL Call Level Interface**, SC41-4806-00
- IBM DB2/400 programming manual — **DB2 for OS/400 Database Programming**, SC41-4701
- IBM redbook about using AS/400 Toolbox for Java, and VisualAge for Java, to access AS/400 data and programs — **Accessing the AS/400 with Java**, SG24-2152-00
- IBM redbook covering performance tuning the AS/400 database server program — **AS/400 Client/Server Performance Using the Windows Clients**, SG24-456-01
- **JDBC Database Access with Java** — **A Tutorial and Annotated Reference** by Hamilton, Cattell, and Fisher, JavaSoft Press, Addison-Wesley, July 1997., ISBN 0-201-30995-5

14

Miscellaneous

Java-Supplied Packages

The Java language is often referred to as a *platform*. Why? Because the intention is for you to write code that is operating system independent. Keep in mind that the Java "compiler" (JAVAC) generates bytecode for the Java Virtual Machine. It does not generate machine code for the specific machine it happens to run on. Furthermore, to achieve the Java "write once, run anywhere" mantra, you need to be able to write Java code that successfully avoids calling operating system APIs or services. That is certainly the case for applets. Applets are not even permitted by the Java security manager to call out to system services and APIs, or to any local program or DLL. Java applications have more options, of course, including the option to invoke native system commands and C code. Again, however, the intent is to decrease (as much as possible) your dependence on the underlying operating system. That will increase the portability of your code. To this end, the Java language must supply to the programmer as much functionality as possible to avoid the *need* to call operating system services. This is the root of the reference to Java as a "platform": programmers are programming to Java and its set of supplied functions. This is in contrast to the traditional style of programming to the target operating system.

By now we are sure you will agree that the Java language itself deserves credit for being a reasonably good language because it has the power of object orientation but is not too complex. On top of this base, further functionality is provided by the class libraries, or packages, that are supplied with the language (see Figure 14-1). This shields you from the need to "break out" (access the operating system). The richer these packages are (and they are getting richer with each release), the more function you have "built-in." Another big advantage is that, because the packages are ported everywhere with the JVM, you can depend on having an impressive amount of function go with you wherever you go.

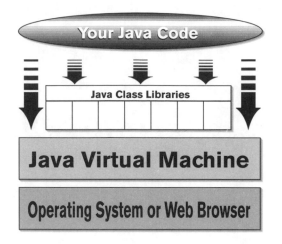

FIGURE 14-1

You are already familiar with some of the class libraries or packages that follow the naming convention "java.xxx." For example, you have seen java.sql (for JDBC) and java.awt, java.awt.event and java.applet (for user interfaces). You have also used many of the classes in java.lang, the "default" package that is automatically imported by Java. You have also seen such classes as java.lang.Object, java.lang.Class, java.lang.Thread, java.lang.String, and more. A list follows of the interesting "core" packages that are supplied with Java at the 1.1.5 level:

Package	Description
java.lang	Base set of language classes, like Object and Class.
java.util	Utility "value add" classes like Vector and Date.
java.awt	Abstract windowing toolkit, user interface components.
java.awt.event	Abstract windowing toolkit, user input events.
java.applet	Base Applet class for creating applets that run in a web browser.
java.image	Classes for working with images like .gif files.
java.text	Internationalization classes for writing "locale sensitive" applications.
java.sql	Framework for JDBC drivers, which is "implemented" by database vendor supplied JDBC drivers.
java.io	Classes and interfaces for working with streams, such as flat files.
java.math	Math classes (hey, just like high school!).
java.net	Networking classes for those interesting in writing their own communications code versus using the AS/400 Toolbox for Java, for example. Makes TCP/IP and http communications relatively easy.
java.rmi	Remote method invocation, the object oriented way to write distributed applications: split your class in two identical pieces — a "proxy" for the client and a server where the work is actually done. See docs/guide/rmi/index.html in your JDK documentation.
java.security	Framework for implementing digital signatures and message digests, with more to come. See docs/guide/security/index.html in your JDK documentation.

The packages we have not described may not be relevant to your first business application, or to Java "GUI" front-end, or to your existing RPG application. The purpose of this book is to provide you with an "RPG slant." It will also, however, give you a new base in Java that will serve you well if you choose to dip deeper into these Java waters by consulting other books that cover Java packages in more detail.

COMMON "HOW DO I?" QUESTIONS

We will round out your introduction to Java by answering some questions that we have been asked by AS/400 programmers who were learning Java, or that arose as we were learning and writing in Java. Although this information refers to packages and/or classes we have not included in this book, once you know where to look you can easily refer to online documentation.

How Do I Determine the Working Directory?

Use the System.getProperty("user.dir") static method call. This returns a String object that contains your current working directory. For example:

LISTING 14-1

```
public class TestWorkingDir
  {
      public static void main(String args[])
      {
          String currDir = System.getProperty("user.dir");
          System.out.println("Current directory: " + currDir);
      }
  }
```

Compiling and running this gives us:

```
C:\JAVA\misc>java TestWorkingDir
Current directory: C:\JAVA\misc
```

How Do I Change the Working Directory?

You have to set the system property "user.dir." The only way to do this is to retrieve all of them, change "user.dir," and then set all of them. This is because, surprisingly, Java does not supply a setProperty method. There is only a setProperties method that sets all of them. For example:

LISTING 14-2

```
public class TestWorkingDir
  {
      public static void main(String args[])
      {
         System.out.println("Was: " + System.getProperty("user.dir"));
          java.util.Properties sysProps = System.getProperties();
          sysProps.put("user.dir", "c:\\phil");
          System.setProperties(sysProps);
          System.out.println("Is : " + System.getProperty("user.dir"));
      }
  }
```

Notice the double backslash. Because the backslash is an "escape" character in Java strings, you must use a double backslash to get just one. This situation is similar to what you find in the C and C++ languages. Compiling and running this example gives us:

```
C:\JAVA\misc>java TestWorkingDir
Was: C:\JAVA\misc
Is : c:\phil
```

We do not recommend using hard coded backslash character here because not all file systems use it. For example on Unix you would need to use a forward slash. A good portable citizen, will use the Java supplied constant java.io.File.pathSeparatorChar. This will be defined properly for each system on which you run your Java application. Keep in mind that applets are not permitted to change the working directory.

How Do I List Files and Directories?

To list files and directories programmatically, use the java.io.File class. It will be worth your while to explore this rich class! This example lists all files in the current working directory:

LISTING 14-3

```
import java.io.File;
public class TestList
{
    public static void main(String args[])
    {
        String currDir = System.getProperty("user.dir");
        File listFiles = new File(currDir);
        String[] allFiles = listFiles.list();
        for (int idx = 0; idx < allFiles.length; idx++)
            System.out.println(allFiles[idx]);
    }
}
```

This gives us:

```
C:\JAVA\misc>java TestList
TestList.java
TestWorkingDir.java
TestWorkingDir.class
TestList.class
```

To subset the list, you can specify a `FilenameFilter` object on the `list` method call. You must create your own class that implements this interface, and code in an `accept` method that takes as input a directory name and a file name. Java will call this method for each file in the directory, and you have to decide whether to return **true**, indicating the name should be considered part of the list. For example, to subset the list to retrieve all `.java` files, you need the following class:

LISTING 14-4

```
import java.io.*;
  public class JavaFileFilter implements FilenameFilter
  {
      public boolean accept(File dir, String name)
      {
          String lcName = name.toLowerCase();
          return (lcName.endsWith(".java"));
      }
  }
```

When calling the list method, the next step is to specify an instance of this class in the previous example:

```
String[] allFiles = listFiles.list(new JavaFileFilter());
```

Now, our previous `TestList` class gives us a subsetted list:

```
C:\JAVA\misc>java TestList
TestList.java
TestWorkingDir.java
JavaFileFilter.java
```

To list files and directories in a user interface, use the supplied `java.awt.FileDialog` class. Do not spend too much time learning the `setFilenameFilter` method because it does not appear to work. Here is an example that is usually tied to a "Browse..." push button:

LISTING 14-5

```
FileDialog browseDlg =
   new FileDialog(parentWindow, "Select File", FileDialog.SAVE);
browseDlg.setDirectory(path);
browseDlg.show();
String newDir  = browseDlg.getDirectory();
String newFile = browseDlg.getFile();
if ((newDir != null) && (newDir.length()>0))
   pathEntry.setText(newDir);
if ((newFile != null) && (newFile.length()>0))
   fileEntry.setText(newFile);
```

For the constructor, it is necessary to specify the parent window, the title of the dialog, and the mode. The mode is either `FileDialog.SAVE` or `FileDialog.LOAD`. If it is `SAVE`, users will get a warning if they select an existing file. Java uses the underlying file system's "open dialog" for this class. On Windows 95 we see the typical open dialog shown in Figure 14-2:

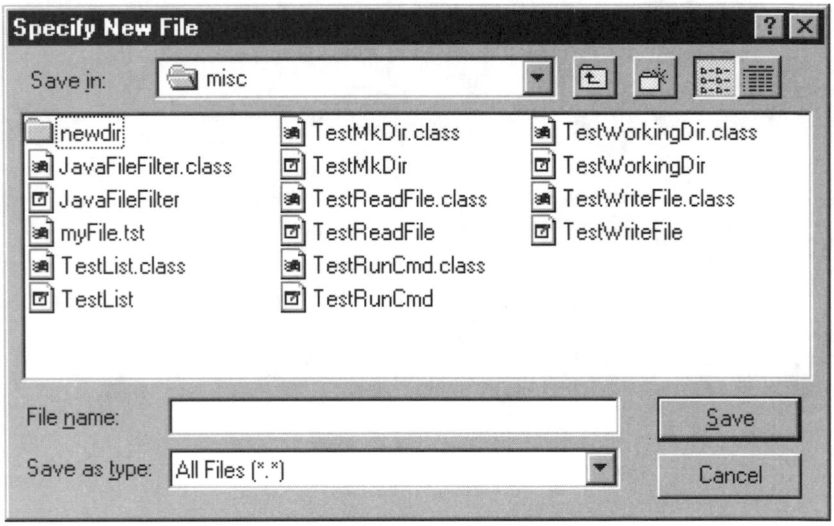

FIGURE 14-2

How Do I Create a Directory?

Once again, you use the `java.io.File` class. The `mkdir` (make directory) method is the one you want. First, however, you must instantiate an instance of `File` that contains the fully qualified new directory name, as follows:

LISTING 14-6

```
import java.io.File;
public class TestMkDir
{
    public static void main(String args[])
    {
        String currDir = System.getProperty("user.dir");
        String newDir = currDir + "\\newdir";
        File dirObject = new File(newDir);
        System.out.println("mkdir " + dirObject.getAbsolutePath());
        boolean ok = dirObject.mkdir();
        System.out.println("result was: " + ok);
    }
}
```

This procedure leads us to the following:

```
C:\JAVA\misc>java TestMkDir
mkdir C:\JAVA\misc\newdir
result was: true
```

How Do I Create or Open a Flat File and Write to It?

Contrary to what you might expect, flat files (such as those on your workstation drives) are not created using the `java.io.File` class. Instead, they are created by using the "zoo" of stream classes in the `java.io` package. This package contains numerous interfaces, classes, and class hierarchies for dealing with streams. (Streams are input or output devices that are read or written bytes at a time.) These classes are designed to be used in a nested fashion. They use one object to create and another to get the desired input/output interface. Some examples are buffered or unbuffered, random or sequential, byte at a time or line at a time, and binary or text. These are described in most Java books, but that level of detail is beyond the scope of *this* book. What you need to know for our purposes is that, to create a file, you will typically use the `FilterOutputStream` class. This passes the `File` object that was created with the file path and intended file name into the constructor. If the file exists, however, it will be replaced. If you want to first check for the existence of a file, use the `File` object's `exist` method. If your intention is to write to the file a line at a time, you would "nest" the `FileOutputStream` object inside a `PrintWriter` object. That will access that class's `println` *(print line)* method, as follows:

LISTING 14-7

```
import java.io.*;
public class TestWriteFile
{
    public static void main(String args[])
    {
        File outFile =
          new File(System.getProperty("user.dir"),"myFile.tst");
        try
        {
          PrintWriter outFileStream =
            new PrintWriter(new FileOutputStream(outFile));
          outFileStream.println("test");
          outFileStream.flush();
          outFileStream.close();
        }
        catch (IOException exc)
        {
        System.out.println("Error opening file " +
         outFile.getAbsolutePath());
          System.exit(1);
        }
        System.exit(0);
    } // end main method
} // end TestWriteFile class
```

The next step is to write lines to this file with the `println` method. As we have done all along, we use the following `System.out.println`:

```
outFileStream.println("Hey, I get it now!");
```

Because `PrintWriter` is a "buffered" stream, `println` does not immediately write to disk. For performance reasons, that happens only when its internal buffer is full. If this causes a problem, specify **true** as a second parameter to its constructor, or explicitly call its `flush` method after every call to `println`.

Finally, you should make it a habit to call `close` when you are done with a file to unlock it and free its resources. Keep in mind that applets cannot read or write local files.

How Do I Read a File (flat)?

For both writing to an output flat file and reading from an input flat file, you use the plethora of classes in the java.io package. We will assume that you want the file to be read efficiently (buffered) and to be read as text versus binary. If that is the case, you open an existing file by using a nested class approach as follows:

LISTING 14-8

```
import java.io.*;
public class TestReadFile
{
    public static void main(String args[])
    {
        File inFile =
          new File(System.getProperty("user.dir"),"myFile.tst");
        try
        {
          BufferedReader inFileStream =
            new BufferedReader(
              new InputStreamReader(
                new FileInputStream(inFile) ) );
          boolean done = false;
          while (!done)
          {
            String line = inFileStream.readLine();
            if (line != null)
              System.out.println(line);
            else
              done = true;
          } // end while loop
          inFileStream.close();
        }
        catch (IOException exc)
        {
          System.out.println("Error reading " +
inFile.getAbsolutePath());
          System.exit(1);
        }
        System.exit(0);
    } // end main method
} // end class TestReadFile
```

Notice that the readLine method was used to read the file a line at a time.

How Do I Call Another Program or Command?

While not heartily recommended for portable applications, there are times when you may deem it necessary to invoke a local program object (such as a local executable file) on your Windows computer. There is an architected way to do this in Java that uses the Runtime class in the java.lang package. This class represents your Java runtime system. To get an instance of this class, you code Runtime.getRuntime(). This returns an object of type Runtime, appropriately enough. You will find a number of useful features in this class that will allow you to perform functions such as tracing calls, querying available memory, and forcing the garbage collector to run. It is also in this class that you find the exec method, which you can use to execute other programs or commands. It is, then, roughly equivalent to the command analyser API (**QCMDEXEC**) on the AS/400. There are actually a number of versions of exec, but typically you need only the one that takes one string, which contains the command and its parameters.

The exec method in Runtime returns an object of type Process for managing the running command. The command will be started as soon as you use the exec method, but there are methods in the returned Process object you can use to wait for the command to finish running and to query its returned value. One example of such a method is one to get the return code the command specifies when it exits. Also, you will probably want to capture and query any messages it issues to standard output or standard error. Process has methods for retrieving these as well.

You can use this ready-made method to run a given command string. It runs the command and captures its standard output and standard error lines as Strings in a Vector object, which you can subsequently cycle through. Because this example also includes a main method, we can test using our new method:

LISTING 14-9

```
import java.util.Vector;
import java.io.*;
public class TestRunCmd
{
    Vector output = new Vector();
    public static void main(String args[])
    {
        TestRunCmd me = new TestRunCmd();
        if (me.runCmd("notepad"))
           me.processOutput();
    } // end main method
    /**
     * helper method to run an external command
     */
    public boolean runCmd(String cmd)
    {
        boolean ok = true;
        System.out.println(cmd);
```

LISTING 14-9

```
      Process process;
      try {
        process = Runtime.getRuntime().exec(cmd);
      }
      catch (IOException exc)
      {
        System.out.println("unexpected error running command:
            " + cmd);
        return false;
      }
      String line;
      // capture standard error
      DataInputStream err = new
        DataInputStream(process.getErrorStream());
    BufferedReader berr = new BufferedReader(new
        InputStreamReader(err));
      try {
        while ((line = berr.readLine()) != null)
          output.addElement(line);
      }
      catch(IOException exc) {}
      // capture standard output
      DataInputStream in = new
        DataInputStream(process.getInputStream());
      BufferedReader bin = new BufferedReader(new
        InputStreamReader(in));
      try {
        while ((line = bin.readLine()) != null)
          output.addElement(line);
        int rc = process.waitFor();
      }
      catch(Exception exc) {}
      return ok;
  } // end runCmd method
  public void processOutput()
  {
    if (!output.isEmpty())
      {
        String line;
        for (int idx = 0; idx < output.size(); idx++)
        {
          line = (String)output.elementAt(idx);
          System.out.println(line);
        }
        output.removeAllElements();
      } // end if !output.isEmpty
  } // end processOutput method
} // end class TestRunCmd
```

You will see the Windows' NOTEPAD edit window comes up when you are running the preceding example. After that window is exited, your Java program exits and returns control to the command line. Had the command been one that produces standard output (say, like the javac.exe command) that output would have been captured and displayed.

How Do I Save and Remember User Profile Information?

In our programs, we often wish to record user profile information, such as preferences. To do this in Java we use a class called `Properties` from the `java.util` package. The properties class is a handy utility class for storing name/value pairs, which Java refers to as *properties*. In other words, it is a table of `Strings` that can hold any information you want to put in it. Each `String` object is indexed in the table using another `String` value for the key. So, you might store information like this about a user:

Name	Value
"LIBRARY"	"MYLIB"
"NUMBER"	"0011001"

These might represent, for example, the values previously entered into entry fields. That will allow you to default these entry fields with the same values on the next use of your application.

To store this information, create an instance of the `Properties` class. Then use the `put` method this class inherits from its parent class, `java.util.Hashtable`. For example:

LISTING 14-10

```
Properties profile = new Properties();
  profile.put("LIBRARY", libraryEntryField.getText());
  profile.put("NUMBER", numberEntryField.getText());
```

At this point, the information only exists in memory. To save it to a local flat file, use the save method. You specify a `FileOutputStream` object for the file to save it to, and a header `String` to be placed as the first line in the file for documentation. We have already discussed how to create or replace an output flat file as follows:

LISTING 14-11

```
File outFile = new File("c:\\", "preferences.dat");
try {
  profile.save(new FileOutputStream(outFile), "User Preferences");
}
catch (Exception exc)
{
 System.out.println("Error saving profile info: " + exc.getMessage());
}
```

You can be as creative as you want to be with the file name and extension. Some common extensions are .dat, .txt, .ini, and .prf, but the choice is yours.

When saving to a local file, it is often safe to assume that there is only one user for that workstation. So, any file name will do. However, if you decide to store the files on a common server, you should probably name the file with the user's ID.

Now that you have this information saved, you need to know how to read it in again. That's a piece of cake. Define a `Properties` object and use its `load` method, specifying a `FileInputStream` as a parameter. This will populate the `Properties` object from disk, after which you can use the `getProperty` method to read individual "values" from it. Here is an example:

LISTING 14-12

```
oldValues = new Properties();
try
{
  File inFile = new File("c:\\", "preferences.dat");
  oldValues.load(new FileInputStream(inFile));
  String oldLibrary = oldValues.getProperty("LIBRARY");
  String oldNumber = oldValues.getProperty("NUMBER");
  libraryEntryField.setText(oldLibrary);
  numberEntryField.setText(oldNumber);
}
catch (Exception exc){ } // no previous values
```

When defining a `Properties` object, you can specify another `Properties` object in the constructor. An example is "new `Properties(defaultProperties);`." The values in the other object are used as defaults that "prime" the new object. This is a convenient way to specify default values for those entries that are not found in the file on disk.

JavaBeans

Now that we have provided examples of some common miscellaneous programming situations in Java, let us turn to some common miscellaneous terms you may have heard in the Java space. For example, can you define "Java beans?" If not, don't be afraid that you don't know beans! The fact is that Java beans are not very mysterious. They are simply "dressed up" Java classes. In other words, they are Java classes that follow a few conventions and, in some cases, add a little functionality to a typical class. Java is all about reuse. The goal is to write Java classes that others can readily use. The conventions and optional added functionality that Java beans offer are designed to make general reuse of Java classes as easy as possible. Thus, it is likely that you will buy Java beans "off the shelves" instead of sticking to simple Java classes. The conventions of Java beans make it easier for Java application development tools to "query" the methods and functions they offer. What's more, the Java beans standard is designed to allow classes with no prior knowledge of each other to cooperate. For example, a database access bean can be used to populate a chart bean.

The optional functionality refers to the ability of one Java class, or bean, to "listen" for changes made to another. Imagine you have an entry field bean in your user interface and you want whatever the user types into it to drive a selection in a list box bean. If "a" is typed, the first entry that starts with "a" is selected; if "ab" is typed, the first entry that starts with "ab" is selected; and so on. Alternatively, imagine that you have a push button labeled "Connect" that connects to the AS/400; You want that button to be disabled when there is a live connection, and enabled when there is not — that is, you want the "enabled" state of the button to be tied to the "connected" state of another AS/400 connection class.

These types of dependencies are very common. Java beans define a way to "tie" one class to another in these situations. You can always code these by hand using traditional means, but the power of Java beans is that you can make these connections between two Java classes without prior "intimate" knowledge of either. This is most important for tools that allow you to graphically "script together" independent Java classes. These tools need a common "component interface" that all Java classes they work with adhere to. This commonality enables you to use Java classes from anyone and yet have the tool work with them as though the tool had intimate knowledge about those classes. All Java tools now support Java beans, including IBM's VisualAge for Java.

The key thing is that the Java beans' standard for writing classes facilitates a world in which anyone can write and sell Java classes — without having to supply the source code — and all tools in the Java application development business can work effectively with those classes. Effectively, in this case, means that you can place those classes in the tool's graphical builder "palette" and connect states of one class to states of another. It also means that there must be a well defined way for these tools to "discover" the states of a Java class that other classes can "monitor."

JavaBean Features

To do this, the Java bean specification defines "features" that the Java classes that adhere to it may contain. These are:

Feature	Description
Properties	Nothing new here, these are simply variables in the class which other beans can monitor. They are defined as `private`, and `getXXX` and `setXXX]isXXX` if the property is `boolean`).
Bound Properties	These are new. Same as a property, in that users can read and optionally write them. However, users can also track the changes in the variable's state.
Methods	Nothing new here, these are just your "`public`" methods in the class — that is, these are the methods others are allowed to call.
Events	These are new. They are triggers that other beans can monitor for, other than a variable state change. They are typically used in user interface classes and correspond to something a user has done. For example, Java defines events in its java.awt classes corresponding to the push of a push button, double clicking on a list entry, selecting of a radio button, and so on. However, you may define an event to be anything, such as inventory falling below a certain threshhold. Other classes can "monitor" for events, just as they can bound property changes. For example, you can define to have a method in your class called when a push button in a `Button` object is pushed. When events "happen" they are said to be *"fired"*.

JavaBean Introspection

Tools that support Java beans typically allow you to see all the features any selected bean supplies. How do the tools do this? They use a built-in Java technique called *introspection*. Keep in mind that you create Java bean features in your classes by using well-defined standards or classes in the `java.beans` package. This means that Java can "query" your class and identify all the properties, methods, and events it supports. This query is referred to as introspection. Java tools use it to extract this list for the user who wants to work with your Java bean. Choosing names for your features that are meaningful and self-describing will make your Java bean much easier to use.

Thinking JavaBeans

Before you begin to design a Java bean class, take some time to consider the needs of the programmer end users of your class: those unknown programmers who will try to use your class without the benefit of your source code. Your thought process might look like the following:

Thought	Description
What variables do I want to allow users to read? What variables do I want to allow users to write?	Define getXXX methods for those variables you want to be readable. Define setXXX methods for those variables you want to be writable. Note, the actual value returned on getXXX need not be a simple private variable, it could be a computed value. Tools determine the name of a property from the XXX string of the getXXX/setXXX methods, not from the variable name.
What variables do I want to enable users to track the state of? Is it enough to be able to query their state, or do users need to be able to be identified when their state changes? These are **bound** properties.	In the setXXX method of these trackable properties, code in a call to the firePropertyChange method of the java.beans.PropertyChangeSuppport class.
What methods do I want to expose for use by the public?	By default, all public methods in a class are exposed through Java introspection, but by supplying a java.beans.BeanInfo class, you can identify a subset of these methods to be exposed.
What events do I want to support? Is there anything that can happen during the life of your class that may be important to others?	If you identify user-initiated or other "trigger" type events that are publicly important, in your code that processes this event, you will use the same event and event listener framework described for Java GUI components. The classes in java.awt, for example, are Java beans and they do fire "events" already, as we have seen in the previous chapter.

JavaBean Example

The procedure for creating beans is beyond the scope of this book. What's more, there is no concept in RPG that is remotely similar! However, a brief introduction to what's involved might be useful. We used the wizards in the VisualAge for Java product to create a simple "Inventory" bean that has the following features:

Feature	Description
"inStock" bound property	This is just an integer representing the number of items in stock. It is bound so users can track its value.
"actionPerformed" event	So we did not have to define a new event type, we reused the java.awt.event.ActionEvent class and put in code to "fire" an event of this type when the inStock value dips below 10.

Figure 14-3 shows what the **BeanInfo** page of VisualAge for Java looks like for this bean:

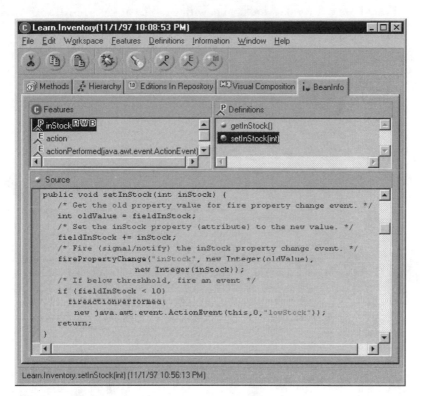

FIGURE 14-3

Notice the use of the superscripts "P" and "E" in the Features list to distinguish Properties from Events. Notice also that the source for the setInStock method is currently displayed. After this code was generated by VisualAge, we changed the line of code "fieldInStock = inStock" to be "fieldInStock += inStock" (that is, we changed "=" to "+="). As a result, the changes are incremental to the existing stock value versus absolute. We also added the lines of code at the end, which will fire the "ActionPerformed" event if the value of fieldInStock is below 10.

To show how easy it is to use Java beans in a Java bean aware tool, we then used the **Visual Composition Editor** in VisualAge to construct a simple little test of this bean. The test frame window initializes the inStock property to 12, then ties two push buttons to the inStock property — "Increment" and "Decrement." The former passes a parameter of 1; the latter passes a parameter of -1. We also did a property to property connection of a read-only TextField (entry field) to our Inventory bean's inStock property so that its value would always be reflected in this TextField. Finally, we connected the "`actionPerformed`" event of our bean to the text property of a `Label` bean at the bottom of the window, and specified the text to be "LOW STOCK!". Figure 14-4 shows what that little test window looks like, with the **Visual Composition Editor** shown in the background:

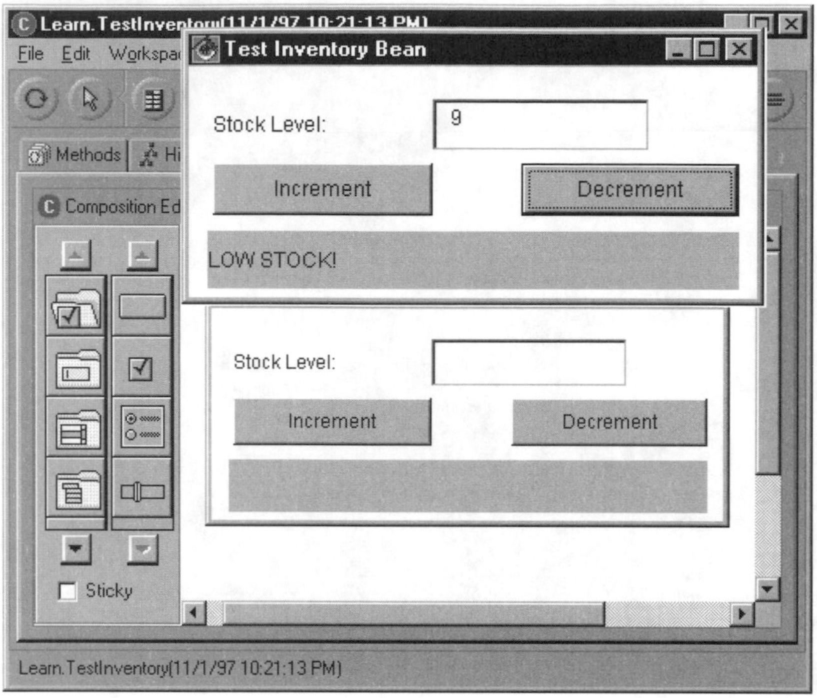

FIGURE 14-4

Figure 14-6 shows what our `Inventory` class looks like in the **Workbench** window of VisualAge:

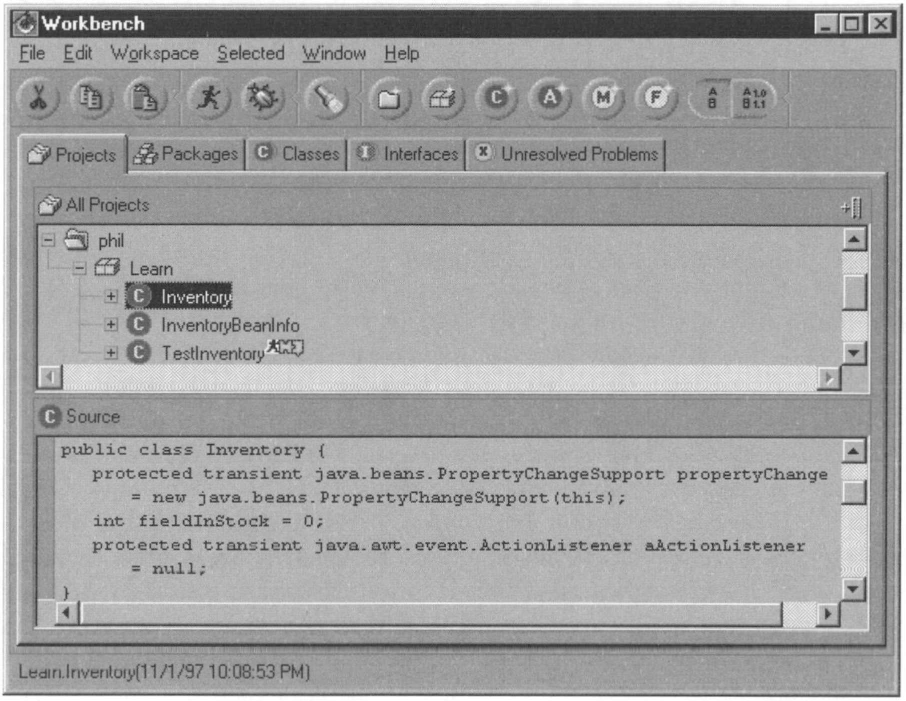

FIGURE 14-5

Notice that we used the **BeanInfo** wizards to generate this code. Don't concern yourself with the use of the `transient` modifier because it is not significant.

JavaBean Grinds

Customization and persistence are only two of the multitude of topics on the subject of Java beans that we've left uncovered. Our purpose here is not to teach you all the details of how to code Java beans. Not only are there lots of books and documentation on the subject, but tools such as VisualAge for Java and Lotus BeanMachinetm are very helpful. What is most important is that you know how to use Java beans. You can assume that any third-party Java code you buy will come in the form of Java beans. Java beans are, after all, effectively a superset of a typical Java class and they offer the most robust reuse framework. It is also important to note that a typical Java class that you write will use get/set methods and public methods, so it will already be a Java bean! It is only for defining bound properties, events, or customizers that it is necessary to delve deeper into the world of defining Java beans. The following Java bean Web site contains everything you need to know about creating, using, and finding beans:

`http://java.sun.com/beans/`

AS/400 Toolbox for Java

There are helper classes to keep in mind when using Java to access the AS/400. IBM Rochester has produced such classes in a product known as the AS/400 Toolbox for Java. This collection (which is a package — like an RPG IV service program) of classes is unique to the AS/400, and can be used by Java applications that run on the AS/400 itself. These classes can also be used by Java applications or applets that run on a client, but want to access AS/400 resources. You should think of them as being similar to a general purpose service program that someone has written and sells for the AS/400. However, you can run these on any client, although they will *always* require an AS/400 as the target server. Thus, you use them with the understanding that your resulting code will not be portable to other servers. That is a tradeoff you have to make to benefit from the programming convenience that these classes offer. (The JDBC classes described in the previous chapter are an exception to this, however.) Having this price to pay is unfortunate, but there's no way to get around it because other servers do not support AS/400 unique services such as data queues and commands. There is nothing magical about these 100 percent Java classes. You could write them yourself. But that, of course, would take time and effort, not to mention the learning curve that would be required to master TCP/IP sockets programming. They use existing server programs on the AS/400 to access resources. However, even if other servers are in your future, the code is relatively small that you would have to rewrite to replace the code. We recommend that you confine all usage of these classes to a few "wrapper" classes that are easily swapped with other implementations for other servers. That way, any possible migration to other servers will be less painful than it would be if you coded explicit references to the classes throughout your code.

At the time of this writing, this product was in a public beta of its second release and was available for download from the AS/400 Web site (**www.as400.ibm.com**, click on "software" then "Java"). Use of the product was designed to be conveniently packaged as part of the V4R2 operating system (optionally installable), and also in Java development tools such as IBM's VisualAge for Java and Borland's Jbuilder/400. These classes, when used for Java applications that run on the AS/400, require V4R2 or above of OS/400. When used for Java applications or applets that run on a client, they require V3R2 or above of OS/400.

We described one set of classes from this product — the JDBC driver for DB2/400 — in the Database Access chapter (chapter 13). This is the one set of classes that is industry standard and, therefore, not a threat to your portability. (However, the SQL you use in these classes will be as portable as SQL is between database vendors.)

At the time of this writing, there were more than three hundred classes in this product, and there are more to come. A brief description follows of the functionality that these classes provide. We refer you to the IBM redbook "**Accessing the AS/400 System with JAVA**," **SG24-2152-00**, for a well done and more detailed introduction to these classes.

The following are offered by the first release of AS/400 Toolbox for Java:

Resource	Description
JDBC database access	SQL driven access to the database. Industry
Record level database access	Direct access to DB2/400 using traditional RPG-sty input/output
Program call	Call any AS/400 program, and exchange parameters. AS/400 error messages are returned to you as well.
Command call	Call any AS/400 non-interactive command. AS/400 error messages are returned.
Print	Work with AS/400 printer, spooler and AFP resources.
Data queue	Work with AS/400 data queues.
Integrated File System	Work with AS/400 IFS files and file lists. By extension, offers access to native QSYS library system via IFS support for this.

These major release 1.0 services are offered through a myriad of classes. In order to use these classes, numerous other helper classes are also supplied that are quite useful in their own right. (Notice that the JDBC classes do *not* require or use these.) A list follows:

Helper Classes	Description
AS/400 object	All service classes except JDBC require one of these as input into their constructor. This class manages AS/400 logins, prompting the user for ID and password, and handling password expired problems.
AS/400 data types	These classes help you easily translate AS/400 values to and from appropriate Java data types.
AS/400 messages	This class represents an AS/400 message returned from a program or command call.
AS/400 record format information	These classes represent DB2/400 field definitions, record formats and actual data records.

USING JAVA ON THE AS/400

What has been covered in this book has been writing Java applications and applets on the client. You may well start there with your Java journey by, for example, adding a graphical user interface onto your existing applications. However, the AS/400 system is committed to being a first-class Java platform based on its own merits. That means you can run Java applications on the AS/400 itself. Because Java is so portable, there are not too many special instructions for doing this. There is, however, some additional information that will give you a leg up. **Building AS/400 Applications with Java**, SG24-2163-00, which is an IBM redbook, covers the topic in depth. What follows, however, will give you the basics.

What Release of OS/400

The IBM Hursley "*Center for Java Technology Development*" is responsible for the initial port of Sun's Java Development Kit or JDK to the AS/400. From their Web site at ncc.hursley.ibm.com/javainfo, you can download a "preview" of JDK 1.1 for the AS/400 that runs on V4R1 or higher of the operating system. This is meant to "get your feet wet," but not necessarily to deploy production level applications. V4R2 of OS/400 from the IBM Rochester team supplies a faster version of the Java Virtual Machine. It more tightly exploits the AS/400 architecture and uses the new OS/400 "native thread" support for faster threads, which is a key part of most Java applications. Furthermore, they supply a "direct execution" compiler that will allow you to optionally compile your Java classes into machine code for the AS/400. This provides the benefit of better performance. Keep in mind that you can mix interpreted and statically compiled classes in the same application. You can also choose to statically compile your classes at "first touch" when running an application. This adds to the AS/400 the benefits of "Just In Time" or JIT compiler technology that many Web browsers support today.

How Do I Use It?

Java on the AS/400 starts with the class file, not the Java source file. Your Java class files live in the Integrated File System, or IFS. They are Unicode based; your RPG source is EBCDIC based. The first step is to choose any of the workstation based development tools. You use them to create your Java source code and then create your Java class files (although the **JAVAC** command is available on the AS/400 too). Next, you copy these to an AS/400 IFS directory for deployment on the AS/400. It will then be possible to run it out of that directory directly. The V4R2 commands you need are **JAVA** or **RUNJVA** *(Run Java Program),* **DLTJVAPGM** *(Delete Java Program),* and **CRTJVAPGM** *(Create Java Program).* You use the last command to statically compile your Java class file into a directly executable format, but you can also do this implicitly as part of the **JAVA** command. Notice that compiling a Java class file does not produce a program object, as you might expect. Instead, it creates a hidden service program and puts a link to it into your Java class file. That way the Java runtime knows it has a compiled version. This link is "invalidated" if the datestamp of the class file is later than the datestamp of the hidden service program. If you are running V4R2 or higher, use **GO CMDJVA** to see all the available Java commands. A menu item you will see listed there is **CMDQSH**, or "Qshell Interpreter Commands," which takes you to another menu that includes a command called **STRQSH** or (Start qsh Shell Interpreter). This starts a shell environment where you can run any of the Java Development Kit commands, such as **JAVAC**, **JAVA**, and **JAVADOC**. The advantage is that when you use **JAVA** in this shell to run a Java program, you can see its console or standard out text, which means that you can enter standard in (command line) information as well. There is also a menu item for **CMDENVVAR** or "Environment Variable Commands" for setting environment variables such as CLASSPATH that may useful for your Java program. Indeed, you must set the CLASSPATH before you can run any Java program on the AS/400.

The AS/400 system debugger will support debugging of AS/400 Java applications. Alternatively, if you want to use a workstation based debugger with a more modern GUI interface, VisualAge for Java's "*AS/400 feature*" that comes with the ***Enterprise*** edition (1.01 or later) includes a remote debugger for debugging AS/400 Java, RPG, COBOL, CL, C, and C++ AS/400 applications from the client. It also includes a number of other unique AS/400 Java utilities. (Borland's Jbuilder product is anticipated to address the AS/400 programmer as well.) The debugger is also available as part of CODE/400. It requires Windows95 or WindowsNT.

OF SERVLETS, ENTERPRISE BEANS, AND MORE

Finally, the world of Java is exploding at an unprecedented rate. You have been given a very brief tour of the core Java language as of JDK 1.1. However, there is much more in the works. This includes ***Java Servlets***, which are similar to Java applets but run on the server versus the client. They work with your Web server software, and effectively allow your HTML and Java clients to invoke Java classes via the Web server, just as you can call RPG and C programs on your server today using CGI *(Common Gateway Interface)*. Servlets will pretty much render CGI obsolete, as well as a number of industry initiatives to improve the CGI performance by offering APIs to run programs in the same address space as the Web server. The AS/400 Web servers, both from IBM and others, will support servlets — indeed some do today.

Enterprise JavaBeans is another interesting initiative that applies to you as a server programmer. These are "grown up" Java beans that support "enterprise" functionality (such as message queuing and CORBA's IIOP networking protocol) and also its services such as transactions. Look for the AS/400 to support these. These Java beans will be supplied by your server vendor, and will run on the server itself.

Another initiative aimed at business critical application development is J/SQL. This is a recognition that JDBC, with its dynamic SQL approach, may not offer the throughput that some very large enterprise applications require. J/SQL is striving to define a form of "embedded SQL" in Java, with the intention of offering better performance. This will have to be implemented and supported by your database vendor just as JDBC is. IBM's DB2, including DB2 for AS/400, will certainly be looking closely at helping define this evolving specification, first championed by Oracle.

Keep an eye on these and numerous other important initiatives at JavaSoft's Web site, `www.javasoft.com`, and IBM's main Java Web site `www.ibm.com/java`.

SUMMARY

In this "wrap up" chapter, we briefly covered the following topics:

- Working with local file system objects
- JavaBeans
- AS/400 Toolbox for Java
- Using Java on the AS/400
- Servlets, Enterprise JavaBeans, and J/SQL

The intent of this chapter is to point you in the right direction for learning more about these topics, rather than offer detailed information. You are probably ready now for a break from all this reading — before diving into your next Java book!

Thanks for coming along for the ride. We are big believers in Java — while not *yet* perfect, its advantages to the AS/400 world are enormous! Finally, we have a general purpose programming language for the AS/400 that is truly open. Plus, we have a single answer to the nagging GUI problem. And we have an object oriented language that is within everyone's grasp. Java will change the face and impressions of the AS/400 — and you will be there, putting your new Java skills and enthusiasm to work! Now it's time to talk to your manager about that raise...

Bibliography

Many books and many Internet Web sites are devoted to Java. The following is a list of a few that we have used in our own adventure learning Java. We recommend that you continue your own Java journey by reading at least one additional Java book, followed by a book on object-oriented analysis and design. Further, the Java manuals that come with V4R2 and higher of OS/400 are worth perusing. Once you start into writing Java code, the Java Development Kit online documentation, as well as the AS/400 Toolbox for Java online documentation will become your best friends.

If this version of this book contains the Java tutorial multimedia CD, we certainly highly recommend that you spend a couple of days exploring it. It has been well received and well reviewed by new and experienced Java programmers alike.

JAVA AND RELATED INTERNET WEBSITES

- `http://www.javasoft.com`, JavaSoft, Sun Microsystems, Inc.
  Sun's Java home page. This site is full of Java-related information, including what's new and what's hot. This is also where to get the latest version of the Java Development Kit for Windows 95, WindowsNT, and Sun Solaris.

- `http://www.ibm.com/java`, IBM Corporation
  IBM's Java home page. Full of all manner of Java-related information, and IBM Java initiatives.

- `http://ncc.hursley.ibm.com/javainfo/hurindex.html`, IBM Corporation
  IBM Hursley laboratory's Center for Java Technology Web site. You can download IBM ports of the Java Development Kit to IBM operating systems here.

- `http://www.as400.ibm.com`, IBM Corporation
  IBM's AS/400 home page. For information on the Java OS/400 JDK, and the AS/400 Toolbox for Java product, follow links for *software* and *Java*.

- `http://www.software.ibm.com/ad/vajava`, IBM Corporation
  IBM's VisualAge for Java home page. You'll find information, technical help, and trial versions of VisualAge for Java, plus links to other worthwhile Internet Web sites for Java programmers.

- `http://www.software.ibm.com/ad/as400/vajava`, IBM Corporation
  IBM's VisualAge for Java home page, catering to the AS/400 programmer. It builds on the VisualAge for Java home page by adding AS/400 unique information, documentation, and links.

- `http://www.software.ibm.com/ad/as400`, IBM Corporation
  IBM's AS/400 application development home page. This includes links to pages on numerous application development products for AS/400 programmers, including CODE/400, VisualAge for RPG and VisualAge for Java.

- `http://www.redbooks.ibm.com`, IBM Corporation
  IBM redbook homepage. You can search here for redbooks, and in some cases download them.

- `http://as400bks.rochester.ibm.com`, IBM Corporation
  IBM whitebook (manual) homepage. You can read all manuals here online, or download PDF formats for printing.

- `http://www.rational.com/uml`, Rational Software Corporation
  This is where you'll find information on the Unified Modeling Language (UML) methodology for object-oriented analysis and design.

- `http://www.blooberry.com/html` A worthwhile reference site developed by author Brian Wilson and devoted to HTML (HyperText Markup Language).

- `http://www.unicode.org`
  A home page for information related to the Unicode Standard.

JAVA, RPG IV AND RELATED BOOKS

- **Accessing the AS/400 with Java**, IBM redbook, SG24-2152-00

- **Building AS/400 Applications with Java**, IBM redbook, SG24-2163-00

- **The Java Programming Language**, by Ken Arnold and James Gosling. Addison-Wesley Publishing Co., 1996. ISBN 0-201-63455-4

- **Core Java, Second Edition**, by Gary Cornell and Cay S. Horstmann. SunSoft Press, 1997. ISBN 0-13-596891-7

- **Java for C/C++ Programmers**, by Michael C. Daconta. Wiley Computer Press, 1996. ISBN 0-471-15324-9

- **Teach Yourself Java in 21 Days**, by Laura Lemay and Charles L Perkins. Sams.net, 1996. ISBN 1-57521-030-4

- **JDBC Database Access With Java - A Tutorial and Annotated Reference**, by Hamilton, Cattell and Fisher. JavaSoft Press, Addison-Wesley Publishing Co., 1997. ISBN 0-201-30995-5

- **Database Design and Programming for DB2/400**, by Paul Conte. Duke Communications, 1997. ISBN 1-88241-906-5

- **Experience RPG IV Tutorial, by Heather Rogers, Maha Masri and Julie Santilli. Advice Press, 1998. ISBN** 1-889671-22-3. See www.advicepress.com/ibm. Highly recommended!!

- **RPG IV By Example**, by George N. Farr and Shailan Topiwala. Duke Communications, 1996. ISBN 1-882419-34-0

- **ILE: A First Look**, by George N. Farr and Shailan Topiwala. Duke Communications, 1994. ISBN 1-884322-22-0

- **Java Language Reference**, by Mark Grand. O'Reilly and Associates, 1997, ISBN 1-56592-204-2

- **HTML Sourcebook** , second edition, by Ian S. Graham. Wiley Computer Publishing, 1996. ISBN 0-471-14242-5

- **1001 Java Programmer's Tips**, by Mark C. Chan, Steven W. Griffith, and Anthony F. Iasi. Jamsa Press, 1997. ISBN 1-884133-32-0

- **Java Programming Explorer**, by Neil Bartlett, Alex Leslie, and Steve Simkin. Coriolis Group Books, 1996. ISBN 1-883577-81-0

- **Client/Server Programming with Java and CORBA**, by Robert Orfali and Dan Harkey. Wiley Computer Publishing, 1997. ISBN 0-471-16351-1

Index

Workbook Available

A workbook that draws on the material presented in the book is available. This workbook is designed for both formal classroom training as well as those using self-study methods. The workbook includes lists of key terms, sample quiz and exam questions as well as a number of hands-on exercises.

This workbook is available through ADVICE Press (**www.advicepress.com**) or directly from the authors at **www.emergingskills.com**

Obtaining the Code and Updates

All of the code samples in this book are provided on the enclosed CD-ROM. If you are using Windows95, open the CD-ROM with a shift click which will give you access to the data and avoid the autostart mechanism for the tutorial program.

The source code and updates are also available through our website **www.advicepress.com/ibm** This site will also be used for other updates, additional materials or errata which may be created after publication of this book.

Individuals without web access should either email the publisher **javarpg@advicepress.com** or send a letter addressed Attn: Java RPG Code and you will be sent the code on diskette for the cost of postage.

ADVICE Press
480 California Avenue
Palo Alto, CA 94306

(650) 321-2197
(650) 321-2199 fax

www.advicepress.com

About The Authors

Phil Coulthard joined the IBM Toronto Laboratory in 1986 and has specialized in tools for the AS/400 programmer (and System/36 before that). He has worked as a developer and team leader on a number of products including Sort, Character Graphics Utility, Screen Design Aid and his pet project CODE/400, the Windows based follow on to ADTS (Application Development ToolSet which includes PDM, SEU, SDA, RLU and DFU). He has been manager of many of the AS/400 application development products, and his current role as of this writing is in architecture and strategy for all of the AS/400 AD languages and utilities.

Phil has a specialized honors degree in mathematics and computer science from the University of Toronto. He is a frequent speaker at COMMON and local user groups, and a frequent author of articles in industry and user group magazines. He also works closely with AS/400 customers on architecture, strategy and tooling decisions for the future. Phil can be reached at `coulthar@ca.ibm.com`.

George Farr joined the IBM Toronto Laboratory in 1985 and has specialized in the RPG language compilers. He has worked as a developer and team leader on all the RPG compilers on the AS/400, including RPG III, RPG IV and VisualAge for RPG. He has also spent time working in an architecture and planning role for RPG. The last few years have seen George working as manager of the VisualAge for RPG language team and recently the RPG IV language team as well.

George has a specialized honors degree in computer science from York University in Toronto. He is a frequent and popular speaker at COMMON and local user groups, and a frequent author of articles in industry and user group magazines. George is also the co-author of the books **ILE: A First Look** and **RPG IV by Example**. George can be reached at `farr@ca.ibm.com`.